Fodor's

MONTRÉAL &
QUÉBEC CITY

Welcome to Montréal and Québec City

France's old-world charm lives on in Montréal and Québec City, two enchanting Canadian cities with rich pasts. Their French heritage is ever-present, from the language to wonderful food to pockets of cobblestoned streets. Cosmopolitan Montréal rocks with lively cultural and shopping scenes; smaller Québec City is jam-packed with history. Visits are lovely year-round: summer brings festivals galore; spring and fall are perfect for city strolls and countryside jaunts; and winter, despite the cold, heats up with Winter Carnival, hot chocolate, and snow sports.

TOP REASONS TO GO

★ **French food:** *Haute* to hearty—including *poutine*, fries with cheese curds and gravy.

★ **Shopping:** Fashion-forward local designers, top-notch cold-weather wear, Inuit art.

★ **Festivals:** From Winter Carnival to Jazz Fest, Quebecers throw great parties all year.

★ **History:** Museums, monuments, and ancient fortifications bring the past to life.

★ **Hockey:** Tickets for Habs games are hard to get, but catch a game on TV at a local bar.

★ **Fun in the snow:** Winter brings ice-skating, tobogganing, skiing, and snowshoeing.

Contents

MAPS

Chapter 1

EXPERIENCE MONTRÉAL AND QUÉBEC CITY

22 ULTIMATE EXPERIENCES

Montréal and Québec City offer terrific experiences that should be on every traveler's list. Here are Fodor's top picks for a memorable trip.

1 Exploring the Old Port

One of the city's most popular parks, Montréal's Old Port is the place to gallery-hop, cycle, stroll, take a jet boat ride on the Lachine Rapids, or just explore the waterfront at your leisure. (Ch. 3)

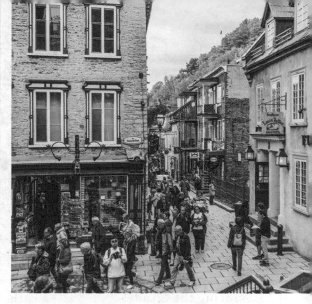

2 Strolling Rue du Petit-Champlain

Take the funicular down to explore lamp-lit Rue du Petit-Champlain, North America's oldest commercial street. (Ch. 5)

3 Carnaval de Québec

One of the world's biggest winter celebrations, this midwinter fête encompasses scores of activities that are bound to make you forget it's below zero. (Ch. 5)

4 Saluting the Citadel

La Citadelle is home to Canada's Royal 22nd Regiment, who turn out in bearskin caps and scarlet tunics for the daily changing of the guard. (Ch. 5)

5 Crossing Montmorency Falls

Ride an aerial cable car to admire the chute from above, or—if you're really daring—cross the suspension bridge above the breathtaking falls. (Ch. 6)

6 Visiting Île d'Orléans

This so-called Garden of Québec is a bucolic wonderland of centuries-old summer cottages, ancient churches, wineries, cider mills, culinary artisans, and produce stands. (Ch. 6)

7 Cheering for the Habs

Nothing is more Canadian than hockey, and the fans' energy and enthusiasm at a Canadiens (aka "Habs") game provide sport for even the most reluctant sports fan. (Ch. 3)

8 Bowing to the Basilique Notre Dame de Montréal

Everything about this magnificent Roman Catholic basilica is grand, from the 228-foot twin steeples to the 7,000-pipe organ to the 24-carat gold stars on the ceiling. (Ch. 3)

9 Posing on Dufferin Terrace

The long boardwalk in front of the Château Frontenac is one of Québec City's most romantic—and photogenic—spots. (Ch. 5)

10 Partying in the Village

Once a tiny nook carved out of Downtown, the Village is great for shopping, strolling, people-watching, and partying. (Ch. 3)

11 Ferrying to Lévis

Treat yourself to views of a lifetime by taking the quick (and inexpensive) 20-minute trip aboard the commuter ferry to the town of Lévis. (Ch. 5)

12 Enjoying Parc du Mont Royal

Snowshoe, ski, or hike a network of trails leading through the dense wooded areas of this hill overlooking the city. (Ch. 3)

13 Eating Poutine

Québec City has some of the best spots to sample poutine (fries drenched in gravy and cheese curds) including the Chez Ashton chain. (Ch. 5)

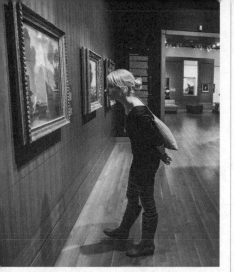

14 Musée des Beaux Arts de Montréal

One of Canada's oldest museums has an exceptional collection of art including works by Rembrandt, Renoir, and Picasso. (Ch. 3)

15 Shopping at Marché du Vieux Port

At this foodies' haven, you'll be tempted by maple syrup products, chocolates, iced cider, and other local specialties. (Ch. 5)

16 Reflecting at the Plains of Abraham

Filled with runners, picnickers, and cyclists, it's hard to imagine the fierce battles between empires that unfolded on this very spot in the 18th century. (Ch. 5)

17 Taking in Old Montréal

Many shops and restaurants are touristy in this part of town, so your time is best spent winding through the old lamp-lit streets and marvelling at the architecture. (Ch. 3)

18 Eating up Jean Talon Market

As well as flowers, fruits, and vegetables, this European-style open market has food stands with crêpes, samosas, Turkish pastries, and more. (Ch. 3)

19 Skiing Mont-Tremblant

With 662 acres of skiable terrain, this peak of the Laurentian Mountains, northwest of Montréal, is one of North America's top ski resorts. (Ch. 4)

20 Grooving at Jazz Fest

Montréal's annual International Jazz Festival is the largest in the world, attracting millions of fans for more than 400 (mostly free!) concerts every summer. (Ch. 3)

21 Marveling at the Oratoire Saint-Joseph

The oratory, gardens, and copper dome of the world's largest and most popular shrine to St. Joseph are a sight to behold. (Ch. 3)

22 Wandering Old Québec

A UNESCO World Heritage site, the enchanting Old City (Vieux Québec) features cobblestone streets lined with cafés, shops, galleries, and cathedrals. (Ch. 5)

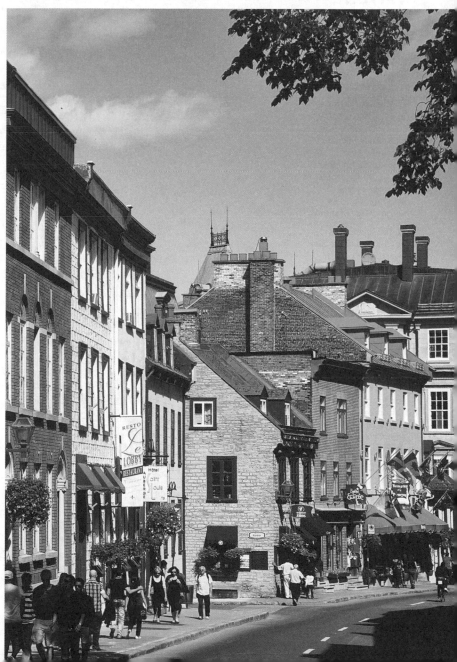

WHAT'S
WHERE

1 Montréal. This is a
bustling, multiethnic
city of neighborhoods,
from the historic Old
City to the hip Plateau.

2 The Laurentians.
The Laurentians (les
Laurentides) encom-
pass thousands of
miles of forests,
mountains, and lakes,
but for many people
the draw is Mont-
Tremblant and its
world-class ski slopes.

**3 The Eastern
Townships.** Called les
Cantons de l'Est in
French, the Eastern
Townships region has
quaint architecture
and rolling hills that
might remind you of
New England. Atop
imposing Mont-Mégan-
tic, you're 3,150 feet
closer to the heavens.
Far from city lights, the
sky here is ideal for
stargazing. Indeed, the
park received its certifi-
cation as an Interna-
tional Dark Sky
Reserve in 2007.

4 The Outaouais.
Bordering the Ottawa
River, the Outaouais is
known for its many
lakes, majestic views,
hiking trails, and inter-
esting wildlife, as well
as the imposing
Château Montebello,
often called the world's
largest log cabin.

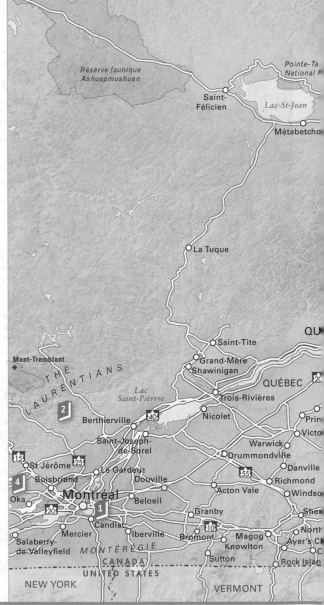

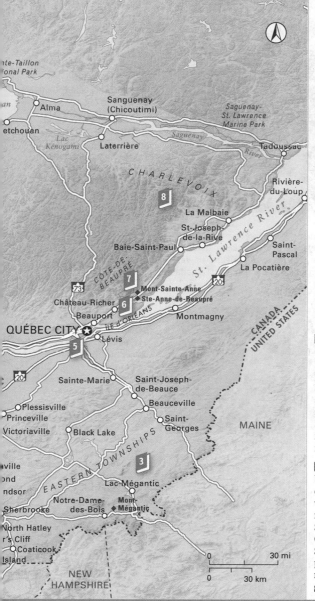

5 Québec City. The capital of the province of Québec is the most French city in North America. Québec's Old City (Vieux Québec) is split into two tiers, separated by steep rock against which are more than 25 *escaliers* (staircases) and a funicular. The surrounding cluster of small, low-rise neighborhoods all have their own charm and flavor.

6 Île d'Orléans. Famed for its wine and cider as well as its strawberry crop and other local produce, the Île d'Orléans is often called the "Garden of Québec." Made up of six small villages, this charming island has several bed-and-breakfasts and fabulous farm stands.

7 Côte-de-Beaupré. The coast hugged by the St. Lawrence River embraces the thundering Montmorency Falls and the impressive Ste-Anne-de-Beaupré shrine. It leads to Mont-Sainte-Anne, famous for its skiing, golfing, and mountain biking.

8 Charlevoix. The big bang of an ancient meteor created picturesque valleys, cliffs, and mountains that brush the St. Lawrence River. This Québec version of Switzerland has inspired painters, poets, and musicians for generations.

What to Eat and Drink in Montréal and Québec City

POUTINE

Canada's national dish, poutine (from Québécois slang meaning "mess"), is a mushy mess of fries covered in melty cheese curds and dark gravy. The take-out mishmash was traditionally a bumpkin's meal until it was named Canada's national dish in 2010.

JULIETTE AND CHOCOLAT

Chocolate is celebrated in all its chocolate-y forms at this beloved dessert shop in Montréal, where highlights include crêpes soufflés, bite-size brownies, candy, milkshakes, and rich hot chocolate, all made from cocoa beans sourced in Peru, Madagascar, and Uganda.

TOURTIÈRE

This rib-sticking meat-and-potatoes pie is a tabletop staple during the cold Québec winters. Named after the old-fashioned cooking vessel that was once used to bake it, tourtière is a dish recognized across the province and is often featured on Christmas eve menus.

MONTRÉAL BAGELS

It's the ultimate rivalry among Montréalers: who makes the better bagel, St. Viateur or Fairmont? Both shops famously sell Montréal bagels, made by hand with sourdough and malt, boiled in honey-sweetened water, wood-fired, and sprinkled with sesame seeds. The result is a firmer, denser bagel than what European Jewish immigrants also brought over to the Big Apple.

SMOKED-MEAT SANDWICH

Smoked-meat sandwiches, like bagels, are another much-loved and much-argued-over classic Montréal eat. Sliced by hand and served over deli countertops, these juicy beef brisket sandwiches, feature cured, spiced meat that is hot-smoked, stacked onto rye bread, and completed with a squirt of yellow mustard.

BOULANGERIE BREAD

In Québec City, there's no better morning start than Le Paingrüel, a longstanding artisanal bakery with daily specials including bread with dark chocolate and dried pear and cranberry-chocolate buns. In Montréal, the Plateau-Mont-Royal is known for its croissant shops, and the La Petite-Patrie neighborhood has several, like the popular Le Pain dans les Voiles.

Treats from The Boulangerie

ÎLE D'ORLÉANS
An island just a 15-minute drive from Downtown Québec City, l'Île d'Orléans is home to the Chocolaterie de l'Île d'Orléans, known for insanely delicious chocolate-dipped soft ice cream cones that have a cult following throughout the province. It's also home to sprawling fruit orchards, producing a bounty of ciders, liqueurs, pies, and pastries that can be purchased at roadside stalls.

ICE CIDER
A Québec specialty, ice cider is a sweet, delicate liqueur that is produced through the alcoholic fermentation of juice from slowly pressed frozen apples. It's a must-try in Québec, if only because it is so complex and complicated to produce.

ARTISAN CHEESES
Québec is home to more than half of Canada's artisan cheese-makers. As such, there's a wealth of craft *fromage* to feast on here. Stock up at farmers' markets.

CRAFT BREWS
Québec takes microbrewing very seriously, specializing in strong beers that'll knock you over faster than you can say "Santé!" Montréal's first craft brewpub, Le Cheval Blanc, opened in the mid-80s, well before the global craft beer revolution, and these days there are several more to choose from.

STREET FOOD AT FIRST FRIDAYS—LES PREMIERS VENDREDIS
On the first Friday of every month from May to October, around 50 food trucks park at Montréal's Olympic Park and dole out their goodies to the hungry masses.

MAPLE SYRUP
Québec produces more than three-quarters of the world's maple syrup, and you'll find it right next to the salt and pepper on most table setups for breakfast, lunch, and dinner. Its origins date to the 1800s when the French learned how to tap trees from the First Nations.

Cool Things to Do in Montréal and Québec City

CROSS-COUNTRY SKIING, SNOWSHOEING, AND SLEDDING ON MONT-ROYAL

Take a guided nighttime snowshoe climb through the snow-covered forest of Mount Royal. By day, make for the summit to Beaver Lake, where a skating rink, tubing lanes, and ski trails facilitate the snow sport of your choice.

DANCING UP A STORM AT IGLOOFEST

Why should below freezing temperatures stop anyone from having an outdoor dance party? Just as the glitter from New Year's parties and resolutions begins to dull, Igloofest takes over the Old Port for nine days and heats things up with electronic sets spun by the hottest local and international DJs. Thousands bundle up and head to Igloo Village to shake off their hats and scarfs on the dance floor under the snow and stars.

COZYING UP AT CRAFT BEER BARS

Montréalers have long been spoiled for choice when it comes to finding warm watering holes with quality brews on tap. Like a hot chocolate but better, Dieu du Ciel!'s dark Aphrodisiaque stout is brewed with cocoa and vanilla beans, creating bourbon and toasty malt notes that will chase the winter blues away. Vices & Versa, L'Amère à Boire, Broue Pub Brouhaha, and MaBrasserie lead a long list of local craft breweries to hunker down in when the forecast reads hyperborean degrees.

PACKING IN THE POUNDS WITH POUTINE

When it comes to winter comfort foods, poutine reigns supreme in *la belle province*. Served with crispy fries, homemade gravy, and requisite squeaky cheese, the carb-heavy medley never fails to grease the arteries and warm the belly. Numerous establishments are dedicated to the dish—including La Banquise, Chez Claudette, Poutineville, and Paul Patates—but it can also be found on the menu at nearly every *casse-croûte* (greasy spoon). For a more gourmet—and gourmand—take, there's Au Pied de Cochon's foie gras poutine and Garde Manger's lobster-heaped frites. Also, look out for La Poutine Week, an annual fry fest that takes place every February in restaurants across the city.

LIGHTING UP WITH MONTRÉAL EN LUMIÈRE AND LUMINOTHÉRAPIE

A little light therapy goes a long way to combat the season's shorter days and longer nights. Every February, the Quartier des Spectacles is illuminated with Montréal en Lumière's light projects and installations, such as a bright, revolving Ferris wheel and a flood-lit toboggan run, and the bundled-up masses, crowding in for the winter fair. Before that, Luminothérapie illumines the square with light art exhibitions from November to January.

Igloofest Music Festival

SKATING IN WINTER WONDERLANDS

Whether for an improvised game of shinny (pick-up hockey) or attempts at the quad, there's ample ice space in the city for every skill level. Outdoor ice rinks can be found in the parks of every neighborhood, like the Plateau's Parc La Fontaine pond or the Old Port's Natrel Rink. If you don't have your own blades to cut the ice with, most places have them for rent. For those who prefer to skate indoors, Atrium Le 1000 brings the best of both worlds together with its large inside rink and centerpiece skylight.

GOING FOR A DIP IN THERMAL SPAS

A warm bath is one of the best antidotes for the chill that settles into your bones midwinter, and a little massage therapy doesn't hurt either. Visit Bota Bota, a riverside boat spa located in the Old Port, for a steamy thermotherapy session to relieve aches and pains and release toxins in the body.

PARTYING WITH THE FAMILY AT FÊTE DES NEIGES

Pack the kids into snowsuits and hop across the river to Parc Jean Drapeau for Fête des Neiges' outdoor snow festival. Among the many attractions are dog sled rides, a 50-foot-high zip line, ice sculptures, a scenic skating path, giant foosball, and a 10-lane tube slide that includes two super-slides and one fitted for a four-seat tube. Plus, a packed program of games and performances for children is sure to keep *les enfants terribles* off thin ice and out of snowball fights during the cold weather season.

SWEETENING UP AT SUGAR SHACKS— CABANES À SUCRE

Before the season melts into spring, head to the sugar bush to tap Canadian maples for their syrupy gold. To enjoy the late winter harvest, Montréalers congregate in a *cabane à sucre* (aka sugar shack), log cabins with long communal tables made for plate passing and syrup swapping. More than just a breakfast garnish, maple is drizzled into courses of the meal, which typically begins with yellow pea soup and is followed with savory traditional dishes such as tourtière meat pies, baked beans, and plenty of pork. The featured ingredient is the star of dessert, too, used generously in super sweet treats like maple pies, taffy, and donuts.

Best Spa Experiences in Montréal and Québec City

SPA WILLIAM GRAY

This luxury spa (in an old greystone colonial home in Old Montréal) is a local favorite. Highlights include warm quartz massages, a Spa Wave sound therapy system, an herbal sauna, and a Himalayan salt room with walls of Himalayan salt bricks.

BOTA BOTA, SPA SUR L'EAU

A unique concept in this Nordic city, this spa is set on a repurposed ferryboat in Old Montréal. The floating spa features a garden, pool, terraces, and hammocks. Other facilities include a sauna, steam room, a water circuit (cold bath, exterior cold shower, lukewarm bath, jet bath). Silence and/or whispering is required everywhere on the boat.

SIBÉRIA SPA

Located in a peaceful woodsy setting a 20-minute drive from le Vieux-Québec, Sibéria Spa offers the opportunity to escape the daily urban grind. Guests can enjoy the hot and cold baths (or for the more daring, there's the invigorating river), choose between 12 massages, and re-energize with a snack or light meal at the spa's adorable café housed in an A-frame chapel.

SPA BOLTON

This spa in the Eastern Townships, set amid natural waterfalls from the Missisquoi River, allows for polar plunging in winter. Guests lie on beds in yurts for massages, while in summer only tent flaps stand between you and the sound of the river. A highlight is the Finnish wood-burning smoke sauna, or Savusauna, the only one of its kind in Canada.

BALNÉA SPA ET RÉSERVE THERMALE

This contemporary spa in the Bromont ski resort is surrounded by trees and overlooks a lake. In addition to treatments and wraps, guests can float outdoors on airbeds among the lily pads, soak up the sun on tiers of sundecks, bliss out in one of the hot or cold pools, or practice yoga by the lake.

STRØM SPA—NUNS' ISLAND

This peaceful respite located minutes from Downtown Montréal boasts outdoor whirlpools, hot and cold baths, Finnish saunas, a eucalyptus-scented steam bath, thermal and Nordic waterfalls, indoor and outdoor fireplaces, and a massage room on stilts.

STRØM SPA—VIEUX QUÉBEC

Overlooking the St. Lawrence River, this spa in Old Québec offers a thermal experience that takes you through outdoor whirlpools, thermal and Nordic baths, Finnish saunas, a eucalyptus steam bath, and indoor and outdoor relaxation areas with fireplaces.

The Nordik Spa-Nature

SCANDINAVE SPA

Located in Old Montréal, Scandinave Spa offers hot and cold baths, a waterfall, and a range of therapeutic massages, including Thai, Swedish, and a fusion of the Hawaiian lomilomi and the re-harmonizing Japanese shiatsu.

THE NORDIK SPA-NATURE

The Nordik Spa-Nature in the Outaouais region is the largest spa in North America and its vast catalog of facilities impress. It's got 10 outdoor baths, nine saunas, an infinity pool, a saltwater flotation pool, a yoga and meditation room, and an outdoor massage pavilion. It also boasts four restaurants, including a biergarten with an outdoor terrace and panoramic view.

SPA NORDIQUE LE GERMAIN

Part of Le Germain Hotel in Charlevoix's Baie St-Paul, Spa Nordique Le Germain provides the usual menu of thermal, hydrotherapy, and beauty treatments, but you'll also find a Nordic shower and a "Snow Fountain" producing finely crushed ice that you rub all over your body.

Best Side Trips from Montréal and Québec City

FARM-HOPPING ON ÎLE D'ORLÉANS
Thousands of tourists and Québec City residents visit this cornucopia of an island each year to go farm-hopping, savoring along the way the local produce and food products, such as maple syrup, fruit jams, apple cider, wine, black currant liqueur, chocolate, bread, pastries, and more.

WENDAKE, HURON-WENDAT NATION VILLAGE
Just half an hour outside Québec City, the village of Wendake, along with its hotel, museum, and traditional longhouse, transport you to the world of the Huron-Wendat Nation before colonization.

EASTERN TOWNSHIPS VILLAGES
The area is known for its green mountains and forests, spas, wineries, ski hills, and charming Loyalist-era towns and villages strung out like beads along the Québec-Vermont border.

ROUTES DES VINS
The official Route des Vins organization of the Brome-Missisquoi area includes 20 wineries, four scenic road trip itineraries, and four cycling routes for your Québec wine-tasting adventure.

CHUTE MONTMORENCY
Plunging 272 feet from the top of a cliff, the spectacular Montmorency Falls stand a full 98 feet higher than Niagara Falls. Daredevils and more active types may prefer to enjoy the falls by zipline, via Ferrata, or from the stair-way climbing up the side of the promontory.

KAMOURASKA AND THE BAS SAINT-LAURENT
With its expansive meadows and farmlands sweeping down to the water, three archipelagos that welcome thousands of seabirds, characteristic painted wooden Victorian homes, and a lively main street, Kamouraska is without a doubt the pretti-est village in the region.

CHARLEVOIX AND THE NORTH SHORE
The Charlevoix is a year-round destination beloved for its painterly landscapes; its ski resort, Le Massif de Charlevoix; its maritime atmosphere in summer and appeal as a whale-watching destination, and, last but not least, its epicurean trail, La Route des Saveurs.

Abbaye St-Benoît-du-Lac

ABBAYE ST-BENOÎT-DU-LAC

Built by the Benedictines in 1912 on a wooded peninsula overlooking Lac Memphremagog, the abbey is inhabited by more than 50 monks. Plan a retreat, pick-your-own apples in season, take a tour of the abbey, shop the delicious homemade cheeses and jellies, and hike the trails.

THE OUTAOUAIS

Less than two hours northeast of Montréal lies the Outaouais, a 33,000 square-mile natural playground numbering 20,000 lakes, 249 miles of hiking trails, and countless rivers. It's beautiful year-round but easier to explore in summer. Be sure to visit Gatineau Park and the iconic Château Montebello.

ASTROLAB IN PARC DU MONT-MÉGANTIC

Located in a wild and mountainous area, the Parc du Mont-Mégantic features 31 miles of hiking, snowshoeing and cross-country skiing trails, and the most powerful observatory in Canada. In 2007, the remote park became the world's first-ever International Dark Sky Reserve.

Montréal and Québec City Today

Ask Quebecers (technically, "Quebecers" are Anglophones and non-native Francophones, while Québécois refers to native Québec Francophones) what they think of their city, and they'll rattle off a grocery list of things to improve: potholes, bureaucratic corruption, construction strikes, snow removal, icy sidewalks, parking meters—the list goes on. Then ask them if they would move anywhere else in the world, and the answer is almost always a resounding no. Any indication that the cold weather is gone, and Quebecers will head to an outdoor terrace (or *terrasse,* pronounced terr-ASS by Anglo Quebecers).

THERE'S MUSIC IN THE AIR

With the massive success of Montréal band Arcade Fire, international record labels are paying more attention to the city. Artists like Milk and Bone, Half Moon Run, Grimes, Kaytranada, Shay Lia, and Béatrice Martin, better known as Coeur de Pirate, are making Montréal concert halls the place to be.

POLITICAL PROGRESS

Politics in Québec can be as entertaining as hockey. Quebecers went to the polling stations in October 2018, and the result surprised not just locals, but all Canadians; the incumbent Liberal party lost by a majority vote to businessman François Legault's Coalition Avenir Québec, ending nearly 50 years of two-party rule in the province. With the CAQ in power until fall 2022, talk of provincial separation has ceased despite renewed conversation around the need to implement further protections of the French language and the declaration by the premier that Québec is a nation, not just a province, in an attempt to unilaterally modify the Canadian Constitution.

One of the issues up for debate in Montréal during the fall 2021 mayoral race was whether the city should secede from Québec to become a city state, much like Monaco or Singapore, or perhaps a non-sovereign city state, such as the German cities of Berlin and Hamburg and the Swiss city of Basel. The point would be to allow Montréal to preserve its unique character and function as a bilingual, multicultural city-state independently from the rest of largely unilingual, unicultural Québec. As fantastical as the idea may seem, this is not the first time discussion around the possibility of Montréal gaining special status as a "distinct society" within Québec has come up.

THE ARTS MAKE A SPLASH

Once the pandemic is over and things fully open up again, Montréal's Downtown arts district, the Quartier des Spectacles, will be ready. The Place-des-Arts' new C$34 million social-minded esplanade is now complete, with a splash pad for the kids in summer and a refrigerated outdoor ice rink in winter.

Be sure to look out for the Cité Mémoire project, an outdoor video-projection installation that recounts the stories of celebrated and lesser-known Montréalers who have helped shape the city's history and identity Films are projected onto building facades, windows, towers, and even trees around Old Montréal.

Québec City, for its part, has been emerging as a premier stop for summer concerts and festivals. On the Plains of Abraham, outdoor performances accommodate more than 250,000 spectators, and people come from all over to watch under the stars. Past performers including Madonna, Céline Dion, Paul McCartney, Rush, and Lady Gaga have helped put Québec City on the entertainment map.

SPORTS FANS IN HIGH PLACES

Montréal's soccer team, CF Montréal (Club de Foot Montréal, formerly known as The Impact) began competing in Major League Soccer in 2012, which helped solidify its fan base. The 2021 additions of top international players Djordje Mihailovic, Bjorn Johnsen, and Victor Wanyama means soccer is continuing to grow as a spectator sport and local attraction.

There has been renewed talk about the return of a major league baseball team to Montréal. However, the city's 2021 mayoral candidates, not to mention many Montréalers, agree that taxpayers should not have to pay for a new stadium, nor should one be built on the site that has been proposed for social housing. One possibility that's been getting a lot of traction these days is for the Tampa Bay Rays to be split between Tampa Bay and Montréal and the team to play in both cities.

Québec City's mayor Régis Labeaume, still sore that his city lost its hockey team in 1995, decided that one of his priorities was to get an NHL team back in town. He built a C$400 million stadium, which opened in September 2015 and has been prospected as a potential venue for a new NHL team in the city. Up to now there is still no hockey team in Québec, but one can still hope.

PEDAL POWER

Montréal has come a long way since its 2009 introduction of BIXI, a bike-sharing scheme similar to those in New York City, London, Chicago, and many other cities. Using the system, you pay to take a bicycle from a rental station and then leave it at a station near your destination. Every year more bike paths are added to city streets (there are at least 500 km [300 miles] of them now), much to the chagrin of some drivers. In 2014, BIXI declared bankruptcy, but city hall stepped in to defend the viability of the initially controversial scheme. In 2019, the scheme enjoyed a record-breaking year, with rides per day increasing from around 31,000 per day in 2018 to more than 36,000 per day in 2019. Since late that year BIXI has been adding more electric bikes to its fleet, and they have proven at least 75% more popular than the regular bicycles. So popular in fact that even with the 700-plus new e-bikes added in summer 2021, they are rarely available.

Montréal and Québec City with Kids

There's no shortage of fantastic activities in Montréal and Québec City for kids. Here's a sampling of what the little ones might enjoy during a visit.

Montréal with Kids

Montréal's popular rent-a-bicycle system, **BIXI,** is a great way for families to see the city. The expanding network of car-free cycling paths now meanders around Parc du Mont-Royal and through Old Montréal, across Parc Jean-Drapeau on Île Notre-Dame, and along the Lachine Canal.

Kids who've had their fill of churches and museums can expend some pent-up energy at the adjacent **Old Port,** which has boats to pedal, a clock tower to climb, and a maze. There's also a water-front beach, but alas, no swimming is allowed.

For culturally adventurous youngsters, there are outdoor dance and theater presentations at **Parc Lafontaine.** Kids can also explore the mysteries of bonsai trees and Chinese gardens at the **Jardin Botanique.**

What soccer is to Brazilians and baseball is to Americans, hockey is to Canadians. It's not a game, it's a religion! If you can score tickets (best to order in advance), catch a **Montréal Canadiens** game at the Centre Bell. A night with the "Habs" and their lively fans is a riveting family experience. Alternatively, take a one-hour tour (ages five and up) of the **Centre Bell,** which includes access to the Canadiens dressing room.

On hot summer days, spend some time at the Quartier des Spectacles, where the large fountains spread along the street will provide some fun and surely cool off your kids. You may even see some adults jumping in, too.

Québec City with Kids

Ice-cream stands, street performers, and (in winter) a steep, thrilling toboggan run make **Terrasse Dufferin** as entertaining for children as for adults, as do the **Plains of Abraham's** open spaces.

Place Royale in the Lower Town brings the 17th and 18th centuries to life for even the youngest children.

La Citadelle's Changing of the Guard ceremony, complete with the Royal 22nd Régiment's mascot, Batisse the Goat, has lots of kid appeal. The hands-on exhibits at the **Musée de la Civilisation** and the 19th-century jail cells preserved in the **Musée de Québec** are both must-see attractions.

Outside Montréal and Québec City with Kids

In the Laurentians, the gentle rides of the **Au Pays des Merveilles** and the **Village du Père Noël** (Santa's Village) are perfect for younger children. There are plenty of thrills at the **Water Parks** at Mont-St-Sauveur in the Laurentians and Bromont in the Eastern Townships.

Montmorency Falls, on the Côte-de-Beaupré, aren't as grand as Niagara, but they're higher, and crossing the suspension bridge above the spectacular chutes of water is a thrill. Farther along the St. Lawrence coast in **Tadoussac,** you can take a boat ride for an up-close encounter with whales (be careful not to get saltwater in your camera or phone).

Free and Cheap

There might be no such thing as a free lunch in Montréal or Québec City, but plenty of other things are free, or nearly so.

ART

Admission to the permanent collections of Montréal's Musée des Beaux-Arts (⊕ www.mbam.qc.ca/en) and Québec City's Musée National des Beaux-Arts (⊕ www.mnbaq.org) is always free. The Musée d'Art Contemporain (⊕ macm.org/en) is half price on Wednesday nights. Every summer the city of Montréal mounts an outdoor exhibit of art or photographs on the sidewalks of avenue McGill College between rues Ste-Catherine and Sherbrooke.

CONCERTS

Montréal's Christ Church Cathedral (✉ 635 rue Ste-Catherine Ouest ☎ 514/843-6577), a magnificent neo-Gothic treasure, and Oratoire St-Joseph (✉ 3800 Chemin Queen-Mary ☎ 514/733-8211) offer free organ recitals on Sunday afternoons at 3:30 pm and 4:30 pm throughout the year. And Les Petits Chanteurs du Mont-Royal, one of the finest boys' choirs in North America, sings the 11 am mass at the Oratoire every Sunday from March to December 24. They also perform several free concerts throughout the year.

Montréal's Festival International de Jazz every June (in 2021 it took place in September due to the pandemic) and Québec City's Festival d'Été in July have dozens of free, open-air concerts. These huge happenings bring thousands, and tens of thousands, of revelers to the streets.

FIREWORKS

From mid-June through July, the sky comes alive with light and color on most Wednesday and Saturday evenings when fireworks teams from around the world compete in the spectacular L'International des Feux Loto-Québec. You can pay for a seat at La Ronde amusement park, or join thousands of Montréalers in the Old Port, on the Jacques Cartier Bridge, and in Parc Champlain on the South Shore and watch for free.

POLITICS

Political junkies can join free guided tours of North America's only French-speaking legislature, the Assemblée Nationale du Québec (☎ 418/643-7239). The parliamentary debates are on Tuesday to Thursday from August to November and February to May.

SCIENCE

McGill University's Redpath Museum (✉ 859 rue Sherbrooke Ouest ☎ 514/398-4086) houses an eclectic collection of dinosaur skeletons, seashells, fossils, minerals, Egyptian mummies, and Stone Age tools in a beautiful 19th-century building. Watch for free lectures.

SIGHTSEEING

For one of the best views of Québec City, take the C$3.75 ferry (✉ 10 rue des Traversiers ☎ 418/643-8420) for a mini cruise across the St. Lawrence River to Lévis and back. Or, also for C$3.75, ride the Funiculaire du Vieux-Québec (✉ 16 rue Petit-Champlain ☎ 418/692-1132), the sharply vertical railway that creaks along the cliff from Lower Town to Upper Town.

What to Read and Watch Before Your Trip

THE APPRENTICESHIP OF DUDDY KRAVITZ BY MORDECAI RICHLER

Duddy Kravitz is a scrappy kid, determined to fight his way out of the Jewish tenements of 1950s Montréal, and this novel is full of colorful characters and classic Montréal neighborhood institutions. The book covers much of the city, and expanses of Québec countryside, from the "cold-water flats" of rue St-Urbain, to the lakes of Québec's Laurentian region. A 1974 movie version stars Richard Dreyfus. Another of Mordecai Richler's novels, *Barney's Version,* is set in Montréal as well, and was adapted into a movie with Paul Giamatti and Rosamund Pike.

SWEET AFFLICTION BY ANNA LEVENTHAL

A series of interweaving, loosely connected stories make up this fresh, funny work of fiction, starring a youthful cast of characters quintessential to Montréal: members of the LGBTQ community, writers, artists, bohemians, and anarchists. Here you'll get slices of Montréal contemporary life, such as in "Moving Day": a story dedicated to Montréal's unique tradition and once-official law in the province, decreeing that any lease in Montréal must end on July 1st, Canada Day—thus forcing all of the city's residents to share the same moving day.

MÃN BY KIM THÚY

Like Thúy's first novel, *Ru, Mãn* is about the Vietnamese immigrant experience in Montréal: this time, with an intimate personal story centered largely around cooking and food. Aside from writing fiction, author Kim Thúy has been a lawyer, cookbook author, and restaurant owner, and her restaurant Ru de Nam was a longtime favorite Vietnamese eatery in Montréal. Ru de Nam is no longer open, but this novel is sure to get you excited about the other great choices in Montréal's Vietnamese dining scene—only some of the great international eating experiences the city has to offer.

THE ARMAND GAMACHE SERIES BY LOUISE PENNY

Chief Inspector Armand Gamache is the hero of Louise Penny's popular mystery crime series, about a provincial police chief solving crimes in the fictional Québec village of Three Pines. The author herself is a longtime resident of Québec's Eastern Townships, just outside Montréal, and bases the series' setting on her own rustic life. Penny's books are a bountiful reading choice for the Québec traveler, as there are seventeen total installments in the series; including and, most recently, *The Madness of Crowds.* Fans will be thrilled to learn that *Three Pines,* based on Penny's beloved novels, is currently being filmed and coming soon to Amazon Prime.

THE PEOPLE'S HISTORY OF QUÉBEC BY JACQUES LACOURSIÈRE AND ROBIN PHILPOT

A concise, well-written account of Québec's colonial history, this book is great preparation before exploring the region. The book touches on the main lives and historical events in this province's rich and complicated past, spanning over 450 years of history: from early French explorers arriving to the Gaspé Peninsula in the 14th century (and their dealings with the Iroquois, Cree, and other First Nations), to the forming of a constitution, ongoing fights for sovereignty, and the creation of a modern society.

COCKROACH BY RAWI HAGE

Canadian author Rawi Hage's second novel is about a cynical, downtrodden man living in Montréal, who often feels—both (meta)physically and metaphorically—as if he is a cockroach. Hage, born in Beirut, introduces the reader to a community of Middle Eastern and European immigrants making life in their adopted city. The story is told through the narrator's dark wit and dry humor, as he struggles with hunger and poverty, desire and pain—and the long, unforgiving Montréal winter.

JESUS OF MONTRÉAL

Jesus of Montréal—along with *The Fall of the American Empire, The Decline of the American Empire,* and *Barbarian Invasions*—is just one of several great films from acclaimed Québécois director Denys Arcand, who makes French-language movies that deal in smart social commentary and Montréal-area settings. In this film, a group of actors are hired by the Catholic Church to create a modernized "Passion of the Christ" play—and end up radicalizing themselves and the audience more than was intended.

LÉOLO

Touching and surreal, this French-Canadian film has plenty of fantasy and enjoyable strangeness (backed up by a Tom Waits soundtrack), telling the story of a boy named Léolo as he comes of age in a very chaotic family. Based in Montréal's Mile End neighborhood, where Léolo's family lives, this critically acclaimed film is full of symbolism and spirituality, with some more realistic commentary on mental illness and familial relations.

THE SCORE

The plot formula in *The Score* will seem familiar: a lone wolf, a convincing rogue sidekick, the big, last job before getting out "for good"—but typical elements are pulled off well here, with plenty of action and entertainment. The target of this classic heist movie (starring Robert De Niro as a Montréal jazz club owner and grand thief) is a $4 million French sceptre stored in the basement of the Montréal Customs House, the most guarded building in Québec, according to the script. Marlon Brando makes a great cameo as an old-time Montréal gangster, and Angela Bassett and Edward Norton complete the cast, in a fun picture with plenty of shots of Montréal's Downtown.

HEATHER O'NEILL

Montréaler Heather O'Neill first came to the attention of Canadian literary circles in 2006 with her Montréal-set novel, *Lullabies for Little Criminals*, the story of Baby, a thirteen-year-old who is drawn into the seedy Montréal underworld of a local pimp. Other novels, also set in Montréal, soon followed: *The Girl Who Was Saturday Night*, about the gorgeous twin children of a famous Québécois folk singer and *The Lonely Hearts Hotel*, which follows two orphan artists who start a circus. O'Neill's latest novel, *When We Lost Our Heads*, tells the story of two best friends in 19th-century Montréal whose intense friendship changes the course of history.

C.R.A.Z.Y.

Often considered one of the most popular Canadian films of all time, Jean-Marc Vallée (director of *Dallas Buyers Club, Big Little Lies, Sharp Objects,* and *Wild*) directed this colorful drama, about a young homosexual man growing up in a conservative Catholic French Canadian family in the 1960s and '70s. This poignant coming-of-age tale is uniquely Québécois—but the late '60s fashion and soundtrack strike a more universal note.

How to Speak Québécois

Français, S'il Vous Plaît

Anytime you visit a foreign country, being familiar with the local language is sure to win you friends. Learn a few phrases, regardless of whether you pronounce them correctly, and the locals will appreciate it. More than 80% of Quebecers claim French as their mother tongue, and while many Quebecers are bilingual or know at least a little English, plenty more don't, especially outside Downtown Montréal and the less touristy areas of the province. Rest assured that you will come across more than a few unilingual Francophones.

As in France, accents and colloquialisms vary widely from region to region. Still, there are several commonly used, uniquely Québécois words and expressions.

Everyday Terms

For starters, Montréal's subway system is known as *le métro*. If you go around asking francophone Quebecers where the closest subway station is, you'll likely be greeted with a blank stare followed by a "*Désolée, mais je ne parle pas l'anglais*" ("I'm sorry, but I don't speak any English"). Similarly, don't go looking for a "convenience store" when you need some last-minute item. Here, even Anglophones call them *dépanneurs*, or "deps" for short.

While here you'll probably spend a lot of time in the *centre-ville* (Downtown) checking out splendid sights like the *Palais de Justice* (not a palace at all, but a courthouse). Except in order to do so you're likely going to need some *argent* (money), or better, *un peu de cash*, which is *franglais* (a curious yet distinct local hybrid of French and English) for

"a bit of money." And where will you be getting that money? Nowhere if you start asking people for the closest ATM. In Québec a bank machine is called a *guichet* (the *gui* pronounced like guitar, the *chet* like "shea").

Dining Out

Of course, many things in Québec, like the menus in most restaurants in Montréal, will be in both French and English, but you'll impress the waitstaff if you order a *steak-frites avec un verre de vin rouge* when you want steak with French fries and a glass of red wine. Later, when you ask for *la facture* or *l'addition* (your bill), and your waiter inquires if you've enjoyed your meal, tell him it was *écoeurant* (the literal translation is "disgusting," or "nauseating," but it's akin to saying something is "sick" for great) and you'll likely see a big amused grin come over his face. It's the rare tourist who's in the know when it comes to Québécois slang and/or colloquialisms, so locals will certainly be impressed if they hear you coming out with the occasional *mon char* (my car) when talking about your wheels or, *ma blonde*, or *ma copine* (girlfriend), when introducing somebody to your female significant other. Conversely, if you're talking about a boyfriend, *mon chum*, or *mon copain*, is how the locals would say it.

Holy Swear Words

Almost all Québécois swear words—aka *sacres*—come courtesy of the Catholic Church, so while the literal translation of words like *tabarnac* (tabernacle) or *câlice* (chalice) might seem pretty tame or nonsensical in English, here they're the equivalent of the dreaded F word.

Chapter 2

TRAVEL SMART

Updated by
Elizabeth Warkentin

⽊ POPULATION
Montréal: 1,700,000

Québec City: 500,000

⌨ LANGUAGE
French

$ CURRENCY
Canadian dollar

☎ AREA CODE
Québec has nine area codes: 354, 367, 418, 438, 450, 514, 579, 581, 819, 873.

⚠ EMERGENCIES
911

🚗 DRIVING
On the right

⚡ ELECTRICITY
110-120V/60Hz; electrical plugs have two flat prongs and a round prong in a V

🕙 TIME
Same as New York

🌐 WEB RESOURCES
www.mtl.org/en
www.quebec-cite.com/en
www.mtlblog.com

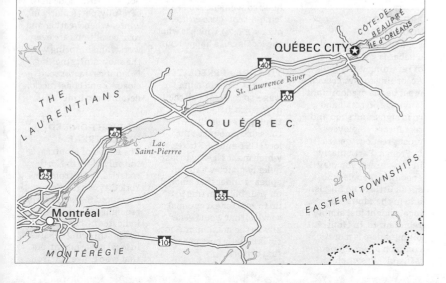

Know Before You Go

You know about poutine and Céline Dion—what else is there? Well, the Canadian province fascinates with a rich culture and history that's been earnestly preserved. Here's what you should know to make the most of your visit.

HISTORY = CONTEXT
The short version: After the English victory in 1759, the francophone people became a minority in the New World. During the 1960s Quiet Revolution, they resolved to uphold their unique culture or risk it being forgotten—defining Québécois identity as separate from that of either English-speaking Canada or France. Quebecers are fiercely proud and protective of their traditions as a result. Remembering this helps to put a lack of English representation into perspective.

BRUSH UP ON YOUR FRENCH
For historical reasons, Québec is very conscious of retaining its language. According to law, French must be the predominant language on retail and road signs, and shop and restaurant employees must greet customers first in French. Particularly in rural areas, you may encounter people who speak little to no English—and in the capital city, locals might just simply be reluctant to. In Montréal, bilingualism is more common and most people will quickly switch to English for you. Nonetheless, attempting a few French phrases is appreciated by locals, and might make traveling easier.

THEY DON'T SPEAK FRENCH
The French language spoken in Québec is a little different than the French you'll hear on the streets of Paris. Mostly it comes down to intonation and accent, but there are many uniquely Québécois words and expressions, too. There are a few that could be helpful like *dépanneur* or "dep" for short: a neighborhood convenience store, or "cinq-à-sept" (also written out as "5-à-7"), which is what the locals call a happy hour.

TIPS ARE APPRECIATED
Servers earn minimum wage, so tips make all the difference. In Québec, tipping is generally 15%—the same amount as the local GST and QST taxes, which makes it easy to just quickly match whatever appears under that amount on your bill. Feel free to tip up to 20% for exceptional service; that would generally be the maximum. A 10% tip is usually customary for taxi drivers.

DOWNLOAD A RIDE-SHARING APP
Having Uber's or its Montréal-based competitor Eva's app on your smartphone will save you a little money and a lot of peace of mind. Montréal's subway only runs until 1:00 am on weekdays and 1:30 am on weekends; starting service again at 5:30 am daily, while Québec City busses and express shuttles always finish at midnight. Particularly in the capital, it might be helpful for those who might get stumped by French signs on public transport.

BRACE YOURSELF FOR BAD ROADS AND CONSTRUCTION
Québec's roads are in abominable shape. In 2018, it was estimated that over C$15 billion in repairs were necessary. The government is set to invest C$135 billion into infrastructure projects such as roads until 2031, so it will take some time for those cracks and potholes to disappear. Drive carefully, particularly in winter when weather and road conditions are even worse, and in spring when the snow starts melting. In summer, factor road closures and construction detours into itineraries.

NO RIGHT-ON-RED IN MONTRÉAL
The Island of Montréal is the only place in North America, aside from New York City, where it's not permitted to turn right on a red light (unless otherwise indicated). Changing the law is still being debated in local government, but that won't save you from

a fine of up to C$200. The SAAQ government website states that elsewhere in Québec, it's not mandatory to turn right on red—in fact, it's a driver's right not to. If you honk at someone for staying put, that can also rack up a C$200 fine if unlucky!

DRINKING IN PUBLIC ISN'T ALWAYS ILLEGAL

Unlike elsewhere in Canada, you are allowed to drink alcohol in public in Québec—but not everywhere. The rule is you must be in a public park and consuming food at the same time so that the liquor is accompanying your meal. A bag of chips won't suffice; the law calls for a picnic-style spread and that you be sitting at a picnic table to do so. The latter caveat is laxer; as long as you're behaving respectfully, authorities will usually turn a blind eye.

GET OUTDOORS IN WINTER

Don't shy away from the chills, as some of Québec's finest joie de vivre happens at -30° Celsius (-22° Fahrenheit). There's skating on the St. Lawrence or at rinks, and festivals like the famed Carnaval de Québec or Igloofest, an electronic music party where guests sport neon snowsuits. Wonderful memories are to be made in the cold.

DRESS FOR THE ELEMENTS—AND COBBLESTONE

Loading up on layers is essential as you never know what Mother Nature's up to. Temperatures can start to plummet as early as

October and linger on until March. Québec winter is notorious for gusty winds and icy sidewalks. Slipping and falling is a Montréaler's rite of passage, but can be avoided by a pair of sturdy shoes. Similarly, the cobblestone streets in historic areas can wreak havoc on high heels, so you may just be better off with flats.

THERE'S AN UNDERGROUND CITY

Montréal's mammoth underground city—known locally as the RÉSO—connects museums, universities, office towers, shopping plazas, hotels, and salons, while providing a welcome escape from the cold or heat and serving as a transport link for 500,000 people per day beneath the city's streets. As well as linking museums like the Place des Arts and the Musée d'art contemporain, the 20 miles of underground is an art network itself. Look for the Art Souterrain festival which showcases contemporary art every February or March in the corridors of Montréal's underground city.

QUÉBEC BEER IS BOOZIER

Québec beers are probably stronger than you're used to unless you're already a craft beer enthusiast. Local and regional microbreweries are known for producing brews with a considerably higher alcohol level, such as darker beers that make the cheeks rosy during winter. Typically, these local beers can be 6% and even rise into the double digits. Know your tipsy limit!

THE LEGAL DRINKING AGE IS 18

In Québec and one other Canadian province, Alberta, the drinking age is 18. That makes Québec a destination for partying, particularly for those who haven't had too much practice doing it yet. Of course, bars and nightclubs cater to different age demographics and crowds—do your research in case you aren't up for getting rowdy.

HAVE THE RIGHT DOCUMENTS

Those with non-U.S. citizenship will likely need to apply for an Electronic Travel Authorization (eTA) from the Canadian government's website. Nationalities that are not eligible for eTAs must apply for visas. Naturalized U.S. residents should carry their naturalization certificate and passport. Permanent residents who aren't citizens should carry their "green card." U.S. residents entering Canada from a third country must have a valid passport, naturalization certificate, or "green card." Regardless of nationality, everyone entering Canada must also download and submit information via the ArriveCAN app to meet the latest COVID-19 health requirements.

Getting Here and Around

Air

Flying time (gate to gate) to Montréal is about 1½ hours from New York, 2½ hours from Chicago, 4 hours from Dallas, and 6 hours from Los Angeles. Flying time to Québec City is about 2 hours from New York, 3 hours from Chicago, 5 hours from Dallas, and 7 hours from Los Angeles.

Trudeau Airport offers self-serve check-in and boarding passes at electronic kiosks throughout the airport. Make sure you arrive at the airport two hours before your flight's scheduled departure.

Security measures at Canadian airports are similar to those in the United States.

AIRPORTS

For service to Montréal, Montréal–Pierre Elliott Trudeau International Airport is 20 km (12.5 miles) west of the city. Québec City's Jean Lesage International Airport is about 13 km (9 miles) northwest of Downtown. Both airports handle domestic and international flights.

GROUND TRANSPORTATION

In Montréal, a taxi from Trudeau International to Downtown costs C$40. All taxi companies must charge the same rate for travel between the airport and Downtown. Taking an Uber might be slightly cheaper.

The least expensive way to get from Trudeau International Airport into the city is to take the 747 Express Bus, operated by Société de transport de Montréal. Shuttles leave from Montréal Central Bus Station, which is connected to Berri–UQAM métro station. They run 24/7—from noon to midnight they leave every 10 minutes or less, while you may wait up to an hour in the early morning hours. The cost is C$10 one-way, payable by card from automated dispensers in the international arrivals area or on the bus in coins only (no bills). The ticket is valid for unlimited travel on the entire Montréal bus and métro system for a 24-hour period.

In Québec City, taxis are available immediately outside the airport exit near the baggage-claim area. A ride into the city costs a flat rate of C$35.10. Taxi Coop Québec is the largest taxi company in the city. You can also take an Uber; depending on the traffic it may save you a few dollars.

FLIGHTS

All the major U.S. airlines, including American, Delta, and United, serve Montréal and Québec City.

Regularly scheduled flights from the United States to Montréal and Québec City as well as flights within Canada are available on Air Canada and the regional airlines associated with it, including Air Canada Express (reservations are made through Air Canada). Porter Airlines also has connecting service to Montréal and Québec City from select U.S. cities, via Toronto's Billy Bishop Airport.

🚲 Bicycle

Québec continues to expand its Route Verte (Green Route), North America's largest network of bike trails totaling over 5,000 km (more than 3,100 miles). Covering the southern half of the province, the bikeways link to Canadian provinces Ontario and New Brunswick, as well as New England and New York. For information and a route planner, head to Route Verte's website or contact Vélo Québec.

☉ Boat and Ferry

The Québec–Lévis ferry, which crosses the St. Lawrence River, gives you a magnificent panorama of Old Québec on its trips to and from Lévis. Although the crossing takes only 12 minutes, the waiting time can increase the trip to an hour. The cost is C$3.65. The first ferry from Québec City leaves weekdays at 6:20 am from the pier at rue Dalhousie, opposite Place Royale. Crossings run every half an hour during weekdays until 6:30 pm. It then runs hourly until 2:20 am. On weekends and holidays, the ferry leaves hourly from 6:30 am to 2:20 am. Schedules can change, so be sure to check the ferry website or call ahead.

☻ Bus

Several private bus lines serve the province. Orléans Express is probably the most convenient, as it offers regular service between Montréal and Québec City and its buses are clean and comfortable. The trip takes a little over three hours. Limocar, another bus line, serves the Eastern Townships, while Greyhound Lines provides interprovincial service. Megabus offers somewhat more luxurious service to the province of Ontario and the city of Buffalo.

Bus terminals in Montréal and Québec City offer service all week. In some small towns the bus station is simply a counter in a local gas station. In rural Québec it's a good idea to bring along a French–English dictionary, although merchants can handle a simple ticket sale in English.

Buses from Montréal to Québec City depart 17 times daily between 6 am and 11 pm. A one-way ticket booked at least a week in advance starts at C$25. All intercity bus lines servicing Montréal arrive at and depart from the city's downtown bus terminal, the Gare d'Autocars de Montréal, which is conveniently located next to the Berri-UQÀM métro station.

Many bus companies offer discounts if you book in advance, usually either 7 or 14 days ahead. Discounts are available for kids.

Most bus lines don't accept reservations for specific seats. You should plan on picking up your tickets at least 45 minutes before the bus's scheduled departure time.

☻ Car

Montréal is accessible from the rest of Canada via the Trans-Canada Highway, which crosses the southern part of the island as Autoroute 20, with Autoroute 720 leading into Downtown. From New York, take I–87 north until it becomes Autoroute 15 at the Canadian border; continue for another 47 km (29 miles) to the outskirts of Montréal. From I–91 through Massachusetts via New Hampshire and Vermont, you can take Route 55 to Autoroute 10.

■TIP➜ At the border you must clear Canadian Customs, so be prepared with your passport and car registration. On holidays and during the peak summer season, expect to wait a half hour or more at the major crossings. Border wait times can be checked on the Transport Québec website.

Getting Here and Around

Montréal and Québec City are linked by Autoroute 20 on the south shore of the St. Lawrence River and by Autoroute 40 on the north shore. On both highways, the ride between the two cities is about 240 km (149 miles) and takes about three hours.

In Québec the road signs are in French, but the important ones have pictograms. Keep in mind the following terms: *centre-ville* (Downtown), *arrêt* (stop), *détenteurs de permis* (permit holders only), *gauche* (left), *droit* (right), *ouest* (west), and *est* (east).

Drivers must carry vehicle registration and proof of insurance coverage, which is compulsory in Canada. Québec drivers are covered by the Québec government no-fault insurance plan. Drivers from outside Québec can obtain a Canadian Non-Resident Inter-Provincial Motor Vehicle Liability Insurance Card, available from any U.S. insurance company, as evidence of financial responsibility in Canada. The minimum liability in Québec is C$50,000. If you are driving a car that isn't registered in your name, carry a letter from the owner that authorizes your use of the vehicle.

GASOLINE
Gasoline is always sold in liters; 3.8 liters make a gallon. As of this writing, gas prices in Québec were around C$1.10 per liter (this works out to about $3 per gallon U.S.). Fuel comes in several grades, denoted as *regulière*, *supérieure*, and *prémium*. Major credit cards are widely accepted. Receipts are provided —ask for a *reçu*.

PARKING
Expect on-street parking in Montréal to be hard to find; your best bet is to leave the car at your hotel garage and take public transportation or a cab. If you must drive, ask your concierge to recommend a garage near your destination. Be extra careful where you park if it snows, to avoid getting towed. Parking in Québec City is much less stressful, although it's also advisable to leave the car at the hotel and walk—especially if you're heading to Vieux-Québec.

The narrow streets of the Old City leave few two-hour metered parking spaces available. Nevertheless, several parking garages at central locations charge about C$12 a day on weekdays or C$7 for 12 hours on weekends. Main garages are at Hôtel de Ville (City Hall), Place d'Youville, Edifice Marie-Guyart, Place Québec, Château Frontenac, rue St-Paul, and the Old Port.

ROAD CONDITIONS
In Montréal and Québec City the jumble of bicycle riders, delivery vehicles, taxis, and municipal buses can be chaotic. In the countryside at night, roads are lighted at exit points from major highways but are otherwise dark. Roads in the province aren't very good, especially during the spring pothole season—be prepared for some spine-jolting bumps and potholes, and check tire pressure once in a while.

In winter, Montréal streets are kept mostly clear of snow and ice, but outside the city the situation can deteriorate. Locals are notorious for exceeding the speed limit, so keep an eye on your mirrors. For up-to-date reports on road conditions throughout the province, go to Transport Québec's website.

ROADSIDE EMERGENCIES
Dial 911 in an emergency. Contact CAA, the Canadian Automobile Association, in the event of a flat tire, dead battery, empty gas tank, or other car-related mishap. Automobile Association of America membership includes CAA service.

RULES OF THE ROAD

By law, you're required to wear seat belts even in the backseat. Infant seats also are required. Radar-detection devices are illegal in Québec; just having one in your car is punishable by fine. Speed limits, given in kilometers, are usually within the 90 kph–100 kph (50 mph–60 mph) range outside the cities.

Right turns on a red light are allowed in most of the province, the island of Montréal being the notable exception, where they're prohibited. Driving with a blood-alcohol content of 0.08% or higher is illegal and can earn you a stiff fine and jail time. Headlights are compulsory in inclement weather. Drivers aren't permitted to use handheld cell phones. The laws here are similar to the rest of North America.

CAR RENTAL

Rates in Montréal start from about C$20 a day for an economy car with air-conditioning and unlimited kilometers. If you prefer a manual-transmission car, check whether the rental agency offers stick shifts; many agencies in Canada don't.

You must be at least 21 years old to rent a car in Québec, and some car-rental agencies don't rent to drivers under 25. Most rental companies don't allow you to drive on gravel roads. Child seats are compulsory for children ages five and under.

Rentals at the airports near Québec City and Montréal are usually more expensive than neighborhood rentals.

🚊 Train

Amtrak offers its daily Adirondack service from New York City's Penn Station to Montréal, although the train sometimes arrives too late to make any connecting trains that evening. Connections are available, often the next day, to Canadian rail line VIA Rail's Canadian routes. The ride takes up to 11 hours, and one-way tickets start at C$92.

VIA Rail trains run from Montréal to Québec City in three hours, arriving at the 19th-century Gare du Palais in Lower Town. Trains on the Montréal—Québec City route run five times daily on weekdays, three to four times daily on weekends. Tickets can be purchased in advance at the station prior to departure or on the VIA Rail website. If you're lucky you can sometimes find discounted fares online for as little as C$37. They are usually nonrefundable.

Business-class tickets start at C$104 each way and include early boarding, seat selection, and a three-course meal with wine.

To save money, look into rail passes. But be aware that if you don't plan to cover many miles, you may come out ahead by buying individual tickets. Senior citizens (60 and older), children (11 and under), and students are often entitled to discounts.

The Train de Charlevoix train system takes you from Québec City to Baie-St-Paul and stops in between, priced at C$88 round-trip. From Baie St Paul, one can go on to La Malbaie, Charlevoix for C$54 round-trip. The small villages and the natural beauty along the route are impressive.

Essentials

Activities

BASEBALL

There is currently one major league baseball team in Canada, the Toronto Blue Jays, founded in 1977. Canada's first major league team, the Montréal Expos, formed in 1969, relocated to Washington, D.C., in 2005. There are proposals to bring the Expos back to Montréal, even part-time, but in the meantime, baseball fans can take in a Capitales game at Québec's Canac stadium. Games are affordable and lively and the stadium, built in 1939, is set in the middle of the city and has trees that are over 200 years old in the outfield. There's also an inflatable dome, affordable concessions, and nice views. ⊕ *capitalesdequebec.com*

BIKING

Weather permitting, one of the best ways to discover Montréal is on a bicycle. This is an incredibly bike-friendly metropolis, and there are thousands of designated bike paths connecting diverse neighborhoods across the island, running along the river, and through parks and forests. The most popular cycling trail on the island begins at the Old Port and winds its way to the shores of Lac St-Louis in Lachine. Pack a picnic lunch; there are plenty of green spaces where you can stop and refuel along the way. If you like to bike but would rather not do it on city streets, ferries at the Old Port can take you to Île Ste-Hélène and the south shore of the St. Lawrence River, where riders can connect to hundreds of miles of trails in the Montérégie region.

HIKING

Canada's second-largest province is packed with hiking trails revealing nature's splendor. The Eastern Townships has a good mix of paths for all fitness levels, including over mountain landscapes with campsites or inns along the way. National parks like La Mauricie and Forillon offer more challenging, remote treks while the Magdalen Islands are perfect for those seeking short and scenic routes.

GOLF

Montréal golf enthusiasts have several excellent golf courses available to them, many less than a half-hour drive from Downtown. If you're willing to trek a bit farther (about 45 minutes), you'll find some of the best golfing in the province. For a complete listing of the many golf courses in the area, Tourisme Québec is the best place to start.

HOCKEY

Ice hockey is nothing short of an institution in Montréal, the city that arguably gave birth to the sport back in the late 19th century. Although variations of the game are said to have been played in other U.S. and Canadian cities as early as 1800, the first organized game of modern hockey was played in Montréal in 1875, and the first official team, the McGill University Hockey Club, was founded in Montréal in 1880. The city's beloved Montréal Canadiens (⊕ *canadiens.nhl. com*) is the oldest club in the National Hockey League and, as Montréalers are keen to tell you, one of the most successful teams in North American sports history. Tickets tend to sell out well before the game—especially if the Habs, as they're nicknamed, play their arch rivals, the Toronto Maple Leafs. You can buy tickets on the NHL website starting from C$54 or show up to the Bell Centre on game day, when scalpers usually drop stubs to half price after the puck drops. During playoffs, the city sets up a massive tailgate party called Fan Jam.

SKIING AND SNOWBOARDING

Skiing makes for a great day trip from either Montréal or Québec City. Near Montréal, is Ski Bromont, a year-round resort with runs for different experience levels, and Mont Saint-Saveur, offering night skiing. As for cross-country skiing, you needn't even leave the city to find choice locations to pursue the sport.

There's a network of winding trails stretching throughout Parc du Mont-Royal, and the Lachine Canal offers a 12-km (7-mile) stretch of relatively flat terrain, making for both a scenic and relatively simple cross-country excursion. There are pros and cons to skiing in the Eastern Townships and the Laurentians. The slopes in the Townships are generally steeper and slightly more challenging, but it requires more time to get out to them. Also, the Townships' centers tend to be quieter and more family-oriented, so if it's après-ski action you're looking for, you might prefer heading out to a Laurentian hill like Mont St-Saveur where, for many, partying is as much the experience as is conquering the slopes.

Québec City has several lodges only an hour's drive or less from Old Québec. Le Relais and Le Massif de Charlevoix are popular with locals, particularly families, while Stoneham Mountain Resort features challenging freestyle runs and outdoor hot tubs for a soothing après-ski.

SWIMMING

Most of the city's municipal outdoor pools are open from mid-June through August. Admission is free on weekdays. On weekends and holidays there's a small fee of no more than C$4 at some pools, depending on the borough. The city's man-made beach, Parc-Plage l'Île Notre-Dame, on the west side of Île Notre-Dame probably has the cleanest water (tested and monitored) in Montréal.

🛏 Accommodations

In Montréal and Québec City you have a choice of luxury hotels, moderately priced modern properties, and small older hotels with fewer conveniences but sometimes more charm. Options in small towns and in the country include large, full-service resorts; small, privately owned hotels; roadside motels; and bed-and-breakfasts. Even outside the cities it's a good idea to make reservations.

Expect accommodations to cost more in summer than in the colder months (except for places such as ski resorts, where winter is high season). When making reservations, ask about special deals and packages. Big-city hotels that cater to business travelers often offer weekend packages, and many city hotels offer rooms at up to 50% off in winter. If you're planning to visit Montréal or Québec City or a resort area in high season, book well in advance. Also be aware of any special events or festivals that may coincide with your visit and fill every room for miles around.

APARTMENT AND HOUSE RENTALS

Airbnb (🌐 www.airbnb.com) has a wide selection of cabins and chalets for rent.

BED-AND-BREAKFASTS

B&Bs, which are also known as gîtes in Québec, can be found in both the country and the cities. For assistance in booking these, be sure to check out B&B websites (🌐 www.bedandbreakfast.com is a good resources for B&Bs throughout the province). Room quality varies from house to house as well, so ask to see a few rooms before making a choice.

The nonprofit organization Association de l'Agrotourisme et du Tourisme Gourmand du Québec has extensive listings of

Essentials

B&Bs, both urban and rural, as well as farms that take paying guests.

HOTELS

Canada doesn't have a national rating system for hotels, but Québec's tourism ministry rates the province's hotels and bed-and-breakfasts; the stars are more a reflection of the number of facilities and amenities than of the hotel's performance. Hotels are rated zero to three stars (B&Bs, zero to four suns), with zero stars or suns representing minimal comfort and few services and three stars or four suns being the very best. All hotels listed have private baths unless otherwise noted.

Montréal is always hosting a festival or an international convention, so the hotels are consistently booked. This takes visitors by surprise. Many of the quaint auberges have a small number of rooms, so they fill up fast. It's necessary to book months ahead for the Grand Prix, the Jazz Festival, the World Film Festival, and all holiday weekends.

⊚ Customs and Duties

U.S. Customs and Immigration has preclearance services at **Pierre Elliott Trudeau International Airport,** which serves Montréal. This allows U.S.-bound air passengers to depart their airplane directly on arrival at their U.S. destination without further inspection and delays.

American visitors may bring in, duty-free, for personal consumption, 200 cigarettes, 50 cigars, 7 ounces of tobacco, and 1 bottle (1.5 liters or 40 imperial ounces) of wine or liquor respectively or up to 8.5 liters of beer or ale. Any alcohol and tobacco products in excess of these amounts are subject to duty, provincial fees, and taxes. You can also bring in gifts for friends or family duty-free, as long as each gift does not exceed C$60 in value.

Cats and dogs must have a certificate issued by a licensed veterinarian that clearly identifies the animal and vouches that it has been vaccinated against rabies during the preceding 36 months. Certificates aren't necessary for Seeing Eye dogs. Plant material must be declared and inspected. There may be restrictions on some live plants, bulbs, and seeds. You may bring food for your own use, as long as the quantity is consistent with the duration of your visit and restrictions or prohibitions on some fruits and vegetables are observed.

Canada's firearms laws are significantly stricter than those in much of the United States. All handguns and semiautomatic and fully automatic weapons are prohibited and cannot be brought into the country. Sporting rifles and shotguns may be imported provided they are to be used for sporting, hunting, or competing while in Canada. All firearms must be declared to Canada Customs at the first point of entry. Failure to declare firearms will result in their seizure, and criminal charges may be made. Regulations require visitors to have a confirmed Firearms Declaration to bring any guns into Canada; a fee of C$25 applies, valid for 60 days but good for one year if renewed before it expires. For more information, contact the Canadian Firearms Centre.

⊕ Emergencies

All embassies are in Ottawa. The U.S. consulate in Montréal is open weekdays from 7:30 am to 5 pm, while in Québec City it's open weekdays 9 am to 4 pm. The U.S. Consulate maintains a list of medical specialists in the Montréal area.

In Montréal, the main English-language hospital is the Montréal General Hospital (McGill University Health Centre). Many pharmacies in Montréal stay open until midnight, including Jean Coutu and Pharmaprix stores. Some are open around the clock, including the Pharmaprix on chemin de la Côte-des-Neiges.

In Québec City, the Centre Hospitalier Universitaire de Québec is the city's largest institution and incorporates the teaching hospitals Pavillon CHUL in Ste-Foy and Pavillon Hôtel-Dieu, the main hospital in Vieux-Québec. Most outlets of the big pharmacy chains in the region (including Jean Coutu, Brunet and Uniprix) are open every day and offer free delivery.

🍴 Dining

French-Canadian fast food follows the same concept as American fast food, though barbecue chicken is also popular. Local chains to watch for include St-Hubert, which serves rotisserie chicken; Chez Cora, which specializes in breakfasts; and La Belle Province, Lafleur, and Valentine, all of which serve hamburgers, hot dogs, and fries. For a vegetarian option, try the excellent Montréal chain Resto Végo.

Many restaurants post their *menu du jour* outside, so you can stroll along and let your cravings guide the way. Nevertheless, bear in mind that reservations are a must at most restaurants during holidays, Winter Carnival, and in the summer months, when the coveted outdoor terraces open. The *table d'hôte*, a cost-cutting special, is a regular at many Montréal restaurants. Upscale restaurants serve elaborate lunch tables d'hôte at reduced prices.

WINES, BEER, AND SPIRITS

Some of the best local microbreweries include Unibroue (Fin du Monde, U Blonde, U Rousse), Brasseurs du Nord (Boréale), and McAuslan (Griffon, St. Ambroise). The local hard cider P.O.M. is also excellent. Caribou, a traditional concoction made from red wine, vodka (or some other liquor), spices, and, usually, maple syrup, is available at many winter events and festivals throughout the province, such as Québec City's winter carnival. Small bars may also offer the drink in season.

The province's liquor purveyor, SAQ, stocks a wide choice of wines (with a heavy emphasis on those from France) and is also the only place you can buy hard liquor; most SAQ stores are open during regular business hours. Supermarkets and convenience stores carry lower-end wines at notably higher prices but they can sell wine and beer until 11 pm all week (long after SAQ stores have closed). The minimum legal age for alcohol consumption is 18.

In Québec, it is illegal to drink alcohol in public with one key exception: in public parks, when consumed with food as part of a meal.

📅 Holidays

Canadian national holidays are as follows: New Year's Day (January 1), Good Friday (late March or early April), Easter Monday (the Monday following Good Friday), Victoria Day (called Fête des Patriotes in Québec; late May), Canada Day (July 1), Labor Day (early September), Thanksgiving (mid-October), Remembrance Day (November 11), Christmas, and Boxing Day (December 26). St. Jean Baptiste Day (June 24) is a provincial holiday.

Essentials

$ Money

Throughout this book, prices are given in Canadian dollars, which at this writing are worth roughly 75¢ to the American dollar. The price of a cup of coffee ranges from C$2.50 or more, depending on how upscale or downscale the place is; beer costs C$3 to C$7 in a bar; a smoked-meat sandwich costs about C$8 to C$10; and museum admission can cost anywhere from nothing to C$20.

■ TIP➜ **Prices throughout this guide are given for adults. Substantially reduced fees are almost always available for children, students, and senior citizens.**

CURRENCY AND EXCHANGE

U.S. dollars are sometimes accepted in Canada, especially in communities near the border. Major U.S. credit cards are accepted in most areas.

The units of currency in Canada are the Canadian dollar (C$) and the cent, in almost the same denominations as U.S. currency ($5, $10, $20, 5¢, 10¢, 25¢, etc.). The exception is 1¢ coins, which are no longer minted and circulated, so expect to pay and receive change rounded up or down by 5¢ accordingly. The C$1 and C$2 bills are also no longer used in Canada; they have been replaced by C$1 and C$2 coins (known as "loonies," because of the loon that appears on the coin, and "toonies," respectively).

At the time of writing, the exchange rate is US$1 to C1.27¢.

Bank cards are widely accepted in Québec and throughout Canada. There are many branches of Québec's financial cooperative, La Caisse populaire Desjardins (a "Caisse Pop" as it's locally referred to), as well as bank machines (ATMs), throughout the region.

▼ Nightlife

If nightlife in Montréal could be distilled into a cocktail, it would be one part sophisticated New York club scene (with the accompanying pretension), one part Parisian joie-de-vivre (and, again, a dash of snobbery), and one part Barcelonan stamina (which keeps the clubs booming until dawn). Montréal's nightlife swings with a robust passion. From the early evening "5-à-7" after-work cocktail circuit, to the slightly later concerts and supper clubs (restaurant–dance club hybrids where people dance on the tables after eating off them), on into the even later dance club scene, all tastes, cultural backgrounds, and legal ages join the melee. Clubbing is, to say the least, huge in Montréal. Some restaurants are even installing discotheques in their basements.

Québec City has a variety of cultural institutions for a town of its size, from the symphony to small theater companies. To sample the nightlife, you'll need to head to the clubs and cafés of rue St-Jean, avenue Cartier, and Grande-Allée, as well as Lower Town. Most bars and clubs stay open until 3 am.

▢ Packing

If you're visiting Montréal anytime between November and May, be sure to bring some warm clothes, or be prepared to purchase some while you're here. Come winter Montréal gets cold—very cold—with temperatures almost always dipping below the freezing mark from December until late March. A good winter coat, scarf, hat (locally called a *toque*), gloves, and warm winter boots are pretty much a necessity in Québec if you want to be comfortable going outside in the winter months. In summer, however, temperatures regularly rise above 86°F (30°C) and Downtown

Montréal, in particular, can get very humid, so bring a few pairs of shorts, sandals, and warm weather clothes.

Passports and Visas

All travelers will need a passport or other accepted secure documents to enter or reenter the United States. Naturalized U.S. residents should carry their naturalization certificate. Permanent residents who aren't citizens should carry their "green card." U.S. residents entering Canada from a third country must have a valid passport, naturalization certificate, or "green card."

■TIP➔ **All American visitors require an Electronic Travel Authorization (eTA) if arriving by plane (an eTA is not necessary if arriving by land or sea).**

Safety

Montréalers are keen to boast they can walk the streets of their city at any time of day or night without fear of incident. And although both Montréal and Québec City are among the safest cities in North America, travelers should nevertheless be on their guard for pickpockets and other petty criminals, especially when traveling on Montréal's often-crowded métro system.

Taxes

A goods and services tax (GST or TPS in Québec) of 5% applies on virtually every transaction in Canada except for the purchase of basic groceries. In addition to imposing the GST, Québec levies a provincial sales tax of 9.975% on most goods and services as well.

Departing passengers in Montréal pay a C$30, plus tax, airport-improvement fee that's included in the cost of an airline ticket.

Time

Montréal and Québec City are both in the Eastern Standard Time Zone. Los Angeles is three hours behind local time and Chicago is one hour behind.

Tipping

Tips and service charges aren't usually added to a bill in Canada. In general, tip at least 15% of the total bill. This goes for waiters and waitresses, barbers and hairdressers, and taxi drivers. Porters and doormen should get about C$2 a bag. For maid service, leave at least C$2 per person a day (C$3 to C$5 in luxury hotels).

Tours

DAY TOURS AND GUIDES

In Montréal, from May through October, Bateau-Mouche runs four harbor excursions and an evening supper cruise daily. The boats are reminiscent of the ones that cruise the canals of the Netherlands—wide-beamed and low-slung, with a glassed-in passenger deck. Boats leave from the Jacques-Cartier Pier at the foot of Place Jacques-Cartier in the Vieux-Port.

Gray Line has nine different types of tours of Montréal from June through October and one tour the rest of the year. There are also day trips to Mont Tremblant and Québec City. The company offers pickup service at the major hotels and at Centre Infotouriste (✉ *1001 Dorchester Square*).

Essentials

In Québec City, Autocar Dupont/Old Québec Tours runs bus tours of the city, departing across the square from the Hôtel Château Laurier (✉ *1230 pl. Georges V*); you can buy tickets at most major hotels. The company runs guided tours in a minibus as well as tours of Côte-de-Beaupré and Île d'Orléans, and whale-watching excursions to Charlevoix. Tours run year-round and cost C$36–C$140. Call for a reservation and the company will pick you up at your hotel.

Croisières AML has day and evening cruises, some of which include dinner, on the St. Lawrence River aboard the MV *Louis-Jolliet*. The 1½- to 4-hour cruises run from May through mid-October and start at C$35 plus tax.

⊙ Visitor Information

In Montréal, Centre Infotouriste, on Dorchester Square, has extensive tourist information on Montréal and the rest of the province of Québec, as well as a currency-exchange service and Internet café. It's open from 9 am to 6 pm daily. The Vieux-Montréal branch is open 9–7 in high season, and 10–6 in low season.

In Québec City, the Québec City Region Tourism and Convention Bureau's visitor information center in Montcalm is open June 21–to August 31, daily 9–7; September through October, daily 9–6; and November 1–June 20, daily 9–5. A mobile information service operates between mid-June and September 7 (look for the mopeds marked with a big question mark).

The Québec government tourism department, Tourisme Québec, has a center open September–June 20, daily 9–5; and June 21–August 31, daily 8:30–7. Tourisme Québec can provide information on specific towns' tourist bureaus.

Montréal and Québec City's Best Festivals

Citizens of Montréal and Québec City always find a good reason to party. Québec City celebrates its long, frigid winters with a carnival that includes a boat race across a frozen river. And Montréal holds February's cold at bay with a sizzling food extravaganza. Throughout the province, the rest of the year is full of festivals celebrating jazz, folklore, film, classical music, theater, fireworks, comedy, and hot-air balloons.

JANUARY AND FEBRUARY

★ Carnaval de Québec (Québec Winter Carnival)

FESTIVALS | The biggest winter carnival in the world takes place on the Plains of Abraham over three weekends from the end of January to mid-February, with winter sports competitions, ice-sculpture contests, and parades. ⊠ *Parc de la Francophonie, Québec City* ☎ *866/422–7628* ⊕ *www.carnaval.qc.ca.*

Fête des Neiges de Montréal

FESTIVALS | Over four weekends from mid-January to mid-February, Montréal celebrates its winter festival at Parc Jean Drapeau across the Port from Old Montréal. Hockey games, tubing, skiing, dog sledding, and a Himalayan zip line are perfect activities to enjoy in the cold winter weather but don't forget your *toque,* pronounced *took* with long O's. ⊠ *Montréal* ☎ *514/872–6120* ⊕ *www. parcjeandrapeau.com/events/fete-des-neiges-de-Montréal* Ⓜ *Jean-Drapeau.*

Montréal en Lumière (Montréal Highlights)

CULTURAL FESTIVALS | This festival brightens the bleak days of February with fabulous food and cultural activities. Leading chefs from around the world give demonstrations and take over the kitchens of top restaurants for special dinners. "Nuit Blanche," held on the last Saturday of this festival, lets you explore the city until the wee hours of the morning. Many of the events are free, and there are shuttle services to take you to the locations. Dress extra warmly. ☎ *514/288–9955, 855/864–3737* ⊕ *www.Montréalenlumiere.com.*

MARCH

Art Souterrain

ART FESTIVALS | Art Souterrain offers an annual free exhibition of contemporary art in an unlikely place: the public corridors of Montréal's Underground City. The ingenious location puts art in front of a prospective daily audience of the nearly 500,000 people that walk beneath Downtown Montréal through vast corridors that connect office towers, shopping centers, hotels, convention halls, universities, restaurants, museums, and performing arts venues. Along over three miles linking the Complexe Guy Favreau to the 1000 de la Gauchetière (as well as nine additional satellite venues aboveground), Art Souterrain exhibits 70 contemporary works in various mediums (sculpture, performance, photography, video, audio, painting), all tied together by a theme that addresses a modern-day social issue. ⊠ *RÉSO Underground City, Montréal* ☎ *800/565–5068* ⊕ *artsouterrain.com.*

APRIL

Blue Metropolis (Metropolis Bleu) Festival

READINGS/LECTURES | Taking place in late April/early May, the multicultural Blue Metropolis Montréal International Literary Festival (⊕ *www.metropolisbleu.org*) presents more than 200 reading, writing, and discussion workshops in English, French, Spanish, Portuguese, and other languages. ⊠ *Montréal* ☎ *514/932–1112* ⊕ *bluemetropolis.org.*

Montréal and Québec City's Best Festivals

MAY

★ Go Bike Montréal Festival

BIKING | The biggest bike celebration in North America, Féria de Vélo de Montréal, includes the Tour la Nuit, a 22-kilometer (14-mile) nighttime ride through the city. The weeklong festival culminates in as many as 50,000 cyclists taking over the streets for the Tour de l'Île, a 50-km (31-mile) ride along a route encircling Montréal. ✉ *Montréal* ☎ *514/521–8356, 800/567–8356* ⊕ *www.velo.qc.ca/en/ event-category/go-bike-Montréal-festival.*

JUNE

Fringe Festival

FESTIVALS | Open to playwrights, acting troupes, dancers, comics, and musicians, the Fringe Festival, during the first three weeks of June, is run on a lottery system to determine which performers get onstage. ✉ *Montréal* ☎ *514/849–3378* ⊕ *www.Montréalfringe.ca.*

Les FrancoFolies de Montréal

MUSIC FESTIVALS |Such major Québécois stars as Isabelle Boulay, Les soeurs Boulay, Coeur de Pirate, Paul Piché, and Nicola Ciccone play to packed concert halls, while lesser-known artists play free outdoor concerts during this mid-June festival celebrating the art of French songwriting. More than 1,000 musicians, many from France, Belgium, Senegal, and Haiti, perform rock, hip-hop, jazz, funk, and Latin. ✉ *Montréal* ⊕ *www. francofolies.com.*

Mondiale de la Bière

FESTIVALS | In Montréal, for five days every June, this beer festival transforms the exhibition hall of Palais des Congrès into a giant indoor beer garden serving some 600 ales, lagers, and ciders from nearly 100 microbreweries from Québec and around the world. Admission is free, tasting coupons are $1 each. ✉ *Montréal* ☎ *514/722–9640* ⊕ *www.festivalmondialbiere.qc.ca/en.*

JULY

Festival d'Été de Québec (Québec City Summer Festival)

MUSIC FESTIVALS | This exuberant 11-day music extravaganza in Québec City features rock, folk, hip-hop, and world-beat music. The main concerts rock nightly with 10 indoor and outdoor stages in early July in or near Old Québec, including one on the Plains of Abraham. ✉ *Québec City* ☎ *418/529–5200, 888/992–5200* ⊕ *www.infofestival.com.*

Festival International de Jazz de Montréal (Montréal International Jazz Festival)

MUSIC FESTIVALS | This major event, held since 1978, attracts more than 1,000 musicians for more than 400 concerts held over a period of nearly two weeks from the end of June through the beginning of July. Past stars have included B.B. King, Ella Fitzgerald, Lauryn Hill, Wynton Marsalis, Chick Corea, Dave Brubeck, and Canada's most famed singer-pianist, Diana Krall. You can also hear blues, Latin rhythms, gospel, Cajun, and world music. ✉ *Montréal* ☎ *514/871–1881, 855/299– 3378* ⊕ *www.Montréaljazzfest.com/en.*

Festival International Nuits d'Afrique

MUSIC FESTIVALS | From France to Jamaica to Cabo Verde, from traditional to contemporary sounds, this eclectic two-week music and dance festival brings together over 700 artists from 30 countries, for the biggest world music gathering in the Americas. At the outdoor stages in the Quartier des Spectacles, you'll find an appealing selection of pop-up restaurants and bars, a family area, open-air workshops with master dancers and drummers, and a Timbuktu market. Check the website for concerts held year-round. ✉ *Montréal* ☎ *514/499–9239* ⊕ *www.festivalnuitsda- frique.com/en/.*

Festival OFF

FESTIVALS | A sidekick of the Festival d'Été International de Québec, this music event takes to the stage in July at the same time as its big brother. Most of the shows are free and take place in offbeat spaces such as in front of Église St-Jean-Baptiste, Bar Le Sacrilège, and the Musée de l'Amérique Française, just to name a few. ⊠ *Québec City* ⊕ *www.quebecoff.org.*

Juste pour Rire (Just for Laughs)

FESTIVALS | Montréal's world-famous comedy festival hosts international comics, in French and English, from the second through third weeks of July. There are tons of shows to watch, from big concert halls to quaint bars. Walk around the Quartier des Spectacles during the festival and giggle your way from one outdoor act to another. The twins parade is not to be missed. ⊠ *Montréal* ☎ *514/845–3155* ⊕ *www.hahaha.com.*

AUGUST

Fêtes de la Nouvelle France (New France Festiva)

CULTURAL FESTIVALS | During this five-day festival, in early to mid-August, Québec City's centuries-old heritage comes alive. The streets of Lower Town are transported back in time, and events range from an old-time farmers' market to games and music—all done in period costume. ⊠ *Québec City* ☎ *418/694–3311* ⊕ *www.nouvellefrance.qc.ca/en.*

International des Montgolfières St-Jean-sur-Richelieu (St-Jean-sur-Richelieu's Hot-Air Balloon Festival)

FESTIVALS | This colorful airborne event, the largest gathering of hot-air balloons in Canada, takes flight about 25 minutes' drive southeast of Montréal. The balloons are so vivid and plentiful that you can sometimes see them from Downtown. ⊠ *Montréal* ☎ *450/346–6000* ⊕ *www.ballooncanada.com.*

OCTOBER

Black and Blue Festival

CULTURAL FESTIVALS | Organized by the Bad Boy Club Montréal, this festival started more than 25 years ago as a gay community fundraiser for AIDS charities. It has grown to be a gay and gay-friendly week (in mid-October) of intense partying, featuring soirées like the Leather Ball, the Military Ball, and the Black and Blue Ball. ⊠ *Montréal* ☎ *514/875–7026* ⊕ *www.bbcm.org.*

HOLI Festival of Colors

CULTURAL FESTIVALS | Inspired by the Indian tradition, this Montréal festival organized by the South Asian Alliance of Québec features live bands, an arts and crafts bazaar, food stalls, and of course, a famous fight of colors. ⊠ *Montréal* ⊕ *www.holiMontréal.com.*

NOVEMBER AND DECEMBER

★ Marché de Noël allemand de Québec (German Christmas Market of Québec City)

FESTIVALS | In the large plaza fronting city hall, as well as the little park across the street, neat rows of darling little wooden huts exactly like those you'd find in Germany offer stollen, steaming hot pretzels, gingerbread, mulled wine, roasted chestnuts, and other aromatic foods, while jewelry designers, wood sculptors, glassmakers, and other artisans chat animatedly with customers, as German Christmas carols play in the background. If you can't get to Europe for the holidays, Québec City's German Christmas market is probably the most magical and most authentic you'll find in North America. The market opens in the third week of November and lasts until December 23rd. ⊠ *Montréal* ⊕ *www.noelallemandquebec.com/en.*

Helpful French Phrases

BASICS

Hello	Bonjour	bohn- zhoor
Yes/No	Oui/non	wee/nohn
Please	S'il vous plaît	seel voo play
Thank you	Merci	mair- see
You're welcome	De rien	deh ree- ehn
I'm Sorry (apology)	Pardon	pahr- don
Good morning	Bonjour	bohn- zhoor
Good evening	Bonsoir	bohn- swahr
Goodbye	Au revoir	o ruh- vwah
Mr. (Sir)	Monsieur	muh- syuh
Mrs.	Madame	ma- dam
Miss	Mademoiselle	mad-mwa- ze
Pleased to meet you	Enchanté(e)	ohn-shahn- tay
How are you?	Comment allez-vous?	kuh-mahn- tahl-ay voo

NUMBERS

one-half	un demi	uhn de-mee
one	un	uhn
two	deux	deuh
three	trois	twah
four	quatre	kaht-ruh
five	cinq	sank
six	six	seess
seven	sept	set
eight	huit	wheat
nine	neuf	nuf
ten	dix	deess
eleven	onze	ohnz
twelve	douze	dooz
thirteen	treize	trehz
fourteen	quartorze	kah-torz
fifteen	quinze	kanz
sixteen	seize	sez
seventeen	dix-sept	deez-set
eighteen	dix-huit	deez-wheat
nineteen	dix-neuf	deez-nuf
twenty	vingt	vehn
twenty-one	vingt-et-un	vehnt-ay-uhn
thirty	trente	trahnt
forty	quarante	ka-rahnt
fifty	cinquante	sang-kahnt
sixty	soixante	swa-sahnt
seventy	soixante-dix	swa-sahnt-deess
eighty	quante-vingts	kaht-ruh-vehn
ninety	quatre-vingts-dix	kaht-ruh-vehn-deess
one hundred	cent	sahn
one thousand	mille	meel
one million	million	meel-ion

COLORS

black	noir	nwahr
blue	bleu	bleuh
brown	brun	bruhn
green	vert	vair
orange	orange	o-rahnj
red	rouge	rouge
white	blanc	blahnk
yellow	jaune	zhone

DAYS OF THE WEEK

Sunday	Dimanche	dee-mahnsh
Monday	Lundi	luhn-dee
Tuesday	Mardi	mahr-dee
Wednesday	Mercredi	mair-kruh-dee
Thursday	Jeudi	zhuh-dee
Friday	Vendredi	vawn-druh-dee
Saturday	Samedi	sahm-dee

MONTHS

January	Janvier	zhahn-vee-ay
February	Février	feh-vree-ay
March	Mars	marce
April	Avril	a-vreel
May	Mai	meh
June	Juin	zhwehn
July	Juillet	zhwee-ay
August	Août	ah-oo
September	Septembre	sep-tahm-bruh
October	Octobre	oc-to-bruh
November	Novembre	no-vahm-bruh
December	Décembre	day-sahm-bruh

USEFUL WORDS AND PHRASES

Do you speak English?	Parlez-vous anglais?	par-lay voo ahn-glay
I don't speak [Language].	Je ne parle pas ...	zhuh nuh parl pah
I don't understand	Je ne comprends pas.	zhuh nuh kohm-prahn pah
I don't know.	Je ne sais pas.	zhuh nnuh say pah
I understand.	Je comprends	zhuh kohm-prahn
I'm American.	Je suis américain.	a-may-ree-kehn
I'm British.	Je suis anglais.	ahn-glay
What's your name?	Comment vous appelez-vous?	ko-mahn voo za-pell-ay-voo
My name is ...	Mon nom est...	zhuh ma-pell
What time is it?	Quelle heure es-il	kel air eh-teel
How?	Comment?	ko-mahn
When?	Quand?	kahn
Yesterday	Hier	yair

Today	Aujourd'hui	o-zhoor-dwee
Tomorrow	Demain	duh-mehn
This morning	Ce matin	suh mah-tin
This afternoon	Cet après-midi	set a-pray mee-dee
Tonight	Ce Soir	suh swahr
What?	Quoi?	kwah
What is it?	Qu'est-ce que c'est?	kess-kuh-say
Why?	Pourquoi?	poor-kwa
Who?	Qui?	kee
Where is ...	Où est	oo ay
...the train station?	la gare?	la gar
...the subway station?	la station de metro?	la sta-syon duh may-tro
...the bus stop?	l'arrêt de bus?	la-ray duh booss
...the airport	l'aéroport?	la-ay ro-porr
...the post office?	la poste?	la post
...the bank?	la banque?	la bahnk
...the hotel?	l'hôtel?	lo-tel
...the museum?	le musée?	luh mew-zay
...the hospital?	l'hôpital?	lo-pee-tahl
...the elevator?	l'ascenseur?	la-sahn-seuhr
Where are the restrooms?	Où sont les toilettes?	oo sohn lay twah-let
Here/there	Ici/là	ee-see /la
Left/right	à gauche/à droite	a goash/a draht
Is it near/far?	Est-ce que c'est près/loin?	say pray/lwehn
I'd like ...	Je voudrais...	zhuh voo-dray...
...a room	une chambre	ewn shahm-bruh
...the key	la clé	la clay
...a newspaper	un journal	uhn zhoor-nah
...a stamp	un timbre	uhn tam-bruh
I'd like to buy ...	Je voudrais acheter...	zhuh voo-dray ahsh-tay...
...a city map	un plan de la ville	uhn plahn de veal
...a road map	une carte routière	ewn cart roo-tee-air
...a magazine	une revue	ewn reh-vu
...envelopes	des enveloppes	dayz ahn-veh-lope
...writing paper	du papier à lettres	dew pa-pee-ay a let-ruh
...a postcard	une carte postale	ewn cart pos-tahl
...a ticket	un billet	uhn bee-yeah
How much is it?	C'est combien?	say comb-bee-ehn
It's expensive/ cheap	C'est cher/pas cher	say sher/pa sher
A little/a lot	Un peu/ beaucoup	uhn peuh/bo-koo
More/less	Plus/moins	plus/mwehn

Enough/too (much)	Assez/trop	a-say/tro
I am ill/sick	Je suis malade.	zhuh swee ma-lahd
Call a doctor	Appelez un docteur	a-play uhn dohk-tehr
Help!	Au secours!	o suh-koor
Stop!	Arrêtez!	a-reh-tay

DINING OUT

A bottle of ...	une bouteille de...	ewn boo-tay duh
A cup of ...	une tasse de...	ewn tass duh
A glass of ...	un verre de...	uhn vair duh
Beer	une bière	ewn bi-yair
Bill/check	l'addition	la-doo-soo-ohn
Bread	du pain	dew pan
Breakfast	le petit-déjeuner	luh puh-tee day-zhuh-nay
Butter	du beurre	dew burr
Cocktail/apéritif	un apéritif	uhn ah-pay-ree-teef
Coffee	un café	uhn ca-fay
Dinner	le dîner	luh dee-nay
Fixed-price menu	la table d'hôte	la ta-bleh doe-teh
Fork	une fourchette	ewn four-shet
I am a vegetarian	Je suis végétarien(ne)	zhuh swee vay-zhay-ta-ree-en
I cannot eat ...	Je ne peux pas manger de...	zhuh nuh puh pah mahn-jay deh
I'd like to order ...	Je voudrais commander...	zhuh voo-dray ko-mahn-day...
Is service included?	Est-ce que le service est compris?	ess kuh luh sair-veess ay comb-pree
I'm hungry/ thirsty	J'ai faim/soif	zay fehn / sua-f
It's good/bad	C'est bon/ mauvais	say bohn/mo-vay
It's hot/cold	C'est chaud/froid	say sho/frwah
Knife	un couteau	uhn koo-toe
Lunch	le déjeuner	luh day-zhuh-nay
Menu	la carte	la cart
Napkin	une serviette	ewn sair-vee-et
Pepper	du poivre	dew pwah-vruh
Plate	une assiette	ewn a-see-et
Please give me ...	Donnez-moi...	doe-nay-mwah...
Salt	du sel	dew sell
Spoon	une cuillère	ewn kwee-air
Tea	du thé	dew tay
Water	de l'eau	duh lo
Wine	du vin	dew vehn

Great Itineraries

MONTRÉAL IN A DAY

Start with a stroll to the peak of Mont-Royal, the city's most enduring natural symbol. Afterward, wander south on avenue du Parc and through McGill University's leafy campus to Downtown. The Musée des Beaux-Arts de Montréal, on rue Sherbrooke, was once the bastion of the Anglo-Canadian establishment, and is worth a visit.

For a more francophone perspective, head from Mont-Royal (the mountain) along rue Mont-Royal (the street) to rue St-Denis, below rue Sherbrooke, which is home to funky boutiques and a boisterous strip of bars near the Université du Québec à Montréal.

In the late afternoon, head down to Old Montréal and pop into the Basilique Notre-Dame-de-Montréal before getting in some nightlife, as in the summer months the Old City is one of the most popular places to party. There are dozens of restaurants to choose from, as well as clubs and bars.

DAY TRIPS AND OVERNIGHTS FROM MONTRÉAL

If you have only a couple of days for a visit and you need to concentrate on one area, the Laurentians are a good choice. Less than an hour's drive from Downtown Montréal, this resort area has recreational options (depending on the season) that include golf, hiking, and superb skiing, both Alpine and cross-country.

Pick a resort town to stay in and use that as a base for visiting some of the surrounding towns. Each town has its own style and appeal: St-Sauveur-des-Monts is lively, Morin Heights is tranquil, and Ste-Adèle, along with the nearby towns of Val Morin and Val David, are a center of gastronomy. Mont-Tremblant, a sophisticated ski and golf resort, is worth a trip, particularly for the picturesque gondola ride to the summit.

You can combine a taste of the Eastern Townships with a two-day visit to the Laurentians. After an overnight stay in the Laurentians, head back south of Montréal to the Townships, which extend to the east along the border with New England. Overnight in Bromont, which is known for golf, skiing, and its water park.

The next day, you can shop in attractive Knowlton (look for signs to Lac Brome) and explore regional history in such towns as Valcourt. Spend a night or two in the resort town of Magog, along Lac Memphrémagog, or in the quieter, and far prettier, North Hatley, on Lac Massawippi. You'll have good dining in either. Save some time for outdoor activities, whether it's golfing, skiing, biking, or hiking.

QUÉBEC CITY IN A DAY

It's inspiring to start your day in Québec's Lower Town, the earliest site of French civilization in North America. Stroll along the narrow streets of the Quartier Pet-it-Champlain, visit the Maison Chevalier, and browse the craft stores and boutiques. From there, head to Place Royale, making a stop at the Église Notre-Dame-des-Victoires, and continue on to Terrasse Dufferin. In the afternoon, when the crowds thin out, check out the Musée National des Beaux-Arts du Québec or the Musée Canadien de l'Histoire.

Catch a gorgeous sunset from the Plains of Abraham—site of the battle that ended France's colonial dreams in North America and marked the beginning of British rule in Canada—before dining anywhere on rue St-Jean, one of the best streets in the city for restaurants and nightlife.

DAY TRIPS AND OVERNIGHTS FROM QUÉBEC CITY

If you want to get out of Québec City for a day or two, take a 20-minute drive to Île d'Orléans, a picturesque island called the "Garden of Québec." In summer, you can explore this idyllic island's boutiques, galleries, and food stands, then dine in a vineyard at Panache Mobile. Stay over in a cozy B&B, or continue on Route 138 northeast to Côte de Beaupré. Here you can visit the impressive Montmorency Falls and the ornate shrine at Ste-Anne-de-Beaupré. Don't miss the classic Québec cuisine of roast goose, *tourtière* (meat pie), and sugar pie at the historical Auberge Baker on Côte-de-Beaupré.

Another option is to take the Train du Massif de Charlevoix, which departs from the spectacular Parc de la Chute-Montmorency outside Québec City. It follows the St. Lawrence shore and the dramatic mountainous landscapes of Charlevoix. You'll visit the artistic community of Baie St-Paul, the impressive mountain Le Massif, and the cliff-top village of La Malbaie. You can do the two-segment rail trip in one day or stay overnight at the castlelike Fairmont Le Manoir Richelieu.

From La Malbaie, it's an hour by car to Tadoussac, at the confluence of the Saguenay and St. Lawrence rivers, where you can hop on a boat for a whale-watching excursion.

MONTRÉAL AND QUÉBEC CITY OVER A LONG WEEKEND

Looking for an ideal four-day getaway? It's possible to see the best of both cities without feeling rushed. Here's one expedient itinerary: Fly into Montréal's Trudeau International Airport on a Thursday evening, take a cab to your Downtown hotel, put down your bags, and head out to grab a late-night bite at a bistro like L'Express or 24-hour poutine hotspot La Banquise. Spend Friday seeing the city's top sights, hit Old Montréal in the evening for dinner and nightlife, and enjoy a leisurely brunch on Saturday morning.

Rent a car from one of the many Downtown rental agencies, then pack up and drive north to Québec City, which takes about three hours. Check into a B&B or boutique hotel in the Old City and spend the rest of the day exploring sights there. Spend Sunday morning in the Old City and dedicate the afternoon to the Fortifications, or take a day trip to the Côte-de-Beaupré or Île d'Orléans. On Monday, fly out of Québec City's Jean Lesage International Airport.

A Food Lover's Tour of Montréal

Many Montréalers are true gourmets, or at least enthusiastic food lovers. And, indeed, the city has thousands of restaurants, markets, and food boutiques catering to just about every conceivable taste, from Portuguese barbecue to Tonkinese soup. Most menus are posted outside.

OLD MONTRÉAL

If you need to stock up on supplies, a good destination would be the cobblestone streets of Old Montréal. Try, for example, a smoked-salmon crêpe or spinach quiche at the tiny **Crêperie Chez Suzette** on rue St-Paul.

DOWNTOWN

Although you can't go wrong starting the day with a bowl of steaming café au lait at **Café Myriade** Downtown, for something a little different head over to Chinatown for a dim sum breakfast at **Maison Kam Fung,** a neighborhood institution.

THE PLATEAU

Fortified with filling dumpling dough, walk up through the streets of the Latin Quarter on rue St-Denis and you'll hit Square St-Louis.

Turn west, then north on boulevard St-Laurent and browse through dozens of ethnic food shops and delis, inhaling the aromas from the Caribbean, the Middle East, Asia, and Eastern Europe. If that reanimates your appetite, stop at the iconic **Schwartz's Delicatessen** and split one of the world's best smoked-meat sandwiches, served piled high on rye (it's best slathered with spicy deli mustard), with your walking companion.

Next work up an appetite for lunch with a walk. Head east along avenue Duluth and take a stroll through Parc Lafontaine. There are two options for a bite to eat: exit the park on the southwest corner to rue Rachel and turn left for **La Banquise,** one of Montréal's top

A Food Lover's Tour of Montréal

HIGHLIGHTS
A fat smoked-meat sandwich at Schwartz's Delicatessen; walking around the Marché Jean-Talon tasting vendors' samples.

WHERE TO START
Chinatown, located in Downtown, at the ornately decorated red gate on St-Laurent off boulevard René-Lévesque.

LENGTH
About 5.5 km (3.5 miles) walking, plus the métro from Laurier to Marché Jean-Talon on the Orange Line.

WHERE TO END
Little Italy. From here, you can walk back to the Orange Line that runs through Downtown.

BEST TIME TO GO
Busy summer Saturday (the crowds are half the entertainment).

WORST TIME TO GO
Dull winter Monday.

EDITOR'S CHOICES
Walking up boulevard St-Laurent, peeking in the delis and offbeat boutiques; the colorful streets of the Plateau; the maple ice cream at Le Glacier Bilboquet.

poutine spots (so popular you may have to wait in line to get in); or go northwest on rue de la Roche until you reach

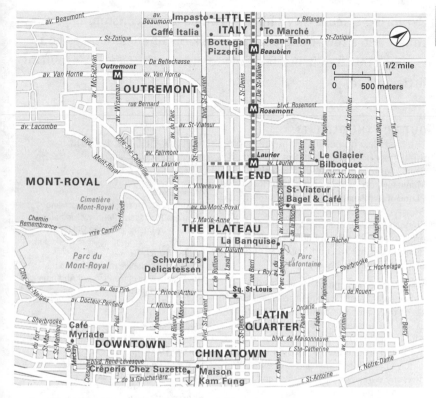

avenue Mont-Royal, a spirited stretch of *terrasses*, tattoo parlors, and thrift shops. Stop for a bagel sandwich on a hot and sweet Montréal-style bagel at **St-Viateur Bagel & Café.** In summer, stop for some ice cream at **Le Glacier Bilboquet** on avenue Laurier Est, or try the Outremont location on rue Bernard.

LITTLE ITALY

Time to cheat on your diet. Hop on the métro at Laurier station and head north to the Jean-Talon stop for an afternoon visit to one of Canada's best markets, **Marché Jean-Talon.** You can spend hours browsing fish, sausage, and cheese shops and sampling everything from smoked buffalo to seasonal produce like heirloom tomatoes.

There's no leaving this area without stopping for dinner, so stroll over to boulevard St-Laurent and find a place to eat in Pétite-Italie (Little Italy). Two restaurants to try are **Impasto** and **Bottega Pizzeria.** Finish with a bracing espresso at **Caffé Italia,** where neighborhood men huddle around the TV to watch soccer.

From here, it's an easy walk back to the Jean-Talon métro stop for a ride back to Old Montréal or Downtown.

A Walk through Québec City's History

Exploring Québec City's history can be an all-consuming pastime—and a rewarding one. The walk outlined here takes you through much of it, but feel free to pursue the Old City's inviting little detours.

OUTSIDE THE OLD CITY

The best place to begin a journey through the history of New France is at the end. Start your tour at the **Wolfe-Montcalm Monument,** on the far west side of the **Plains of Abraham.** It was here in 1759 that British general James Wolfe extinguished France's dreams of a North American empire and set off the English-French divergence that has both enriched and plagued Canada's history.

The Plains of Abraham was where the famous Battle of Québec (also called Battle of the Plains of Abraham) took place, in which General Wolfe's forces were victorious against Marquis de Montcalm's surprised French troops. Today this hilltop patch of green is a pleasant and expansive city park with trees, lawns, and meandering paths with sweeping views of the St. Lawrence River.

Make your way over to the Fortifications and the Old City via the northern side of the Plains of Abraham, along the **Grande Allée,** through the residential neighborhood of **Montcalm,** home to gorgeous 19th-century neo-Gothic and Queen Anne–style mansions and **Hôtel du Parlement.**

THE FORTIFICATIONS

The end of the Grand Allée is Porte St-Louis. Turn right down the Côte de la Citadelle, which leads to **La Citadelle.** Something of a microcosm of Canada's sometimes contrarian cultural character, the fortress is home to the Royal 22e Régiment, a crack military unit that speaks French but dresses in the

A Walk through Québec City's History

HIGHLIGHTS
Exploring La Citadelle; leisurely strolling along the Terrasse Dufferin; walking along rue du Petit-Champlain in the Old City.

WHERE TO START
The Wolfe-Montcalm Monument, on the far western side of the Plains of Abraham outside the walls of the city.

LENGTH
About 3 km (2 miles).

WHERE TO END
On rue du Petit-Champlain, in the Lower Town section of the Old City.

BEST TIME TO GO
A weekday summer morning.

WORST TIME TO GO
A cold winter day.

EDITOR'S CHOICE
Strolling along the tree-lined streets off Grande Allée in Montcalm; riding the funicular from Upper Town to Lower Town; standing in historic Place Royale.

bearskin hats and red tunics of a British guards unit for ceremonial parades. Don't miss the daily Changing of the Guard ceremony.

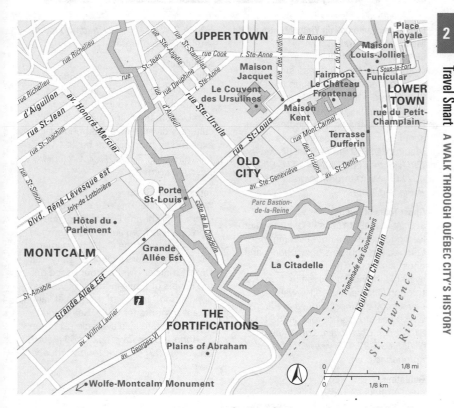

UPPER TOWN

Beyond **Porte St-Louis,** you can imagine yourself in 17th- and 18th-century France. Steep-roofed houses with small windows crowd a tangle of narrow, curving streets and the rattle of horse-drawn carriages on ancient cobblestones adds to the illusion.

The **Maison Jacquet** on rue St-Louis looks exactly as it did when it was built in 1677 and the **Maison Kent** was once the home of Queen Victoria's father, the Duke of Kent. **Le Couvent des Ursulines** at 12 rue Donnacona has a museum featuring an exhibit of magnificent lace embroidery created by Ursuline nuns in the 19th and early 20th centuries.

Québec City's most famous building, the **Fairmont Le Château Frontenac,** is at the beginning of **Terrasse Dufferin,** which is worth a stroll for sweeping views of the St. Lawrence River before you get on the funicular to reach Lower Town.

LOWER TOWN

Once at the base of this cable-connected elevator, you end up in the 17th-century **Maison Louis-Jolliet,** built before he paddled off to explore the Mississippi River. From here, it's a short walk to **Place Royale,** a square graced by a statue of the Sun King Louis XIV, and considered to be the birthplace of New France. The last jaunt is along **rue du Petit-Champlain,** the oldest street in the city, lined with shops and cafés.

Montréal and Québec City's Best Walking Tours

Circuit des Fantômes du Vieux Montréal (Old Montréal Ghost Trail).

SPECIAL-INTEREST TOURS | From May to October, you can join these street theater walking tours (C$26) through the Old City, where a host of spirits are said to still roam the streets. Tours begin at 8:30 pm and the haunted journey lasts about 90 minutes. Reservations are required. ✉ *360 rue St-François-Xavier, Old Montréal* ☎ *514/844–4021, 800/363–4021* ⊕ *www.fantomMontréal.com* Ⓜ *Place-d'Armes.*

Ghost Tours of Québec.

SPECIAL-INTEREST TOURS | Costumed actors lead ghoulish 90-minute evening tours of Québec City murders, executions, and ghost sightings. The tours (C$22) are available in English or French, from May through October. After the walk, you can buy a copy of *Ghost Stories of Québec,* which has stories not told on the tours. ✉ *34 boul. Champlain, Lower Town* ☎ *855/692–9770* ⊕ *www.ghosttoursofquebec.com.*

Guidatour.

GUIDED TOURS | You can walk through various historic, cultural, or architecturally diverse areas of the city with a guide. Popular tours include Old Montréal, the Underground City, the Christmas Secrets of Old Montréal, and the elite 19th-century neighborhood known as the Golden Square Mile. Reservations are required. ✉ *360 rue St-François-Xavier, Suite 400, Old Montréal* ☎ *514/844–4021,* *800/363–4021* ⊕ *www.guidatour.qc.ca/ en/?* Ⓜ *Place-d'Armes.*

Kaleidoscope.

GUIDED TOURS | This company offers a range of 70 different guided tours, from architecture tours to Montréal's Red Light district, and the city's many culturally diverse neighborhoods can be explored by foot, bike, or bus. ✉ *Montréal* ☎ *514/277–6990* ⊕ *www.tourskaleidoscope.com.*

Tours Voir Québec.

WALKING TOURS | This tour company offers English- and French-language (and Spanish from June to September) walking tours of the Old City, starting at C$25. Other tours include a "Bury Your Dead" murder mystery tour based on the novels of Louise Penny, as well as a popular food tour with tastings at various establishments for C$55. Self-guided audio tours are also available. ✉ *12 rue St-Anne, Upper Town* ☎ *418/694–2001, 866/694–2001* ⊕ *www.toursvoirquebec.com.*

Contacts

✈ Air

AIRLINE CONTACTS Air Canada. ☎ 888/247–2262 ⊕ www.aircanada. com. **American Airlines.** ☎ 800/433–7300 ⊕ www. aa.com. **Delta Airlines.** ☎ 800/221–1212 for U.S. reservations, 800/241–4141 for international reservations ⊕ www. delta.com. **Porter Airlines.** ☎ 888/619–8622 ⊕ www. flyporter.com.

AIRPORT INFORMATION Montréal–Pierre Elliott Trudeau International Airport. (YUL). ✉ 975 Roméo-Vachon Blvd. North, Dorval ☎ 800/465–1213, 514/633–3333 ⊕ www. admtl.com. **Jean Lesage International Airport.** (YQB). ✉ 505 rue Principale, Québec City ☎ 418/640–3300, 877/769–2700 ⊕ www.aeroportdeque-bec.com.

AIRPORT SECURITY ISSUES Transportation Security Administration. ⊕ www.tsa.gov.

GROUND TRANSPORTA-TION Société de transport de Montréal. ✉ Montréal ☎ 514/786–4636 ⊕ www. stm.info. **Taxi Coop Québec.** ☎ 418/525–5191 ⊕ www. taxicoop-quebec.com.

🚲 Bike

BIXI. ✉ Montréal ☎ 514/789–2494, 877/820–2453 ⊕ Mon-tréal.bixi.com.

🚌 Bus

Gare d'autocars de Montréal. ✉ 1717 rue Berri, Montréal ☎ 514/842–2281 ⊕ www. gamtl.com. **Gare du Palais Bus Station.** ✉ 320 rue Abraham-Martin, Québec City ☎ 418/525–3000 ⊕ www.orleansexpress. com. **Greyhound Lines.** ☎ 800/231–2222 in the U.S., 800/661–8747 in Can-ada ⊕ www.greyhound. com. **Limocar.** ☎ 866/692–8899, 819/562–8899 ⊕ www.limocar.ca. **Orléans Express.** ☎ 833/449–6444, 450/640–1477 ⊕ www. orleansexpress.com.

🚗 Car

EMERGENCY SERVICES CAA. ☎ 800/222–4357, 800/686–9243, 800/222–4357 Roadside assistance ⊕ www.caaquebec.com.

MAJOR RENTAL AGENCIES Alamo. ☎ 844/357–5138 ⊕ www.alamo.com. **Avis.** ☎ 800/879–2847 ⊕ www.avis.com. **Budget.** ☎ 800/268–8900 from Can-ada, 800/218–7992 from U.S. ⊕ www.budget.com. **Hertz.** ☎ 800/654–3001

⊕ www.hertz.com. **National Car Rental.** ☎ 844/382–6875 in the U.S., 844/307-8014 in Canada ⊕ www.nationalcar. com.

🚆 Train

INFORMATION Amtrak. ☎ 800/872–7245 ⊕ www. amtrak.com. **Train de Char-levoix.** ☎ 844/737–3282, 418/240–4124 ⊕ www. traindecharlevoix.com. **VIA Rail Canada.** ☎ 888/842–7245 from U.S. ⊕ www. viarail.ca.

🛏 Accommodations

BED AND BREAKFASTS Association de l'Agro-ourisme et du Tourisme Gourmand du Québec. ☎ 514/252–3138 ⊕ www. agrotourismeettouris-megourmand.com. **BB Canada.** ⊕ www.bbcan-ada.com. **Bed and Break-fasts Québec.** ⊕ www.bed-breakfastsquebec.com. **Vrbo.** ☎ 877/202–9331 ⊕ www.vrbo.com.

➕ Emergencies

FOREIGN EMBASSIES AND CONSULATES U.S. Consulate General. ✉ 1155 rue St-Alexandre, Montréal ☎ 514/398–9695 ⊕ ca.usembassy.gov/ embassy-consulates/ Montréal. **U.S. Consulate**

Contacts

General. ✉ 2 pl. Terrasse Dufferin, Québec City ☎ 418/692–2095 ⊕ ca. usembassy.gov/embassy-consulates/quebec. **U.S. Embassy.** ✉ 490 Sussex Dr., Ottawa ☎ 613/688–5335 ⊕ ca.usembassy.gov.

HOSPITALS Centre Hospitalier Universitaire de Québec, Pavillon Hôtel-Dieu. ✉ 11 côte du Palais, Upper Town ☎ 418/525–4444, 418/691–5042 emergencies ⊕ www.chudequebec.ca/centre-hospitaliers/l'hotel-dieu-de-quebec.aspx. **Montréal General Hospital (McGill University Health Centre).** ✉ 1650 av. Cedar, Downtown ☎ 514/934–1934 ⊕ www.muhc.ca/mgh Ⓜ Guy-Concordia.

PHARMACIES Pharmaprix. ☎ 800/746–7737 ⊕ www1.pharmaprix.ca/en/home. **Pharmaprix.** ✉ 1500 rue Ste-Catherine Ouest, Downtown ☎ 514/933–4744 ⊕ www1.pharmaprix.ca Ⓜ Guy-Concordia.

❸ Tours

CONTACTS Bateau-Mouche. ☎ 514/849–9952, 800/361–9952 ⊕ www.bateaumouche.ca. **Croisières AML.** ✉ 10 rue Dalhousie, Lower Town ☎ 866/856–6668 ⊕ www.croisieresaml.com. **Fitz and Follwell Co.** ✉ 1251 Rue Rachel E, The Plateau ☎ 438/792–6480 ⊕ www.fitzMontréal.com. **Gray Line.** ✉ Montréal ☎ 800/472–9546 ⊕ www.grayline.com. **Old Québec Tours.** ☎ 418/664–0460, 800/267–8687 ⊕ www.oldquebectours.com.

❾ Visitor Information

CONTACTS Association Touristique des Cantons de l'Est. ✉ 20 rue Don Bosco Sud, Sherbrooke ☎ 866/963–2020 administration, 800/355–5755 ⊕ www.cantonsdelest.com. **Association Touristique des Laurentides.** ✉ La Porte-du-Nord rest area, Autoroute des Laurentides, Exit 51 ☎ 450/224–7007, 800/561–6673 ⊕ www.laurentides.com. **Association Touristique Régionale de Charlevoix.** ✉ 495 boul. de Comporté, C.P. 275, La Malbaie ☎ 418/665–4454, 800/667–2276 ⊕ www.tourisme-charlevoix.com. **Canadian Tourism Commission.** ☎ 604/638–8300 ⊕ www.travelcanada.ca. **Centre d'Interpretation de la Côte-de-Beaupré.** (Beaupré Coast Interpretation Center). ✉ 7976 av. Royale, C.P. 40, Château-Richer ☎ 418/824–3677, 877/824–3677 ⊕ www.histoire-cotedebeaupre.org. **Centre Info-Touriste.** ✉ 1255 rue Peel, suite 100, Downtown ☎ 514/873–2015, 877/266–5687 ⊕ www.bonjourquebec.com Ⓜ Peel or Bonaventure. **Parks Canada.** ☎ 819/420–9486, 888/773–8888 ⊕ www.pc.gc.ca. **Québec City Tourist Information.** ✉ 12 rue Sainte-Anne, Upper Town ☎ 418/641–6290, 877/266–5687 ⊕ www.quebec-cite.com/en. **Sépaq.** ☎ 800/665–6527 ⊕ www.sepaq.com. **Terroir & Saveurs.** ✉ Montréal ☎ 514/252–3138 ⊕ www.terroiretsaveurs.com. **Tourisme-Montréal.** ☎ 877/266–5687 ⊕ www.mtl.org/en/contact-us. **Tourisme Québec.** ✉ 1001 rue du Sq. Dorchester, No. 100, C.P. 979, Downtown ☎ 877/266–5687, 514/873–2015 ⊕ www.bonjourquebec.com.

💲 Money

CURRENCY CONVERSION Oanda.com. ⊕ www.oanda.com. **XE.com.** ⊕ www.xe.com.

💲 Taxes

INFORMATION Canada Customs and Revenue Agency. ✉ Summerside Tax Centre, 275 Pope Rd., Suite 104, Summerside ☎ 800/668–4748 in Canada, 902/432–5608 ⊕ www.ccra-adrc.gc.ca.

MONTRÉAL

3

Updated by
Elizabeth Warkentin

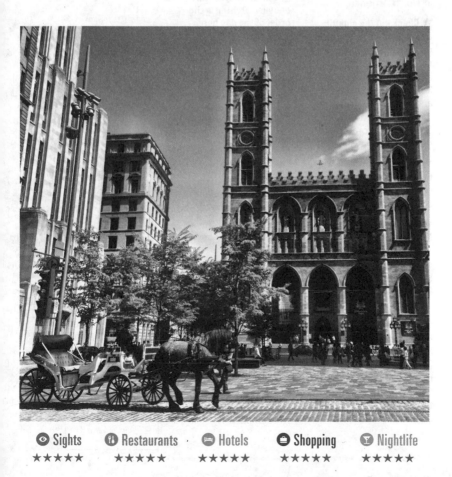

◉ Sights	🍴 Restaurants	🛏 Hotels	🛍 Shopping	🍸 Nightlife
★★★★★	★★★★★	★★★★★	★★★★★	★★★★★

WELCOME TO MONTRÉAL

TOP REASONS TO GO

★ **Browse public markets:** Amble through Marché Atwater, one of the city's oldest public markets, and the bustling Marché Jean-Talon, the largest open-air market in North America.

★ **Check out the nightlife:** Enjoy Canada's unrivaled party capital at famous nightlife spots that include rue Crescent, boulevard St-Laurent, and the Latin Quarter, as well as Old Montréal and the Village, Montréal's epicenter of gay life.

★ **Get a dose of multiculturalism:** Explore ethnic neighborhoods and sample global cuisine.

★ **Celebrate Jazz Fest:** Montréal's biggest musical event, Jazz Fest, happens every year in late June and early July. Reserve early: hotels book up months in advance.

★ **Stroll Old Montréal:** Historic Vieux-Montréal has cobblestone streets, a great waterfront, fine restaurants and bed-and-breakfasts, and the Old Port, which buzzes with nightlife.

1 **Old Montréal (Vieux-Montréal).** The oldest part of the city.

2 **Downtown.** Montréal's largest shopping district.

3 **Westmount.** An affluent "suburb," or independent municipality within the city.

4 **The Latin Quarter.** People-watching is the order of the day here.

5 **The Village.** Lively, diverse, and great nightlife.

6 **The Plateau Mont-Royal and Mile End.** Trendy cafés and upscale boutiques and galleries.

7 **Outremont.** Chic fashion boutiques and stylish cafés.

8 **Little Italy.** All the best pastry shops and grocery stores.

9 **Parc du Mont-Royal.** The Central Park of Montréal.

10 **Côte-des-Neiges.** A vibrant and ethnically diverse neighborhood.

11 **Hochelaga-Maisonneuve.** See the site of the 1976 Olympics.

12 **Sud-Ouest and Lachine.** A magnet for creatives and foodies.

13 **The Islands.** Île Ste-Hélène and Île Notre-Dame.

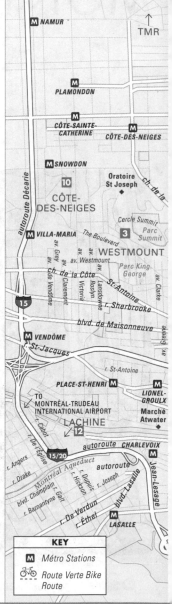

KEY

Ⓜ Métro Stations

Route Verte Bike Route

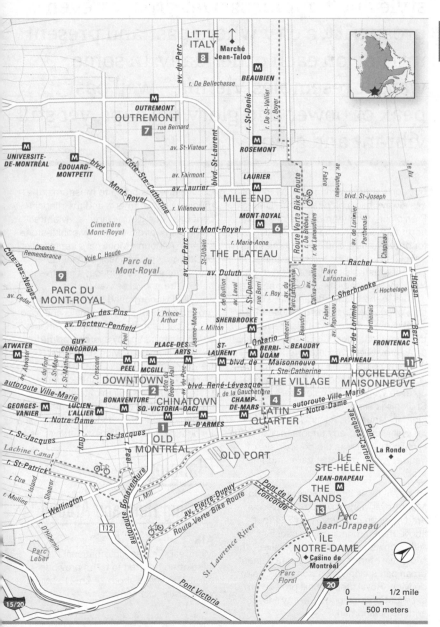

Canada's most diverse metropolis, Montréal is an island city that favors style and happiness over order or even prosperity, a city where past and present intrude on each other daily. In some ways it resembles Vienna—well past its peak of power and glory, perhaps, yet still vibrant and grand.

But don't get the wrong idea. Montréal has always had a bit of an edge. During Prohibition, thirsty Americans headed north to the city on the St. Lawrence for booze, music, and a good time, and people still come for the same things. Summer festivals celebrate everything from comedy and French music and culture to the circus arts and fireworks, and, of course, jazz. And on those rare weeks when there isn't a planned event, the party continues. Clubs and sidewalk cafés are abuzz from late afternoon to the early hours of the morning. Montréal is also a city that knows how to mix it up even when it's 20 below zero. Rue St-Denis is almost as lively on a Saturday night in January as it is in July, and the festival Montréal en Lumière, or Montréal Highlights, enlivens the dreary days of February with concerts, balls, and fine food.

Montréal takes its name from Parc du Mont-Royal, a stubby plug of tree-covered igneous rock that rises 764 feet above the surrounding cityscape. Although its height is unimpressive, "the Mountain" forms one of Canada's finest urban parks, and views from the Chalet du Mont-Royal atop the hill provide an excellent orientation to the city's layout and major landmarks.

Old Montréal is home to museums, the municipal government, and the magnificent Basilique Notre-Dame-de-Montréal within its network of narrow cobblestone streets. Although Montréal's *centre-ville*, or Downtown, bustles like many other major cities on the surface, it's active below street level as well, in the so-called Underground City—the underground levels of shopping malls and food courts connected by pedestrian tunnels and the city's subway system, or *métro*. Residential Plateau Mont-Royal and trendy neighborhoods like Griffintown/St-Henri thrum with the kinetic energy of restos, *boîtes de nuit* (nightclubs), bars, art galleries, and cafés. The greener areas of town include Parc du Mont-Royal, Parc Lafontaine, and the Jardins Botaniques.

Planning

Getting Here and Around

AIR
Montréal's Trudeau International Airport (also often referred to by its previous name, Dorval) is about 24 km (15 miles) west of the city center.

GROUND TRANSPORTATION

The easiest way to get in is to take a cab for a fixed fare of C$41, unless your hotel provides transportation. The cheapest way to get into town is the 747 express bus, a 24-hour shuttle service from the airport to the main bus terminal with stops at the Lionel-Groulx métro station and several additional stops near Downtown hotels. The one-way fare is C$10 (accepted in coins only)—with 24 hours of unlimited bus and métro travel included in the price. Plan on it taking about a half hour outside rush hour to get to Downtown from the airport. Another alternative is the 204 bus, with a one-way fare of C$3.25, taking you from the Dorval train terminal straight to the airport.

BICYCLE

An extensive network of bike paths and relatively flat terrain make Montréal ideal for bicycles. The BIXI (a contraction of "bicycle" and "taxi") system—with more than 3,000 sturdy aluminum-frame bikes and e-bikes at more than 300 credit card–operated stands (or you can download the app or your phone) throughout the city—makes two-wheel exploring easy. There's a one-way unlocking fee of C50¢, plus +C10¢ a minute for a regular bike and C25¢ a minute for an e-bike.

CAR

If you're driving in to the city, take I–91 or I–89 from Vermont, I–87 from New York, and Autoroute 20 (also known as Autoroute Jean-Lesage) from Québec City.

Having a car Downtown isn't ideal—garages are expensive and on-street parking can be a hassle. The city has a diligent tow-away and fine system for double-parking or sitting in no-stopping zones during rush hour, and ticket costs are steep. In residential neighborhoods, beware of alternate-side-of-the-street-parking rules and resident-only parking. In resident-only parking, residents' cars will bear a special sticker on the upper left-hand side of the back window. In winter, street plows are ruthless in dealing with parked cars in their way. If they don't tow them, they'll bury them.

PUBLIC TRANSPORTATION

The Société de transport de Montréal (STM) operates both the métro (subway) and the bus system. The métro is quiet (it runs on rubber tires), and will get you to most of the places you want to visit. For those few places that are more than a 15-minute walk from the nearest métro station, bus connections are available.

Métro hours on the Orange, Green, Blue, and Yellow lines are weekdays 5:30 am to 12:30 am and weekends 5:30 am to 12:30, 1, or 1:30 am (it varies by line). Trains run every three minutes or so on the most crowded lines—Orange and Green—at rush hours. The cash fare for a single ticket is C$3.50. One- and three-day unlimited-use cards are also available for C$10 and C$20.50.

TAXI

Taxis in Montréal all run on the same rate: C$3.45 minimum and C$1.70 per kilometer (roughly ½ mile). They're usually easy to hail on the street, outside train stations, in shopping areas, and at major hotels. You can also call a dispatcher to send a driver to pick you up at no extra cost. A taxi is available if the white or orange plastic rooftop light is on.

⇨ For more information on getting here and around, see Travel Smart.

Planning Your Time

Put Old Montréal and the Old Port at the top of your sightseeing list. Spend a full day walking around this area, head back to your hotel for a late-day break, and return for dinner. Aside from finding several of the city's top restaurants here, city hall, Marché Bonsecours, and other grand and charming buildings are illuminated at night. Also dedicate a full day to wandering around Downtown, rue Ste-Catherine, and Chinatown. Visit the

Latin Quarter and the area around McGill University—both have a busy student life, but shouldn't be dismissed as places where only under-20s frequent. Even if you're too tired to go out on the town, take a nighttime walk down rue Crescent or rue St-Denis for a taste of the city's *joie de vivre.*

For browsing, shopping, and dining out, explore Outremont, Mile End/the Plateau, Griffintown/St-Henri, and Westmount. For kid-friendly activities, check out Hochelaga-Maisonneuve and the Islands for the Biôdôme, La Ronde, and the Jardin Botanique.

A city landmark not to miss is St. Joseph's Oratory, Canada's largest church, in the west end of the city.

When to Go

To avoid crowds and below-freezing temperatures, Montréal's short spring, which typically starts in late April or early May but doesn't normally end until early June, is ideal. Fall is gorgeous—and touristy—when the leaves change color, so expect traffic on weekends. Early September after Labor Day until the end of the month is another good time to visit.

Restaurants

Montréal has one of Canada's most cosmopolitan restaurant scenes, and with—at least before the pandemic—trendy new eateries popping up regularly, their menus heavily influenced by flavors from around the globe, and often with an added touch of French flair.

Montréal's top dining destinations are plentiful, especially as young chefs move to hip destinations in Mile End, the Plateau, and the Griffintown/St-Henri areas to open new restaurants. Downtown,

convenient to many hotels, finds most of its restaurants clustered between rues Guy and Peel and on the side streets that run between boulevard René-Lévesque and rue Sherbrooke. Rue St-Denis and boulevard St-Laurent, between rues Sherbrooke and Jean-Talon, have long been, convenient and fashionable areas, with everything from sandwich shops to high-price gourmet shrines. Old Montréal, too, has a collection of well-regarded restaurants, most of them clustered on rue St-Paul, avenue McGill, and place Jacques-Cartier.

You can usually order à la carte, but make sure to look for the table d'hôte, a two- to four-course package deal. It's often more economical, offers interesting specials, and may also take less time to prepare. For a splurge, consider a *menu dégustation,* a five- to seven-course tasting menu that generally includes soup, salad, fish, sorbet (sherbet; to cleanse the palate), a meat dish, dessert, and coffee or tea. A menu dégustation for two, along with a good bottle of wine, will cost around C$250.

Most restaurants will have an English menu or, at the very least, a bilingual menu—but some might only be in French. If you don't understand what a dish is, don't be too shy to ask; a good server will be happy to explain. If you feel brave enough to order in French, remember that in Montréal an *entrée* is an appetizer, and what Americans call an entrée is a *plat principal,* or main dish.

WHAT IT COSTS in Canadian Dollars

	$	$$	$$$	$$$$
RESTAURANTS				
	under C$12	C$12–C$20	C$21–C$30	over C$30

Where Should I Stay?

	Neighborhood Vibe	Pros	Cons
Old Montréal	Cobblestone streets, boutique hotels, designer clothes, and historic architecture; very touristy, especially at the eastern end, although it quiets down at night.	Quaint; easy access to bike paths; nice to walk along the waterfront; hip restaurants and mixology options are in the Old Port.	Can be desolate in the late evening outside hotel lobbies; parking is scarce; depending on the exact location, métro and bus access can be limited.
Downtown	Montréal's center for hustle and bustle, mostly on rue Sherbrooke, rue Ste-Catherine, and boulevard de Maisonneuve.	Extremely convenient; big-name hotel chains and luxury hotels; central location; pools; garage parking; perfect for families as well as business travelers; near the outdoor Quartier des spectacles.	Traffic congestion is relentless; not as many dining options as other neighborhoods, and what is there tends to be at either extreme—fast food or very pricey (and not always worth it).
The Latin Quarter	Hopping with university kids and moviegoers, this area boasts a crazy mix of cafés, bars, handmade-chocolate shops, and folks carrying library books.	Festival central; easy métro access; right between the Plateau and Downtown; local characters abound.	Uneven gentrification means dodgy pockets; litter; bad roads.
The Plateau Mont-Royal and Mile End	Scattered auberges, Airbnb rentals, and B&Bs host the artsy crowd and academics, with streets filled with local boutiques and hip restaurants; perfect for strolling.	Stumbling distance to the best bistros and pubs; unique shopping that focuses on local designers and craftspeople.	Limited métro and taxi access; limited hotel options; can be noisy at night; panhandlers galore.

Hotels

Montréal is a city of neighborhoods with distinct personalities, which creates a broad spectrum of options when it comes to deciding on a place to stay. The Downtown core has many of the big chain hotels you'd find in any city, but also several luxury hotels, such as the Ritz-Carlton and the Four Seasons. Old Montréal, the Plateau, and other surrounding areas have unique *auberges* (inns) and boutique hotels.

Most of the major hotels in Down-town—the ones with big meeting rooms, swimming pools, and several bars and restaurants—are ideal for those who want all the facilities along with easy access to the department stores and malls on rue Ste-Catherine, the museums of the Golden Square Mile, and nightlife on rues Crescent and de la Montagne. If you want something a little more histori-cal, consider renting a room in one of the dozen or so boutique hotels that occupy the centuries-old buildings lining the cobbled streets of Old Montréal. Most of them offer all the conveniences along with the added charm of stone walls, casement windows, and period-style furnishings.

If your plans include shopping expe-ditions to avenue Mont-Royal and rue Laurier with maybe a few late nights at the jazz bars and dance clubs of Boulevard St. Laurent and rue St-Denis, then the place to bed down is in one of Plateau Mont-Royal's small, but comfort-able hotels. Room rates in the area tend to be quite reasonable, but be careful: the hotels right in the middle of the action—on rue St-Denis, for example—can be noisy, especially if you get a room fronting the street.

WHAT IT COSTS in Canadian Dollars

	$	$$	$$$	$$$$
HOTELS				
	under C$200	C$200–C$300	C$301–C$400	over C$400

Nightlife

If nightlife in Montréal could be distilled into a cocktail, it would be one part sophisticated New York club scene (with the accompanying pretension), one part Parisian joie-de-vivre (and, again, a dash of snobbery), and one part Barcelonan stamina (which keeps the clubs booming until dawn).

Hot spots are peppered throughout the city. There are compact clusters along rue Crescent, boulevard St-Laurent (known as "The Main"), avenue Mont-Royal, and rue St-Denis. Prominent rue Ste-Cath-erine plows through town, connecting most of these nighttime niches, and farther east, near Beaudry métro station, it becomes the main drag for the Village, also called the Gay Village. For whatever reason, the streets named after saints contain most of the clubs: rue Ste-Cath-erine, boulevard St-Laurent, rue St-Paul, and rue St-Denis. The Old Port/Old Montréal is currently Montréal's hottest neighborhood. Before COVID, a steady stream of chic venues were opening in this cobblestone district.

Montréal's nightlife swings with a robust passion. From the early evening "5-à-7" after-work cocktail circuit, to the slightly later concerts and supper clubs (restau-rant–dance club hybrids where people dance on the tables after eating off them), on into the even later dance club scene, all tastes, cultural backgrounds, and legal ages join the melee. Clubbing is, to say the least, huge in Montréal. Some restaurants are even installing discotheques in their basements.

Money-Saving Tips

There are several good ways to save money during your trip. If you'll be visiting three or more of the city's museums, consider buying a museum pass. They start at $C50 for 2, 3, 4 or 5 consecutive days. ⊕ *museesMontréal. org/en/cards/the-passes*

Tourist transit passes, which give you unlimited access to the transit system, also may be worth your while; one-day passes are C$10 while three-day

passes will set you back C$20.50. Weekly passes cost C$28, but they're loaded electronically on a special Opus card that costs C$6. ⊕ *www.stm.info/ en#view-tariffs*

Hitting the town earlier in the evening is a good way to save as well, by stopping into cafés and bars for food and drink specials offered during cinq-à-sept (5 to 7), Montréal's happy hour.

The bars stop serving around 3 am and shut down shortly thereafter (with the exception of sanctioned "after-hour" haunts). On the weekends, expect them to be packed to the gills until closing. The club scene picks up right after the bars close, and then extends until dawn.

Performing Arts

Montréal is the home of nearly a dozen professional companies and several important theater schools, but there's also a lively English-language theater scene and one of the few remaining Yiddish theaters in North America. As for venues, the Quartier des Spectacles is a 70-acre entertainment district in Downtown with stages for outdoor performances and nearly 80 venues for dance, music, theater, and art.

For a city its size, Montréal offers a remarkable number of opportunities for fans of classical music to get their fill, from operas and symphonies to string quartets.

As for dance, there are several modern dance companies of note, including Montréal Danse and Québec's premier ballet company, Les Grands Ballets Canadiens.

Shopping

Montréalers *magasinent* (shop) with a vengeance, whether they're scurrying down busy Ste-Catherine St. Downtown, checking out department store bargains, hunting for Danish mid-century antiques in the Gay Village, browsing designer wares on St-Laurent, or sampling gourmet eats at one of the city's markets. For many locals, doing the *magasinage* is practically an art form.

Yet, even before COVID-19 struck, one of North America's top shopping cities was in a state of flux. Where, until recently, boulevard St-Laurent and rue St-Denis, were the "it" streets to shop, increasingly this honor is being shared with Old Montréal, an area that has been enjoying a renaissance among locals. In the decade before the pandemic, Montréal's patron saint of shopping streets, Ste-Catherine, was undergoing a metamorphosis as a significant cohort of young, educated professionals moved into condos Downtown and retailers scrambled to meet their needs and tastes. Along with the pandemic, the changing face of retail and the prevalence of online shopping have also contributed to the transformation of Ste-Catherine and other Downtown streets, with the corresponding downward slide of many traditional brick-and-mortar stores. That being said, Montréal's most important shopping street has also welcomed new arrivals such as the trendy Vancouver-based Aritzia; Lolë, Montréal's more stylish version of Lululemon; an elegant Club Monaco spread out over two floors of the Beaux Arts–style Dominion Square Building; and a branch of hip Montréal-brand, Frank and Oak, initially an online-only retailer. And, at long last, after years of talk, the city's two luxury department stores, Ogilvy and Holt Renfrew, merged in early 2020 into one giant upmarket department store directly attached to the brand new Four Seasons Hotel, opened in Summer 2019.

Meanwhile, the iconic rue Sainte-Catherine is currently in Phase I of a major infrastructure and street design facelift. According to the City of Montréal website, the usually congested thoroughfare will consist of only a single traffic lane, with wide sidewalks on either side and the addition of numerous trees, placing pedestrians at the heart of the new public space. The plan is also to create cool spaces for locals during the city's oppressive heat waves by connecting and consolidating existing green spaces in the downtown core and increasing plant cover. Plans may also include heated sidewalks in winter, an idea that has been under discussion for many years.

Activities

Most Montréalers would probably claim they hate winter, but the city is full of cold-weather sports venues—skating rinks, cross-country ski trails, and toboggan runs—that see plenty of action. During warm-weather months, residents head for the tennis courts, bicycle trails, golf courses, and two lakes for boating and swimming.

You don't have to travel far from Montréal to find good downhill skiing or snowboarding. The many ski centers in the Laurentians and Eastern Townships are within an hour's drive from the city. As for cross-country, excellent trails can be found right in Parc du Mont-Royal, or on the Islands (Île Ste-Hélène and Île Notre-Dame).

Despite the bitter winters (or perhaps because of them), Montréal has fallen in love with the bicycle, with enthusiasts cycling year-round. More than 600 km (372 miles) of bike paths crisscross the metropolitan area, and bikes are welcome on the first car of métro trains during off-peak hours.

The city is truly passionate about Canada's national sport, hockey. If you're here during hockey season, try to catch a Montréal Canadiens game at Centre Bell, or at the very least find yourself a good sports bar.

Old Montréal (Vieux-Montréal)

Old Montréal, which was once enclosed by thick stone walls, is the oldest part of the city. It runs roughly from the waterfront in the south to ruelle des Fortifications in the north and from rue McGill in the west to rue Berri in the east. The churches and chapels here stand as testament to the religious fervor that inspired the French settlers who landed here in 1642 to build a "Christian commonwealth" under the leadership of Paul de Chomedey, Sieur de Maisonneuve, and the indomitable Jeanne Mance. Stone warehouses and residences are reminders of how quickly the fur trade commercialized that lofty ideal and made the city one of the most prosperous in 18th-century Nouvelle France. And finally, the financial houses along rue St-Jacques, bristling with Victorian ornamentation, recall the days when Montréalers controlled virtually all the wealth of the young Dominion of Canada.

History and good looks aside, however, Old Montréal still works for a living. Stockbrokers and shipping companies continue to operate out of the old financial district. The city's largest newspaper, *La Presse*, has its offices here. Lawyers in black gowns hurry through the streets to plead cases at the Palais de Justice or the Cour d'Appel; the city council meets in the Second Empire city hall on rue Notre-Dame; and tech innovators and creatives in film, animation, visual effects and video gaming hustle off to meetings in airy lofts and ornate co-working spaces.

GETTING HERE AND AROUND

The easiest way to get from Downtown to Old Montréal is aboard Bus 515, a shuttle that provides a quick direct link to several sites in the Old City and Old Port. It runs from 7 am to midnight. You can also take the Métro's Orange line to the Place-d'Armes and Square-Victoria stations, or you can walk, but the primary routes from Downtown go through some drab and somewhat seedy, although not especially dangerous, areas. If you feel like biking, it's better to rent a BIXI bicycle at a Downtown stand and drop it off at one in Old Montréal. Biking to Old Montréal is a breeze because it's all downhill, but the return trip to is a challenging workout, unless you can snag an e-bike.

Taxis can whisk you here from Downtown in about 10 minutes.

The best way to get around the Old City is on foot, but wear good shoes because the cobbles can be hard on the feet.

TIMING

Having enough time to see the sights, stroll around, and try some of the area's notable restaurants means dedicating at least one day. If it's your first time in the city and you're only here for an extended weekend, consider staying in one of Old Montréal's auberges or boutique hotels.

👁 Sights

★ Basilique Notre-Dame-de-Montréal

(*Our Lady of Montréal Basilica*)

CHURCH | Few churches in North America are as wow-inducing as Notre-Dame. Everything about the Gothic Revival–style church, which opened in 1829, seems designed to make you gasp—from the 228-foot twin towers out front to the tens of thousands of 24-karat gold stars that stud the soaring blue ceiling.

Nothing in a city renowned for churches matches Notre-Dame for sheer grandeur—or noise-making capacity: its 12-ton brass bell is the largest in North America, and its 7,000-pipe Casavant organ can make the walls tremble. The pulpit is a work of art in itself, with an intricately curving staircase and fierce figures of Ezekiel and Jeremiah crouching at its base. The whole place is so overwhelming it's easy to miss such lesser features as the stained-glass windows from Limoges and the side altars dedicated to St. Marguerite d'Youville, Canada's first native-born saint; St. Marguerite Bourgeoys, Canada's first schoolteacher; and a group of Sulpician priests martyred in Paris during the French Revolution.

For a peek at the magnificent baptistery, decorated with frescoes by Ozias Leduc, you'll have to tiptoe through the glassed-off prayer room in the northwest corner of the church. Every year dozens of brides—including Céline Dion, in 1994—march up the aisle of Chapelle Notre-Dame-du-Sacré-Coeur (Our Lady

Montréal OLD MONTRÉAL (VIEUX-MONTRÉAL)

of the Sacred Heart Chapel), behind the main altar, to exchange vows with their grooms before a huge modern bronze sculpture that you either love or hate.

Notre-Dame is an active house of worship, so dress accordingly. The chapel can't be viewed weekdays during the 12:15 pm mass, and is often closed Saturday for weddings. ■TIP➜ Don't miss the 45-minute multimedia spectacle, "Aura," which celebrates the basilica's exquisite features through light and sound. See website for schedule (⊕ www. aurabasiliqueMontréal.com/en). ✉ 110 rue Notre-Dame Ouest, Old Montréal ☎ 514/842–2925, 866/842–2925 for Aura tickets ⊕ www.basiliquenotredame.ca/ en ☑ C$14 +C$1 service fee (self-guided tour); multimedia show "Aura" C$32.00 + C$2 service fee ⚠ Reserve online or by phone. Ⓜ Place-d'Armes.

Centre des Sciences de Montréal
CHILDREN'S MUSEUM | FAMILY | You—or more likely, your kids—can design an energy-efficient bike, create a television news report, explore the impact that manufacturing one T-shirt has on the environment, find out what it's like to ride a unicycle 20 feet above the ground, create an animated film, or just watch an IMAX movie on a giant screen at Montréal's interactive science center. Games, puzzles, and hands-on experiments make it an ideal place for rainy days or even fair ones. The center also has a bistro serving light meals, a coffee and pastry shop, and a food court. ✉ Quai King Edward, Old Montréal ☎ 514/496–4724, 877/496–4724 ⊕ www.centredessciencesdeMontréal.com ☑ Exhibitions C$22, IMAX only C$12 Ⓜ Place-d'Armes.

Chapelle Notre-Dame-de-Bon-Secours (Our Lady of Perpetual Help Chapel)
CHURCH | Mariners have been popping into Notre-Dame-de-Bon-Secours for centuries to kneel before a little 17th-century statue of the Virgin Mary and pray for a safe passage—or give thanks for one. Often, they've expressed their gratitude by leaving votive lamps in the shape of small ships, many of which still hang from the barrel-vaulted ceiling. This is why most Montréalers call the chapel the Église des Matelots (the Sailors' Church), and why many people still stop by to say a prayer and light a candle before leaving on a long trip.

These days, the statue of Our Lady of Perpetual Help guards the remains of St. Marguerite Bourgeoys, who had the original chapel built in 1657 and is entombed in the side altar next to the east wall of the chapel. The current chapel dates from 1771; a renovation project in 1998 revealed some beautiful 18th-century murals that had been hidden under layers of paint.

The 69-step climb to the top of the steeple is worth the effort for the glorious view of the harbor, as is the equally steep climb down to the archaeological excavations under the chapel for a glimpse into the history of the chapel and the neighborhood. The dig is accessible through the adjacent Musée Marguerite Bourgeoys, which also has exhibits on the life of St. Marguerite and the daily lives of the colonists she served. The chapel is closed weekdays January through February except for the 10:30 am mass on Sunday. ✉ 400 rue St-Paul Est, Old Montréal ☎ 514/282–8670 ⊕ margueritebourgeoys.org/en ☑ Museum (includes archaeological site) and tower C$14; Chapel free ⊙ Closed Mon. mid-Oct.–mid-May Ⓜ Champ-de-Mars.

Fondation PHI pour l'art contemporain
ART GALLERY | Housed in two heritage buildings, this nonprofit organization aims to showcase compelling contemporary art from around the world. The Foundation presents two to three major exhibitions a year in addition to a series of public events, special collaborative projects, and a forward-thinking education program. A free app takes you through the exhibits, and podcasts provide a fascinating look at the artists

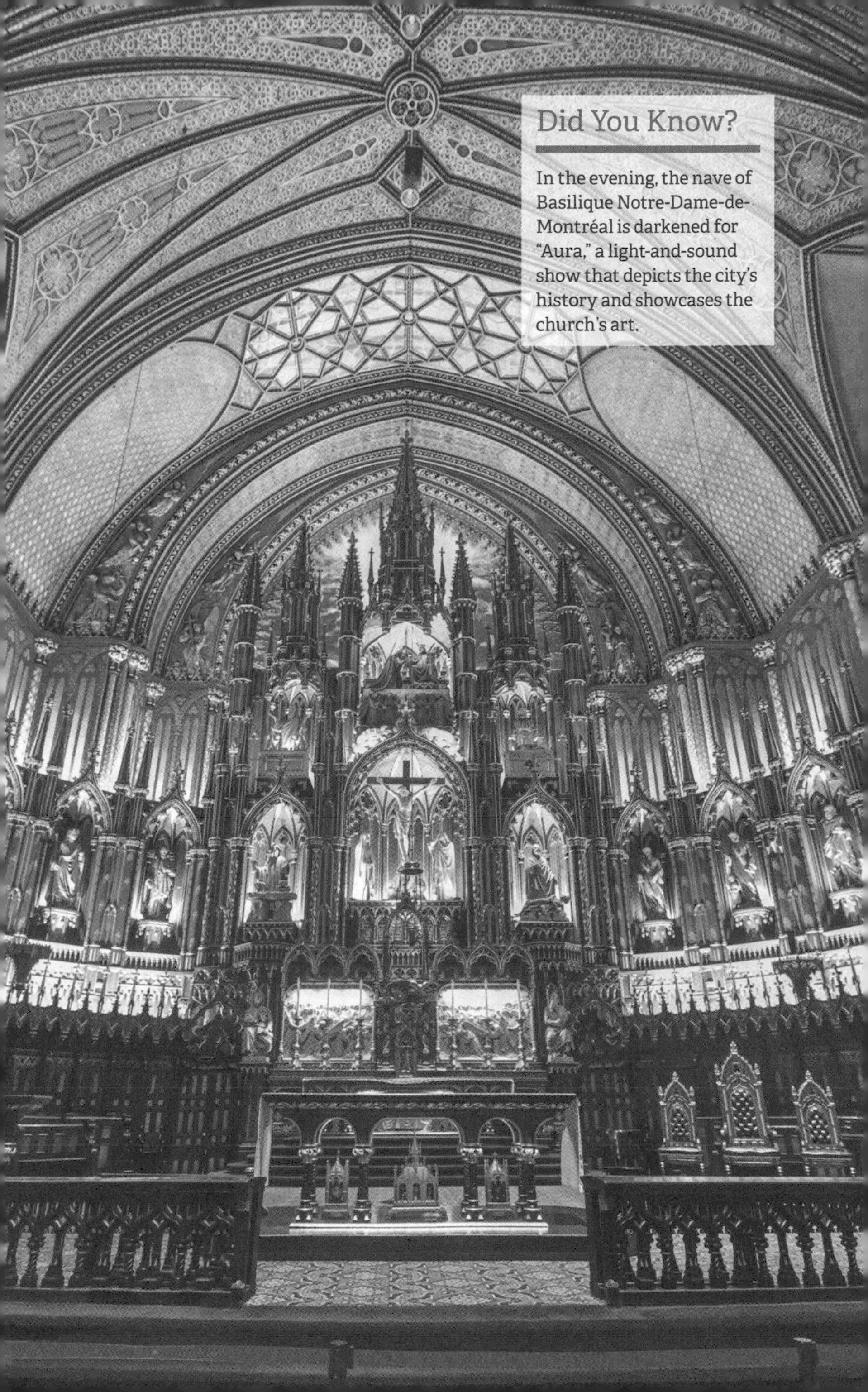

Did You Know?

In the evening, the nave of Basilique Notre-Dame-de-Montréal is darkened for "Aura," a light-and-sound show that depicts the city's history and showcases the church's art.

themselves. ■TIP→ Check the website or call before you visit as the Fondation Phi closes regularly for installations. ✉ *451–465 rue St-Jean, Old Montréal* ☎ *514/849–3742, 888/934–2278* ⊕ *phi.ca/fr/fondation/* ⊘ *Closed Mon. and Tues.* ☞ *Reservations essential* Ⓜ *Square-Victoria or Place-d'Armes.*

Maison St-Gabriel

HISTORIC HOME | Thick stone walls, a steep roof, and mullioned windows mark the Maison St-Gabriel as one of Montréal's rare surviving 17th-century houses. But it's the interior and the furnishings that will sweep you back to the colonial days when Sainte-Marguerite Bourgeoys and the religious order she founded used this house to train *les filles du roy* (king's daughters) in the niceties of home management. Les filles were young women without family or fortune but plenty of spunk who volunteered to cross the Atlantic in leaky boats to become the wives and mothers of New France. It wasn't an easy life, as the Maison's hard, narrow beds, primitive utensils, and drafty rooms attest—but it had its rewards, and the prize at the end was a respectable, settled life. Ste-Marguerite also had some state-of-the-art domestic equipment—the latest in looms and butter churns, labor-saving spit turners for roasting meat, and an ingenious granite sink with a drainage system that piped water straight out to the garden. Located on the little island of New France and deep in the working-class neighborhood of Pointe St-Charles, Maison St-Gabriel is off the beaten path, but it's well worth a 10-minute taxi ride from Old Montréal. ✉ *2146 place Dublin, Pointe-St-Charles* ☎ *514/935–8136* ⊕ *www.maisonsaintgabriel.ca/en/* 🎟 *C$15 weekdays; C$17 summer* ⊘ *Closed Mon. and Tues.* ☞ *Guided tours in English Thurs.–Sun. at 2 pm. In French, 1 pm and 3 pm. The restaurant is currently closed.* Ⓜ *Square-Victoria, then Bus 61.*

Marché Bonsecours (*Bonsecours Market*)

NOTABLE BUILDING | You can't buy fruits and vegetables in the Marché Bonsecours anymore, but you can view an exhibit; shop for local fashions, crafts, and souvenirs in the row of upscale boutiques that fill its main hall; lunch in one of the cafés or restaurants; or grab a craft beer. But the Marché is best admired from the outside. Built in the 1840s as the city's main market, it is possibly the most beautifully proportioned neoclassical building in Montréal, with its six cast-iron Doric columns and two rows of meticulously even sash windows, all topped with a silvery dome. Perhaps the marché was too elegant to be just a farmers' market. ✉ *350 rue St-Paul Est, Old Montréal* ☎ *514/872–7730* ⊕ *www.marchebonsecours.qc.ca* Ⓜ *Champ-de-Mars.*

★ Musée d'Archéologie et d'Histoire Pointe-à-Callière (PAC) (*Pointe-à-Callière Archaeology and History Museum*)

RUINS | A modern glass edifice built on the site of Montréal's first European settlement, the PAC impresses. The museum presents new local and international temporary exhibitions each year, but the real reason to visit the city's most ambitious archaeological museum is to take the elevator ride down to the 17th century.

It's dark down there, and just a little creepy thanks to the 350-year-old tombstones teetering in the gloom, but it's worth the trip. This is a serious archaeological dig that takes you to the very foundations of the city. A more lighthearted exhibit explores life and love in multicultural Montréal. For a spectacular view of the Old Port, the St. Lawrence River, and the Islands, ride the elevator to the top of the tower, or stop for lunch in the museum's glass-fronted café. In summer there are re-creations of period fairs and festivals on the grounds near the museum.

Built on the actual foundations of the city, the impressive Pointe-à-Callière museum takes visitors back in time to 17th-century Montréal.

The Fort Ville-Marie pavilion showcases the remains of the forts and artifacts from the first Montréalers. The 360-foot underground William collector sewer, built in the 1830s and considered a masterpiece of civil engineering at that time, connects the original museum space with the new pavilion and features a sound-and-light show projected onto the walls of the collector sewer. ⊠ *350 place Royale, Old Montréal* ☎ *514/872–9150* ⊕ *www.pacmusee.qc.ca* ⊠ *C$24* Ⓜ *Place-d'Armes.*

Musée du Château Ramezay

HISTORIC HOME | Claude de Ramezay, the city's 11th governor, was probably daydreaming of home when he built his Montréal residence, now a UNESCO-listed "1001 Historic Sites You Must See Before You Die." Its thick stone walls, dormer windows, and steeply pitched roof make it look like a little bit of 18th-century Normandy dropped into the middle of North America—although the round, squat tower is a 19th-century addition. The extravagant mahogany paneling in the Salon de Nantes was installed when Louis XV was still king of France. The British used the château as headquarters after their conquest in 1760, and so did the American commanders Richard Montgomery and Benedict Arnold. Benjamin Franklin, who came north in a failed attempt to persuade the locals to join the American Revolution, stayed here during that winter adventure.

Most of the château's exhibits are a little staid—guns, uniforms, and documents on the main floor and tableaux depicting colonial life in the cellars—but they include some unexpected little eccentricities that make it worth the visit. Head outside, through the back door, and you'll enter gardens full of 18th-century tranquility. ⊠ *280 rue Notre-Dame Est, Old Montréal* ☎ *514/861–3708* ⊕ *www.chateauramezay. qc.ca/en* ⊠ *C$10.44* ⊗ *Closed Mon. late Oct.–late May* Ⓜ *Champ-de-Mars.*

Montréal's History

Montréal is the second-largest French-speaking city in the Western world, but it's not only francophone culture that thrives here. About 14% of the 3.3 million people who call Greater Montréal home claim English as their mother tongue.

Yet the two cultures are not as separate as they once were. Chatter in the bars and bistros of rue St-Denis east of boulevard St-Laurent still tends to be in French, and crowds in restaurants on rue Crescent in the Downtown core speak English. But the lines have blurred, with more conversations taking place in a uniquely Montréal mixture of the two languages.

Both linguistic groups have had to come to grips with no longer being the only player. So-called *allophones*—people whose mother tongue is neither French nor English—make up 19% of the city's population.

The first European settlement on the island of Montréal was Ville-Marie, founded in 1642 by 54 men and women under the leadership of Paul de Chomedey, Sieur de Maisonneuve, and Jeanne Mance, a French noblewoman, who hoped to create a new Christian society. The settlement's location near the confluence of the St. Lawrence and Ottawa rivers also meant a lucrative trade in beaver pelts, as the fur was a staple of European hat fashion for nearly a century.

The French regime in Canada ended with the Seven Years' War, also known as the French and Indian War. The Treaty of Paris ceded all of New France to Britain in 1763.

American troops under generals Richard Montgomery and Benedict Arnold occupied the city during their 1775–76 campaign to conquer Canada, but their efforts failed and troops withdrew. Soon invaders of another kind—English and Scottish settlers—poured into Montréal. By 1832, the city became a colonial capital. But 1837 brought anti-British rebellions, and this led to Canada's becoming a self-governing dominion in 1867.

The city's ports continued to bustle until the St. Lawrence Seaway opened in 1957, allowing ships to sail from the Atlantic to the Great Lakes without having to stop in Montréal to transfer cargo.

The opening of the métro in 1966 changed the way Montréalers lived, and the next year the city hosted the World's Fair. But the rise of Québec separatism in the late 1960s under René Lévesque created political uncertainty, and many major businesses moved to Toronto. By the time Lévesque's separatist Parti Québécois won power in Québec in 1976—the same year the summer Olympics came to the city—Montréal was clearly Canada's No. 2 city.

Uncertainty continued through the 1980s and '90s, with the separatist Parti Québécois and the federalist Liberals alternating in power in Québec City. Since 1980, the city has endured two referenda on the future of Québec and Canada. In the cliff-hanger of 1995, just 50.58% of Quebecers voted to remain part of Canada. Montréal bucked the separatist trend and voted nearly 70% against independence.

Old Port (*Vieux Port*)
CITY PARK | FAMILY | Montréal's favorite waterfront park is your ideal gateway to the St. Lawrence River. Rent a pedal boat, take a ferry to Île Ste-Hélène, sign up for a dinner cruise, or, if you're really adventurous, ride a raft or a jet boat through the turbulent Lachine Rapids. If you're determined to stay ashore, however, there's still plenty to do, including riding the Grande Roue, the tallest Ferris wheel in Canada; soaking in the rays at the Clock Tower Beach (you can't swim, though); and enjoying street performances, sound-and-light shows, or art displays and exhibitions. Visiting warships from the Canadian navy and other countries often dock here and open their decks to the public. You can rent a bicycle or a pair of in-line skates at one of the shops along rue de la Commune and explore the waterfront at your leisure. In winter, rent a pair of skates and glide around the outdoor rink. You can also, quite literally, lose the kids in Shed 16's Labyrinthe, a maze of alleys, surprises, and obstacles built inside an old waterfront warehouse. With the rope and aerial courses aboard life-size replicas of pirate and royal ships, kids will also go crazy for the Voiles en Voiles adventure park. ✉ *Old Montréal* ☎ *514/496–7678, 800/971–7678* ⊕ *www. oldportofMontréal.com* Ⓜ *Place-d'Armes or Champ-de-Mars.*

Place-d'Armes
PLAZA/SQUARE | When Montréal was under attack, citizens and soldiers would rally at Place-d'Armes, but these days the only rallying is done by tourists, lunching office workers, and flocks of voracious pigeons. The pigeons are particularly fond of the triumphant statue of Montréal's founder, Paul de Chomedey, with his lance upraised, perched above the fountain in the middle of the cobblestone square. Tunnels beneath the square protected the colonists

from the winter weather and provided an escape route; unfortunately, they are too small and dangerous to visit. ✉ *Bordered by rues Notre-Dame Ouest, St-Jacques, and St-Sulpice, Old Montréal* Ⓜ *Place-d'Armes.*

Place de la Grande-Paix
PLAZA/SQUARE | If you're looking for peace and quiet, the narrow strip of grass and trees on Place d'Youville just east of Place Royale is an appropriate place to find it. It was here, after all, that the French signed a major peace treaty with dozens of aboriginal nations in 1702. It was also here that the first French colonists to settle in Montréal landed their four boats on May 17, 1642. An obelisk records the settlers' names. ✉ *Between Place d'Youville and rue William, Old Montréal* Ⓜ *Place-d'Armes.*

Place Jacques-Cartier
PLAZA/SQUARE | The cobbled square at the heart of Old Montréal is part carnival, part flower market, and part sheer fun. You can pause here to have your portrait painted, buy an ice cream or watch the street performers. If you have more time, try to get a table at one of the sidewalk cafés, order a beer or a glass of wine, and watch the passing parade. During the holiday season you can order a mulled wine or hot cider in the market and warm up by one of the wood-burning stoves from your perch on an Adirondack chair. The 1809 monument honoring Lord Nelson's victory over Napoléon Bonaparte's French navy at Trafalgar angers some modern-day Québec nationalists. The campaign to raise money for it was led by the Sulpician priests, who were engaged in delicate land negotiations with the British government at the time and were eager to show what good subjects they were. ✉ *Bordered by rues Notre-Dame Est and de la Commune, Old Montréal* Ⓜ *Champ-de-Mars.*

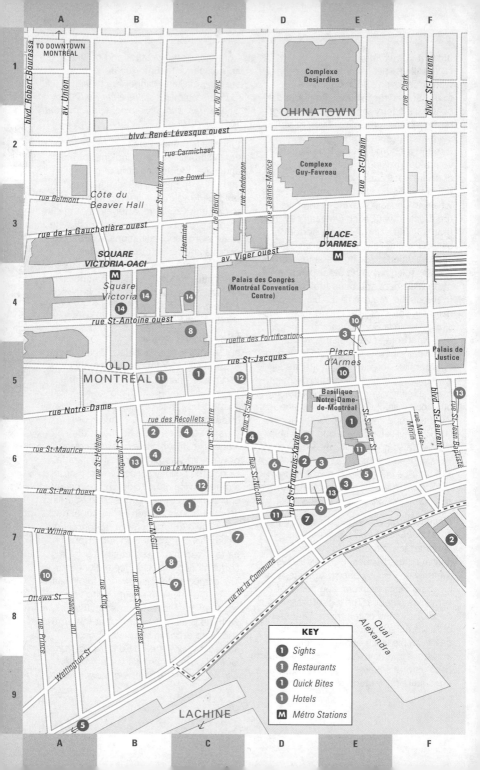

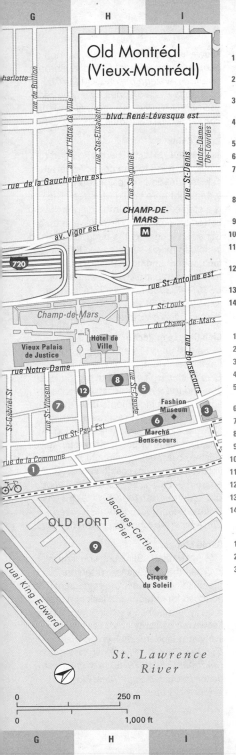

Old Montréal (Vieux-Montréal)

Sights ▼

1 Basilique Notre-Dame-de-Montréal............. E6
2 Centre des Sciences de Montréal............. F7
3 Chapelle Notre-Dame-de-Bon-Secours..........I5
4 Fondation PHI pour l'art contemporain...... D6
5 Maison St-Gabriel...... A9
6 Marché Bonsecours... H6
7 Musée d'Archéologie et d'Histoire Pointe-à-Callière (PAC)........... D7
8 Musée du Château Ramezay................. H5
9 Old Port.................. H7
10 Place d'Armes........... E5
11 Place de la Grande-Paix............. D7
12 Place Jacques-Cartier........ H5
13 Place Royale............. E6
14 Square Victoria......... B4

Restaurants ▼

1 Bloom.................... C7
2 Boris Bistro............. B6
3 Brasserie 701............. E5
4 Brit & Chips............. B6
5 Club Chasse et Pêche................... H5
6 Garde Manger.......... D6
7 Gibbys.................... C7
8 Ikanos................... B7
9 Le Cartet................. B8
10 Le Serpent.............. A7
11 Monarque.............. B5
12 Olive + Gourmando...... C6
13 Restaurant Helena...... B6
14 Toqué!.................... C4

Quick Bites ▼

1 Crew Collective Café.... C5
2 Le Petit Dep............. D6
3 Maison Christian Faure.......... E6

Hotels ▼

1 Auberge du Vieux-Port............... G6
2 Hôtel Bonaparte........ D6
3 Hôtel Épik Montréal.... D6
4 Hôtel Gault................ C6
5 Hôtel Nelligan............ E6
6 Hôtel St. Paul............ B7
7 Hôtel William Gray...... G5
8 InterContinental Montréal.................. C4
9 Le Petit Hôtel........... D6
10 Le Place d'Armes Hôtel & Suites............ E5
11 Le Saint-Sulpice......... E6
12 LHotel..................... C5
13 Springhill Suites by Marriott............... F5
14 W Montréal............. B4

3

Montréal OLD MONTRÉAL (VIEUX-MONTRÉAL)

Place Royale

PLAZA/SQUARE | The oldest public square in Montréal, dating to the 17th century, was a market during the French regime and later became a Victorian garden. ✉ *Bordered by rues St-Paul Ouest and de la Commune, Old Montréal* Ⓜ *Place-d'Armes.*

Square Victoria

PLAZA/SQUARE | Although Square Victoria officially lies within the Quartier International, or International District, Montréalers consider it a part of Old Montréal. The square nicely blends its French and English heritage with an 1872 statue of Queen Victoria on one side and an authentic Parisian métro entrance and a flower market on the other. Both are framed by a two-block stretch of trees, benches, and fountains that makes a pleasant place to relax and admire the handsome 1920s office buildings on the east side. The art nouveau métro entrance, incidentally, was a gift from the French capital's transit commission. ✉ *Rue du Square Victoria, between rues Viger and St-Jacques, Old Montréal* Ⓜ *Square-Victoria.*

🍴 Restaurants

Old Montréal is home to some of the city's most in-vogue bistros and fine-dining establishments—all tucked into gorgeous heritage buildings. Foodies eat wild game, fresh seafood, and inventive plant-based dishes while tasting local and imported wine. Daily changing menus written on chalkboards are a common sight, since market-fresh food is popular.

Brasserie 701

$$$ | **BRASSERIE** | Inspired by Paris's golden-age brasseries, Brasserie 701's spectacular setting features high ceilings, neoclassical architecture, giant arched windows, and lovely chandeliers. The menu incudes the usual suspects expected at a brasserie, from tartares, filet mignon, and escargot to foie gras.

Known for: packed with locals; salmon or beef tartare; homemade wild mushroom ravioli. Ⓢ *Average main: C$30* ✉ *701 côte de la Place-d'Armes, Old Montréal* ☎ *514/904–1201* ⊕ *www.brasserie701. com/en* Ⓜ *Place-d'Armes.*

Brit & Chips

$$ | **BRITISH** | **FAMILY** | There's no need to cross the pond to find perfectly battered fish and delicious chips, as they can be found right here in Old Montréal. The cod is a staple, but the salmon dipped in beer batter is also a menu favorite, and for a Canadian touch, try the haddock covered in golden maple syrup batter. **Known for:** popcorn shrimp; fish-and-chips; maple syrup batter. Ⓢ *Average main: C$15* ✉ *433 rue McGill, Old Montréal* ☎ *514/840–1001* ⊕ *www.britandchips. com* Ⓜ *Square-Victoria.*

Club Chasse et Pêche

$$$$ | **CANADIAN** | Despite the name—French for "Hunting and Fishing Club"—this isn't a hangout for the local gun-and-rod set. Impeccable service and top-notch ingredients have made this one of the best restaurants in the city; the name is simply referencing the wood-and-leather decor. **Known for:** terroir cuisine; *chasse* (filet mignon) *et pêche* (lobster) dish; impeccable service. Ⓢ *Average main: C$42* ✉ *423 rue St-Claude, Old Montréal* ☎ *514/861–1112* ⊕ *www. leclubchasseetpeche.com* ⊙ *Closed Sun.–Tues. No lunch* Ⓜ *Champ-de-Mars.*

Garde Manger

$$$$ | **CANADIAN** | Blink and you'll miss it. While the address is written on the building's facade, the restaurant's nondescript exterior and lack of a sign mean you may be searching for a while. **Known for:** celebrity chef; seafood bar; lively atmosphere. Ⓢ *Average main: C$50* ✉ *408 rue St-François-Xavier, Old Montréal* ☎ *514/678–5044* ⊕ *gardemanger.ca* ⊙ *Closed Sun.–Tues. No lunch* Ⓜ *Place-d'Armes.*

Gibbys

$$$$ | **STEAKHOUSE** | A culinary landmark like few others in the city, Gibbys is one of Montréal's most famous steak houses. Part of what makes it so attractive is the 200-year-old historic building in which it's located, featuring vaulted-ceilings, wood beams, stone walls, and candlelit dining rooms. **Known for:** extensive wine list; aged steaks; historic building. [$] *Average main: C$60* ✉ *298 place d'Youville, Old Montréal* ☎ *514/282–1837* 🌐 *www.gibbys.com* 🕒 *No lunch* [M] *Square-Victoria.*

★ **Ikanos**

$$$$ | **MODERN GREEK** | A far cry from the cliché-clad tavernas found elsewhere in the city, Ikanos serves refined Aegean gastronomy in an elegant and sleek environment. No blue-and-white checkered tablecloths in sight; the muted neutral palette puts the spotlight on the food. **Known for:** *loukoumades* (Greek donuts); *mezzes* (Greek tapas); Greek wines. [$] *Average main: C$60* ✉ *112 rue McGill, Old Montréal* ☎ *514/842–0867* 🌐 *promo.ikanos.ca* 🕒 *Closed Sun.–Tues. No lunch* [M] *Square-Victoria.*

Le Cartet

$$ | **FRENCH** | As a gourmet grocery shop, takeout counter, and French restaurant rolled into one, this splendid space was quickly adopted by local foodies. Instead of being dejected by the brunch queues on Saturday and Sunday, visitors should take advantage of that time to browse the restaurant's inviting grocery shop for gourmet souvenirs to take home. **Known for:** gazpacho; brunch; mimosas. [$] *Average main: C$17* ✉ *106 rue McGill, Old Montréal* ☎ *514/871–8887* 🌐 *www.lecartet.ca* 🕒 *No dinner* [M] *Square-Victoria.*

★ **Le Serpent**

$$$$ | **MODERN ITALIAN** | The expertise and irreproachable service at Le Serpent truly make it an essential stop on any Montréal foodie itinerary. The industrial-looking space caters to trendy diners, and almost paradoxically, serves sublime Italianate plates that could be mistaken for comfort food if they weren't so elegantly presented. **Known for:** friendly service; oysters doused in maple mignonette sauce; industrial chic vibe. [$] *Average main: C$35* ✉ *257 rue Prince, Old Montréal* ☎ *514/316–4666* 🌐 *www.leserpent.ca* 🕒 *Closed Sun.–Tues. No lunch* [M] *Square-Victoria.*

Monarque

$$$$ | **CANADIAN** | For fine dining in Old Montréal, head to this chic, contemporary restaurant serving expertly presented Canadian fare, from oysters to PEI *côte de boeuf*. A chic, illuminated bar showcases the wine collection, with 400 selections including some Québécois bottles. **Known for:** wine and cheese selection; classic salle à manger; top-notch service. [$] *Average main: C$35* ✉ *406 rue Saint-Jacques, Old Montréal* ☎ *514/875–3896* 🌐 *restaurantmonarque.ca/en* [M] *Square-Victoria-OACI.*

★ **Olive + Gourmando**

$$ | **CAFÉ** | **FAMILY** | Influential types arrive at lunchtime en masse for a table at this bustling bakery and sandwich shop where vegetables are organically grown in a nearby garden and fresh crab is flown in for salads. Crowd pleasers include Le Cubain panini (pancetta, roasted pork, Gruyère with lime, cilantro, and chipotle) and the vegan sandwich with chickpea and harissa spread, pickled beets, creamy sauce, and minty slaw. **Known for:** popular brunch; organic produce; affordable sandwiches. [$] *Average main: C$16* ✉ *351 rue St-Paul Ouest, Old Montréal* ☎ *514/350–1083* 🌐 *www.oliveetgourmando.com* 🕒 *Closed Mon. and Tues. No dinner* [M] *Square-Victoria.*

Restaurant Helena

$$$$ | **PORTUGUESE** | Housed inside a welcoming space with alcove windows and stone walls, this airy, colorful restaurant serves traditional Portuguese with plenty of seafood dishes. Share a few tapas plates, like the grilled sardines fillets, cod fritters, the grilled asparagus, or the baby

potatoes with herbs before delving into the main course. **Known for:** *caldo verde*; historic building; Portuguese tapas. [$] *Average main: C$40* ✉ *438 McGill, Old Montréal* ☎ *514/878–1555* 🌐 *www.restauranthelena.com* 🕘 *Closed Sun. No lunch Sat.* [M] *Square-Victoria.*

★ Toqué!
$$$$ | CANADIAN | Frequently named one of Montréal's best restaurants and Canada's third best by canadas100best.com, a meal at Toqué! is not so much about sustenance but rather experience. Toqué is slang for "a little stubborn," as in the chef's insistence on using fresh, local ingredients; consequently, the menu changes daily in accordance with market offerings but foie gras, duck, and wild venison are on constant rotation. **Known for:** wine pairings; tasting menu; market cuisine. [$] *Average main: C$55* ✉ *900 pl. Jean-Paul-Riopelle, Old Montréal* ☎ *514/499–2084* 🌐 *www.restaurant-toque.com* 🕘 *Closed Sun. and Mon. No lunch* [M] *Square-Victoria.*

☕ Coffee and Quick Bites

★ Crew Collective Café
$ | CAFÉ | Undoubtedly the most strikingly beautiful coffee shop in Montréal, perhaps even in North America, Crew Collective & Café is housed inside a former 1920s-era bank that's fitted with 50-foot-high vaulted ceilings, intricate tiling, and bronze chandeliers. It's no wonder Forbes named it of the five most beautiful co-working spaces in the world. **Known for:** cold brew; architectural, lavish space; curated coffee beans. [$] *Average main: C$6* ✉ *360 rue Saint-Jacques, Old Montréal* ☎ *514/285–7095* 🌐 *crewcollectivecafe.com* [M] *Place-d'Armes.*

★ Le Petit Dep
$ | CANADIAN | You'll want to keep coming back again and again to this adorable little gourmet convenience store and café with its mint-green facade and single origin coffee. Le Petit Dep proudly stocks local products, including prêt-à-manger soups, salads, and comfort foods such as chili, pasta, and vegan shepherd's pie. **Known for:** delicious sweets; prêt-à-manger meals; delightful setting. [$] *Average main: C$8* ✉ *179 rue St-Paul Ouest, Old Montréal* ☎ *514/284–9162* 🌐 *www.lepetitdep.ca* [M] *Place-d'Armes or Square-Victoria.*

Maison Christian Faure
$ | BAKERY | FAMILY | This elegant patisserie is housed in a historic, beautifully renovated three-story graystone in Old Montréal. Baskets of buttery brioches and flaky croissants await, and the prominent pastry display holds rows of seasonal fruit tarts and classic French desserts like *mille-feuilles* (made of delicate layers of puff pastry and airy vanilla-scented custard) and Paris-Brest (made of choux pastry and a praline-flavored cream). **Known for:** acclaimed pastry chef; French-style pâtisseries; historic building. [$] *Average main: C$7* ✉ *355 Place Royale, Old Montréal* ☎ *514/508–6453* 🌐 *www.maisonchristianfaure.ca/en* 🕘 *Closed Mon.–Wed.* ☞ *Reduced hours due to pandemic; takeout only.* [M] *Place-d'Armes.*

The City's Oldest Patisserie ☕

A light croissant or rich pastry from **Duc de Lorraine**, the city's oldest patisserie, makes for a nice break. Try to snag an almond paste croissant before the café runs out. For lunch, try one of the quiches, sandwiches, or the soupe du jour followed by a scoop of homemade ice cream or a *tartelette poire et amande* (pear and almond tart). ✉ *5002 Chemin de la Côte-des-Neiges, Montréal,* ☎ *514/731-4128,* 🌐 *www.ducdelorraine.ca.*

Hotels

Let's start with the name. Nobody says "Old Town." That's an American phrase. You may call it Old Montréal, but street signs are in French and say "Vieux-Montréal." Either way, it's full of charm—from narrow, cobblestone streets to quaint outdoor terraces, or *terrasses* in French. You can find boutique hotels, auberges, and cozy bed-and-breakfasts nestled inside heritage buildings. Most properties have exposed beams, stone walls, wooden floors, and thick, casement windows. History buffs find this area pleasing, as do people who want to wander around boutiques and art galleries. But know that this is no place for stilettos. Bring your walking shoes and expect to stumble on film crews and the occasional Hollywood actor taking a smoke break. We're talking to you, Brad Pitt.

★ Auberge du Vieux-Port

$$$ | **B&B/INN** | This showcase for 19th-century architecture—think casement windows, exposed beams and brick—is the gold standard for intimate boutique hotels, attracting A-listers and well-heeled romantics with its mix of old-world charm and modern comfort. **Pros:** some rooms have decks and fireplaces; loft options offer more space and high ceilings; expansive rooftop deck. **Cons:** breakfast not included in base price; some rooms are very small; sometimes noisy in street-facing rooms. [$] *Rooms from: C$325* ✉ *97 rue de la Commune Est, Old Montréal* ☎ *514/876–0081, 888/660–7678* 🌐 *www.aubergedu-vieuxport.com* 🛏 *75 rooms* 🍴 *No Meals* [M] *Place-d'Armes or Champ-de-Mars.*

Hôtel Bonaparte

$$ | **B&B/INN** | Housed inside a 19th-century building, the Auberge Bonaparte is a gem. **Pros:** perfect for theater lovers—the Centaur Theatre is next door; excellent location; some rooms have balconies. **Cons:** parking lot is down the street; not family-friendly; downstairs restaurant can be a bit noisy on weekends. [$] *Rooms from: C$289* ✉ *447 rue St-François-Xavier, Old Montréal* ☎ *514/844–1448* 🌐 *www.bonaparte.com* 🛏 *36 rooms and one suite* 🍴 *Free Breakfast* [M] *Place-d'Armes.*

★ Hôtel Épik Montréal

$$ | **B&B/INN** | With its rustic stone walls and exposed beams, this inn was the first of its kind in the Old Port when it opened in the late 1980s, and the new owners continue to honor its tradition of calm excellence while adding modern comfort and contemporary design accents throughout. **Pros:** bountiful breakfast; refrigerator downstairs for guest to use in a pinch (if there's space); soundproof shutters. **Cons:** no elevator; king beds are pricey; rooms need to be booked far in advance. [$] *Rooms from: C$289* ✉ *171 rue St-Paul Ouest, Old Montréal* ☎ *514/842–2634, 877/841–2634* 🌐 *www.epikMontréal.com* 🛏 *10 rooms* 🍴 *Free Breakfast* [M] *Place-d'Armes.*

★ Hôtel Gault

$$$ | **HOTEL** | Once a cotton factory in the 1800s, this five-story heritage boutique hotel has loftlike rooms, suites, apartments, and terrace-suites with soaring ceilings, French windows, cast-iron columns, and an artsy vibe that doesn't sacrifice comfort for style. **Pros:** quiet location; some rooms have private terraces; 24/7 room service. **Cons:** no pool; C$35 valet; a bit hard to find. [$] *Rooms from: C$386* ✉ *449 rue Ste-Hélène, Old Montréal* ☎ *514/904–1616, 866/904–1616* 🌐 *www.hotelgault.com* 🛏 *30 suites* 🍴 *No Meals* [M] *Square-Victoria.*

Hôtel Nelligan

$$$ | **HOTEL** | This boutique hotel, named for Quebec's most passionate poet, Emile Nelligan, is known for its romance-inspiring lobby atrium and rooftop terrace offering views of the Old City and the harbor. **Pros:** Le Labo toiletries; cozy rooms with brick walls, king-size beds, and enormous bathrooms, some

with whirlpool bathtubs and showers; in summer, breakfast or cocktails with a view on rooftop terrace. **Cons:** no pool; pricey valet parking; popular event space. $ *Rooms from: C$350* ⊠ *106 rue St-Paul Ouest, Old Montréal* ☎ *514/788–2040, 877/788–2040* ⊕ *www.hotelnelligan. com* ↻ *105 rooms* ⦿| *No Meals* Ⓜ *Place-d'Armes.*

Hôtel St. Paul

$$$ | HOTEL | Forget fussy oil paintings or rococo furniture—behind its 19th-century Beaux-Arts facade, the St. Paul boasts a chic lobby furnished with jewel-toned velvet sofas and a giant alabaster fireplace built of backlit blocks of "ice." Rooms have also undergone a redo with an airier, more contemporary feel and design, in line with the lobby. **Pros:** great location on a north–south artery; pets allowed (C$55 per night); designer lobby. **Cons:** no pool; modern furniture and bright colors not for everyone; underlie hallways and elevators can be spooky. $ *Rooms from: C$315* ⊠ *355 rue McGill, Old Montréal* ☎ *514/380–2222, 866/380–2202* ⊕ *www. hotelstpaul.com* ↻ *119 rooms* ⦿| *No Meals* Ⓜ *Square-Victoria.*

Hôtel William Gray

$$$ | HOTEL | Popular with A-listers and the millennial crowd, the Hotel William Gray marries the deep history and contemporary cool of Old Montréal, with its two 18th-century stone buildings topped by an eight-story glass tower. **Pros:** Himalayan salt room in the spa; magnificent views of Old Montréal and Jacques Cartier bridge from popular rooftop terrace; small, tranquil outdoor pool, a rarity in Old Montréal hotels. **Cons:** most rooms don't have bathtubs; pool too small for laps; older travelers may not appreciate the trendy scene in the restaurant or two rooftop bars. $ *Rooms from: C$325* ⊠ *421 rue Saint Vincent, Old Montréal* ☎ *514/656–5600* ⊕ *www.hotelwilliamgray.com* ↻ *127 rooms* ⦿| *No Meals* Ⓜ *Champ-de-Mars.*

InterContinental Montréal

$$$ | HOTEL | After extensive room renovations in 2016, the InterContinental definitely got its groove back, catering to a variety of travelers—from families and their pets, to the business and fitness cliques. **Pros:** outdoor terrace on sixth floor; saltwater swimming pool; easy underground access to shopping and nightlife. **Cons:** 1990 building lacks character; dull ground-floor entry; gets the convention crowd. $ *Rooms from: C$380* ⊠ *360 rue St-Antoine Ouest, Old Montréal* ☎ *514/987–9900, 877/660–8550* ⊕ *www.Montréal.intercontinental.com* ↻ *357 rooms* ⦿| *No Meals* Ⓜ *Square-Victoria or Place-d'Armes.*

Le Petit Hôtel

$$$ | HOTEL | FAMILY | Little sister of Auberge du Vieux Port, this boutique hotel marries creative design with old stone walls, exposed beams, a narrow lobby with a counter coffee bar and a seven-foot orange sculpture, and—contrary to its name—not-so-petite rooms. **Pros:** cribs, playpens, and babysitters available; bicycles to borrow; elevator. **Cons:** lobby not especially elegant or cozy; steep fee for valet parking; small bathrooms have no tubs and some can be cramped. $ *Rooms from: C$319* ⊠ *168 rue St-Paul Ouest, Old Montréal* ☎ *514/405–3729, 877/530–0360* ⊕ *www. petithotelMontréal.com* ↻ *28 rooms* ⦿| *Free Breakfast* Ⓜ *Square-Victoria.*

★ Le Place d'Armes Hôtel & Suites

$$$ | HOTEL | FAMILY | Four splendidly ornate Victorian commercial buildings were merged to create Old Montréal's largest boutique hotel, pleasing honeymooners and business execs alike with its old-fashioned grandeur, exposed brick walls in rooms, *hammam* (Middle Eastern–style steam bath), rooftop terrace, and unobstructed views of the Basilique Notre-Dame-de-Montréal. **Pros:** rooftop bar; best (Turkish) spa in town; Japanese tavern (*hamachi bibimbap* [marinated yellowtail]). **Cons:** rooms in new building

have no bathtubs, only multi–jet showers; steep approach from métro is slippery in winter; late sleepers may be disturbed by the noontime Angelus bells at the basilica. $ *Rooms from: C$386* ✉ *55 rue St-Jacques, Old Montréal* ☎ *514/842–1887, 888/450–1887* ⊕ *www.hotelplacedarmes.com* ➥ *169 rooms* ⊠ *No Meals* Ⓜ *Place-d'Armes.*

Le Saint-Sulpice

$$$ | HOTEL | With its sought-after address beside the basilica's chapel, this boutique hotel is blessed with a magical garden terrace, casement windows that actually open, luxurious suites—both in space and decor—and a lively lobby restaurant with one of the city's best menus. **Pros:** proximity to the Basilique Notre-Dame de Montréal; in-room massage service; celebrity-spotting. **Cons:** pricey summer rates; too posh for comfort with kids; church bells may disturb late sleepers. $ *Rooms from: C$345* ✉ *414 rue St-Sulpice, Old Montréal* ☎ *514/288–1000, 877/785–7423* ⊕ *www.lesaintsulpice.com* ➥ *108 rooms* ⊠ *No Meals* Ⓜ *Place-d'Armes.*

LHotel

$$$ | HOTEL | Housed in a stately 19th-century bank in the financial district, the dignified facade accurately suggests the grand interior with its high ceilings, antique furnishings, and large windows. **Pros:** excellent art collection and close to other galleries; Botero wine bar has distinct character; spacious high-ceiling rooms. **Cons:** rue St-Jacques is dull after 6 pm; buffet continental breakfast is pricey and not included; some rooms are dated. $ *Rooms from: C$369* ✉ *262 rue St-Jacques Ouest, Old Montréal* ☎ *514/985–0019, 877/553–0019* ⊕ *www. lhotelMontréal.com* ➥ *59 rooms* ⊠ *No Meals* Ⓜ *Square-Victoria.*

Springhill Suites by Marriott

$$$ | HOTEL | FAMILY | Convenient and quiet, with large rooms and underground parking—rarities in Old Montréal—this all-suites hotel attracts families and business travelers who return for the free breakfast buffet, lobby market, saltwater pool, and fitness center. **Pros:** well-stocked lobby store; free, bountiful breakfast with healthy options; saltwater pool. **Cons:** poor views; difficult access on a narrow street; popular with families so pool can be crowded. $ *Rooms from: C$315* ✉ *445 rue St-Jean-Baptiste, Old Montréal* ☎ *514/875–4333, 866/875–4333* ⊕ *www. springhillsuites.com* ➥ *124 rooms* ⊠ *Free Breakfast* Ⓜ *Champ-de-Mars.*

★ W Montréal

$$$$ | HOTEL | A chic showcase for your Prada luggage, the W Montréal lives up to the brand's reputation for a hip take on luxury and style, providing its A-list clientele with excellent service and sleek, modern decor, notably peekaboo bathrooms, a trendy bar, and a lobby designed for lingering and entertaining. **Pros:** Bluetooth speakers in rooms; bright, airy rooms; well-connected concierge. **Cons:** showers afford no privacy; lobby noisy at night; nonmember fee for in-room Wi-Fi (free in the lobby). $ *Rooms from: C$435* ✉ *901 Square Victoria, Old Montréal* ☎ *514/395–3100, 888/627–7081* ⊕ *www. whotels.com/Montréal* ➥ *152 rooms* ⊠ *No Meals* Ⓜ *Square-Victoria.*

❶ Nightlife

Once a tourist trap full of overpriced souvenirs, Old Montréal is now home to a mix of top-notch restaurants and chic lounges. During the summer you can enjoy stunning views of the river from some of the city's best rooftop terraces. Excellent dining can be found along rue St-Paul, while rue McGill is a big part of the 5-à-7 scene.

BARS AND LOUNGES

Coldroom

BARS | No advertised street number. A secret, nondescript back door. Imaginative, award-winning mixologists. A cocktail selection that changes with the seasons. Twists on old classics; think: old fashioned with mezcal. Clear, no-nonsense house rules like:

"Act your age, or you'll be required to be accompanied by a parent or guardian."

"For all make out purposes, may we suggest our next door neighbour The William Grey hotel? Get a room."

And just for the men: "Know your alcohol limits. Stay classy."

"Erase the word 'slut' and 'gay' and any other abusive language from your vocabulary."

"Learn some dance moves. If you need help, ask our manager Dan."

What more could you want in a speakeasy? ⊠ *401a rue St-Vincent, Old Montréal* ⚜ *Adjacent to El Pequeño Bar (same owners). The entrance is via the large black door with "Sortie" written above it. Press the doorbell. Be patient* ☎ *514/903–6887* ⊕ *www.thecoldroommtl.com* Ⓜ *Champ-de-Mars.*

Maison St-Paul

WINE BARS | Sharpen your swords! This chic bar for Champagne and other bubblies is the perfect place to break open a bottle—literally. The staff like to open the bottles of Champagne with sabers, a practice that adds an element of fun and drama to an accessible venue. Finger foods include oysters, steak (and other kinds of) tartares, and caviar. ⊠ *343 rue St-Paul Est, Old Montréal* ☎ *514/903–9343* ⊕ *www.maisonsaintpaul.ca* ☾ *Closed Mon. and Tues.* Ⓜ *Champs-de-Mars.*

Philémon Bar

WINE BARS | You can grab a glass of one of Philémon's well-priced private import Cavas, Proseccos, or Champagnes to accompany the menu at this sleek bar, which serves more than the usual pub fare (oysters, anyone?). It's packed with locals Thursday through Saturday—in fact, it's become quite the singles hangout. Bouncers keep the ratio of guys to gals at a comfortable level. ⊠ *111 rue St-Paul Ouest, Old Montréal* ☎ *514/289–3777* ⊕ *www.philemonbar.com* Ⓜ *Place-d'Armes.*

Terrasse sur l'Auberge

BEER GARDENS | For an unbeatable view of the Old Port and numerous Montréal landmarks, head to this unpretentious patio on the roof of the Auberge du Vieux-Port Hotel. Open from the end of May through mid-October (2–11 weekdays, 1–11 on weekends), it's a great place to watch the International Fireworks Festival—if you're early enough to snag a table—and enjoy cocktails and a light tapas menu. ■**TIP**➔ **Try the clear sangria (made with peach Ciroc, Cointreau, white wine, and Sprite).** ⊠ *97 rue de la Commune Est, Old Montréal* ☎ *514/419–1349* ⊕ *www.terrassesurlauberge.com* Ⓜ *Place-d'Armes or Champs-de-Mars.*

LIVE MUSIC

Modavie Wine Bar

WINE BARS | With a French and Mediterranean menu, an attractive sidewalk terrasse, and a sophisticated interior that contrasts dark wood against stone walls, this jazz bar is pleasing to the eyes *and* ears. Despite being spread out over two floors, the space still feels cozy. Live duos play during the first part of the week, while weekends showcase full bands. There's never a cover charge. ⊠ *1 rue St-Paul Ouest, Old Montréal* ☎ *514/287–9582* ⊕ *www.modavie.com* Ⓜ *Champ-de-Mars.*

🎭 Performing Arts

THEATER

Centaur Theatre

THEATER | Montréal's best-known English-language theater company stages everything from frothy musical revues to serious works, and prominently features works by local playwrights. Its home is in the former stock-exchange building in Old Montréal. ⊠ *453 rue St-François-Xavier, Old Montréal* ☎ *514/288–3161* ⊕ *www.centaurtheatre. com* Ⓜ *Place-d'Armes.*

Centre Phi

ARTS CENTERS | Packed with intimate screening rooms, recording facilities, exhibition spaces, and a performance space, this center promotes artist-driven film, design, and music from locals as well as international artists. Films are in English and French. ⊠ *407 rue St-Pierre, Old Montréal* ☎ *514/225–0525, 855/526–8888* ⊕ *phi.ca/fr/centre* Ⓜ *Place-d'Armes or Square-Victoria.*

🛍 Shopping

The historic part of the city still has its fair share of garish souvenir shops, but there remain a few fashion boutiques and shoe shops with low to moderate prices lining rues Notre-Dame and St-Jacques, from rue McGill to Place Jacques-Cartier. However, with gentrification in the west end of the area, this is increasingly the exception rather than the norm as high-end fashion boutiques and spas, especially along rue St-Paul Ouest, oust the holdouts out of business. The area is also rich in art galleries and crafts shops along rue St-Paul and tucked inside the narrow rue des Artistes. Use the Place-d'Armes, Champ-de-Mars, or Square-Victoria métro stations.

ART

Images Boréales

ART GALLERIES | If the friendly and knowledgeable staff don't win you over, the vast collection of Inuit and First Nations art certainly will. Images Boréales represents the best-known Inuit artists while also making a point of working with young, emerging Inuit talent with strong potential. With more than 2,000 pieces of sculpture in soapstone and serpentine, the store will give you the biggest challenge in deciding what to buy. ⊠ *4 rue St-Paul Est, Old Montréal* ☎ *514/439–1987* ⊕ *www.imagesboreales.com* Ⓜ *Champ-de-Mars.*

CLOTHING

Boutique Denis Gagnon

WOMEN'S CLOTHING | This innovative designer, whose creations have been exhibited at the Montréal Museum of Fine Arts, is much loved on the Montréal fashion scene. In this sleek, subterranean boutique, Gagnon's couture designs stand alongside his ready-to-wear collection. He's also well-known for his shoes. More recently he added the "bazaar," a collection of vintage tableware, furniture, and curios. ⊠ *170 rue St-Paul Ouest, Old Montréal* ☎ *514/935–6360* ⊕ *www.denisgagnon.ca* Ⓜ *Place-d'Armes.*

Boutique Sarah Pacini | Sarah Pacini MAN | Philippe Dubuc

MEN'S CLOTHING | One of the city's favorite menswear designers, Philippe Dubuc has merged his collections with international women's fashion brand, Sarah Pacini. Dubuc's collections are characterized by exquisitely tailored classic cuts in richly textured fabrics in blues, grays, blacks, and beiges, perfectly complementing Sarah Pacini's timeless yet contemporary styles. ⊠ *90 Rue Saint-Paul O, Montréal* ☎ *514/844–7424* ⊕ *ca.sarahpaciniman. com* Ⓜ *Place d'Armes.*

Top Montréal Shopping Experiences 🛍

Some of the best deals can be found at **La Maison Simons** department store, where there's something cheap and chic for everyone, from teeny-boppers to mesdames and messieurs, on a budget. Montréal's luxury lane runs from **Holt Renfrew Ogilvy**, the Saks 5th Avenue of Montréal, on rue Ste-Catherine, and north up rues de la Montagne and Crescent to rue Sherbrooke, with local designer fashions such as **Marie Saint Pierre** and **Arthur** lining the route.

The path of luxury continues west along rue Sherbrooke, where you'll find the Montréal Museum of Fine Arts, as well as high-end galleries and antiquarians such as **Le Petit Musée** and **Galerie Alan Klinkhoff.**

Funky fashionistas will want to hit Mile End and the Plateau. In Mile End, hipster territory includes **General 54** and **Unicorn**, with **Citizen Vintage** for recycled fashions. Moving down Montréal's beloved Main—boulevard St-Laurent—check out vintage, decor, fashion, and design shops.

Closer to Downtown, **Boutique 1861** and **M0851** are worth the walk. One-of-a-kind independent shops line avenue Mont-Royal and rue St-Denis.

Delano Design

WOMEN'S CLOTHING | Fashion, art, and design unite under one architecturally stunning roof. Sartorial offerings from Canadian and European designers hang alongside works from the contemporary painter Yunus Chkirate. ⊠ 70 rue St-Paul Ouest, Old Montréal ☎ 514/286–5005 ⊕ www.delanodesign. com Ⓜ Place-d'Armes.

★ **Maison Pepin**

HOUSEWARES | Talented owner and painter Lysanne Pepin has an eye for design. Her boutiques, located a few addresses apart on the same block, are beautiful and intriguing spaces to explore. They are filled with romantic clothes, funky shoes, and a carefully edited mix of local and international labels, as well as eclectic housewares and furniture for home and office. ⊠ 350 and 378 rue St-Paul Ouest, Old Montréal ☎ 514/844–0114 ⊕ the-pepinshop.com Ⓜ Square-Victoria.

Signatures Québécoises

WOMEN'S CLOTHING | Housing a streamlined selection of Québécois fashion designers, the loftlike space inside Marché Bonsecours sells luxe lines that include Ricardo, Christian Chenail, and the fanciful creations of Ophelie Hats. But it's the owner's own exotic kimonos that steal the show. ⊠ Marché Bonsecours, 350 rue St-Paul Est, Old Montréal ☎ 514/398–0761 ⊕ signaturesquebecoises.com Ⓜ Champ-de-Mars.

U&I

MIXED CLOTHING | Stylish locals flock to this sleek boutique in Old Montréal, which is stocked with unisex avant-garde finds from North America and Europe, with an emphasis on Montréal and Canadian brands. Cydwoq and Canada Goose hang alongside coats from the sleek Montréal label Mackage and pieces from U&I's own label. ⊠ 235 rue St. Paul Ouest, Old Montréal ☎ 514/508–7704 ⊕ www.boutiqueuandi.com Ⓜ Place-d'Armes.

SHOES

John Fluevog

SHOES | Unusually curved lines, from the heels of his shoes to the interior design of his funky boutique, have cultivated a devout following for the Canadian shoe designer. Belts and bags are also available, letting you create a quirky yet

Biking in Montréal

Weather permitting, one of the best ways to discover Montréal is on a bicycle. This is an incredibly bike-friendly metropolis, and there are thousands of designated bike paths connecting diverse neighborhoods across the island, running along the river, and through parks and forests. If you like to bike but would rather not do it on city streets, ferries at the Old Port can take you to Île Ste-Hélène and the south shore of the St. Lawrence River, where riders can connect to hundreds of miles of trails in the Montérégie region.

Go Bike Montréal Festival. The biggest bike celebration in North America, Féria de Vélo de Montréal, includes the Tour la Nuit, a 22-kilometer (14-mile) nighttime ride through the city. The weeklong festival culminates in as many as 50,000 cyclists taking over the streets for the Tour de l'Île, a 50-km (31-mile) ride along a route encircling Montréal. ✉ *Montréal* ☎ *514/521–8356, 800/567–8356* ⊕ *www.*

velo.qc.ca/en/event-category/ go-bike-Montréal-festival.

Fitz & Follwell Co. This company's bike tour of Montréal highlights is popular, but go deeper and try "Hoods & Hidden Gems" to really learn what makes the city tick. They also offer bike rentals, walking tours, and snow tours in winter. ✉ *1251, rue Rachel Est, The Plateau* ☎ *514/521–8356 ext. 311* ⊕ *fitz. tours* Ⓜ *Bus 11, 97 or 30 from Mont-Royal station.*

Lachine Canal. The most popular cycling trail on the island begins at the Old Port and winds its way to the shores of Lac St-Louis in Lachine. Pack a picnic lunch; there are plenty of green spaces where you can stop and refuel along the way. ✉ *Montréal.*

Le Pôle des Rapides. This 100-km (62-mile) network of bicycle trails follows lakefronts, canals, and aqueducts. The trails are open April 15 to October 15. ✉ *Montréal* Ⓜ *Verdun, Angrignon, LaSalle, Charlevoix, Lionel-Groulx.*

coordinated outfit. Look to the soles for curious and inspiring messages. ✉ *180 rue St-Paul O., Old Montréal* ☎ *514/379–1970* ⊕ *www.fluevog.com* Ⓜ *Place d'Armes.*

 Activities

BOATING

In Montréal, you can climb aboard a boat at a Downtown wharf and be crashing through Class V white water minutes later.

Lachine Rapids Tours

(*Jet Boating Montréal*)
BOATING | FAMILY | Discover the rapids aboard a large jet boat—and bring a change of clothes. There are

daily departures (every two hours) May through October from the Clock Tower Pier in the Old Port. The price includes all gear, and the trip lasts an hour. Another option is a 20-minute ride in a 12-passenger boat that reaches speeds up to 80 kph (50 mph). Boats leave the Old Port's Jacques-Cartier Pier every half hour between 10 am and 6 pm from May to October. Trips are narrated in French and English. ✉ *47 rue de la Commune Ouest, Old Montréal* ☎ *514/284–9607* ⊕ *jetboatingMontréal.com* 💺 *Jet boat C$71; 20-minute speed boat ride C$23; 45-minute panoramic trip (much calmer) C$46* Ⓜ *Champ-de-Mars.*

3

Montréal OLD MONTRÉAL (VIEUX-MONTRÉAL)

SPAS

Le Scandinave Les Bains Vieux-Montréal

SPAS | A bastion of urban chic in historic Old Montréal, this spa is especially popular on cold winter days. Inspired by the age-old tradition of public baths, the Scandinave prides itself on offering guests an authentic, yet contemporary experience with an accent of privacy and total relaxation. The posh interior of slate, marble, and wood contrasts nicely with the bubbling pool and misty steam rooms. The ultimate meltdown is the zero-stress chamber of absolute quiet and darkness to intensify the peacefulness. All you need to bring along is your bathing suit; the spa provides sandals, bathrobes, and towels. For extra relaxation, sign up for a massage with one of their professional masseuses. ⊠ *71 rue de la Commune Ouest, Old Montréal* ☎ *844/220–2009, 844/220–2009 Reservations* ⊕ *www.scandinave.com* Ⓜ *Place-d'Armes.*

Downtown

The heart of Downtown (or *centre-ville* in French)—with its department stores, boutiques, bars, restaurants, theaters, art galleries, bookstores, and even a few churches—runs from avenue Atwater to boulevard St-Denis. Ste-Catherine is also the main drag of the Quartier des Spectacles, which runs west to east from rue Bleury to rue St-Hubert. Inside this arts and entertainment district are the Place des Arts and several other cultural venues; it also serves as the Downtown home to most of Montréal's many summer festivals.

Walk farther north on rue Crescent to rue Sherbrooke and the lower slopes of Mont-Royal and you come to what was once the most exclusive neighborhood in Canada—the **Golden Square Mile.** During the boom years of the mid-1800s, baronial homes covered the mountain north of rue Sherbrooke. Many are gone, replaced by high-rises or modern town houses, but there are still plenty of architectural treasures to admire, most of them now foreign consulates or university institutes.

And underneath it all—the entire Downtown area and then some—is Montréal's **Underground City,** a vast network of more or less anything you'd find on the street above.

GETTING HERE AND AROUND

Getting to and around Downtown is easy, thanks to the métro. There are several stations along boulevard de Maisonneuve, which is a block away from and runs parallel to rue Ste-Catherine. Many of them link directly to the Underground City.

◉ Sights

Arsenal Art Contemporain

ART GALLERY | Housed in a repurposed shipyard boasting 80,000 square feet of exhibition space, Arsenal Art Contemporain dedicates itself to the support, promotion, and development of contemporary art and has been credited with helping revitalize the old industrial area of Griffintown. The largest private art center in Canada, it was originally founded in Montréal in 2011 but also has locations in Toronto and New York City. ⊠ *2020 rue William, Downtown* ☎ *514/931–9978* ⊕ *www.arsenalcontemporary.com* ⊠ *C$15* ⊗ *Closed Mon.* Ⓜ *Georges-Vanier or Lionel-Groulx.*

Cathédrale Marie-Reine-du-Monde

(*Mary Queen of the World Cathedral*)

CHURCH | The best reason to visit this cathedral is that it's a quarter-scale replica of St. Peter's Basilica in Rome—complete with a magnificent reproduction of Bernini's ornate baldachin (canopy) over the main altar and an ornately coffered ceiling. When Bishop Ignace Bourget (1799–1885) decided to build his cathedral in the heart of the city's Protestant-dominated commercial quarter, many fellow Catholics thought he was

Did You Know?

The baroque-style Cathédrale Marie-Reine-du-Monde, or Mary, Queen of the World Cathedral in English, is the third-largest church in Quebec.

crazy. But the bishop was determined to assert the Church's authority—and its loyalty to Rome—in the British-ruled city. Bourget didn't live to see the cathedral dedicated in 1894, but his tomb holds a place of honor among those of his successors in the burial chapel on the east side of the nave. ⊠ *1085 rue de la Cathédrale, Downtown* ✛ *Enter through main doors on boul. René-Lévesque.* ☎ *514/866–1661* ⊕ *microsites.dioceseMontréal.org/microsites/cathedralecatholiquedeMontréal (French only)* ⊠ *Free* Ⓜ *Bonaventure.*

Centre Bell

SPORTS VENUE | **FAMILY** | The Montréal Canadiens haven't won the Stanley Cup since 1993, though they came very close in June 2021, ultimately losing the finals against Tampa Bay. Most of the team's fans can't remember the golden 1960s and '70s, when *Les Glorieux* virtually owned the trophy. The superstitious blame the team's fallen fortunes on its 1996 move from the hallowed Forum to the brown-brick Centre Bell arena. Still, Montréal is a hockey-mad city and the Habs, as locals call the team, are still demigods here, and there are even university courses based on this superstar team. (When they celebrated their 100th season in 2009–10, the city changed the name of the strip of rue de la Gauchetière in front of the Centre Bell to Avenue des Canadiens-de-Montréal.) The Bell Centre is also a venue for blockbuster acts like Coldplay, Drake, and Trevor Noah. ⊠ *1260 av. des Canadiens-de-Montréal, Downtown* ☎ *877/668–8269, 855/310–2525 for hockey tickets* ⊕ *www.centrebell.ca* ⊠ *Tours: C$20* Ⓜ *Bonaventure or Lucien-l'Allier.*

★ Christ Church Cathedral

CHURCH | The seat of the Anglican (Episcopalian) bishop of Montréal offers downtown shoppers and strollers a respite from the hustle and bustle of rue Ste-Catherine, with free noontime concerts and organ recitals. Built in 1859, the cathedral is modeled on Snettisham Parish Church in Norfolk, England, with some distinctly Canadian touches. The steeple, for example, is made with aluminum plates molded to simulate stone, and inside, the Gothic arches are crowned with carvings of the types of foliage growing on Mont-Royal when the church was built. The stained-glass windows behind the main altar, installed in the early 1920s as a memorial to the dead of World War I, show scenes from the life of Christ. On the wall just above and to the left of the pulpit is the Coventry Cross; it's made of nails taken from the ruins of Britain's Coventry Cathedral, destroyed by German bombing in 1940. ■ **TIP→ Free Saturday group tours can be arranged by calling the office.** ⊠ *635 rue Ste-Catherine Ouest, Downtown* ☎ *514/843–6577 ext. 241* ⊕ *www.Montréalcathedral.ca* ⊠ *Free* ☞ *Sat. tour not offered during COVID* Ⓜ *McGill.*

Church of St. Andrew and St. Paul

CHURCH | Montréal's largest Presbyterian church—sometimes affectionately called the A&P—is worth a visit, if only to see the glorious stained-glass window of the risen Christ that dominates the sanctuary behind the white-stone communion table. It's a memorial to members of the Royal Highland Regiment of Canada (the Black Watch) who were killed in World War I. ⊠ *3415 rue Redpath (main entrance on rue Sherbrooke), Downtown* ☎ *514/842–3431* ⊕ *www.standrewstpaul.com* ⊠ *Free* ☞ *For guided visit, phone in advance to make arrangements* Ⓜ *Guy-Concordia.*

McGill University

COLLEGE | Merchant and fur trader James McGill would probably be horrified to know that the university that he helped found in 1828 has developed an international reputation as one of North America's best party schools. McGill also happens to be one of the two or three best universities in Canada, and certainly one of the prettiest. Its campus is an island

The Musée des Beaux-Arts has one of Canada's largest permanent collections of Canadian art, as well as a gallery where you can buy paintings by local artists.

of grass and trees in a sea of traffic and skyscrapers. The statue of James McGill himself was removed in Summer 2021 after several bouts of vandalism aimed at the representation of the deceased slave owner. Take the time to stroll up the drive that leads from the Greek Revival Roddick Gates to the austere neoclassical Arts Building and meander over to the splendid Romanesque Redpath Hall building. McGill's first dedicated library is now a grand 300-seat concert hall (⊕ *www.mcgill.ca/music/about-us/ halls/redpath-hall*), though the newer library building next door still bears the generous benefactor's name. If you have an hour or so, drop into the temple-like Redpath Museum of Natural History (⊕ *www.mcgill.ca/redpath*) to browse its eclectic collection of dinosaur bones, old coins, African art, and shrunken heads. ✉ *859 rue Sherbrooke Ouest, Downtown* ☎ *514/398–3000 main switchboard, 514/398-4861 museum* ⊕ *www.mcgill.ca* 🎫 *Suggested donation: C$10* Ⓜ *McGill.*

Musée d'art contemporain
(*Museum of Contemporary Art*)
ART MUSEUM | If you have a taste for pastoral landscapes and formal portraits, you might want to stick with the Musée des Beaux-Arts, but for a walk on the wild side of art, head to the Musée d'art contemporain (MAC) and see what you can make of the jagged splashes of color that cover the canvases of the "Automatistes," as Québec's rebellious artists of the 1930s styled themselves. The works of the Automatistes form the core of this museum's collection of 5,000 pieces. The museum often has weekend programs and art workshops, some of which are geared toward children, and almost all are free. And for a little romance and music with your art, try the Vendredi Nocturnes (Nocturnal Fridays) with live music, bar service, and guided tours of the exhibits. Hours for guided tours vary. ✉ *Temporary address: 1 Place Ville Marie, Downtown* ☎ *514/847–6226* ⊕ *www. macm.org* 🎫 *C$15; half price 5–9 pm Wed.* ⊙ *Closed Mon.* Ⓜ *Place-des-Arts.*

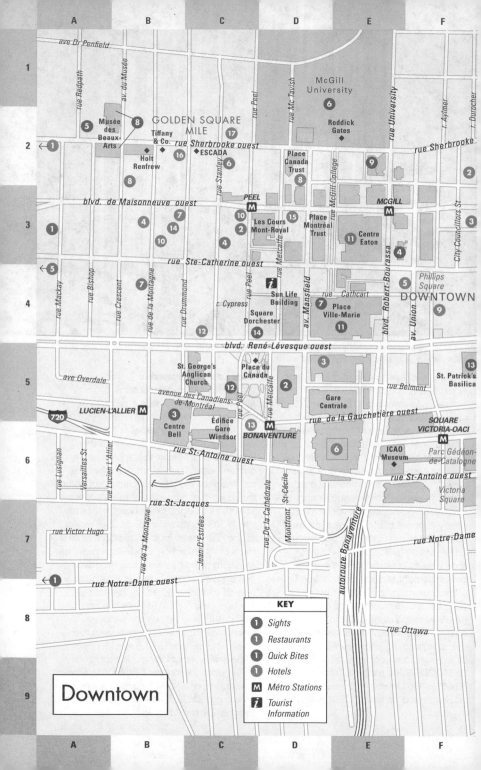

Downtown

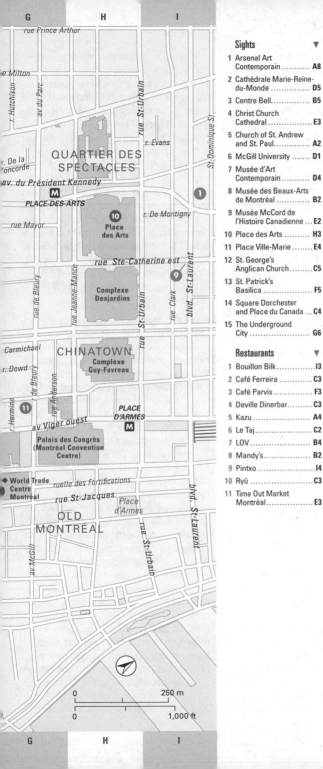

Sights ▼

1 Arsenal Art Contemporain **A8**
2 Cathédrale Marie-Reine-du-Monde **D5**
3 Centre Bell............... **B5**
4 Christ Church Cathedral **E3**
5 Church of St. Andrew and St. Paul............. **A2**
6 McGill University **D1**
7 Musée d'Art Contemporain **D4**
8 Musée des Beaux-Arts de Montréal **B2**
9 Musée McCord de l'Histoire Canadienne ... **E2**
10 Place des Arts **H3**
11 Place Ville-Marie **E4**
12 St. George's Anglican Church......... **C5**
13 St. Patrick's Basilica **F5**
14 Square Dorchester and Place du Canada ... **C4**
15 The Underground City **G6**

Restaurants ▼

1 Bouillon Bilk **I3**
2 Café Ferreira **C3**
3 Café Parvis **F3**
4 Deville Dinerbar.......... **C3**
5 Kazu **A4**
6 Le Taj **C2**
7 LOV **B4**
8 Mandy's.................. **B2**
9 Pintxo **I4**
10 Ryū **C3**
11 Time Out Market Montréal................. **E3**

Quick Bites ▼

1 Café Myriade............. **A3**

Hotels ▼

1 Château Versailles...... **A2**
2 Delta Montréal **F2**
3 Fairmont Le Reine Elizabeth **D5**
4 Four Seasons Montréal................. **B3**
5 Hôtel Birks............... **F4**
6 Hotel Bonaventure Montréal.................. **E6**
7 Hôtel Chez Swann...... **B3**
8 Hôtel Le Germain **D2**
9 Hôtel le Square-Phillips et Suites **F4**
10 Hôtel Vogue **B3**
11 Humaniti **G5**
12 Le Centre Sheraton...... **C4**
13 Le Marriott Chateau Champlain..... **C6**
14 Le Mount Stephen Hotel...................... **B3**
15 Le St-Martin Hôtel Particulier **D3**
16 Ritz-Carlton Montréal .. **B2**
17 Sofitel Montréal.......... **C2**

3

Montréal DOWNTOWN

★ **Musée des Beaux-Arts de Montréal**
(*Montréal Museum of Fine Arts*)
ART MUSEUM | Not surprisingly, Canada's oldest museum has one of the finest collections of Canadian art anywhere. The works of such luminaries as Paul Kane, the Group of Seven, Paul-Émile Borduas, and Marc-Aurèle Fortin are displayed here in a space built onto the back of the neoclassical Erskine and American United Church, one of the city's most historic Protestant churches. The nave has been preserved as a meeting place and exhibition hall and also displays the church's 18 Tiffany stained-glass windows, the biggest collection of Tiffany's work outside the United States. The rest of the gallery's permanent collection, which includes works by everyone from Rembrandt to Renoir, is housed in its two other pavilions: the neoclassical Michal and Renata Hornstein Pavilion, across Avenue du Musée from the church, and the glittering, glass-fronted Jean-Noël-Desmarais Pavilion, across rue Sherbrooke. All three are linked by tunnels. If you visit the museum in summer, spring or fall, you'll be greeted outside the main entrance by bright, twisted glass sculpture, now part of the MMFA's permanent collection. ■ **TIP→ Admission is free from 5 to 9 pm Wednesday.** *1380 rue Sherbrooke Ouest, Downtown* ☎ *514/285-2000* ⊕ *www.mbam.qc.ca/en* ✉ *C$24; half price on Wed. after 5 pm; Discovery exhibitions and collections free first Sun. of the month* ⊙ *Closed Mon.* Ⓜ *Guy-Concordia.*

Musée McCord de l'Histoire Canadienne
(*McCord Museum of Canadian History*)
HISTORY MUSEUM | David Ross McCord (1844–1930) was a wealthy pack rat with a passion for anything that had to do with Montréal or Canadian history. His collection of paintings, costumes, toys, tools, drawings, and housewares provides a glimpse of what city life was like for all classes in the 19th century. If you're interested in the lifestyles of the elite, however, you'll love the photographs that William Notman (1826–91) took of the rich at play. One series portrays members of the posh Montréal Athletic Association posing in snowshoes on the slopes of Mont-Royal, all decked out in Hudson Bay coats and woolen hats. Each of the hundreds of portraits was shot individually in a studio and then painstakingly mounted on a picture of the snowy mountain to give the impression of a winter outing. There are guided tours (call for schedule), a reading room, a documentation center, a gift shop, a bookstore, and a café. ■ **TIP→ Admission is free from 5 to 9 pm Wednesday.** ✉ *690 rue Sherbrooke Ouest, Downtown* ☎ *514/861-6701* ⊕ *musee-mccord.qc.ca/en/* ✉ *C$19* ⊙ *Closed Mon.* Ⓜ *McGill.*

Place des Arts
PERFORMANCE VENUE | Montréal's primary performing-arts complex has been hosting performances since 1963, and since 2010 the complex has been undergoing a major makeover to stunning effect. The glass-walled Maison symphonique 2,000-seat concert hall is the permanent home of the Montréal Symphony Orchestra; with state-of-the-art acoustics and only 75 feet between the end of the stage and the last row, it's an intimate place for concerts. The Salle Wilfrid Pelletier performance space is used by three resident companies: the Opéra de Montréal, Les Grands Ballets Canadiens, and the popular Jean Duceppe theater company. The venue's four other performance spaces host dance, theater, and festival events. Place des Arts is also the centerpiece of the city's Quartier des Spectacles, a square kilometer dedicated to arts and culture, with performance halls, dance studios, broadcasting facilities, and recording studios. The huge plaza, or esplanade, in front of the complex is a favorite gathering place for locals and visitors—especially during the Jazz Festival and Just for Laughs, when it's packed with free concerts and entertainment.

■TIP→ **Even if you don't have tickets to something, you can walk around the quartier during festival season (pretty much all summer) to take in a variety of shows and concerts for free.** ☒ *175 rue Ste-Catherine Ouest, Downtown* ☎ *514/842–2112 tickets, 514/285–4200 administration, 866/842–2112 tickets* ⊕ *www.placedesarts.com* Ⓜ *Place-des-Arts.*

Placé Ville-Marie

STORE/MALL | The cross-shaped 1962 office tower of Place Ville-Marie was Montréal's first modern skyscraper; the mall complex underneath it was the first link in the Underground City. The wide expanse of the building's plaza, just upstairs from the mall, makes a good place to relax with coffee or a snack. Benches, picnic tables, potted greenery, and fine views of Mont-Royal make it popular with walkers, tourists, and office workers. While there you'll surely want to try out the new (2019) glass-encased gastro food pavilion, Le Cathcart Restaurants et Biergarten (⊕ *lecathcart.com/en*). For more great views of the city, the building's 44th floor is home to a rooftop gourmet brasserie, Les Enfants Terribles, which boasts a year-round terrace. ☒ *Bordered by boul. René-Lévesque and rues Mansfield, Cathcart, and University, Downtown* ☎ *514/861–9393* ⊕ *www. observatoire360.com/en* Ⓜ *McGill or Bonaventure.*

Square Dorchester and Place du Canada

PLAZA/SQUARE | On sunny summer days you can join the office workers, store clerks, and Downtown shoppers who gather in these two green squares in the center of the city to eat lunch under the trees and perhaps listen to an open-air concert. If there are no vacant benches or picnic tables, you can still find a place to sit on the steps at the base of the dramatic monument to the dead of the Boer War. Other statues honor Scottish poet Robert Burns (1759–96) and Sir Wilfrid Laurier (1841–1919), Canada's first French-speaking

prime minister. Meanwhile, the statue of Sir John A. MacDonald, Canada's first prime minister, has been removed for he was one of the architects of Canada's inhumane residential school system for Indigenous children. ☒ *Bordered by boul. René-Lévesque and rues Peel, Metcalfe, and McTavish, Downtown* Ⓜ *Bonaventure or Peel.*

St. George's Anglican Church

CHURCH | This is possibly the prettiest Anglican (Episcopalian) church in Montréal. Step into its dim, candle-scented interior and you'll feel you've been transported to some prosperous market town in East Anglia, England. The double hammer-beam roof, the rich stained-glass windows, and the Lady Chapel on the east side of the main altar all add to the effect. It certainly seems a world away from Centre Bell, the modern temple to professional hockey that's across the street. ☒ *1001 av. des Canadiens-de-Montréal, Downtown* ☎ *514/866–7113* ⊕ *www.st-georges.org* ▢ *Free* Ⓜ *Bonaventure.*

St. Patrick's Basilica

CHURCH | Built in 1847, this is one of the purest examples of the Gothic Revival style in Canada, with a high-vaulted ceiling glowing with green and gold mosaics. The tall, slender columns are actually pine logs lashed together and decorated to look like marble, so that if you stand in one of the back corners and look toward the altar you really do feel as if you're peering at the sacred through a grove of trees. St. Pat's—as most of its parishioners call it—is to Montréal's Anglophone Catholics what the Basilique Notre-Dame is to their French-speaking brethren—the mother church and a monument to faith and courage. One of the joys of visiting the place is that you'll probably be the only tourist there, so you'll have plenty of time to check out the old pulpit and the huge lamp decorated with six 2-meter- (6-foot-) tall angels hanging over the main altar. And if you're named after some

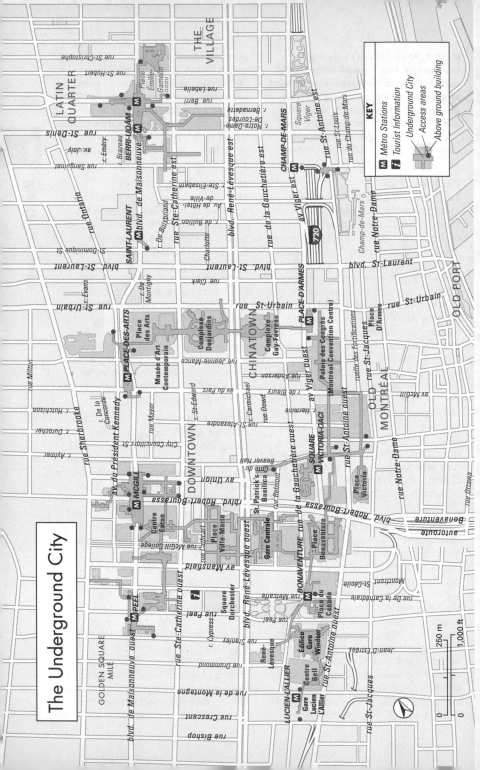

relatively obscure saint like Scholastica or Aeden of Fleury, you can search for your namesake's portrait among the 170 painted panels on the walls of the nave. ■ TIP→ **For a solemn experience visit on the third Sunday of the month (September through June), when the mass is sung completely in Latin.** ⊠ *454 boul. René-Lévesque Ouest, Downtown* ☎ *514/866–7379* ⊠ *Free* Ⓜ *Square-Victoria.*

The Underground City (*La ville souterraine*) STORE/MALL | Place Ville-Marie, the cruciform skyscraper designed by I. M. Pei, was the tallest structure in the city when it opened in 1962. Located in the heart of Downtown, it signaled the beginning of Montréal's subterranean city. Montréalers were skeptical that anyone would want to shop or even walk around in the new "down" town, but more than five decades later they can't live without it, especially in winter.

About half a million people use the 32-km (20-mile) Underground City, or *la ville souterraine*, daily. The tunnels link 10 métro stations, 7 hotels, 200 restaurants, 1,700 boutiques, and 60 office buildings—not to mention movie theaters, concert halls, convention complexes, the Centre Bell, two universities, and a college. In 2004, the Underground City was rebranded as the "RESO," a play on the word "réseau," which means network. You'll see the signs for it in the Downtown area and can find a map of the network at Montréalvisitorsguide.com/the-underground-city-map. ⊠ *Downtown.*

🍴 Restaurants

From top-quality steak to gourmet burgers, there is lots of meat to be found Downtown. That said, plant-forward restaurants are increasingly stepping on to the scene and making a big splash with meat eaters and veggies alike. You'll find everything Downtown from Indian curries, simple Chinese dumplings, whole-animal cooking, dry-aged beef, designer veggie burgers, mouth-watering shawarma and falafel, and Mediterranean and Middle Eastern dishes that stretch the definition. The dress code can be as formal as at the Ritz or completely toned down and hip—it all depends on where you go.

Bouillon Bilk
$$$$ | MODERN FRENCH | The decor at this restaurant reflects its philosophy: fresh, thoughtful, and simplified (yet not simple). The market-based menu changes often and includes dishes that are just as beautiful to look at as they are delicious. **Known for:** sleek, modern decor; private-import wines; market cuisine. Ⓢ *Average main: C$38* ⊠ *1595 boul. St-Laurent, Downtown* ☎ *514/845–1595* ⊕ *www.bouillonbilk.com* ☉ *No lunch on weekends* Ⓜ *St-Laurent.*

Café Ferreira
$$$$ | PORTUGUESE | The open-concept kitchen is renowned for its for "haute" Portuguese cuisine, including roasted salted cod, seafood bouillabaisse, and a whole array of appetizers like giant shrimp and grilled octopus or the roasted sardine fillets. Wine connoisseurs are attracted to the impressive list of Portuguese wines. **Known for:** ceviche; seafood bouillabaisse; intimate Portuguese experience. Ⓢ *Average main: C$40* ⊠ *1446 rue Peel, Downtown* ☎ *514/848–0988* ⊕ *www.ferreiracafe.com* ☉ *No lunch weekends* Ⓜ *Peel.*

Café Parvis
$$ | ECLECTIC | What was once a fur showroom in the 1970s now hosts Café Parvis, a stylish yet eclectic eatery with floor-to-ceiling windows, half-stripped mint-green paint, and luxuriant plants hanging from the ceiling. If morning visits are for artisan coffee and pâtisserie du jour, dinner is for ordering shareable wood-oven baked pizzas enhanced by

fresh salads and the on-point selection of organic wines. **Known for:** organic wines; quality coffee; wood-oven baked pizzas. $ *Average main: C$18* ✉ *403 rue Mayor, Downtown* ☎ *514/764–3589* ⊕ *cafeparvis.com* ⊘ *Closed Mon. No dinner Sun.* Ⓜ *Place-des-Arts.*

Deville Dinerbar

$$$$ | DINER | FAMILY | Located in Montréal's Downtown core, Deville Dinerbar is a whimsical alternative to the otherwise rather serious dining options in the area. A palette of neon pink, white, and black keeps the dining room sleek, sexy, and exciting (but not diner-kitschy). **Known for:** diner-like decor; Deville Food Cake; substantial burgers. $ *Average main: C$37* ✉ *1425 rue Stanley, Downtown* ☎ *514/281–6556* ⊕ *www.devilledinerbar.com* ⊘ *Closed Sun.-Mon. No lunch Sat.-Wed.* Ⓜ *Peel.*

Kazu

$$ | JAPANESE | You could almost walk right by this tiny establishment on this seedier stretch of Ste-Catherine St., but the line of people waiting to get in is a telltale sign. Popular plates include the tuna rice bowl or the messy barbecue pork neck—you'll be licking sauce off your hands, but you won't be sorry. **Known for:** Japanese comfort food; long lines; housemade tofu. $ *Average main: C$18* ✉ *1862 rue Ste-Catherine Ouest, Downtown* ☎ *514/937–2333* ⊕ *www.kazuMontréal.com* ⊘ *Closed Tues. and Wed. No lunch* Ⓜ *Guy-Concordia.*

LOV

$$ | VEGETARIAN | With its airy, all-white and green, plant-filled decor, dining at LOV (Local, Organic, Vegan) is like sitting in a beautiful greenhouse. This fashionable restaurant is the kind of plant-based establishment that even die-hard carnivores will line up to enter. **Known for:** upscale vegan cuisine; LOV poutine; biodynamic and natural wines. $ *Average main: C$17* ✉ *1232 rue de la Montagne, Downtown* ☎ *514/287–1155* ⊕ *www.lov.com* ⊘ *No lunch Mon.-Thurs.* Ⓜ *Peel.*

★ Le Taj

$$$ | INDIAN | Refined Le Taj carries a piece of Montréal's history with its ornate mud wall originally made for India's pavilion at World Expo '67. With northern Indian cuisine in mind, which isn't as spicy as its southern counterpart, *thalis*—platters comprising a variety of curries—are ideal for sampling unfamiliar flavors. **Known for:** samosas and pakoras made with herb-flavored batter; vegetarian-friendly; multiflavored platters. $ *Average main: C$22* ✉ *2077 rue Stanley, Downtown* ☎ *514/845–9015* ⊕ *www.restaurantletaj.com* ⊘ *Closed Sun. No lunch* Ⓜ *Peel.*

Mandy's

$$ | CONTEMPORARY | If you're in the mood for a big, nourishing, market-fresh salad served in a colorful ceramic bowl in a pastel setting, Mandy's is the place to go. Choose from among 15 different varieties of salads, such as the Habibi salad with quinoa, parsley, mint, chickpeas, roasted sweet potato, cherry tomatoes, red onion, and feta, mixed with tahini dressing; the Clean Green with basil, cilantro, mint, broccoli, cucumber, edamame, purple cabbage, green onions, and pumpkin seeds, garnished with tamari dressing; or the Crunchy Sesame with romaine lettuce, mixed greens, avocado, mandarin oranges, cherry tomatoes, shredded carrots, crunchy noodles, and toasted sesame seeds with the Asian sesame vinaigrette. **Known for:** always fresh ingredients; nourishing salads; attractive setting in soothing colors. $ *Average main: C$14* ✉ *2067 rue Crescent, Downtown* ☎ *514/419–0779* ⊕ *www.mandys.ca* Ⓜ *Guy.*

Ryū

$$ | JAPANESE | The salmon and avocado tartare is a must at this surprisingly affordable Japanese tapas restaurant and lounge. Vegans and vegetarians will appreciate plates like the shiitake lettuce cups, avocado tacos, and black truffle mushroom dumplings. Carefully selected wines and classic cocktails combine with

sleek lighting (the dragon changes color throughout the night) for a memorable dining experience. **Known for:** omakase; high-end sushi; traditional and contemporary dishes. ⓢ *Average main: C$18* ✉ *1468 rue Peel, Downtown* ☎ *514/446–1468* ⊕ *www.ryupeel.com* ◔ *No lunch* Ⓜ *Peel.*

Time Out Market Montréal

$$ | **CONTEMPORARY** | Time Out Market, the popular "anti-food courts" gastro halls opening in cities around the globe, unveiled its Montréal location in late 2019. The industrial-chic, dimly lit 40,000 square-foot space features a black ceiling, gray and concrete surfaces, and warm, oil-finished maplewood floors. **Known for:** great mocktails; arts and events space; curated selection of some of Montréal's best eateries all under one roof. ⓢ *Average main: C$18* ✉ *Centre Eaton, 705 rue Ste-Catherine O., Downtown* ☎ *514/370–3883* ⊕ *timeoutmarket. com/Montréal/en* Ⓜ *McGill.*

🄲 Coffee and Quick Bites

Café Myriade

$ | **CAFÉ** | Aficionados are willing to wait for a seat at this small café, where the foam on your latte or café au lait is artfully arranged in waves, hearts, or curlicues. The delicious coffee is imported from Ethiopia, Guatemala, Brazil, Bolivia, and elsewhere via the famed 49th Parallel Coffee Roasters in Vancouver. **Known for:** photogenic location; high-quality coffee; latte art. ⓢ *Average main: C$7* ✉ *1432 rue Mackay, Downtown* ☎ *514/939–1717* ⊕ *www.cafemyriade. com* Ⓜ *Guy-Concordia.*

🛏 Hotels

The hub for countless festivals, Downtown Montréal is a convenient place to unpack your bags. This is where you'll find the major chain hotels, with underground parking, pools, and all the amenities that families enjoy. A few new boutique hotels have appeared in recent years, providing more options for couples without kids. From Downtown, it's just a short trip—via bike path, métro, or taxi—to the city's other neighborhoods of interest, so this is a good central point from which to see the city. Traffic often crawls in the city, and since the outdoor festival "quartier," Le Quartier des Spectacles, was revamped even more people are attracted to Downtown's hotels. So leave your car at the hotel and go by foot or métro whenever possible.

Château Versailles

$$ | **HOTEL** | History lovers and lovers of the romantic variety, too, appreciate the luxury within the Versailles' two elegant beaux arts mansions, with high ceilings, plaster moldings, antique furnishings, and a twinkling chandelier in the entryway. **Pros:** easy access to museum district and to nearby Westmount; elaborate decor and breakfast; spacious rooms with fireplaces. **Cons:** no elevator; staid decor and furnishings could use a refresh; at busy intersection. ⓢ *Rooms from: C$220* ✉ *1659 rue Sherbrooke Ouest, Downtown* ☎ *514/933–3611, 888/933–8111* ⊕ *chateauversaillesMontréal.com* ⮥ *65 rooms* ⓘⓞⓘ *Free Breakfast* Ⓜ *Guy-Concordia.*

Delta Montréal

$$ | **HOTEL** | **FAMILY** | Business travelers and jazz festival performers cycle through the Delta's airportlike lobby every year, taking advantage of the hotel's minimalist and quiet rooms, saltwater pool, squash courts, high-tech gym, and family-friendly restaurant. **Pros:** kid- and pet-friendly amenities; two squash courts and saltwater pool; excellent soundproofing. **Cons:** restaurant not great; fee for a safe in room; drab lobby needs a makeover. ⓢ *Rooms from: C$250* ✉ *475 av. du Président-Kennedy, Downtown* ☎ *514/286–1986, 844/860–3753* ⊕ *marriott.com/hotels/travel/yuldb-delta-hotels-Montréal* ⮥ *456 rooms* ⓘⓞⓘ *No Meals* Ⓜ *McGill or Place-des-Arts.*

★ Fairmont Le Reine Elizabeth
$$$ | **HOTEL** | Reopened in summer 2017 after a $140 million renovation, Le Reine Elizabeth's retro-chic makeover boasts contemporary mid-century-modern interiors; a huge market and food hall; a gorgeous pool redo and new spa; and creative meeting hubs, all the while preserving the property's iconic heritage (John and Yoko's 1969 "bed-in" suite [1742] has been carefully restored and enhanced with artifacts from the day). **Pros:** stylish, luxurious rooms; craft cocktails at Nacarat Bar and outdoor terrace; excellent dining options. **Cons:** some bathrooms are small; conventioneers abound; daily fee for Wi-Fi unless you are a member. [$] *Rooms from: C$359* ✉ *900 boul. René-Lévesque Ouest, Downtown* ☎ *514/861–3511, 866/540–4483 reservations* 🌐 *www.fairmont.com/queen-elizabeth-Montréal* 🛏 *952 rooms* 🍴 *No Meals* [M] *Bonaventure.*

★ Four Seasons Montréal
$$$$ | **HOTEL** | The city's most highly anticipated hotel opening of the 2010s, the Four Seasons Montréal opened its doors in 2019 and offers all you would expect from the iconic brand: world-class design, luxurious rooms, chic social areas, and impeccable service. **Pros:** spa offers Kneipp water therapy with hot and cold foot baths; celebrity chef restaurant and bar, MARCUS; elegant, contemporary bar and lounge. **Cons:** no outdoor spaces; exorbitant nightly rates; only an indoor pool. [$] *Rooms from: C$825* ✉ *1440 rue de la Montagne, Downtown* ☎ *514/843–2500* 🌐 *www.fourseasons.com/Montréal* 🛏 *169 rooms* 🍴 *No Meals* [M] *Guy-Concordia or Peel.*

★ Hôtel Birks
$$$$ | **HOTEL** | Opened in fall 2018, the glamorous Hôtel Birks was once the Canadian headquarters of the Birks jewelry empire, Canada's equivalent of Tiffany's, and it wisely preserved the jewelry store's original stained glass, pendant lamps, and ornate crown moldings. **Pros:** many rooms have gas fireplaces; richly appointed lobby in historic building; stunning, atmospheric brasserie popular with locals. **Cons:** no pool; parking can be a challenge; not all rooms have bathtubs. [$] *Rooms from: C$420* ✉ *1240 rue du Square Phillips, Downtown* ☎ *514/370–3000* 🌐 *www.hotelbirksMontréal.com* 🛏 *132 rooms* 🍴 *No Meals* [M] *McGill.*

Hotel Bonaventure Montréal
$$ | **HOTEL** | **FAMILY** | From the Brutalist concrete facade to its modern and comfortable new lobby (latest renovation in 2019), the Bonaventure delivers style and value, along with a heated outdoor pool, 2½ acres of rooftop gardens, a pond and waterfalls inhabited by dozens of mallard ducks, and updated bedrooms (most renovated in 2021) with white bedding, gray walls, dark-wood, granite countertops, and modern bathrooms. **Pros:** year-round heated pool; almost every room has a view of the rooftop garden; easy access to the métro and the Underground City. **Cons:** modernist exterior not for everyone; elevator ride to reception is not very welcoming; high volume of business and convention traffic. [$] *Rooms from: C$259* ✉ *900 rue de la Gauchetière O., Downtown* ☎ *514/878–2332, 800/267–2575* 🌐 *www.hotelbonaventure.com* 🛏 *397 rooms* 🍴 *No Meals* [M] *Bonaventure.*

Hôtel Chez Swann
$$ | **HOTEL** | Drawn to its Baz Luhrmann–style flamboyance, young culture vultures love that Chez Swann fully commits to the idiosyncratic design, with swirly black ceilings in the hallways, original art, custom furniture, textured rugs, sink-in sofas, a spin room, and free calls within North America. **Pros:** Downtown location; quirky design; in-room spa treatments. **Cons:** not suitable for kids; no pets; no bathtubs. [$] *Rooms from: C$245* ✉ *1444 rue Drummond, Downtown* ☎ *514/842–7070, 877/568–7070* 🌐 *www.hotelchezswann.com* 🛏 *23 rooms* 🍴 *Free Breakfast* [M] *Peel.*

Hôtel Le Germain

$$$ | **HOTEL** | Le Germain Montréal was popular with creative types and international hipsters who appreciate contemporary design and stylish details even before the 2019 top to bottom overhaul. **Pros:** fabulous views, especially from the new glass-walled rooms; late check out; unlimited filtered water on each floor. **Cons:** glassed-in showers, sometimes visible from the room, not for everyone; parking is scarce, and the valet isn't cheap; breakfast no longer included in the rate. [$] *Rooms from: C$362* ✉ *2050 rue Mansfield, Downtown* ☎ *514/849–2050, 877/333–2050* 🌐 *germainhotels.com* 🛏 *136 rooms* 🍴 *No Meals* [M] *Peel or McGill.*

Hôtel le Square-Phillips et Suites

$$ | **HOTEL** | **FAMILY** | Often accommodating movie crews and performers who make themselves at home in the sun-filled laundry room and glassed-in rooftop pool, this apartment-style hotel is full of basic rooms and suites—all with fully equipped kitchens and living rooms with flat-screen televisions. **Pros:** good shopping nearby; full in-room kitchens; excellent rooftop pool, gym, and sunbathing. **Cons:** drab decor; not much nightlife nearby; uninspired lobby. [$] *Rooms from: C$259* ✉ *1193 Pl. Phillips, Downtown* ☎ *514/393–1193, 866/393–1193* 🌐 *www.squarephillips.com* 🛏 *164 rooms* 🍴 *Free Breakfast* [M] *McGill.*

Hôtel Vogue

$$$$ | **HOTEL** | Committed shoppers like the location—just a five-minute walk from Holt Renfrew Ogilvy and other destination fashion boutiques on rue Ste-Catherine and the Golden Mile. **Pros:** Clear Inc. technology to ensure purification of water and air throughout hotel; chic lobby; some mobility accessible rooms and bathrooms. **Cons:** no pool; steep valet parking fee; no spa. [$] *Rooms from: C$525* ✉ *1425 rue de la Montagne, Downtown* ☎ *514/285–5555, 844/442–8746* 🌐 *www.hilton.com/en/hotels/yulm-qqq-vogue-Montréal-downtown* 🛏 *142 rooms* 🍴 *No Meals* [M] *Peel.*

Humaniti

$$$$ | **HOTEL** | At the junction of Downtown, Old Montréal, and Chinatown, Humaniti, which is part of the Marriott Autograph Collection, is a brand new uber-modern design hotel and condo construction that opened in June 2021. **Pros:** rooftop pool and poolside bistro and terrace; gorgeous lobby filled with art works by local artists; bakery in building and grocery store across the courtyard. **Cons:** windows in rooms don't open; pool only open in summer; views not great. [$] *Rooms from: C$439* ✉ *40 rue de la Gauchetière O., Downtown* ☎ *514/657–2595* 🌐 *www.humanitiMontréal.com* 🛏 *193 rooms* 🍴 *No Meals* [M] *Place des Arts or Champ-de-Mars.*

Le Centre Sheraton

$$$ | **HOTEL** | **FAMILY** | After a long day of networking and conventions, the lobby area's atrium cafe bar welcomes thanks to its two-story panel of floor-to-ceiling windows and quiet lounging nook by the fire. **Pros:** close to the Centre Bell; two outdoor terraces; rooms have views of the mountain or St. Lawrence River. **Cons:** Sheraton Club lounge on the 37th floor costs extra; lively scene not for everyone; lobby marred by convention signs. [$] *Rooms from: C$350* ✉ *1201 boul. René-Lévesque Ouest, Downtown* ☎ *514/878–2000, 888/627–7102* 🌐 *www.marriott.com/hotels/travel/yulsi-le-centre-sheraton-Montréal-hotel* 🛏 *825 rooms* 🍴 *No Meals* [M] *Bonaventure or Peel.*

Le Marriott Château Champlain

$$$$ | **HOTEL** | An icon from Expo1967, this 36-floor skyscraper overlooking Place du Canada is always full of business guests, families, and prom parties,

Old meets new at Le Mount Stephen, where sleek contemporary guest rooms are housed in a grand neoclassical building.

due to its expansive views of the city from its distinctive half moon windows and the indoor links to the métro and Underground City. **Pros:** some rooms have Japanese multi-function toilets and shower towers; expansive views; park-side location. **Cons:** no bathrobes or slippers provided; A/C can be very loud; can be noisy with parties. [$] *Rooms from: C$465* ✉ *1050 rue de la Gauchetière Ouest, Downtown* ☎ *514/878–9000, 800/200–5909* 🌐 *www.marriott.com/hotels/travel/yulcc-Montréal-marriott-chateau-champlain* 🛏 *614 rooms* 🍴 *No Meals* [M] *Bonaventure.*

★ Le Mount Stephen Hotel

$$$$ | **HOTEL** | Set in a restored neoclassical landmark once owned by a Canadian railway pioneer (as well as a new 11-story tower behind the original mansion) this modern boutique hotel features contemporary guest rooms with state-of-the-art comforts (chromatherapy showers, Japanese [Toto] toilets, heated floors, and Nespresso machines) as well as ornate interiors that include original features, such as 300-year-old stained-glass windows and intricate woodwork. **Pros:** Insta-worthy Bar George; unique historic property with opulent interior; high-end experience. **Cons:** British-inspired restaurant may be too proper for some; rates match the luxury; not family-friendly. [$] *Rooms from: C$529* ✉ *1440 rue Drummond, Downtown* ☎ *514/313–1000, 844/838–8655* 🌐 *www.lemountstephen.com* 🛏 *90 rooms* 🍴 *No Meals* [M] *Peel.*

Le St-Martin Hôtel Particulier

$$$ | **HOTEL** | **FAMILY** | Sober and chic, this tasteful hotel is in a great location for shopping, museums, and restaurants, and made special with features like a year-round heated pool, hardwood accents, fireplaces, soundproofed windows, and a French fusion restaurant. **Pros:** very good restaurant with stylish decor; windows are soundproof; soaker tub and TV in bathrooms. **Cons:** guests must be over the age of 25; small outdoor pool often in shade; reception is just steps from the sidewalk and gets crowded at checkout. [$] *Rooms from: C$330*

✉ *980 boul. de Maisonneuve Ouest, Downtown* ☎ *514/843–3000, 877/843–3003* 🌐 *www.lestmartinMontréal.com* 🛏 *123 rooms* 🍴 *No Meals* [M] *Peel.*

★ Ritz-Carlton Montréal

$$$$ | HOTEL | The legacy, the elegance, the celebrity chef, the newish pool (2012)—all good reasons to splurge on a room at the "Ritz," the city's grandest hotel and icon in the Golden Square Mile, near museums, McGill University, and all the best boutiques. **Pros:** infinity pool with patio; revived style, but still plenty of history; state-of-the-art bathrooms and soundproof windows; high-end shopping and galleries within a five-minute walk. **Cons:** not all rooms have a picturesque view; Sherbrooke Street can be dull on weeknights; poor métro access. [$] *Rooms from: C$700* ✉ *1228 rue Sherbrooke Ouest, Downtown* ☎ *514/842–4212, 800/363–0366* 🌐 *www.ritzMontréal.com* 🛏 *129 rooms* 🍴 *No Meals* [M] *Peel or Guy-Concordia.*

★ Sofitel Montréal

$$$ | HOTEL | At the foot of Mont-Royal, in the heart of Downtown, this exquisite 17-story hotel uses its understated elegance (if the beautiful lobby carpets, made by the same company that carpeted Versailles for King Louis XIV can be called understated), excellent service and details, and convenient location to attract a well-heeled international crowd. **Pros:** within walking distance of museums, McGill, the Bell Centre, and destination boutiques; bright and tailored rooms; chef Olivier Perret helms the exceptional restaurant Renoir. **Cons:** obstructed views in the east-facing rooms; scarce street parking; no pool. [$] *Rooms from: C$359* ✉ *1155 rue Sherbrooke Ouest, Downtown* ☎ *514/285–9000* 🌐 *www.sofitel.com* 🛏 *258 rooms* 🍴 *No Meals* [M] *Peel.*

Nightlife

From expensive restaurants to lowly bars, Downtown offers something for every taste and budget. Rue Crescent, with its lively mix of restaurants, pubs, and clubs, is where you'll find most of the action, with neighboring rue Bishop and rue Mackay not far behind.

BARS AND LOUNGES

★ Bar Furco

GATHERING PLACES | Making its name through word of mouth alone, Furco has become one of the trendiest Downtown bistro bars, and for good reason. It's all about the industrial-chic interior, the warm amber lighting, and the relaxed, inviting vibe. A nice mix of clientele, great food (the menu changes weekly), and good pours also help make this a popular after-work hangout for locals, and the perfect retreat from the Quartier des Spectacles, a stone's throw away. ✉ *425 rue Mayor, Downtown* ☎ *514/764–3588* 🌐 *www.barfurco.com* ☞ *They take a small proportion of reservations online, otherwise you'll have to stand in the queue outside* [M] *Place-des-Arts or McGill.*

★ Brutopia

BREWPUBS | House-brewed concoctions like Raspberry Blond Beer or Mango Session IPA attract locals and tourists alike, and lately the kitchen has been serving up delicious tapas-style pub food, including some healthy vegetarian and vegan options. In addition to the unique brews, check out the sprawling outdoor seating, the art gallery on the third floor, and nightly live music. A typical crowd at Brutopia is under 30, but older folk shouldn't feel out of place. With live music ranging from traditional Irish folk to the occasional punk or psychedelic '60s garage band, this pub serves as a refreshing alternative to the slightly more upscale, trendy bars and nightclubs that mark the Crescent Street strip. ✉ *1219 rue Crescent,*

*Downtown ☎ 514/393–9277 ⊕ www.
brutopia.net Ⓜ Guy-Concordia.*

Hurley's Irish Pub
PUBS | For years this pub has been serving up a bounty of whiskeys and brews (19 different beers on tap), with a healthy dose of Irish atmosphere on the side. Despite its cavernous size, the arrangement of seating areas, flanked by bars, makes it feel cozy, and there's a stage for live entertainment. It still fills up quickly, so unless you don't mind standing while you sip your Guinness, come early to snag a seat. ✉ *1225 rue Crescent, Downtown ☎ 514/861–4111 ⊕ www.hurleysirishpub.com Ⓜ Guy-Concordia.*

★ Pullman
WINE BARS | At this sophisticated yet relaxed wine bar, let yourself be guided by the expertise of the sommeliers. The tapas-style cuisine is top-notch, and the green beans with truffle oil and roasted almonds are scrumptious. During cooler months things get going at 4:30 pm, but in summer don't arrive until the sun starts to set. ✉ *3424 av. du Parc, Downtown ☎ 514/288–7779 ⊕ www.pullman-mtl.com ☾ Closed Sun.–Tues.* Ⓜ *Place-des-Arts.*

Stogies Lounge
BARS | If the surprisingly trendy interior and views of rue Crescent aren't a big enough draw, then check out the conspicuous glass humidor housing a seemingly infinite supply of imported cigars. Thanks to being grandfathered in, the bar still allows smoking Cubans on site, despite Québec's tough no-smoking law. ✉ *2015 rue Crescent, Downtown ☎ 514/848–0069, 877/848–0069 ⊕ www.stogiescigars.com Ⓜ Guy-Concordia or Peel.*

COMEDY CLUBS
The Montréal Just For Laughs comedy festival, which takes place every July, has been the largest such festival in the world since its inception back in 1983.

But Montréalers don't have to wait until summer to get their comedy fix, as there are several Downtown clubs covering all things funny.

The Comedy Nest
COMEDY CLUBS | For decades, this comedy club has been showering Montréalers with humor from some of the biggest names out there: Jim Carrey, Tim Allen, and Russell Peters included. For a mere C$6, Newbie Tuesdays and Comedy Lab Wednesdays, when novice comedians and local comics work out new material, are always good for a laugh and will also secure you one free ticket for a Thursday or Friday late show. Arrive early to get a decent spot near the stage (or perhaps away from it). ✉ *Pepsi Forum, 2313 rue Ste-Catherine Ouest, 3rd floor, Downtown ☎ 514/932–6378 ⊕ www.comedynest.com Ⓜ Atwater.*

Montréal Improv
COMEDY CLUBS | The heart of the city's improv comedy scene offers shows in both English and French. The Friday night Main Event Smackdowns, where the audience determines the winner, are especially good for a laugh. ■**TIP→** Get **here early, as the C$10 tickets usually sell out quickly.** ✉ *3716 rue Notre-Dame Ouest, Downtown ⊕ www.Montréalimprov.com Ⓜ Place Saint-Henri.*

DANCE CLUBS
Club Electric Avenue
DANCE CLUBS | Generations X and Y will get along just fine here, as classics from the '80s and '90s boom out over a devoted, nostalgic crowd. In the basement of the Newtown lounge, these digs have great sound, excellent service, and sexy interior design. It's open Thursday to Saturday from 10 pm. ✉ *1476 rue Crescent, Downtown ☎ 514/285–8885 ⊕ clubelectricavenue.ca Ⓜ Guy-Concordia or Peel.*

Foufounes Electriques
LIVE MUSIC | "Foufs," as it's affectionately known, has been going strong for almost 40 years—since 1983. Attracting

Classical Music

The performing arts thrive in Montréal, from dance troupes to classical music groups to theater. Place des Arts, Montréal's main concert hall in Downtown Montréal, is a popular venue for large-scale productions, but some groups, such as I Musici, perform at venues throughout town.

■TIP➜ **Note that many performing arts groups take to the road or are on hiatus in summer.**

I Musici de Montréal Chamber Orchestra. Arguably the best chamber orchestra in Canada, I Musici, under the direction of Jean-François Rivest, performs at several places around town, including the Salle Bourgie at the Musée des Beaux-Arts and the Place des Arts' Nouvelle Salle. ⊠ *4672 B rue Saint-Denis, Montréal* ☎ *514/987–6919 tickets* ⊕ *www.imusici.com.*

a cult following of alternative rock and heavy metal fans, it gets packed on weekends. You can enjoy a cheap beer on one of two summer terraces under the playful eyes of skulls and spiders. It's open Thursday to Saturday from 4 pm. ⊠ *87 rue Ste-Catherine Est, Downtown* ☎ *514/844–5539* ⊕ *www.foufouneselectriques.com* Ⓜ *St-Laurent.*

Salsathèque
DANCE CLUBS | Though neon lights and disco balls abound, this flashy club is all about the Latin lover—dance lover, that is. Merengue, bachata, and salsa (of course) are the specialties, but themed evenings keep things interesting with R&B, reggae, and Top 40 hits. Check the website to learn the week's schedule and sign up for the guest list to avoid a cover. Open Friday to Sunday. ⊠ *1220 rue Peel, Downtown* ☎ *514/875–0016* ⊕ *www.salsatheque.ca* Ⓜ *Peel.*

LIVE MUSIC
Club Soda
LIVE MUSIC | The grandaddy of the city's rock clubs has evolved into one of the dominant venues for jazz, reggae, techno, and rhythm and blues. Club Soda is a tall, narrow concert hall with high-tech design and 500 seats—all of them with great sight lines. ⊠ *1225 boul. St-Laurent, Downtown* ☎ *514/286–1010* ⊕ *www.clubsoda.ca* Ⓜ *St-Laurent.*

McKibbin's Irish Pub
LIVE MUSIC | This beautiful old sandstone mansion includes three floors of food, drink, and good Irish *craic* (a Gaelic term that means having fun with affable companions). This isn't hard to do with more than 20 different stouts, lagers, and ales on tap. There's live entertainment nearly every night of the week, so head to the basement if you're looking for a bit of quiet (or a good chin-wag). The house fries are excellent for noshing, but beware of the Rim Reaper—chicken wings made with the world's hottest pepper. ⊠ *1426 rue Bishop, Downtown* ☎ *514/288–1580* ⊕ *www.mckibbinsirishpub.com* Ⓜ *Guy-Concordia.*

★ Upstairs Jazz Bar & Grill
LIVE MUSIC | Five nights a week, the cheerful Joel Giberovitch greets you personally near the entrance to his club, which despite the name is actually downstairs. Giberovitch loves what he does, and the constant stream of local and imported jazz musicians makes this the favored jazz hangout in the city. The eclectic menu makes a nice accompaniment to the live music—try the home-cut fries with smoky mayo. Cover charges start at C$6 and range up to C$45 for big-ticket performers during Jazz Fest. The third set is free (usually around 11 pm), and other sets are also free if you sit on one of the cozy terraces.

■ **TIP➜ Parking costs only C$5. Ask your server for a ticket.** ✉ *1254 rue Mackay, Downtown* ☎ *514/931–6808* ⊕ *www. upstairsjazz.com* Ⓜ *Guy-Concordia.*

⭐ Performing Arts

CLASSICAL MUSIC

Opéra de Montréal

OPERA | This renowned opera company, the largest francophone opera in North America, has a varied schedule of classics, including *Le Nozze di Figaro*, *Rigoletto*, and *Silent Night*. Seventy-five minutes before each show, the "pre-Opera" program, done in French with a summary in English, gives attendees a look at the history, music, and artists of the Opéra de Montréal. ✉ *Place des Arts, 260 boul. de Maisonneuve, Downtown* ☎ *514/985–2258, 877/385–2222.* ⊕ *www. operadeMontréal.com* Ⓜ *Place-des-Arts.*

Orchestre Métropolitain du Grand Montréal

CONCERTS | The Met may lie in the shadow of the Orchestre Symphonique de Montréal, but its talented conductor and artistic director, Yannick Nézet-Séguin, continues to draw the spotlight. He's in high demand across the world; in addition to his role here, he's the musical director at the Philadelphia Orchestra and New York City's Metropolitan Opera, and honorary conductor at the Rotterdam Philharmonic. His charismatic approach has brought in the crowds since 2000 and produced highly acclaimed performances. Most shows take place at Place des Arts or Maison Symphonique de Montréal. ✉ *486 rue Ste-Catherine Ouest, #401, Downtown* ☎ *514/842–2112 tickets* ⊕ *www.orchestremetropolitain. com* Ⓜ *Place-des-Arts.*

★ **Orchestre symphonique de Montréal**

MUSIC | Montréal's beloved OSM plays programs that include masterful renditions of the classics, with contemporary works thrown into the mix. The orchestra's home, the Maison symphonique de Montréal, is part of the Place des Arts complex. ✉ *1600 rue St-Urbain, Downtown* ☎ *514/842– 9951, 888/842–9951* ⊕ *www.osm.ca* Ⓜ *Place-des-Arts.*

Pollack Concert Hall

CONCERTS | McGill University's concert hall showcases the best talents from its formidable music faculty, with concerts by the McGill Symphony, Opera McGill, the McGill Baroque Orchestra, and the Montréal Chamber Orchestra, among others. ✉ *555 rue Sherbrooke Ouest, Downtown* ☎ *514/398–4547* ⊕ *www. mcgill.ca/music/about-us/halls/pollack-hall* Ⓜ *McGill.*

DANCE

Agora de la Danse

MODERN DANCE | More than just a performance space for contemporary dance, this center actively works in the dance community to encourage creativity and experimentation. Hosting acclaimed artists and companies from around the world, the company is also affiliated with the Université du Québec à Montréal dance faculty. ✉ *1435 rue de Bleury, Downtown* ☎ *514/525–1500 for tickets* ⊕ *www.agoradanse.com* Ⓜ *Place-des-Arts.*

BJM Danse Montréal

BALLET | Under newly appointed (2021) French artistic director Alexandra Damiani, BJM Danse Montréal fuses contemporary music and visual arts with extraordinary technique. Performances are held at Place des Arts and Agora de la Danse, and there are free shows at Théâtre de Verdure in Parc Lafontaine during the summer months. ✉ *Downtown* ☎ *514/982–6771* ⊕ *www.bjmdanse.ca.*

La Fondation de Danse Margie Gillis

MODERN DANCE | Margie Gillis, one of Canada's most exciting and innovative soloists, works with her own company and guest artists to stage performances at Place des Arts, Agora de la Danse, and other area venues. ⊠ *Downtown* ☎ *514/845–3115* ⊕ *www.margiegillis.org.*

★ Les Grands Ballets Canadiens de Montréal

BALLET | One of Canada's premier ballet companies, Les Grands have been moving audiences since 1957. Under the artistic direction of Ivan Cavallari, the company has continued to evolve a rich body of both classic and contemporary work. Its annual presentation of *The Nutcracker*, which often sells out, has become a Christmas tradition. Performances take place at the Place des Arts. ⊠ *Downtown* ☎ *514/849–0269 tickets* ⊕ *www.grandsballets.com.*

Montréal Danse

MODERN DANCE | Lavish sets and dazzlingly sensual choreography have helped make Montréal Danse one of Canada's most popular contemporary repertory companies. It has a busy touring schedule, but also regularly performs at Place des Arts, Agora de la Danse, and the Théâtre de Verdure. ⊠ *Downtown* ☎ *514/871–4005* ⊕ *www.Montréaldanse.com.*

Tangente

MODERN DANCE | For more than 40 years, Tangente has hosted weekly performances of contemporary and experimental dance between September and May on various Montréal stages (there are currently three venues in the city). It also acts as an archive for contemporary dance and experimental performance art, with more than 2,000 files focusing on major international dance schools and festivals, companies, and choreographers. Tangente encourages national and international exchanges between dance companies and artists. ⊠ *The Wilder, 1435 rue de Bleury, Downtown* ✛ *rue De Bleury and rue Sainte-Catherine Ouest* ☎ *514/525–5584* ⊕ *www.tangentedanse. ca* Ⓜ *Station Place-des-Arts.*

FILM

★ Cinéma du Parc

FILM | A favorite of Montréal moviegoers for years, this theater focuses on first-run movies from around the world. Retrospectives based on interesting themes and prominent directors are also screened. Located inside the Galeries du Parc mall, near McGill University, it primarily caters to an Anglophone audience. ∎TIP➔ The cinema offers parking at C$3 for three hours. Just ask for your coupon at the box office. ⊠ *Galeries du Parc Mall, 3575 av. du Parc, Suite 6100, Downtown* ☎ *514/281–1900* ⊕ *www.cinemaduparc. com* Ⓜ *Place-des-Arts.*

Cinéma Impérial

FILM | Recognized by the Québec government as a historical monument in 2001, this grand Renaissance-style movie theater, complete with ornate ceilings, decorative molding, and red-velvet seats, screens independent films, though on a somewhat irregular basis. It plays host to many cultural events, including the Montréal World Film Festival. ⊠ *1432 rue de Bleury, Downtown* ☎ *514/884–7187* ⊕ *www.cinemaimperial.com* Ⓜ *Place-des-Arts.*

THEATER

Black Theatre Workshop

THEATER | The only Black English-language company in Québec (and the longest-running in Canada) continues to support and nourish the careers of many prominent artists on the national scene. Expect innovative new productions performed alongside classic plays, such as *A Raisin in the Sun*. Shows take place at the Centaur Theatre and other venues around the city. ⊠ *Downtown* ☎ *514/932–1104* ⊕ *www.blacktheatreworkshop.ca.*

Geordie Productions

THEATER | Promoting itself as a theater for all audiences, this accomplished English company has been delighting kids and adults since 1982. Most productions are performed at the Centaur Theatre. ✉ *Downtown* ☎ *514/845–9810* ⊕ *www. geordie.ca.*

Monument-National

THEATER | The highly regarded École Nationale de Théâtre du Canada—aka National Theatre School of Canada—supplies world stages with a steady stream of well-trained actors and directors. It works and performs in the historic and glorious old theater that has played host to such luminaries as Edith Piaf and Emma Albani. (Québec's first feminist rallies in the early 1900s also took place here.) Graduating classes perform professional-level plays in both French and English. The theater also plays host to an assortment of touring plays, musicals, and concerts. ✉ *1182 boul. St-Laurent, Downtown* ☎ *514/842–7954, 866/547– 7328* ⊕ *ent-nts.ca/en* Ⓜ *St-Laurent.*

Théâtre Jean Duceppe

THEATER | Named for one of Québec's most beloved actors, this theater makes its home in the smallest and most intimate of the four auditoriums in Place des Arts. It primarily stages major French-language productions. ✉ *175 rue Ste-Catherine Ouest, Downtown* ☎ *514/842–2112* ⊕ *www.duceppe.com* Ⓜ *Place-des-Arts.*

★ Théâtre du Nouveau Monde

THEATER | Celebrating 70 years in 2021 on the Montréal theatre scene, the Théâtre du Nouveau Monde plans to expand its current space. A season's offerings at this renowned French-language theatre might include works by locals Michel Tremblay and Patrice Robitaille, as well as works by Shakespeare, Molière, Camus, Ibsen, Chekhov, and Arthur Miller. ✉ *84 rue Ste-Catherine Ouest, Downtown* ☎ *514/866–8668* ⊕ *www.tnm.qc.ca* Ⓜ *St-Laurent.*

🛍 Shopping

Montréal's largest retail district takes in rues Sherbrooke and Ste-Catherine, boulevard de Maisonneuve, and the side streets between them. Because of the density and variety of the stores, it's the best shopping bet if you're in town overnight or for a weekend. The area bounded by rues Sherbrooke, Ste-Catherine, de la Montagne, and Crescent, anchored by the Museum of Fine Arts to the north and the newly merged luxury department stores Holt Renfrew and Ogilvy (now Holt Renfrew Ogilvy) to the south, is the corridor of chic. You'll find a tempting blend of antiques shops, art galleries, designer salons, and luxury jewelry shops displayed beneath colorful awnings. Rue Ste-Catherine is the main shopping thoroughfare, with most of the chain stores and department stores. To get here, take the métro to the Peel, McGill, or Guy-Concordia stations.

ANTIQUES

Antiquités Pour La Table

ANTIQUES & COLLECTIBLES | Armoires and sideboards brimming with fine crystal and china line the walls at this beautiful shop, while chandeliers, linens, and other vintage pieces make up the rest of the treasures. ■TIP→ **Phone before you visit, as hours can vary** ✉ *762 av. Atwater, Downtown* ☎ *514/989–8945* ⊕ *www. antiquesforthetable.com* ☾ *Closed Sun. and Mon.* Ⓜ *St-Henri.*

Grand Central

ANTIQUES & COLLECTIBLES | "Grand" is the right word to describe this antiques emporium—it's filled to the brim with elegant chandeliers and candelabras, armchairs and secretaries, and other decorative elements from the 18th and 19th centuries. These items would add a touch of refinement to almost any home. ✉ *2448 rue Notre-Dame Ouest, St-Henri, Downtown* ☎ *514/935–1467, 514/935–1269* ⊕ *www.grandcentralinc.ca* ☾ *Closed Sun.* Ⓜ *Lionel-Groulx.*

Le Petit Musée

ANTIQUES & COLLECTIBLES | The Kleins have been selling and acquiring exquisite antiques and antiquities from around the globe for four generations. One of

Montréal's most prestigious antiques galleries, Le Petit Musée has been a fixture in Downtown's Golden Square Mile for over half a century. The shop, which is housed in a gorgeous greystone on Sherbrooke St., is a veritable treasure trove covering various rooms over four floors. You'll need a few hours and a lot of stamina to take in the nicely arranged and meticulously cataloged Inuit sculptures, African masks, Chinese bronzes, Japanese screens, Egyptian earthenware, Greco-Roman works, Pre-Columbian pottery, Persian textiles, European furniture, oriental jewelry, and more. ✉ 1494 rue Sherbrooke O., Downtown ☎ 514/937–6161 ⊕ petitmusee.com ◷ Closed Sun. and Mon. Ⓜ Guy-Concordia. Antiques

ART
Edifice Belgo
ART GALLERIES | Built more than a century ago, Edifice Belgo houses more than two dozen art galleries and artists' studios exhibiting the works of both established and emerging artists. Galerie Hugues Charbonneau and Galerie Bellemare Lambert feature the work of contemporary artists working in Québec and Canada. For wearable art, visit designer Véronique Miljkovitch's atelier on the second floor. ■TIP➜ **Each gallery or atelier maintains different hours, so it's best to call ahead.** ✉ 372 rue Ste-Catherine Ouest, Downtown ☎ 514/861–2953 Ⓜ Place-des-Arts.

★ Galerie Alan Klinkhoff
ART GALLERIES | From Lawren Harris and Emily Carr to Jean-Paul Riopelle and Jean Paul Lemieux, the Klinkhoffs know art, especially Canadian art. Open since 1950, the gallery showcases several floors of Canadian works from both contemporary and historical artists. ✉ 1448 rue Sherbrooke Ouest, Downtown ☎ 514/284–9339, 416/233–0335 Toronto location ⊕ www.klinkhoff.ca ◷ Closed Sat. and Sun. ☞ Also open by appointment Ⓜ Guy.

BOOKS AND STATIONERY
Paragraphe
BOOKS | This cornerstone of Montréal's English-language literary scene carries the usual selection of mysteries and thrillers, but it also stocks a wide range of Canadian works. It's a favorite with visiting authors, who stop by to read from their latest releases. Sip on a coffee from the adjacent Second Cup coffee shop while you peruse the stacks. ✉ 2220 av. McGill College, Downtown ☎ 514/845–5811 ⊕ www.paragraphbooks.com Ⓜ McGill.

Renaud-Bray
BOOKS | Tucked away in the basement level of the Complexe Desjardins shopping mall, this outlet of the vast French-language book chain is chockablock with French and English books, magazines, and music. ✉ Complexe Desjardins, 150 Ste-Catherine Ouest, Downtown ☎ 514/288–4844 ⊕ www.renaud-bray.com Ⓜ Place-des-Arts.

★ The Word
BOOKS | Deep in the heart of the McGill University neighborhood, this award-winning Montréal landmark is bursting with used books (including first editions) and specializes in philosophy, poetry, and literature. Despite its dilapidated appearance, the Lilliputian shop is beloved by locals and visitors alike. As celebrated Montréal novelist Heather O'Neill says, "Everyone says a prayer before walking in so that the roof won't collapse." Open since 1975, the owners shunned modern technology (including a cash register) until just a few years ago. There's not even a sign, so keep your eyes peeled as you walk along Milton, though the bargain books lining the window are a good clue. ■TIP➜ **The Word recently made an appearance in the Netflix movie *Pieces of a Woman* starring Vanessa Kirby and Shia LaBeouf.** ✉ 469 rue Milton, Downtown ☎ 514/845–5640 ⊕ www.wordbookstore.ca ◷ Closed Sun. Ⓜ McGill.

Montréal-based Frank and Oak is hugely successful in Canada with 23 boutiques and a thriving Web presence.

CLOTHING

Aritzia

WOMEN'S CLOTHING | At more than 10,000 square feet, Aritzia's gleaming glass-fronted, two-story location on Ste-Catherine St. is the Vancouver brand's largest in Canada. Offering dressy and casual classics in addition to youthful contemporary fashions, this is the place to shop if you're looking for on-trend women's clothing at mid-range prices. Along with its own collections, Aritzia also carries popular labels like Mackage, Citizens of Humanity, and AGOLDE. ✉ *1125 rue Ste-Catherine Ouest, Downtown* ☎ *514/285–0791* ⊕ *www.aritzia. com* Ⓜ *Peel.*

★ Arthur

MEN'S CLOTHING | Everything about this shop, from the handsome Crescent St. location to the immaculate hardwood floors to the classic bespoke men's shirts with damask silk lining and hand-sewn button holes speaks of quality, tradition, and style. Armenian-Canadian tailor Arthur Der Shahinian has been creating custom-made suits for men (and some women) since 1978, first from his modest digs at Marché Jean-Talon, and now from his elegant atelier-cum-boutique on Crescent St. Still, Mr. Der Shahinian and his sons Tavit and John haven't compromised their principles of quality and friendly, professional service. At 70, Der Shahinian is the youngest shirtmaker in Montréal, a fact that speaks volumes about what has been happening to the fashion industry in the last quarter century. The Der Shahinians also custom-make men's shoes. ✉ *2165 rue Crescent, Downtown* ☎ *514/843–0522* ⊕ *www. arthurMontréal.com* Ⓜ *Guy-Concordia.*

Café Boutique Eva B

SECOND-HAND | On the secondhand fashion map for decades, Eva B has all kinds of clothes, shoes, jewelry, and even eyeglasses on offer. Budget at least 30 minutes to scour the labyrinth of racks and the "pool," a large platform in the back where everything is a dollar. Just watch your step; the floor is uneven. If you get hungry in the process, nosh on a samosa or cookie from the in-store café. There is now a second location, Eva D at 1611 boul. Saint-Laurent. ✉ 2015 boul. St-Laurent, Downtown ☎ 514/849–8246 ⊕ boutiqueevab.com Ⓜ St-Laurent.

Editorial Boutique

WOMEN'S CLOTHING | Designer duds happily share space with inexpensive but in-vogue items at this low-key Downtown boutique with a devoted cult following. Brands include Citizens of Humanity, Dickies, Erin Wasson, Luv U Always, For Love of Lemons, Unif, and Jeffrey Campbell. ✉ 1455 rue Stanley, Downtown ☎ 514/849–3888 ⊕ www.editorialboutique.com Ⓜ Peel.

★ E.R.A. Vintage Wear

WOMEN'S CLOTHING | With a reputation as the best vintage shop in the city, this upscale boutique specializes in vintage clothing, shoes, and accessories from the 1920s through the mid-1980s. Each handpicked item is carefully cleaned, repaired, and altered as necessary to give it a more contemporary flair and using no new materials. High-profile clients like Julianne Moore and Cate Blanchett have been known to drop by. This location is bright, spacious, and loaded with irresistible treasures. ✉ 999 rue du College, Loft 41, Downtown ☎ 514/543–8750 ⊕ www.eravintagewear.com ◔ Closed Sun.–Tues. Ⓜ Place St-Henri.

★ Frank and Oak

MIXED CLOTHING | From its humble beginnings in a kitchen, this popular Canadian brand outfits young creatives and professionals in casual, contemporary fashions using ecologically friendly fabrics like hemp, kapok, seawool (a yarn made from recycled polyester and oyster shell composites), SeaCell (biodegradable fibers made from renewable raw materials found in seaweed and natural cellulose) and recycled cottons, polyesters, nylons, and wools. ✉ 1420 and 1432 rue Stanley, Downtown ☎ 514/228–3761 Menswear store, 514/360–0553 Womenswear store ⊕ www.frankandoak.com ☞ Menswear: 1420 rue Stanley; Womenswear: 1432 rue Stanley Ⓜ Peel.

Harry Rosen

MEN'S CLOTHING | This is Canada's premier high-end menswear destination. Stocked with both casual and formal attire, wallets, watches, and hats, this 22,000-square-foot flagship store caters to the classically tailored male. Brands include 7 For All Mankind, Michael Kors, Cole Haan, Tom Ford, and Armani. ✉ Cours Mont-Royal, 1455 rue Peel, Downtown ☎ 514/284–3315 ⊕ www.harryrosen.com Ⓜ Peel.

★ Henri Henri

HATS & GLOVES | A Montréal tradition since 1932, the best men's hat store in Canada carries a huge stock of homburgs, fedoras, and derbies, as well as cloth caps and other accessories. Prices range from about C$150 to C$1,000, the top price fetching you a top-of-the-line Panama hat. Lots of women's hats on offer as well. ✉ 189 rue Ste-Catherine Est, Downtown ☎ 514/288–0109, 888/388–0109 ⊕ www.henrihenri.ca Ⓜ St-Laurent or Berri-UQAM.

La Senza

LINGERIE | This Québec-based lingerie chain is known for its bright, cheerful push-up bras, panties, and negligees. It also sells sleepwear and sportswear. ✉ Place Montréal Trust, 705 rue Ste-Catherine Ouest, Downtown ☎ 514/288–8775 ⊕ www.lasenza.com Ⓜ Peel.

Lululemon

MIXED CLOTHING | This Canadian sports-and-yoga wear chain offers plenty of styles, colors, and cuts to please both guys and gals. You'll also find headbands, scarves, jewelry, and more. ✉ 1232 rue Ste-Catherine Ouest, Downtown ☎ 514/394–0770 ⊕ www.lululemon.com Ⓜ Peel.

L'Uomo Montréal

MEN'S CLOTHING | You'll come to this store for the selection of European menswear and accessories, but you'll stay for the impeccable service and attention to detail. Expect suits from Kiton and Borrelli, bags from Prada, shoes from U.K. brand Edward Green, and ties from Massimo Bizzocchi. ✉ *1452 rue Peel, Downtown* ☎ *514/844–1008, 877/844–1008* ⊕ *www.luomo-Montréal. com* ☙ *Closed Sun.* Ⓜ *Peel.*

★ Marie Saint Pierre

WOMEN'S CLOTHING | The leading female designer in Québec (and one who's celebrated throughout Canada), Marie Saint-Pierre is known for her signature pleats and ruffles—think sleek and sophisticated rather than frilly. Now she's lending her avant-garde touch to bridal, with a wedding collection that's available only at this flagship boutique. ✉ *2081 rue de la Montagne, Downtown* ☎ *514/281–5547* ⊕ *www.mariesaintpierre.com* Ⓜ *Peel or Guy-Concordia.*

Olam

WOMEN'S CLOTHING | The fashions here don't come cheap, but French-influenced owner Charles Abitbol believes in quality fashion for women of all ages. Abitbol sources funky and whimsical fashions for the younger set, as well as more classic pieces with clean lines from European, American, and local Québec designers such as Yumi, Sanctuary Clothing, Desigual, and Mélissa Nepton. The Fat Boy beanbag chairs may entice you to hang a while in the vast loftlike upstairs space, but like the Taschen design books and the colonial-inspired Québec and French-made furniture, these are also for sale. There's a second location at 433 rue Saint-Denis. ✉ *1374 rue Ste-Catherine Ouest, Downtown* ☎ *514/875–9696* ⊕ *olam-mousseline.com* Ⓜ *Peel.*

Roots

MIXED CLOTHING | Bring the great outdoors in, courtesy of this beloved Canadian chain with a beaver emblem. There are lots of casual neutrals for men, women, and kids, with pops of colorful sportswear thrown in for good measure. Quality leather goods are also available. ✉ *1025 rue Ste-Catherine Ouest, Downtown* ☎ *514/845–7995* ⊕ *www.roots. com* Ⓜ *Peel.*

★ Tozzi

MIXED CLOTHING | Known around Montréal as one of the top menswear destinations, Tozzi is a one-stop shop for the dapper gentleman. Suits, polos, jeans, watches, sunglasses, and cologne—this boutique offers just about everything in a minimalist, serene environment. ■TIP➡ **Two doors down you'll find the Tozzi women's fashions boutique.** ✉ *2085, 2095, and 2115 rue Crescent, Downtown* ☎ *514/285–2444* ⊕ *www.boutiquetozzi. com* Ⓜ *Guy-Concordia or Peel.*

Winners

OUTLET | Tucked away on the lowest level of Place Montréal Trust lies this huge discount store stocked with clothing, shoes, housewares—you name it. Allow adequate time if you really want to rummage, but if you're not at leisure, head straight to the runway collections and the sale racks for the best bargains. ■TIP➡ **The Alexis Nihon (Atwater métro) location, on the edge of Westmount, can also also be a good bet for snagging a deal on designer labels and Italian shoes.** ✉ *Place Montréal Trust, 1500 av. McGill College, Downtown* ☎ *514/788–4949* ⊕ *www.winners.ca* Ⓜ *McGill.*

DEPARTMENT STORES

Holt Renfrew Ogilvy

DEPARTMENT STORE | These two iconic Canadian luxury department stores (Holt Renfrew and Ogilvy) merged into one brand, undergoing a monumental expansion of the original Ogilvy building.

Unveiled as Holt Renfrew Ogilvy in 2019, the posh department store is linked, physically, to the equally glamorous Four Seasons Hotel, also opened in 2019. The exclusive mega-store features loads of clean, white-on-white decor (white pillars, white walls, white floors, white marble), showcasing fashions and accessories for men and women from the world's premier designer labels. Many of these are housed in intimate, partitioned boutique settings within the larger department store. On the fifth floor, clients can enjoy a private shopping experience in one of five personal shopping suites. Especially noteworthy is the new Café Holt, all 1940s Hollywood-inspired glamour, with a remarkable light that recalls a solar orb set above a square orange bar, Breccia Pernice marble and chocolate wood surfaces, and gently curved seating in plush orange velvet upholstery. The café menu emphasizes fresh, local ingredients, with the chef highlighting his Canadian and international influences. ✉ *1307 rue Ste-Catherine Ouest, Downtown* ☎ *514/842–7711* ⊕ *www.holtrenfrew.com/en/stores?location=holtrenfrewogilvy* Ⓜ *Peel.*

Hudson's Bay (formerly La Baie or The Bay)
DEPARTMENT STORE | Hudson's Bay department store is a descendant of the Hudson's Bay Company, the iconic 17th-century fur-trading company that played a pivotal role in Canada's development. The Bay, as it's known by Canadians, has been a department store since 1891 and is known for its duffel coats and signature red-, green-, and white-striped blankets. Besides fashions, housewares, and toys, there's also a beauty salon and spa, an optician, and a watch and jewelry repair services. ✉ *585 rue Ste-Catherine Ouest, Downtown* ☎ *514/281–4422* ⊕ *www.thebay.com* Ⓜ *McGill.*

La Maison Simons
DEPARTMENT STORE | Find the *trends du jour* at a great price from the youth-oriented labels on the ground floor of this

Montréal's Markets 🍴

Marché Jean-Talon in the north end of the city has an Italian flavor; the surrounding streets are home to some of the finest pizza and cafe lattes anywhere. **Marché Atwater** has an indoor hall, packed with eateries, butchers, bakeries, and fine food emporiums.

The markets are a great place to pick up nonperishables such as jam from Île d'Orléans or cranberries harvested late September to mid-October; or maple syrup and butter, year-round.

bustling department store. Upstairs, the fare is more "mature," ranging from respectable and affordable twin sets to luxe offerings from the likes of Chloé and Missoni. The store's fashion-forward men's suits and casual wear are also worth checking out. ✉ *977 rue Ste-Catherine Ouest, Downtown* ☎ *514/289–1840, 877/666–1840* ⊕ *www.simons.ca* Ⓜ *Peel.*

FOOD
★ **Divine Chocolatier**
CHOCOLATE | Tucked away in a small basement space on Crescent Street, this precious little chocolaterie owned by Belgian *maître chocolatier* Richard Zwierzynski has lived here for 30 years, and been in existence since 1976. With its stuffed teddy bears, shoe- and bottle-shaped chocolate decorations, and antique porcelain plates adorning the walls, a visit to Divine is like stepping into a 19th-century ice-cream parlor. Chocolate massage oil and chocolate tablets made from the mold of an illustration from the Kama Sutra will tickle the fancy, but it's the chocolate truffles, assorted chocolates, and the dark chocolate ganache cheesecake that will have you returning

again and again. ✉ *2158 rue Crescent, Downtown* ☎ *514/282–0829* ⊕ *www. divinechocolatier.com* Ⓜ *Guy-Concordia.*

Marché Atwater

MARKET | Heading down Atwater Avenue toward Lachine Canal, you can't miss the art deco tower of Atwater Market. This is the best spot to pick up local produce, fresh flowers, and gourmet meats and cheeses. In summer, bring a blanket and enjoy a picnic by the canal or have a drink at the Canal Lounge, a café and bar on a barge. During the winter holidays there is now the added bonus of an outdoor Christmas market. ✉ *138 av. Atwater, Downtown* ☎ *514/937–7754 for all Montréal's public markets* ⊕ *www.marchespublics-mtl.com* Ⓜ *Lionel-Groulx.*

JEWELRY

Birks

JEWELRY & WATCHES | The Canadian equivalent of Tiffany's (with its own version of the iconic blue box) has been selling diamond engagement rings, exquisite jewelry, and fine crystal since 1879. Recently renovated and redesigned and now part of the new Hôtel Birks, the luxury jewelry store now contains partitioned boutiques within a larger boutique and sells items by brands such as Messika, Van Cleef & Arpels, Rolex, Cartier, and Breitling, in addition to Birks Collections. Even if diamonds or watches aren't on your shopping list, it's still worth a visit to the elegant new hotel and the seriously stunning Henri Brasserie Française (restaurant and bar lounge), serving French-inspired cuisine highlighting seasonal Québec and Canadian products (⊕ *www.restauranthenri.com*) ✉ *Hôtel Birks, 620 rue Ste-Catherine O., Downtown* ☎ *514/397–2511* ⊕ *www. maisonbirks.com/en/maison-birks-Montréal-centre-ville* ⊙ *Closed Sun. and Mon.* Ⓜ *McGill.*

★ **Bleu Comme Le Ciel**

JEWELRY & WATCHES | In French they call costume jewelry *bijoux de fantaisie,* and that's exactly what you'll find here: a fantastic array of colorful crystal baubles. Elegant lines from Ginette NY contrast with the bold designs of Reminiscence Paris. The glass-walled boutique is easy to miss, as it blends into the surrounding building. ✉ *1143 boul. de Maisonneuve Ouest, Downtown* ☎ *514/847–1128* ⊕ *www.bleucommeleciel.com* ⊙ *Closed Sun.* Ⓜ *Peel.*

Château d'Ivoire

JEWELRY & WATCHES | Whether you're considering a watch, diamond bracelet, or engagement ring, Château d'Ivoire might just have what you're looking for (as long as a significant price tag doesn't deter you). Brands at the newly built, ultra modern two-story veneration of all things luxury include Chopard, Piaget, Rolex, IWC, and Cartier, among others. ✉ *2020 rue de la Montagne, Downtown* ☎ *514/845–4651, 888/883–8283* ⊕ *www. chateaudivoire.com* ⊙ *Closed Sun. and Mon.* Ⓜ *Peel or Guy-Concordia.*

Kaufmann de Suisse

JEWELRY & WATCHES | Walk the red carpet (literally) beyond the black-and-white marble exterior into an elegant room filled with precious jewels. Founded in Montréal more than 60 years ago by a Swiss master jeweler and goldsmith, Kaufmann de Suisse is known for its flowing bands of gold and platinum. The posh, yet friendly family-run boutique recently expanded to include a VIP Philippe Patek corner, showcasing wares from the exclusive Swiss watchmaker. ✉ *2195 rue Crescent, Downtown* ☎ *514/848–0595* ⊕ *www.kaufmanndesuisse.ca* ⊙ *Closed Sun.* Ⓜ *Guy-Concordia or Peel.*

The Route Verte

Stretches of what's called the most extensive route of biking trails in North America pass right through the very heart of Downtown Montréal.

The Route Verte (Green Route) is a free 5,000-km (3,100-mile) network of paths, shared roadways, and paved shoulders that traverse the province of Québec.

The cycling group Vélo Québec first began talking about the possibility of a province-wide bike network back in the 1980s, but it wasn't until 1995 that the government announced it would fund the C$88.5-million project to be built over the next 12 years.

More than 320 km (200 miles) of the Route Verte cover the streets of the city. It passes through Downtown, stretches up Mont-Royal, hugs the shore near the Lachine Canal, and extends out to Parc Jean-Drapeau, to name just a few of the major areas covered.

For more information, including maps, suggested routes, and other trip-planning tools, visit ⊕ *www. routeverte.com*

3

Montréal DOWNTOWN

MALLS AND SHOPPING CENTERS

Les Cours Mont-Royal

MALL | A variety of chic independent boutiques are mixed in with quality chains like DKNY and Desigual in this graceful mall, once a grand hotel. Drop by Spa Diva or the top-notch salon Pure if you're in need of a beauty break. The elegant atrium sometimes hosts runway shows. ■TIP➔ **Be sure to stop by the Barbie Expo, a collection of more than 1,000 Barbie dolls rocking some of the biggest names in fashion, including Christian Dior, Donna Karen, Armani, Vera Wang, Oscar De La Renta, Christian Louboutin, Carolina Herrera, and Zac Posen.** ⊠ *1455 rue Peel, Downtown* ☎ *514/842–7777* ⊕ *www.lcmr.ca* Ⓜ *Peel.*

Place Ville Marie

MALL | Stylish shoppers head to the 80-plus retail outlets in Place Ville Marie, part of the city's vast underground network. New to the mall is Le Cathcart restaurants et biergarten, an upscale food hall and beer garden inside a glass pavilion. Also, as of December 2021, the Musée d'art contemporain has its temporary digs here while the museum building undergoes a renovation and expansion (⊕ *macm.org/en*).

⊠ *Boulevard René-Lévesque and rue University, Downtown* ☎ *514/861–9393* ⊕ *www.placevillemarie.com* Ⓜ *McGill or Bonaventure.*

SHOES

Browns

SHOES | In business since 1940, this local institution stocks fashionable footwear and accessories for men and women. Besides its own label, Browns carries shoes by Emporio Armani, Michael Kors, Cole Haan, Steve Madden, Stuart Weitzman, and more. Comfortable couches make shopping a pleasant experience inside this gleaming white-and-silver flagship. ⊠ *1191 rue Ste-Catherine Ouest, Downtown* ☎ *514/987–1206, 866/720–7463 customer care* ⊕ *www.brownsshoes.com* Ⓜ *Peel.*

Ⓐ Activities

HOCKEY

Ice hockey is nothing short of an institution in Montréal, the city that arguably gave birth to the sport back in the late 19th century. Although variations of the game are said to have been played in other U.S. and Canadian cities as early as

Ice-Skating in Montréal

Come the winter months and you don't have to look very far to find an ice-skating rink in Montréal. There are municipally run outdoor—and some indoor—rinks in virtually every corner of the city. Outdoor rinks are open from December until mid-March and admission is free, though there is a few for skate rental. The rinks on Île Ste-Hélène and at the Old Port are large, but note that there is a C$6.95 admission charge (free admission for children under 6) to skate at the Old Port one.

All in all, there are at least 195 outdoor and 21 indoor rinks spread across Montréal. So lace up those skates and make some figure eights!

For information on the numerous ice-skating rinks in the city call or check the city's website. ☎ *514/872–1111 Montréal.ca/en/places?q=skating*

1800, the first organized game of modern hockey was played in Montréal in 1875, and the first official team, the McGill University Hockey Club, was founded in Montréal in 1880. The city's beloved Montréal Canadiens is the oldest club in the National Hockey League and, as Montréalers are keen to tell you, one of the most successful teams in North American sports history—even though they haven't won the Stanley Cup since 1993!

McGill University Redbirds Hockey

HOCKEY | Formed in 1877, this was the first organized hockey club in Canada. It is now one of the top university men's ice hockey programs in Canada, and the Redmen (now known as the the Redbirds) were a Canadian University cup finalist in 2011. Games against cross-town rivals, the Concordia Stingers or the UQTR Patriotes, are always emotional duels. Home games take place at Percival Molson Stadium. ■ **TIP→ In 2020, McGill University announced that its sports teams would henceforth be known as the Redbirds (instead of by their former offensive moniker, the Redskins)** ✉ *475 av. des Pins Ouest, Downtown* ☎ *514/398–7006* ⊕ *mcgillathletics.ca/sports/mens-ice-hockey* Ⓜ *McGill.*

Montréal Canadiens

HOCKEY | The Montréal Canadiens meet National Hockey League rivals at the Centre Bell from October through April (and even later if they make the playoffs). The "Habs" (the nickname's taken from Habitants, or early settlers) have won 24 Stanley Cups, although they've been struggling in the standings for several years now and haven't won a cup since the 1992–93 season. (They did make it to the finals in July 2021 but lost to Tampa Bay.) Nevertheless, Les Canadiens are a great source of pride to the city's sports fans, and tickets for their local games continue to be a hot commodity. Buy tickets in advance to guarantee a seat. ✉ *1909 av. des Canadiens-de-Montréal, Downtown* ☎ *877/463–2674, 514/989–2841 Bell Centre* ⊕ *nhl.com/canadiens* Ⓜ *Lucien-L'Allier or Peel.*

ICE-SKATING

Atrium le 1000 de la Gauchetière

ICE-SKATING | FAMILY | Inside the tallest building (currently, buildings in Montréal are not permitted to be taller than the height of Mount Royal) in the city, this skating rink lies under a glass atrium, allowing sunlight to shine down on the rink year-round. After working up an appetite, hit any one of the 12 restaurants in the surrounding food court.

✉ *1000 rue de la Gauchetière, Downtown* ☎ *514/395–0555* 🌐 *le1000.com/en/skate* 🎫 *C$9; skate rental C$9* 🕓 *Closed Mon. and Tues.* ☞ *Reservations required* [M] *Bonaventure.*

Westmount

The upscale neighborhood of Westmount is predominantly anglophone, a far cry from the French-speaking Montréal foreigners and people from the ROC (Rest of Canada) often picture. Around Victoria Village, a shopping area, you'll see Victorian shopfronts frequented by polished moms in Prada sunglasses and Lululemon leggings driving Land Rovers and pushing strollers, as well as dressed-down locals walking their dogs along rue Sherbrooke and avenue Victoria. The largely residential neighborhood has lovely parks for strolling and the homes are beautiful, but there aren't many tourist sights around here. Thanks to inflated property taxes and rents in the last decade, as well as a private management company buying up many of the commercial buildings that make up the neighborhood, many of the more characterful, independent boutiques have been replaced by expensive brands that can be found Downtown like l'Occitane, Sarah Pacini, Rudsak, and James Perse, in addition to ubiquitous ones such as Starbucks and Lululemon. Despite this, Westmount is still a good place to go for high end shopping. Rue Sherbrooke Ouest and avenue Victoria are a pleasant mix of hip shops, fine florists, patisseries, cafes, home decor/kitchenware shops, a cookbook store/cooking school, a mom-and-pop hair salon, grocery/produce stores, and a Japanese sushi-cum-grocery that's lived on Victoria Avenue since the 1970s. The neighborhood also has some interesting dining choices, especially on Victoria.

GETTING HERE AND AROUND

The closest métro to Westmont is Vendôme, or you can take Bus 24 west from Downtown.

🍴 Restaurants

Westmount is a relatively new foodie destination, and provides much-needed sustenance after hitting the area's luxury boutiques.

Aux Vivres

$$ | VEGETARIAN | FAMILY | A favorite among vegans, celiacs, and vegetarians—and even omnivores—Montréal's first vegan restaurant serves comfort food dishes and beverages that are creative and delicious—not to mention packed with vitamins. A large chalkboard holds specials of the day. **Known for:** vegan- and celiac-friendly; Dragon bowl; vegan cheesecake (*gâteau fauxmage*). [$] *Average main: C$14* ✉ *4896 rue Sherbrooke O., Westmount* ☎ *514/842–3479* 🌐 *www.auxvivres.com* [M] *Vendôme.*

★ Park

$$$$ | JAPANESE FUSION | Sustainable, organic, and fresh every day is the philosophy of this high-end sushi restaurant. The menu is eclectic, with excellent sashimi—some specimens flown in directly from Japan—noodles, and some vegetarian-friendly Japanese dishes mixed with a variety of influences from chef Antonio Park's multiple backgrounds—Korean, Argentinian, and Canadian. **Known for:** exquisite desserts; creative menu; omakase. [$] *Average main: C$40* ✉ *378 av. Victoria, Downtown* ☎ *514/750–7534* 🌐 *www.parkresto.com* 🕓 *Closed Sun. and Mon.* [M] *Vendôme.*

Petros

$$$$ | GREEK | FAMILY | A local favorite in Westmount, this BYOW Greek *estiatorio* (more upscale than a taverna) specializes in seafood and has a warm, welcoming atmosphere. With its Grecian-blue tiles and shutters, white walls, traditional Greek music, and ultrafriendly, bona-fide

Greek waiters, Petros makes you feel as if you've stepped through a portal straight onto a Cycladic isle. **Known for:** BYOB—bring your own wine; jumbo shrimp; excellent vegan and vegetarian meze. [$] *Average main: C$37* ✉ *4785 rue Sherbrooke, Westmount* ☎ *514/938–5656* 🌐 *www.restaurantpetros.ca/en* ⏲ *No lunch Sat.–Tues.* [M] *Vendôme, then bus 24.*

Coffee and Quick Bites

Café Bazin

$$ | **FRENCH** | A melange between a patisserie, a café, and a French bistro, this little restaurant has been a darling of food critics since it opened in 2017. Serving deftly executed French dishes like quiche, *vol au vent*, and *tartines niçoises* in a fresh, modern setting of white subway tiles, decorative brass struts, richly patinated wooden tables, and mint green–velvet seating, Café Bazin is a little corner of France in the heart of Anglo Westmount. **Known for:** charming decor; French classics; exquisite pastries. [$] *Average main: C$17* ✉ *380 av. Victoria, Westmount* ☎ *438/387–3070* 🌐 *www.cafebazin.com* ⏲ *Closed Sun. and Mon.* [M] *Vendôme.*

Shopping

Stylish locals, quaint architecture, and upscale boutiques make this a chic shopping destination. Victoria Village (rue Sherbrooke Ouest and avenue Victoria) is an eclectic blend of hip shops, fine florists, home decor/kitchenware shops, a cookbook store/cooking school, grocery/produce stores, a Japanese sushi-cum-grocery that's lived on Victoria Avenue since the 1970s, and mid-range to expensive chain brands like Lululemon, UGG, and Roots.

ANTIQUES

★ Ruth Stalker Antiques

ANTIQUES & COLLECTIBLES | The original owner made her reputation finding and salvaging fine pieces of early Québec and Canadian pine furniture, but she also developed a good instinct for folk art, such as exquisitely carved hunting decoys, weather vanes, and pottery. Now her two children continue the tradition. ✉ *155 Hillside avenue, Westmount* ☎ *514/931–0822* ⏲ *Closed Sun. and Mon.* [M] *Atwater.*

ART

Galerie de Bellefeuille

ART GALLERIES | This gallery has a knack for discovering important new talents. It represents many of Canada's top contemporary artists as well as some international ones. Its 5,000 square feet hold a good selection of sculptures, paintings, and limited-edition prints. There is another location at 1455 rue Sherbrooke O. ✉ *1366 and 1367 av. Greene, Westmount* ☎ *514/933–4406* 🌐 *www.debellefeuille.com* ⏲ *Closed Sun.* [M] *Atwater.*

CLOTHING

James

WOMEN'S CLOTHING | The home of hippie chic in Montréal, this boutique is packed with flowing tunics, embroidered blouses, and white-cotton dresses. Add a good mix of designer jeans and funky moccasins by Minnetonka and you'll understand why James is a Victoria Village mainstay. ✉ *4910 rue Sherbrooke Ouest, Westmount* ☎ *514/369–0700* [M] *Vendôme.*

Courval Fine Lingerie

LINGERIE | Whether you're looking for a sheer lace eye mask to enhance your bedroom eyes, a sexy body suit, a sensible bra, or cozy flannel PJs to snuggle up with fireside, Courval, in business since 1918, has it all. ✉ *4861 rue Sherbrooke, Westmount* ☎ *514/484–5656* 🌐 *courvalfinelingerie.com* ⏲ *Closed Sun.* [M] *Vendôme.*

HOUSEWARES
Ben & Tournesol

HOUSEWARES | A Westmount fixture since 1993, this boutique is the place to go for plush pillows, linens, and duvets from Designers Guild, which may inspire you to redesign your bedroom (if not your whole house). There are also products by Hermès, Fred Perry, and others. Ask the friendly staff for guidance on the perfect gift. ⊠ *4937 rue Sherbrooke Ouest, Westmount* ☎ *514/481–5050* ⊕ *www. benandtournesol.com* Ⓜ *Vendôme.*

SHOES
★ **Scarpa**

SHOES | One of the top shoe stores in Montréal, hands down, Scarpa, which means "shoe" in Italian, opened in 2008. From espadrilles, flats, and pumps to winter boots, sneakers, and strappy sandals, Scarpa shoes are always high quality and consistently on point. The company has its own footwear brand and atelier, which aptly enough is called Ateliers. A smaller collection of men's shoes is also available. ⊠ *4901 rue Sherbrooke O., Westmount* ☎ *514/484–0440* ⊕ *scarpa.ca* Ⓜ *Vendôme or Bus 24 from Downtown.*

TOYS
Oink Oink

TOYS | FAMILY | This pigtail-covered boutique offers three levels of fun for babies, kids, and young adults. Innovative and kooky gifts, books, clothing, and even scooters are available. ⊠ *1343 av. Greene, Westmount* ☎ *514/939–2634* ⊕ *www.oinkoink.com* Ⓜ *Atwater.*

The Village

Often referred to as **the Gay Village,** this area is the center of one of the most vibrant LGBTQ communities in the world, widely supported by residents of this proudly liberal, open-minded city. In recent years the municipal, federal, and provincial governments have taken it upon themselves to promote the Village and Montréal's LGBTQ-friendly climate as a reason for tourists to visit, but its restaurants, mid-century modern antiques shops (on rue Atateken), and bars make it a popular destination for visitors of all persuasions. The lively strip of rue Ste-Catherine running east of the Latin Quarter is the backbone of the Village.

In late July, the Village's Pride Parade, widely considered the biggest and most outrageous party of the year, attracts more than a million people.

GETTING HERE AND AROUND
The Village is centered around the Beaudry métro station, which has its entrance adorned with rainbow pillars. Its borders are considered rue Ste-Catherine Est from rue Atateken to de Lorimier, and on the north–south axis from René-Lévesque to Sherbrooke.

⊙ Sights

Galerie Blanc

ARTS CENTER | Blanc is an open-air art gallery whose mission is to bring the general public closer to art. Open 24/7, rain, snow, or shine, exhibitions showcase the work of different artists and change regularly. The gallery is open to anyone and there is no admission fee. It's located on rue Ste-Catherine E. between rue Wolfe and rue Atateken. ⊠ *rue Ste-Catherine E., The Village* ✛ *Between rue Wolfe and rue Atateken* ⊕ *galerieblanc.com* ▣ *Free* Ⓜ *Beaudry.*

❿ Restaurants

A little outside the hustle and bustle of the busy Downtown Montréal core, the Village is quite charming. During the summer months (May to September), rue Ste-Catherine in the Village is closed off to cars, which makes it pleasant to explore the shops and restaurants.

Le Mousso

$$$$ | **MODERN CANADIAN** | Regularly lauded on Canadian best-of dining lists, Le Mousso is run by chef Antonin Mousseau-Rivard, who dreams up beautifully plated, northern European-inspired dishes that are as much works of art as they are imaginative combinations of flavor and texture for the taste buds. Using mostly local and seasonal ingredients, the seven-course tasting menu might feature dishes such as bortsch *décomposé* (beet soup), grilled scallops lightly smoked with fir and served on coals with wild plum butter, or tataki Wagyu beef accompanied by cream, New Brunswick caviar, and nasturtium leaves. **Known for:** innovative cuisine highlighting the terroir; tasting menus only; minimalist decor. [$] *Average main: C$225* ✉ *1023 rue Ontario Est, The Village* ☎ *438/384–7410* 🌐 *www.lemousso.com* 🕒 *Closed Sun.–Wed. No lunch* ☞ *One service only per evening, starting at 7:30 pm* [M] *Berri-UQAM.*

Tendresse

$$ | **VEGETARIAN** | This lovely new bistro, with its minimalist interior in coral pink, seafoam green, and golden ochre, attracts locals for its casual yet stylish atmosphere, appetizing vegan cuisine, gourmet cocktails and mocktails, and natural and organic vegan wines. So flavorsome and satisfying are dishes like the seared cauliflower with panisse and green goddess sauce; the cabbage, bok choy, and tofu dumplings served with sesame sauce and cilantro; and the sautéed mushroom waffles sprinkled with dill, mint, cilantro, and maple and truffle mayo, that even hardcore meat advocates will soon forget they're eating plant-based dishes. **Known for:** sautéed mushroom waffles; some gluten free dishes; inspired cocktails/mocktails and vegan organic wines. [$] *Average main: C$17* ✉ *1259 rue Ste-Catherine E., The Village* ☎ *438/387–1471* 🌐 *bistrotendresse.com* [M] *Beaudry.*

🍸 Nightlife

Head east along rue Ste-Catherine to enjoy the colorful Gay Village—you'll know you've arrived when you're amid a sea of pretty pink balls and rainbow flags hung in the streets. It's developing a bit of a reputation for fine dining as of late, though it's still mainly known as a place for late-night partying.

BARS AND LOUNGES

★ Club Unity

BARS | Small, semiprivate lounges are scattered throughout the two-story complex, and the beautiful rooftop terrace is one of the finest in the Village. Unity is one of the longest running, most popular gay dance clubs in town—although, despite some complaints, you'll often find as many straight girls here as you will gay men. Open weekends from 10 pm to 3 am. ✉ *1171 rue Ste-Catherine Est, The Village* ☎ *514/523–2777* 🌐 *www.clubunity.com* [M] *Beaudry.*

Le Stud

BARS | Once a men-only establishment, Le Stud has been known to let in some women. A small dance floor and trance music have brought in a whole different crowd. It's packed most nights. ✉ *1812 rue Ste-Catherine Est, The Village* ☎ *514/598–8243* 🌐 *www.studbar.com* [M] *Papineau.*

Renard

BARS | Big brother to Bistro Tendresse, this stylish bar with huge ceiling mirrors that make the space appear twice as large, gets packed in the evenings. Despite its prime location in the Gay Village, Renard appeals to a diverse clientele who love its inclusive, convivial atmosphere, festive happy hours, and signature seasonal cocktails. ✉ *1272 rue Ste-Catherine E., The Village* ☎ *514/903–0648* 🌐 *bar-renard.com* [M] *Beaudry.*

Montréal's Chinatown

Sandwiched between Downtown and Old Montréal, the center of the action in Montréal's Chinatown is at the intersection of rue Clark and rue de la Gauchetière, where part of the street is closed to traffic. On weekends, especially in summer, it's particularly busy, crowded with tourists as well as residents shopping in the Asian markets for fresh produce, meat and fish, and health supplements.

Chinese immigrants first came to Montréal in large numbers after 1880, following the construction of the transcontinental railroad, and there's been a steady influx of people from Asia and Southeast Asia—including the Vietnamese—since then. Now the city's Chinatown covers about an 18-block area between boulevard René-Lévesque and avenue Viger to the north and south, and near rue de Bleury and avenue Hôtel de Ville to the west and east.

The best way to enter Chinatown is through the ornate gates on boulevard St-Laurent—Place d'Armes is the closest métro station—then head for the hub at rue de la Gauchetière at the intersection of rue Clark. Chinatown has four gates or *paifangs*. The most prominent one is probably the South Gate at the corner of boulevard Saint-Laurent and avenue Viger.

Where to Eat

Maison Kam Fung. This family-run restaurant for three generations offers more than 60 dishes on rotation on any given day, making this *the* place for dim sum feasts. Waiters clatter up and down the aisles pushing a parade of trolleys bearing such treats as firm dumplings stuffed with pork and stir-fried squid and shrimp. **Known for:** Cantonese and Szechuan dishes; dim sum; Peking duck. ✉ *1111 rue St-Urbain, #M05, Chinatown* ☎ *514/878–2888* ⊕ *www.restaurantchinatownkimfung. com* Ⓜ *Place-d'Armes.*

Noodle Factory. The dining room is small and not much to look at, but no matter—the food here is the main attraction, and locals come in droves for the homemade noodles and dumplings. If you time your visit right, you might see the staff through the huge kitchen window working on the dough. **Known for:** homage noodles and dumplings; cash only; General Tao chicken. ✉ *1018 rue St-Urbain, Chinatown* ☎ *514/868–9738* ⊕ *www. restonoodlefactory.com* ▭ *No credit cards* ☾ *Closed Mon.* Ⓜ *Places-d'Armes.*

Qing Hua Dumplings. Groups of students and other budget-conscious connoisseurs of hearty chows crowd the tables at this hole-in-the-wall restaurant for traditional Chinese *jiaozi*, or soup dumplings, just like they make them in northeast China, with a price that's right: just C$12 for 15 dumplings. Demand is high for the lamb-and-coriander dumplings; the boiled shrimp, leek, and egg version; and the fried dumplings with chicken and curry. **Known for:** affordable eats; soup dumplings; cash only. ✉ *1019 boul. St-Laurent, Chinatown* ☎ *514/903–9887* ⊕ *qinghuadumpling.com* ▭ *No credit cards* Ⓜ *Place-d'Armes.*

DANCE CLUBS
Cabaret Mado
CABARET | Makeup, glitter, and glamorous costumes abound at this nightclub with drag-queen entertainment. Mado herself is a Québec celebrity (so much so that she was immortalized in wax at the now-defunct Grévin museum inside the Centre Eaton). During karaoke and improv evenings, even the clientele can get involved. ⊠ 1115 rue Ste-Catherine Est, The Village ☎ 514/525–7566 ⊕ www.mado.qc.ca Ⓜ Beaudry.

★ Sky
BARS | This massive complex houses a bar, restaurant, and dance club popular with both gay men and women. Weekly themed events include hip hop, cabaret, and a Western saloon. The best time to come is during the summer, as the pièce de résistance is the beach-like roof deck with city views and a pool (possibly the hottest destination in the Village). ⊠ 1474 rue Ste-Catherine Est, The Village ☎ 514/529–6969 ⊗ Closed Mon. Ⓜ Beaudry.

Stereo
DANCE CLUBS | Some of the most beautiful cross-dressers sashay on the huge dance floor of this converted theater. It's popular with both men and women, straight and gay, and often attracts hip-hop hordes near dawn on Friday and Saturday. Don't even bother arriving before 2 am. ⊠ 858 rue Ste-Catherine Est, The Village ☎ 514/658–2646 ⊕ www.stereonightclub.net ☞ Check Facebook for updated information Ⓜ Beaudry or Berri-UQAM.

◉ Shopping

The Gay Village is known for its excellent furniture stores as much as it is for its vibrant nightlife. Rue Atateken counts several antiques shops. Plenty of unique treasures are just waiting to be discovered, most being midcentury modern. The Beaudry métro station is your best bet.

ANTIQUES
★ Antiquités Curiosités
ANTIQUES & COLLECTIBLES | A sea of chairs, lamps, and other 1930s to 1980s furnishings and accessories awaits you at Antiquités Curiosités, but it's the beautifully restored Mad Men–era teak pieces that are the biggest draws. Retro curiosities like rotary phones also tickle the fancy. ⊠ 1769 rue Atateken, The Village ☎ 514/525–8772 ⊕ a-lantiquite-curiosite.business.site Ⓜ Beaudry.

★ Boutique Spoutnik
ANTIQUES & COLLECTIBLES | Mod, space-aged, kitsch—this boutique has it all. From Russell Spanner dressers to vintage needlepoint dog-portraits-turned-cushions to ceramic lamps in atomic designs circa 1950, Spoutnik is a veritable Aladdin's Cave of retro treasures. Owner Sylvie Rochon takes her work seriously, carefully curating her collection and adding her own artistic touches to vintage objects. Not surprisingly, her gorgeous boutique has been featured in several Québec publications. ⊠ 2120 rue Atateken, The Village ☎ 514/525–8478 ⊕ www.boutiquespoutnik.com ⊗ Closed Sun. and Mon. Ⓜ Sherbrooke.

Espace Vintage
ANTIQUES & COLLECTIBLES | This vintage shop specializing in pieces from the 1950s to the 1980s sells antique furniture, lamps, vases, wall clocks, and other household collectibles from the era. ⊠ 1691 rue Atateken, The Village ☎ 514/561–8491 ⊕ espace-vintage.business.site ⊗ Closed Mon. and Tues. Ⓜ Beaudry.

The Latin Quarter

The **Latin Quarter** (Quartier Latin), just south of the Plateau, has been a center of student life since the 18th century, when Université de Montréal students gave the area its name (courses were given in Latin), and today it continues

Montréal Jazz Fest offers a series of ticketed concerts that take place at a dozen or so Montréal venues as well as six stages of free diverse programming in the heart of Downtown Montréal.

to infuse the city with youthful energy. When night falls, its streets are filled with multinational hordes—young and not so young, rich and poor, established and still studying.

The Université de Québec à Montréal (UQAM) spreads across the district, along with theaters, bars, bookstores, and movie theaters. Some area businesses cater to a young clientele and their penchant for the loud and flashy, but the quarter is also home to some of the city's trendiest nightspots. In summer, the streets of the Latin Quarter are busy with summer festival events, such as the Jazz Fest in late June/early July and the Just for Laughs Festival in July.

GETTING HERE AND AROUND

The Latin Quarter is concentrated on boulevard de Maisonneuve and rue St-Denis. The busy Berri-UQAM métro station is the closest.

◉ Sights

Chapelle Notre-Dame-de-Lourdes

(*Our Lady of Lourdes Chapel*)

CHURCH | Artist and architect Napoléon Bourassa called his work here *l'oeuvre de mes amours,* or a labor of love—and it shows. He designed the little Byzantine-style building himself and set about decorating it with the exuberance of an eight-year-old making a Mother's Day card. He covered the walls with murals and encrusted the altar and pillars with gilt and ornamental carving. It's not Montréal's biggest monument to the Virgin Mary, but it's the most unabashedly sentimental. ✉ *430 rue Ste-Catherine Est, Latin Quarter* ☎ *514/845–8278* ⊕ *www. cndlm.org* ▦ *Free* Ⓜ *Berri-UQAM.*

Square St-Louis

PLAZA/SQUARE | This large, leafy square is an oasis in the middle of Montréal's urban jungle of noise, traffic jams, and construction. Entering the square, which is surrounded by colorful and ornate Second Empire-style graystone homes,

Ruelles Vertes

Almost as emblematic of Montréal as its winding staircases fronting duplexes and triplexes, are the city's back alleys, or *ruelles*, with their jumble of ramshackle tin and wood sheds, circular staircases, and rambunctious kids playing hockey. Originally intended for back door coal and heating oil deliveries, garbage pickups, and telephone line and electrical services, they fell out of use by the 1970s. However, in the last 15 or 20 years, many of these back alleys have been lovingly embellished with plants, flowers, murals, and other art work, thanks to a lot of hard work and dedication on the part of residents. In some cases, asphalt has given way to grassy paths, giving an even greater impression of being in the countryside. In French, these vibrant and imaginative green spaces are known as *Ruelles Vertes*. There are currently more than 400 officially designated *ruelles vertes*, representing about 43 miles in terms of distance, and making Montréal one of the world's top cities for green laneways.

Green laneways and *éco-quartiers* (eco-neighborhoods) can be found all over the city, but the prettiest tend to be located around the Plateau, the Latin Quarter, Mile End, Outremont, Parc Extension, Rosemont—La Petite-Patrie, and NDG. If you're in the Latin Quarter, be sure to visit the one between rues Drolet and Henri-Julien and av. des Pins and Square St-Louis or Ruelle Demers, between rues Henri-Julien and Hôtel-de-Ville. In the Plateau, try Ruelle Milton between rues Clark and Saint-Urbain. More information about the green laneway and *éco-quartier* citywide initiative can be found, in French only, at ⊕ www.eco-quartiers.org/les-eco-quartiers.

feels a little like entering a children's picture book, especially in winter, when the ground and the houses are blanketed with snow and the white stuff muffles all sound. In summer, locals spread out on the grass by the fountain or take a bistro table at the little gray kiosk (formerly a public toilet) café that serves sandwiches, salads, ice cream, and other cold refreshments—it even offers a book exchange. And for an unexpected bonus, some of the lanes to the side and rear of the square's beautiful houses have been lovingly "greened up" with street art and vegetation, thanks to a lot of hard work and effort on the part of the neighbors. ⊠ *Bordered by av. Laval and rue St-Denis between rue Sherbrooke Est and av. des Pins Est, Latin Quarter* Ⓜ *Sherbrooke.*

🍴 Restaurants

Institut de tourisme et d'hôtellerie du Québec

$$$ | CONTEMPORARY | Long held in disdain by Montréal food critics, the restaurant at the Institut de tourisme et d'hôtellerie du Québec (ITHQ) has upped its epicurean game. These days the restaurant's top-notch cuisine pays homage to Québec's terroir with enticingly presented dishes served in a contemporary yet elegant setting (think white table cloths, cloche plate covers, and impeccable service). **Known for:** evening menu wine pairings for additional C$49; wild mushroom risotto with mushroom foam; duck magret. Ⓢ *Average main: C$22* ⊠ *3535 rue St-Denis, Latin Quarter* ☎ *514/282–5155, 855/229–8189 select option 2 from the voice message menu* ⊕ *www.ithq.*

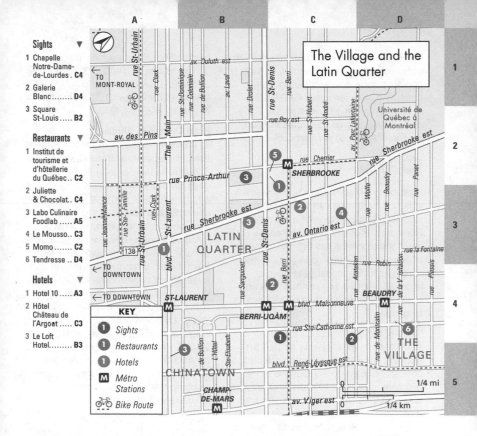

Sights ▼

1 Chapelle Notre-Dame-de-Lourdes . **C4**

2 Galerie Blanc........ **D4**

3 Square St-Louis..... **B2**

Restaurants ▼

1 Institut de tourisme et d'hôtellerie du Québec.. **C2**

2 Juliette & Chocolat.. **C4**

3 Labo Culinaire Foodlab..... **A5**

4 Le Mousso.. **C3**

5 Momo....... **C2**

6 Tendresse .. **D4**

Hotels ▼

1 Hotel 10..... **A3**

2 Hôtel Château de l'Argoat..... **C3**

3 Le Loft Hotel......... **B3**

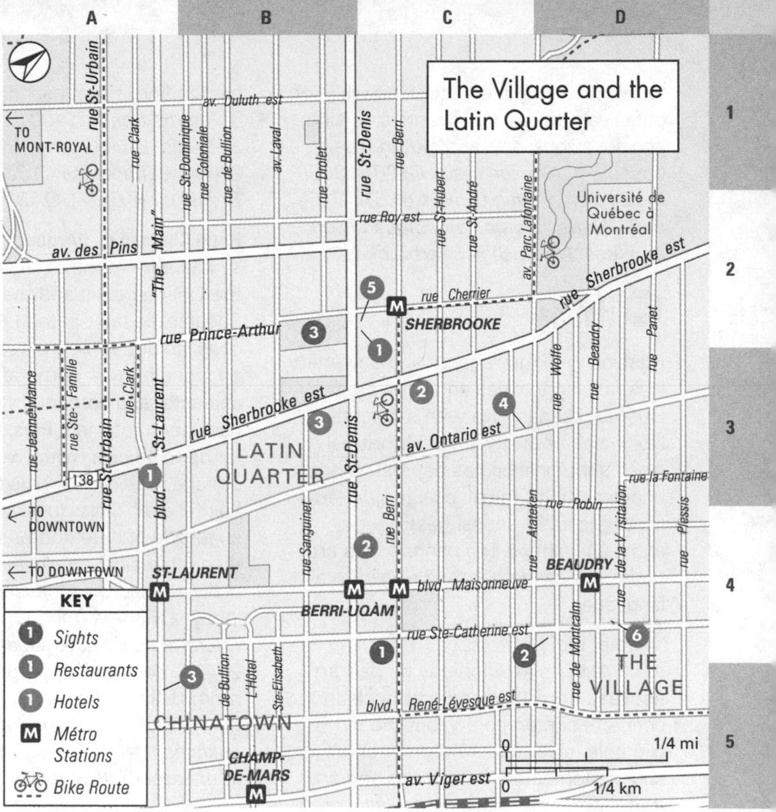

qc.ca/en/restaurants/restaurant-de-lithq ⏰ *Closed Sun. and Mon. No lunch Sat.* [M] *Sherbrooke.*

Juliette & Chocolat

$$ | **CONTEMPORARY** | **FAMILY** | This popular Québec restaurant/chocolate bar chain is the brainchild of Juliette Brun, a self-confessed chocoholic since she was a child. First opened in 2003 when Juliette was only 22, there are now nearly 30 locations across the province. **Known for:** brunches; all things chocolate; crepes and waffles. [$] *Average main: C$16* ✉ *1615 rue St-Denis, Latin Quarter* ☎ *514/287–3555* 🌐 *www.juliettetchocolat.com* [M] *Berri-UQAM.*

★ Labo Culinaire Foodlab

$$$ | **ECLECTIC** | Take cutting-edge experimental art and mix it up with food and what you get is Labo Culinaire Foodlab. Located on the third floor of Montréal's Society of Arts and Technology (SAT), Foodlab is an ongoing culinary experiment with rotating themes that range from destinations (i.e., Jerusalem) to dishes inspired by chefs (i.e., Julia Child's cookbook). **Known for:** natural wines; trendsetting chefs; lovely terrace. [$] *Average main: C$22* ✉ *Société des Arts Technologiques building, 1201 boul. St-Laurent, Latin Quarter* ☎ *514/844–2033 ext. 225* 🌐 *www.sat.qc.ca/en/restaurant-foodlab-labo-culinaire* ⏰ *Closed Sun.–Tues. No lunch* [M] *St-Laurent.*

★ Momo

$$ | **JAPANESE** | A darling of Montréal food critics since it opened in 2014, Canada's first vegan sushi restaurant is an innovative twist on the traditional sushi eatery. The setting, fresh from a renovation and redesign in early 2021, is replete with brick walls, natural woods and soothing

tones, including a few stunning walls of botanicals. **Known for:** inventive cuisine; eco-conscious; soy- and gluten-free options. $ *Average main: C$20* ✉ *3609 rue St-Denis, Latin Quarter* ☎ *514/825-6363* 🌐 *sushimomo.ca* 🕒 *Closed Mon. and Tues. No lunch* [M] *Sherbrooke.*

Hotels

Bustling with moviegoers and university kids rushing to cafés and libraries, the Quartier Latin is alive with expectation. No, it isn't as pretty as Old Montréal, since gentrification has been slow and uneven, but it's full of local flavor—artisanal chocolate shops, gastropubs, and hippie shops. The panhandlers are funny, not dangerous, and beg in two languages.

★ Hotel 10

$$ | **HOTEL** | Its exterior may be part art nouveau from 1914 and part brick-and-concrete contemporary, but the hip clientele, sleek and modern interiors, and contemporary furnishings and art throughout, make this centrally located hotel *all* cool. **Pros:** proximity to nightlife on the Main; rooms are bright and modern; on-site car-rental. **Cons:** trendy is not everyone's cup of tea; weekend party atmosphere can be alienating for some; drivers must choose between iffy street parking, C$28 parking underground or C$30 valet parking. $ *Rooms from: C$285* ✉ *10 rue Sherbrooke Ouest, Latin Quarter* ☎ *514/843-6000, 855/390-6787* 🌐 *www.hotel10Montréal.com* 🛏 *136 rooms* 🍴 *No Meals* [M] *St-Laurent.*

Le Loft Hotel

$$$$ | **HOTEL** | Inside an art deco landmark, this chic hotel has loftlike rooms with high ceilings and lots of space, as well as sleek IKEA kitchens, king beds, funky art, leather sectionals, and expansive views of the cityscape. **Pros:** superior soundproofing; 10-foot ceilings; good for longer stays. **Cons:** dark hallway—some complaints about lack of security; a bit hard to find; street parking is scarce. $ *Rooms from: C$400* ✉ *334 Terrasse St-Denis, Latin Quarter* ☎ *514/439-1818* 🌐 *www.lofthotel.ca* 🛏 *30 rooms* 🍴 *Free Breakfast* [M] *Berri-UQAM.*

Hôtel Château de l'Argoat

$ | **B&B/INN** | At the nexus of the Plateau, the Quartier Latin and the Quartier des Spectacles, the Château de l'Argoat consists of two Victorian-era cream-colored stone homes, some of whose original character and gorgeous wood features have been retained. **Pros:** free parking for up to 15 cars, with two EV chargers; storage for bicycles, plus tools; friendly, helpful staff. **Cons:** superior rooms and suite side of hotel rooms much nicer than other side; no elevator and not really wheelchair accessible; unappealing lobby. $ *Rooms from: C$150* ✉ *524 rue Sherbrooke E., Latin Quarter* ☎ *514/842-2046* 🌐 *hotel-chateau-argoat.com* 🛏 *25 rooms* 🍴 *Free Breakfast* ☞ *No breakfast during COVID, but guests may store food in kitchen's refrigerator if there isn't one in their room.* [M] *Sherbrooke.*

Nightlife

Though tiny, the Quartier Latin is known for its theaters, cafés, and student population. (One of the major French-language universities, UQAM, is located here.) Concentrated on lower rue St-Denis, there are copious bars if you're looking for some nightlife.

BARS AND LOUNGES

Le Cheval Blanc

BREWPUBS | Unchanged for four decades and showing its age, this hole-in-the-wall-with-atmosphere was Montréal's first artisanal brew pub. It's a lively pub, where music combines with the buzz of arty and political dialogue. There is outdoor seating and it often hosts art exhibits. ✉ *809 rue Ontario E, Latin Quarter* ☎ *514/522-0211* 🌐 *www.lechevalblanc.ca* [M] *Berri-UQAM.*

The projections on the wall at the pavilion of the Université du Québec à Montréal (UQÀM) change according to the different festivals happening there year-round.

Le Sainte-Elisabeth
PUBS | In between the Quartier des Spectacles (the local performing-arts district) and the Quartier Latin, this European pub is popular in part because of its friendly service and good selection of domestic and imported beers, as well as whiskey and cognac. With one of the city's most beautiful backyard terraces, this is a great place to enjoy the fall colors. ✉ *1412 rue Ste-Elisabeth, Downtown* ☎ *514/286–4302* ⊕ *www.facebook.com/ PubSteElisabeth* Ⓜ *Berri.*

🎟 Performing Arts

FILM
★ Grande Bibliothèque – Bibliothèque et Archives Nationales du Québec
FILM | Spread over five floors, Montréal's largest public library is a modern, light-filled, and spacious place to while away an afternoon perusing an impressive film collection. With 18 screening stations and new titles acquired monthly, they offer a wide range of genres to suit film buffs. ✉ *Grande Bibliothèque, 475 boul.*

de Maisonneuve Est, Latin Quarter ☎ *514/873–1100* ⊕ *www.banq.qc.ca* ⊘ *Closed Mon.* Ⓜ *Berri-UQAM.*

Cinémathèque Québécoise
FILM | With more than 35,000 films in its collection, and a ticket price of just C$10, Montréal's Museum of the Moving Image is the best place in the city to catch a foreign flick in its original language (with subtitles), in addition to Québécois and other Canadian productions. The museum also stocks scripts, television shows, and various new media, with a permanent display of vintage cinema equipment. ✉ *335 boul. de Maisonneuve Est, Latin Quarter* ☎ *514/842–9763* ⊕ *www.cinematheque. qc.ca* Ⓜ *Berri-UQAM.*

THEATER
Théâtre Ste-Catherine
THEATER | With approximately 100 comfortable seats, this independent alternative theater features comedy and improv shows most nights. On Sunday, there's a free improv workshop that's open to all, with participants later showing off what

they learned as that evening's entertainment. The theater also houses a café/bar as well as Le Nouveau International, a nonprofit organization run by a thriving community of artists working year-round to produce theater, comedy, improv, films, a bimonthly magazine, and sketch shows. ⊠ *264 rue Ste-Catherine Est, Latin Quarter* ☎ *514/284–3939* ⊕ *www.theatresaintecatherine.com* Ⓜ *Berri-UQAM.*

Théâtre St-Denis

CONCERTS | This is one of several theaters hosting events that are part of the Just for Laughs Festival, and touring Broadway productions, concerts, musicals, and dance performances can often be seen here. ⊠ *1594 rue St-Denis, Latin Quarter* ☎ *514/849–4211, 514/790–1111 tickets, 800/848–1594 tickets* ⊕ *www.theatrestdenis.com* Ⓜ *Berri-UQAM.*

The Plateau Mont-Royal and Mile End

Plateau Mont-Royal—or simply **the Plateau** as it's more commonly known—is still home to a strong Portuguese community, though gentrification of the Plateau has pushed up rents and driven many students, immigrant families, and single young graduates to neighborhoods farther north and east. As a result, much of the housing originally built for factory workers has been bought and renovated by professionals, artists, performers, and academics eager to find a place to live close to all the action. The Plateau is always bustling, even in the dead of winter, but on sunny summer weekends it's packed with Montréalers who come here to shop, dine, and people-watch.

Many of the older residences in the Plateau and the nearby neighborhoods have the wrought-iron balconies and twisting staircases that are typical of Montréal. The stairs and balconies, treacherous in winter, are often full of families and couples gossiping, picnicking, and partying come summer. If Montréalers tell you they spend the summer in Balconville, they mean they don't have the money or the time to leave town and won't get any farther than their balconies.

Blending almost seamlessly with the Plateau is **Mile End,** one of the hippest neighborhoods in town, the world's second "coolest" after Brooklyn's Williamsburg, according to HuffPo. This funky area starts buzzing the moment restaurants open for brunch. Historically home to Montréal's working-class Jewish community, it is now full of inexpensive, often excellent restaurants as well as shops selling handicrafts, design furniture, and secondhand clothes. Head east from Parc off streets like Bernard, St-Viateur, and Fairmount. By day it's a great place to take a stroll or sit on a café's *terrasse* (patio) to watch the passers-by—from artsy bohemians to Hasidic Jews.

GETTING HERE AND AROUND
The Plateau's most convenient métro station is Mont-Royal on the Orange Line. It's a large district, but relatively flat and easy to walk around. If you want to cover more ground without resorting to a taxi, there are several Bixi bicycle stands in the area, and plenty of bike lanes.

Mile End borders the Plateau and Outremont. To reach Mile End by public transit, take the métro's Orange Line to Laurier or Bus 55 from Place d'Armes métro station; get off at Fairmount or St. Viateur and walk west from there.

◉ Sights

★ **Boulevard St-Laurent**
STREET | A walk here is a walk through Montréal's multicultural history. The shops, restaurants, synagogues, and churches that line the 10-block stretch north of rue Sherbrooke reflect the various waves of immigrants that have called it home. Keep your eyes open and you'll see Jewish delis, Hungarian and

Slovenian charcuterie shops, Chinese grocery stores, Italian coffee bars, Greek restaurants, Vietnamese sandwich shops, and Peruvian snack bars. You'll also spot some of the city's trendiest restaurants, cafés, and galleries, as well as the dernier cri in skateboard fashion. The first immigrants to move into the area in the 1880s were Jews escaping pogroms in Eastern Europe. It was they who called the street "the Main," as in Main Street—a nickname that endures to this day. Even Francophone Montréalers sometimes call it "La Main." ⊠ *The Plateau* ⊕ *boulevardsaintlaurent.com/en* Ⓜ *St-Laurent, Sherbrooke, or Mont-Royal.*

Musée des Hospitalières de l'Hôtel-Dieu
HISTORY MUSEUM | The nuns of the Religieuses Hospitalières de St-Joseph ran Montréal's Hôpital Hôtel-Dieu for more than 300 years, until the province and the Université de Montréal took it over in the 1970s. The first sisters—girls of good families caught up in the religious fervor of the age—came to New France with Jeanne Mance in the mid-1600s to look after the poor, the sick, and the dying. The order's museum—tucked away in a corner of the hospital the nuns built but no longer run—captures the spirit of that age with a series of meticulously bilingual exhibits. Just reading the excerpts from the letters and diaries of those young women helps you to understand the zeal that drove them to abandon the comforts of home for the hardships of the colonies. The museum also traces the history of medicine and nursing in Montréal. ∎TIP➜ **Guided tours are available for groups of 10 or more by reservation. Hours vary depending on the season.** ⊠ *201 av. des Pins Ouest, The Plateau* ☎ *514/849–2919* ⊕ *www.museedeshospitalieres.qc.ca* ⊠ *C$10 (cash only)* ⊗ *Closed Mon., 12 pm–1pm Tues.–Sun., and Christmas and Easter* Ⓜ *Sherbrooke, then Bus 144; or Place-des-Arts, then Bus 129 or 80.*

Parc Lafontaine
CITY PARK | You could say that Parc Lafontaine is a microcosm of Montréal: the eastern half is French, with paths, gardens, and lawns laid out in geometric shapes; the western half is English, with meandering paths and irregularly shaped ponds that follow the natural contours of the land. In summer, you can take advantage of bowling greens, tennis courts, an open-air theater (Théâtre de Verdure), where there are free events, and two artificial lakes with paddleboats. In winter, one lake becomes a large skating rink. The park is named for Sir Louis-Hippolyte Lafontaine (1807–1864), a pioneer of responsible government in Canada. His statue graces a plot on the park's southwestern edge. ∎TIP➜ **Théâtre de Verdure is temporarily closed while it undergoes reconstruction/redevelopment.** ⊠ *3933 av. Parc Lafontaine, The Plateau* ☎ *514/872–6381* Ⓜ *Sherbrooke or Mont-Royal.*

🍴 Restaurants

Peppered with bistros and cafés, the Plateau has a bohemian edge that can't be found anywhere else in the city. Chef-owned eateries favor market cuisine served in a decor of brick walls and hardwood floors. Noisy French-style bistros, like L'Express, are local institutions, as are cafés populated by poets and academics with laptops. There's vegan haute cuisine, and Thai, along with sushi and stubborn little bakeries that refuse to mechanize.

As Montréal's equivalent of Brooklyn and Shoreditch, Mile End caters mostly to hip creatives. Between hipster-run cafés and locally sourced revisited British gastropubs, this neighborhood sets the trends and constantly pushes the limits of culinary experimentation.

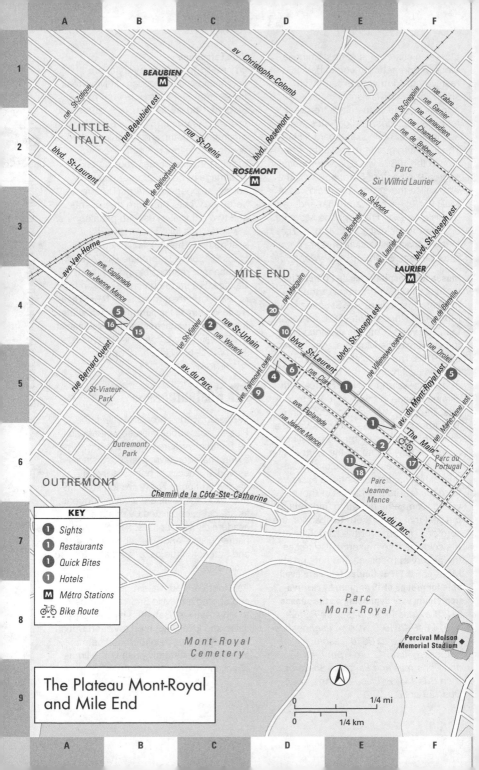

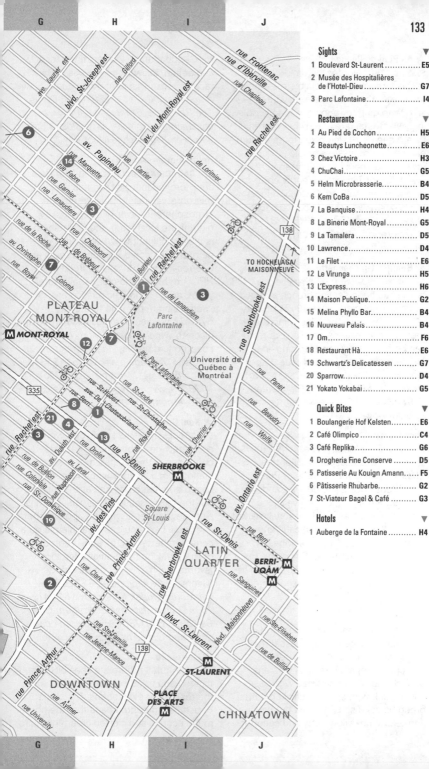

★ Au Pied de Cochon

$$$$ | BISTRO | Not for the timid, the menu at this famous 20-year-old bistro—one of the late Anthony Bourdain's favorites—is an ode to gluttony and nose-to-tail cooking. Wild restaurateur and chef Martin Picard serves pickled bison tongue, guinea hen liver mousse, a whole pig's head for two, and pork hocks braised in maple syrup. **Known for:** local celebrity chef; foie gras poutine; Au Pied de Cochon food truck. Ⓢ *Average main: C$36* ⊠ *536 av. Duluth Est, The Plateau* ☎ *514/281–1114* ⊕ *www.aupieddecochon.ca* ☾ *Closed Mon. and Tues. No lunch* Ⓜ *Mont-Royal.*

★ Beautys Luncheonette

$$ | DINER | FAMILY | The Schkolnick family has been serving brunch at this Montréal landmark since 1942 and very little here has changed, including the menu. On weekends, the line out front can be daunting. **Known for:** long lines on the weekend; historic venue; bagel with lox. Ⓢ *Average main: C$15* ⊠ *93 av. du Mont-Royal Ouest, The Plateau* ☎ *514/849–8883* ⊕ *www.beautys.ca* Ⓜ *Mont-Royal.*

Chez Victoire

$$$ | MODERN FRENCH | A beacon of the French cultural diaspora in Montréal, Chez Victoire is the epitome of Plateau-Mont-Royal's joie de vivre and warmth. Fittingly, the creative menu features French-inspired seasonal market cuisine. **Known for:** roasted cauliflower and truffles dish; organic wines; homemade charcuterie. Ⓢ *Average main: C$22* ⊠ *1453 av. du Mont-Royal Est, The Plateau* ☎ *514/521–6789* ⊕ *chezvictoire. com* ☾ *No lunch* Ⓜ *Mont-Royal.*

ChuChai

$$$ | THAI | Vegans, vegetarians, and meat eaters alike love this casual Thai restaurant where no meat is served. The chefs prepare meatless versions of such classics as calamari with basil, crispy duck with spinach, chicken with green beans, fish with three hot sauces, and beef with yellow curry and coconut milk—substituting the real thing for soy and seitan. **Known for:** "Thaïpas" (Thai tapas); vegan Thai fare; mock duck. Ⓢ *Average main: C$21* ⊠ *4088 rue St-Denis, The Plateau* ☎ *514/843–4194* ⊕ *www. chuchaimontMontréal.ca* ☾ *Closed Sun. and Mon. No lunch* Ⓜ *Mont-Royal.*

Helm Microbrasserie

$$ | CANADIAN | Few places in Montréal are more Québécois than this lively microbrewery/gastropub, where the atmosphere is electrifying on hockey night if the local team, the Canadiens, is playing. With its own set of brews named after iconic Mile End streets and a terroir-inspired, locally sourced menu, HELM (which stands for barley, water, yeast, and malt in French) is in and of itself a vibrant homage to the city's dynamic beer culture. **Known for:** great place to watch hockey; Montréal-inspired micro brews; locally sourced meals. Ⓢ *Average main: C$15* ⊠ *273 rue Bernard Ouest, Mile End* ☎ *514/276– 0473* ⊕ *www.helmmicrobrasserie.ca* Ⓜ *Rosemont.*

★ Kem CoBa

$ | ICE CREAM | FAMILY | Only one word accurately describes the all-natural goodness at this ice cream and sorbet stand: *yum.* Flavors change frequently based on what chefs find at the market, but the lightly salted butter ice cream is a staple; partner it with the apple sorbet and you'll have yourself an apple pie on a cone. Or, better yet, give the "soft serve of the week" a taste. **Known for:** local favorite; cash only; eccentric soft-serve flavors. Ⓢ *Average main: C$5* ⊠ *60 av. Fairmount Ouest, Mile End* ☎ *514/419– 1699* ⊕ *www.facebook.com/Kem-Co-Ba-158923114173515* ⊟ *No credit cards* ☾ *Closed Oct.–Apr.* Ⓜ *Laurier.*

★ Lawrence

$$$ | CANADIAN | There are lines outside this hip and trendy establishment before the restaurant even opens. The chef's British background means that the homemade scones and clotted cream here are

required eating. **Known for:** butcher shop, Boucherie Lawrence; British-inspired fare; arctic char and sea urchin. [$] *Average main: C$22* ✉ *9 ave. Fairmount E., Mile End* ☎ *514/796–5686* 🌐 *lawrence-mtl.com* 🕒 *Closed Sun.–Tues. No lunch* [M] *Laurier.*

★ La Banquise

$ | **CANADIAN** | **FAMILY** | Québec is notorious for poutine—French fries topped with cheese curds and gravy—and La Banquise has been the place for an authentic experience since 1968 with an extensive menu featuring 31 varieties. Neophytes might want to stick with La Classique, but mouthwatering novelties like La Taquise (guacamole, sour cream, tomatoes), L'Obélix (smoked meat), La Veggie Reggie (pickles, tomatoes, creamy coleslaw, and Banquise sauce), and La Véganomane (vegan sauce and cheese) are quite alluring. **Known for:** smoked-meat poutine; open 24 hours; cash only. [$] *Average main: C$12* ✉ *994 rue Rachel Est, The Plateau* ☎ *514/525–2415* 🌐 *www.labanquise.com* 💳 *No credit cards* [M] *Mont-Royal.*

★ L'Express

$$$ | **FRENCH** | **FAMILY** | This iconic Montréal bistro hasn't changed much since its opening in 1980, and it's just as well—regulars would throw a fit if it did. Quintessential French fare is fairly priced and appetizing, outstanding even, with dishes like steak tartare with fries, salmon with sorrel, and calf's liver with tarragon. **Known for:** late-night dining; steak tartare; lively atmosphere. [$] *Average main: C$25* ✉ *3927 rue St-Denis, The Plateau* ☎ *514/845–5333* 🌐 *restaurantlexpress.com* [M] *Sherbrooke.*

Le Filet

$$$$ | **MODERN CANADIAN** | A study in contrasts, Le Filet has a discreet blink-and-you'll-miss-it facade with a glitzy black-and-gold interior and a hot-spot buzz. Though it's been around a while, there is no mixed messaging when it comes to the exacting presentation and superb food and wine. **Known for:** garnished oysters; voted a top three seafood restaurant in city by ThreeBestRated Canada; expert sommeliers. [$] *Average main: C$35* ✉ *219 av. Mont-Royal Ouest, The Plateau* ☎ *514/360–6060* 🌐 *lefilet.ca* 🕒 *Closed Sun. and Mon.* [M] *Mont-Royal.*

La Tamalera

$$ | **MEXICAN** | **FAMILY** | The kitschy-cool décor includes a display of religious icons as well as vibrantly colorful furniture, while the menu is haute Mexican street cuisine at its best. The food here is simple and the menu small, but everything is fresh and delicious. **Known for:** vibrant decor; corn-based homemade tacos; Mexican-inspired brunch. [$] *Average main: C$12* ✉ *226 av. Fairmount Ouest, Mile End* ☎ *438/381–5034* 🌐 *www.latamaleraMontréal.com* 💳 *No credit cards* 🕒 *Closed Mon. No dinner weekends* [M] *Laurier.*

★ Le Virunga

$$$$ | **AFRICAN** | A mother-daughter team helm this delightfully cozy pan-African Québécois fusion restaurant in Le Plateau. Innovative and well executed dishes like cassava couscous with okra and goat stew celebrate local produce and sub-Saharan flavors for an experience you won't soon forget. **Known for:** homey, high-end cooking in an intimate setting; goat stew; excellent cocktails and South African wine. [$] *Average main: C$35* ✉ *851 rue Rachel E., The Plateau* ☎ *514/504–8642* 🌐 *www.levirungarestaurant.ca* 🕒 *Closed Sun.–Tues. No lunch* [M] *Mont-Royal.*

Maison Publique

$$$$ | **CANADIAN** | Local celebrity chef Derek Dammann teamed up with famed British chef Jamie Oliver to open this pub-style restaurant that perfectly blends Canadian and British traditions. The interior is dark and cozy; the handwritten menu changes frequently based on what's in season. **Known for:** celebrity chef owners; Welsh rarebit; dishes intended for sharing. [$] *Average main:*

C$37 ✉ *4720 rue Marquette, The Plateau* ☎ *514/507–0555* 🌐 *maisonpublique.com* 🕓 *Closed Mon. and Tues.* [M] *Laurier.*

Melina Phyllo Bar
$ | **GREEK** | **FAMILY** | It may be in the heart of trendy Mile End, but this "phyllo bar" looks like it was transported directly from Athens, with food arriving on checkered cobalt-blue wax paper. The spanakopita, with a perfect crunchy exterior, makes for an excellent lunch on the go, as does the Melina sandwich, with its spicy feta spread, kalamata hummus, cucumbers, tomatoes, and graviera. **Known for:** take-out Greek; bougatsa pastry; vegan and vegetarian eats. [$] *Average main: C$7* ✉ *5733 av. du Parc, Mile End* ☎ *514/270–1675* 💳 *No credit cards* [M] *Parc.*

Nouveau Palais
$$ | **CANADIAN** | **FAMILY** | Hipsters head to this laid-back '70s diner for one thing: delicious, classic greasy spoon dishes with a modern twist (a close second is the décor; think wood paneling and vinyl seats). The Palace Hamburger (Palais Burger) is gaining a reputation among Montréalers as one of the best in the city, and the sweet-potato pie also has fans. **Known for:** 1970s vibe; fish and chips; house burger (meat and veggie versions). [$] *Average main: C$16* ✉ *281 rue Bernard Ouest, Mile End* ☎ *514/273–1180* 🌐 *www.nouveaupalais.com* 🕓 *Closed Mon. No lunch* [M] *Rosemont.*

Restaurant Hà
$$$ | **VIETNAMESE** | Located at the foot of Mount Royal, this unassuming but contemporary local hot spot serves some of the best Vietnamese fare in the city on one of the most enjoyable patios in Montréal. "Simple yet edgy" are the operative words to describe the menu here. Steamed buns attractively blackened with squid ink, ginger-carrot crispy tofu, and grilled chicken à la citronelle with napa cabbage are among the surprising novelties. **Known for:** squid ink steamed buns; authentic Vietnamese food; lovely terrace. [$] *Average main: C$22* ✉ *243 av. du Mont-Royal Ouest, The Plateau* ☎ *514/848–0336* 🌐 *www.restaurantha.com* 🕓 *Closed Mon.–Wed. No lunch* [M] *Mont-Royal.*

★ Schwartz's Delicatessen
$$ | **JEWISH DELI** | **FAMILY** | You simply haven't really eaten in Montréal if you haven't eaten at Schwartz's, Canada's oldest deli. This Montréal classic has zero frills décor-wise, yet crowds have been coming since 1928 for a thick and legendary smoked-meat sandwich on rye with mustard. **Known for:** long wait for a table; local institution; sandwiches with smoked meat marinated in herbs and spices. [$] *Average main: C$14* ✉ *3895 boul. St-Laurent, The Plateau* ☎ *514/842–4813* 🌐 *www.schwartzsdeli.com* [M] *Sherbrooke.*

Sparrow
$$ | **MODERN BRITISH** | Part cocktail bar, part British restaurant, this in-vogue spot has welcoming aviary décor motifs. Diners can get a traditional English breakfast in the morning, followed by a Sunday roast and a good old-fashioned basil gimlet. **Known for:** great cocktails; organic, hormone-free burgers; brunch. [$] *Average main: C$15* ✉ *5322 boul. St-Laurent, Mile End* ☎ *514/507–1642* 🌐 *www.lesparrowbar.com* [M] *Laurier.*

Yokato Yokabai
$$ | **JAPANESE** | Frequently cited as the best ramen house in Montréal bar none, Yokato Yokabai is indeed a discreet restaurant that deserves to be visited by all noodle lovers—especially when temperatures drop below freezing point here. The décor—dark-wood paneling and minimal knickknacks—immediately transports diners to a Japanese hole-in-the-wall. **Known for:** long waits; Tonkotsu ramen; atmospheric décor. [$] *Average main: C$15* ✉ *4185 Drolet, The Plateau* ☎ *514/282–9991* 🌐 *www.yoka.ca* [M] *Mont-Royal.*

Coffee and Quick Bites

Boulangerie Hof Kelsten

$ | **BAKERY** | The mastermind behind this photogenic bakery had been making bread for Montréal's best restaurants for years before he decided to open up his own place. His own shop is a favorite with locals, who line up every weekend for fresh baguettes. **Known for:** panettone; chocolate babka; Jewish cuisine. [$] *Average main: C$10* ✉ *4524 boul. St-Laurent, The Plateau* ☎ *514/649–7991* 🌐 *hofkelsten.com* [M] *Mont-Royal.*

★ **Café Olimpico**

$ | **CAFÉ** | **FAMILY** | Ranked one of the world's best cafés by the U.K.'s *Telegraph*, this unpretentious 1970s-style café is popular with locals for Italian pastries like cannoli and pistachio bomboloni and, of course, great espresso made from a secret blend of six different coffee beans. It's also a good place to get a feel for authentic Montréal. **Known for:** local spot; gourmet coffee; sunny patio. [$] *Average main: C$5* ✉ *124 rue St-Viateur Ouest, Mile End* ☎ *514/495–0746* 🌐 *www.cafeolimpico.com* [M] *Rosemont.*

Café Replika

$ | **TURKISH** | **FAMILY** | Students, freelancers, and local hipsters flock to this understated Turkish café for two reasons: the gourmet coffee and the food. Between the Nutella and sea salt cookie, and the feta and sausage omelet, and the boreks (a traditional flaky pastry sprinkled with sesame seeds), it's hard to pick just one thing off Replika's menu. **Known for:** Turkish fare; friendly owners; latte art. [$] *Average main: C$7* ✉ *252 rue Rachel Est, The Plateau* ☎ *514/903–4384* 🌐 *www.cafereplika.com* [M] *Mont-Royal.*

Pâtisserie Au Kouign Amann

$ | **BAKERY** | **FAMILY** | The compact bakery serves some of the best croissants in Montréal, but the specialty here is the eponymous *kouign amann*, a multilayered butter and sugar cake originally from Brittany. The aroma of freshly baked bread is alluring to say the least and the passion for pastries is evident and sometimes demonstrated by perfectionist owner Breton Nicolas Henri. **Known for:** tiny gem; kouign amman; perfect croissants. [$] *Average main: C$7* ✉ *316 av. du Mont Royal Est, The Plateau* ☎ *514/845–8813* 🌐 *aukouingamann.com* 💳 *No credit cards* ⏲ *Closed Sun. and Mon.* [M] *Mont-Royal.*

★ **Pâtisserie Rhubarbe**

$ | **BAKERY** | **FAMILY** | This small and tastefully decorated bakery is, simply put, a Montréal treasure. Locals come from all over the city to pick up delicious desserts like lemon tarts and Paris-Brest that taste as good as they look. **Known for:** long wait for a table; afternoon tea; Paris-Brest. [$] *Average main: C$8* ✉ *1479 av. Laurier Est, The Plateau* ☎ *514/316–2935* 🌐 *www.patisserierhubarbe.com* ⏲ *Closed Mon.–Wed.* [M] *Laurier.*

★ **St-Viateur Bagel & Café**

$ | **CAFÉ** | **FAMILY** | Even New Yorkers have been known to (collective gasp!) prefer Montréal's light and crispy bagel to its bulkier Manhattan cousin, due to the dough of the Montréal version being boiled in honey-sweetened water before baking in a wood-burning oven. St-Viateur Bagel & Café is a great place to get them, especially with smoked salmon. **Known for:** local favorite; delicious bagels; classic and creative options. [$] *Average main: C$10* ✉ *1127 av. Mont-Royal Est, The Plateau* ☎ *514/528–6361* 🌐 *www.stviateurbagel.com* [M] *Laurier.*

Hotels

Full of artists and academics, the Plateau and Mile End are bustling neighborhoods with a high density of bistros, brewpubs, martini bars, bakeries, designer boutiques, and parks. This is no place for quiet contemplation. In summer, join the crowds at outdoor markets and street fairs. There aren't many places to stay, but they include some lovely auberges and B&Bs.

Auberge de la Fontaine
$$ | **B&B/INN** | **FAMILY** | Built out of two adjoining houses with a signature yellow front door, lacquered-barn-board facade, and welcoming flower boxes, this turn-of-the-20th-century residence overlooks Parc Lafontaine and one of the city's major bicycle trails. **Pros:** some rooms have private balconies with park views; near bars and restaurants; most rooms have whirlpool baths. **Cons:** parking can be difficult; some rooms are unrenovated and quite small; lobby is serviceable, but lacking glamour. [$] *Rooms from: C$235* ✉ *1301 rue Rachel Est, The Plateau* ☎ *514/597–0166, 800/597–0597* 🌐 *www.aubergedelafontaine.com* 🛏 *21 rooms* 🍴 *Free Breakfast* [M] *Mont-Royal.*

🍸 Nightlife

The restaurants and bars along St-Denis and Mont-Royal are popular with everyone from rambunctious students to serious food-lovers. Boulevard St-Laurent ("The Main"), especially between rue Sherbrooke and avenue des Pins, is home to the see-and-be-seen crowd, with merrymakers spilling out of bars and clubs at all hours of the night.

Mile End has become well-known for inspired cuisine, affordable lounges, and relaxed bars, and is slowly becoming a second village to the hipster gay crowd, who tend to forgo the main Village.

BARS AND LOUNGES

Bar Waverly
BARS | Named for the street that epitomizes the Mile End, this neighborhood bar has a warm staff, friendly atmosphere, and a great selection of scotch. Owners Richard Holder and Olivier Farley have been in the business for years, and it shows. Nightly DJs provide an edgier vibe, while huge floor-to-ceiling windows make it perfect for people-watching. ✉ *5550 boul. St-Laurent, Mile End* ☎ *514/903–1121* 🌐 *www.barwaverly.com* 🕒 *Closed Sun.–Tues.* [M] *Laurier.*

★ Bily Kun
BARS | This Czech-themed bar is a favorite hangout of Plateau locals. There's live jazz during the cocktail hour and a DJ or classical performances later in the evening. Try an absinthe-laced apple cocktail from the extensive alcohol menu as you nibble on a few tapas. Bily Kun gets packed, though the high ceilings help alleviate the feeling of claustrophobia. ✉ *354 av. du Mont-Royal Est, The Plateau* ☎ *514/845–5392* 🌐 *www.bilykun.com* [M] *Mont-Royal.*

Dieu du Ciel!
BREWPUBS | A chalkboard scribbled with rotating craft beers and a convivial atmosphere set the scene for this neighborhood-favorite brewpub. Small bites such as flatbreads can be ordered to accompany your IPAs and ales. ✉ *29 Laurier Ave. W, Mile End* ☎ *514/490–9555* 🌐 *dieuduciel.com/en.*

Le Bowhead
PUBS | Opened in 2019, this is Montréal's first meat-free pub. In addition to plant-based comfort foods, Le Bowhead sources beers, wines, and spirits that are 100% vegan, meaning that no animal-based fining agents have been used in the filtration process. The decor is fuss-free, with white walls and marine blue faux wood-paneling, utilitarian tables, and diner-style chairs. The only ornamentation is a series of small, old-fashioned copper diving helmets on one wall—a sort of nautical theme, sans fish. The menu features old-school pub fare like sliders, popcorn "chicken," Frito pie, and even ANML fries and po' boy sandwiches. Neither the meatless dishes nor menu descriptions give away that it's a vegan pub; the only telltale sign of this fact is the small print in the bottom righthand corner of the menu stating that all ingredients are "100% plant-based." ✉ *3723 boul. St-Laurent, The Plateau* ☎ *514/977–0838* 🌐 *bowheadpub.com* 🕒 *Closed Sun. and Mon.* [M] *St-Laurent.*

Art in the Métro

Montréal was ahead of the curve in requiring all construction in the métro system to include an art component, resulting in such dramatic works as Frédéric Back's mural of the history of music in Place des Arts and the swirling stained-glass windows by Marcelle Ferron in Champs-de-Mars. The art nouveau entrance to the Square-Victoria station, a gift from the city of Paris, is the only original piece of Hector Guimard's architectural-design work outside the City of Light.

Operating since 1966, the métro is among the most architecturally distinctive subway systems in the world, with each of its 65 stations individually designed and decorated.

The newer stations along the Blue Line are all worth a visit as well, particularly Outremont, with a glass-block design from 1988. Even Place-d'Armes, one of the least visually remarkable stations in the system, includes a treasure: look for the small exhibit of archaeological artifacts representing each of Montréal's four historical eras (aboriginal, French, English, and multicultural).

La Buvette chez Simone

WINE BARS | Lively but not obnoxious, this easygoing wine bar is a great place to visit with friends. Arrive early (it opens at 4 pm but the kitchen only gets going at 5 pm), because it's always busy and it doesn't take reservations. Many wines are available by the glass, in 2- and 4-ounce pours, with an emphasis on French varietals. Dress is casual, though the after-work crowd ups the glam factor. ⊠ 4869 av. du Parc, Mile End ☎ 514/750–6577 ⊕ www.buvettechezsimone.com Ⓜ Laurier or Mont-Royal.

★ Le Majestique

WINE BARS | With its unappealing store-front, bric-à-brac décor, retro knick-knacks, and sceney vibes, Majestique is a quirky wine bar that's open until the wee hours with an excellent selection of small plates. The snazzy surroundings only add to the charm of this fine-dining-meets-casual-savoir-faire; the salmon confit, the quinoa croquette, and rotating choice of fresh oysters are musts. Whatever you do, though, do not skimp on the legendary foot-long piglet hotdog. It's absolutely worth it. Note that minors are not allowed on the premises. ⊠ 4105 boul. St-Laurent, The Plateau ☎ 514/439–1850 ⊕ www.restobarmajestique.com ⊗ Closed Sun. ☞ Check Facebook for updated information Ⓜ Mont-Royal.

★ Reservoir

BREWPUBS | It's all about the beer at this friendly restaurant and bar, where it's all brewed right on the premises. Packed almost every night of the week, this bar has everything from India pale ales to German-inspired wheat beers. The upstairs patio is the ideal spot for watching locals stroll along the quaint cobblestone avenue. ⊠ 9 av. Duluth Est, The Plateau ☎ 514/849–7779 ⊕ reservoirbrasseur.com ⊗ Closed Mon. Ⓜ Sherbrooke.

Suwu

BARS | This self-described "hip hop eatery" and neighborhood bar invites you to relax and pull up a chair or cozy couch. Simple but intense dishes like truffle-oil popcorn and a grilled cheese mac-and-cheese sandwich (yes, you read that right) are paired with powerful cocktails (try the signature Wu-Tang) to help make this one of the hottest destinations on The Main—without any of the usual pretension. Open nightly from 5 to 3. They also serve brunch on weekends. ✉ *3581 boul. St-Laurent, The Plateau* ☎ *514/564–5074* ⊕ *www.suwuMontréal. com* Ⓜ *St-Laurent.*

Whisky Café
BARS | Known for its happy hour, this bar, café, and cigar lounge is elegant but unpretentious—it's the perfect spot for a romantic rendezvous. The selection of more than 150 varieties of scotch, plus an impressive choice of wines, champagnes, and ports, leaves most everyone's thirst quenched. ✉ *5800 boul. St-Laurent, Mile End* ☎ *514/278–2646* ⊕ *www.whiskycafe.com* Ⓜ *Rosemont.*

LIVE MUSIC
Barfly
LIVE MUSIC | Fans of blues, punk, country, and bluegrass jam into this tiny hole-in-the-wall, which has some of the cheapest drink prices on St-Laurent. A very popular hangout for locals, Barfly is arguably the premier dive bar in the city. ✉ *4062A boul. St-Laurent, The Plateau* ☎ *514/284–6665* Ⓜ *Sherbrooke or St-Laurent.*

Casa del Popolo
LIVE MUSIC | One of the city's treasured venues for indie rock, jazz, reggae, blues, folk, and hip-hop, this neighborhood bar is ideal for discovering up-and-coming local acts or forgotten international giants still touring. While you enjoy the music, take a look at the original art and sample some of the tasty vegetarian food. ✉ *4873 boul. St-Laurent, The Plateau* ☎ *514/284–3804 café, 514/284–0122 office* ⊕ *www.casadelpopolo.com* Ⓜ *Mont-Royal.*

🎭 Performing Arts

THEATER
Mainline Theatre
THEATER | Operated by the same people who present the Montréal Fringe Festival every summer, the Mainline opened in 2006 to serve the city's burgeoning

Anglo theater community and has been going strong ever since. ✉ *3997 boul. St-Laurent, The Plateau* ☎ *514/849–3378* ⊕ *www.mainlinetheatre.ca* Ⓜ *St-Laurent or Mont-Royal.*

Théâtre du Rideau Vert
THEATER | The oldest professional French theater company in North America, Théâtre du Rideau Vert has been winning over audiences with its contemporary productions since 1948. Many popular francophone actors got their big break here. ✉ *4664 rue St-Denis, The Plateau* ☎ *514/844–1793* ⊕ *www.rideauvert.qc.ca* Ⓜ *Mont-Royal.*

🛍 Shopping

The Plateau has long been recognized as one of North America's hippest neighborhoods, and though trends typically come and go, its certain cachet endures. Rue St-Denis is home to both independent boutiques and chain stores selling local and international fashion, as well as jewelry stores, all at prices for every budget. Boulevard St-Laurent and avenue Mont-Royal both offer opportunities for vintage shopping, with St-Laurent also known for contemporary furniture and décor stores.

Just north of the Plateau, the Mile End offers an eclectic mix of artsy boutiques and shops stocked with up-and-coming Montréal designers.

BOOKS AND STATIONERY
★ **S.W. Welch Bookseller**
BOOKS | Everyone from casual readers to serious book collectors will find something at this Mile End gem, where the stacks of literature are complemented by a vast selection of books on philosophy, science, and religion. The owner and his employees are friendly and well-read. ✉ *225 rue St-Viateur Ouest, Mile End* ☎ *514/848–9358* ⊙ *Closed Mon. and Tues.* Ⓜ *Laurier.*

CLOTHING

atelier b

WOMEN'S CLOTHING | Set in an old button factory, this retro, multipurpose space (boutique, design/sewing workshop, and sewing school) makes and sells simple and sustainable clothing for women, men, and children, as well as toys, underwear, and homewares. Having embraced the concept of a circular economy, many of their products, such as pencil cases and bags, are made from recycled scraps of organic cotton and linen, sometimes even turning these into pulp to make lamp shades. atelier b also produces made to order pieces and does repairs and alterations. ⊠ *5758 boul. St-Laurent, Mile End* ☎ *514/769–6094* ⊕ *atelier-b.ca* Ⓜ *Rosemont.*

Bodybag by Jude

WOMEN'S CLOTHING | When Nicole Kidman wore one of this designer's zip denim dresses, Judith Desjardins's star was set. The designer has a penchant for all things British, so look for cheeky checks and plaids. ⊠ *17 rue Bernard Ouest, Mile End* ☎ *514/274–5242* ⊕ *www.bodybagby-jude.com* Ⓜ *Rosemont.*

Boutique 1861

WOMEN'S CLOTHING | This boutique stocks romantic, lacy, and affordable finds from local and international designers, including Arti Gogna and Champagne & Strawberry. With everything white—hardwood floors, couches, and armoires—the boudoir vibe is irresistible. Just look for the pink-and-black cameo signage. The name comes from the smaller branch at 1861 rue Ste-Catherine. ⊠ *3670 boul. St-Laurent, The Plateau* ☎ *514/670–6110* ⊕ *www.1861.ca.*

Citizen Vintage

SECOND-HAND | If you're a believer in buying stylish upcycled clothing, then this Mile End vintage boutique has your name on it. Bright, spacious, and carefully curated by the owners (who scour North America for their finds), this store makes shopping easy, as everything is arranged by color. The stock changes almost daily, so don't feel you can only visit once. ■ **TIP→ There's a second location in the Plateau at 4059 boul. Saint-Laurent** ⊠ *5330 boul. St-Laurent, Mile End* ☎ *514/439–2774* ⊕ *www.citizenvintage. com* Ⓜ *Laurier.*

★ Deuxième Peau

LINGERIE | Tucked away in a basement, the tiny "Second Skin" sells a fine assortment of French lingerie. It's hard to miss the curvy mannequins in their ground-floor window, adorned in the likes of Aubade, Chantelle, and Prima Donna. While you're feeling brave and beautiful, kill two birds with one stone and try on a bathing suit from the shop's tasteful collection of French, Spanish, and Australian designers. ⊠ *4457 rue St-Denis, The Plateau* ☎ *514/842–0811* Ⓜ *Mont-Royal.*

★ Éditions de Robes

WOMEN'S CLOTHING | Owner Julie Pesant has stocked her boutique with top-quality Montréal-made-and-designed dresses in a multitude of styles that can easily be dressed up or down with a simple change of accessories. From peplums to lace, satin to jersey, long and short, they're all here. ⊠ *5334 boul. Saint-Laurent, Mile End* ☎ *514/271–7676* ⊕ *www. editionsderobes.com* ☽ *Closed Sun. and Mon.* Ⓜ *St-Laurent, then bus 55.*

Général 54

WOMEN'S CLOTHING | The Mile End neighborhood earned its reputation for all things cool with funky shops like this one. The natural-hue clothes—most by local designers—are feminine and elegant, and owner Jennifer Glasgow sells her eponymous clothing line here. The location on The Main is warm and welcoming, with exposed brick and intricately patterned floors. ⊠ *5145 boul. St-Laurent, Mile End* ☎ *514/271–2129* ⊕ *www.general54.com* Ⓜ *Laurier.*

Kanuk

MIXED CLOTHING | This company's snowy owl trademark has become something of a status symbol among the shivering urban masses. The Québec-made coats and parkas sold here are built to keep an Arctic explorer warm and dry. Try on coats in a variety of styles and lengths, with optional fur hoodies. Rain gear is also available. ⊠ *485 rue Rachel Est, The Plateau* ☎ *514/284–4494, 877/284–4494* ⊕ *www.kanuk.com* Ⓜ *Mont-Royal.*

★ M0851

LEATHER GOODS | Sleek, supple leather clothing and bags from the Québec designer Frédéric Mamarbachi have a cult following from Antwerp to Tokyo. The rough-hewn wood floors and concrete walls of this branch give it an industrial-chic vibe. ⊠ *3526 boul. St-Laurent, The Plateau* ☎ *514/849–9759* ⊕ *www.m0851. com* Ⓜ *St-Laurent or Sherbrooke.*

Mousseline

WOMEN'S CLOTHING | With sizes running from 2 to 22, this place makes finding the perfect fit a snap. Choosing from among the casual wear by fashion labels like James Perse, Pas de Calais, and Odd Mooly might be a bit more difficult. Be sure to pick up a comforting sweater from Autumn Cashmere. ⊠ *220 av. Laurier Ouest, Mile End* ☎ *514/878–0661* ⊕ *olam-mousseline.com* Ⓜ *Laurier.*

Muse

WOMEN'S CLOTHING | Designer Christian Chenail's contemporary take on fashion always has a French twist, and his daring black gowns are showstoppers. His flirty skirts and dresses usually come in cheerful shades of red and blue and call to mind the styles of the '50s. ⊠ *4467 rue St-Denis, The Plateau* ☎ *514/848–9493* ⊕ *www.muse-cchenail.com* ⊙ *Closed Sun.* Ⓜ *Mont-Royal.*

Unicorn

WOMEN'S CLOTHING | Young Québécois designers like Barilà, Valérie Dumaine, and Mélissa Nepton are the stars of this beautiful Mile End boutique, which also stocks unique national and international labels. All the black and white in the window display hints at the minimalist aesthetic within. ⊠ *5135 boul. St-Laurent, Mile End* ☎ *514/544–2828* ⊕ *www. boutiqueunicorn.com* Ⓜ *Laurier.*

WANT Les Essentiels

MIXED CLOTHING | Established in Montréal in 2007, WANT's new (2021) flagship boutique in hipster Mile End draws inspiration from travel and transitional spaces like airports, train stations, airplane cabins, and Montréal's metro cars, complementing the label's minimalist, gender neutral clothing, footwear and bags in muted blacks, whites, and grays. In addition to its own brand, WANT also carries apothecary, jewelry, and accessories from labels such as Grown Alchemist, Susanne Kaufmann, and All Blues, among others. ■**TIP→ Shoppers can also enjoy a VIP WANT experience by booking an appointment online.** ⊠ *5445 av. de Gaspé, Mile End* ⊕ *wantlesessentiels. com* Ⓜ *Laurier.*

★ Clark Street Mercantile: Boutique pour Gentlemen

MEN'S CLOTHING | Featured in publications like the *Guardian*, *GQ* and *Goop*, this authentically retro locale is a hipster's dream. Little has changed on the building's main floor, with the old, scuffed up brownish gray terrazzo flooring still in attendance and few embellishments made to the premises. The focus here is on the clothing and other products like leather goods, apothecary and homewares, each item handpicked for quality, craftsmanship and the story behind the brand. In addition to their own locally produced in-house brand, Clark Street Mercantile sources casual and classic men's clothing from labels like Portuguese Flannel, La Paz, and orSlow; apothecary from Rockwell, Groom and Baxter; and other lifestyle products, including books, from Barebones, Kinto, and Monocle. ✉ *5200 rue Clark, Mile End* ☎ *514/508–6090* ⊕ *clarkstreetmercantile. com* ◔ *Closed Mon.* Ⓜ *Laurier, then bus 51 west or walk.*

FOOD

★ La Vieille Europe

OTHER SPECIALTY STORE | For a taste of the old Main, where generations of immigrants came to shop, look no farther than this deli packed with sausages, cheeses, European chocolates, jams, and loads of atmosphere. Pick up a rich shot of espresso on your way out. ■**TIP→ Call ahead as hours vary seasonally.** ✉ *3855 boul. St-Laurent, The Plateau* ☎ *514/842–5773* ⊕ *www.facebook.com/LaVieilleEurope* Ⓜ *St-Laurent or Sherbrooke.*

★ Librarie Espagnole

OTHER SPECIALTY STORE | A fixture on boulevard St-Laurent since 1964, this is your one-stop shop for all things Spanish and Latin American in Montréal. The name is really a misnomer today since few books are sold here anymore. However, the friendly staff at this unpretentious establishment sell just about everything else from Spanish and Latin American foods to ceramic ware and cookware to flamenco shoes and a large assortment of *espadrilles.* ✉ *3811 boul. St-Laurent, The Plateau* ☎ *514/849–3383* ⊕ *lespanola.com* ◔ *Closed Sun.* Ⓜ *Sherbrooke, then bus 144 Ouest.*

HOUSEWARES

★ Zone

HOUSEWARES | This multilevel labyrinth of affordable housewares is filled with fine and funky designs for the kitchen, bath, and living room. ■**TIP→ There is also an outpost on Monkland, in NDG.** ✉ *4246 rue St-Denis, The Plateau* ☎ *514/845–3530* ⊕ *www.zonemaison.com* Ⓜ *Sherbrooke or Mont-Royal.*

Outremont

Above the Plateau and next to Parc du Mont-Royal, **Outremont** has long been Montréal's more affluent residential francophone enclave (as opposed to Westmount, always stubbornly English right down to its neo-Gothic churches and lawn-bowling club). It has grand homes, tree-shaded streets, perfectly groomed parks, and two upscale shopping and dining strips along rue Laurier and avenue Bernard. The latter, with wide sidewalks and shady trees, is particularly attractive. The eastern fringes of Outremont are home to Montréal's thriving Hasidic community.

GETTING HERE AND AROUND

By métro, take the Blue Line to Outremont station. You can also get to Outremont from Downtown on Bus 55, which goes along St. Laurent Boulevard, or Bus 80, which goes through Mont-Royal Park along avenue du Parc. Both bus routes can be picked up outside the Place-des-Arts métro, and you need to get off at rue Laurier and walk west from there. (Outremont begins on the west side of Parc; the east side of Parc is Mile End.)

Alternately, you could stay on Bus 80 for a few more stops until you come to Bernard and then walk west. Both Laurier and Bernard avenues are Outremont's primary hubs for commercial activity. The Outremont métro stop lets you off on avenue Van Horne, another commercial hub but without the fun, interesting boutiques and restaurants of Laurier and Bernard. If you're coming from Downtown and feeling fit you could walk to Outremont in roughly 30–45 minutes, or, for that matter, just hop on a BIXI bicycle, taking the same route as Bus 80 and getting there in half the time.

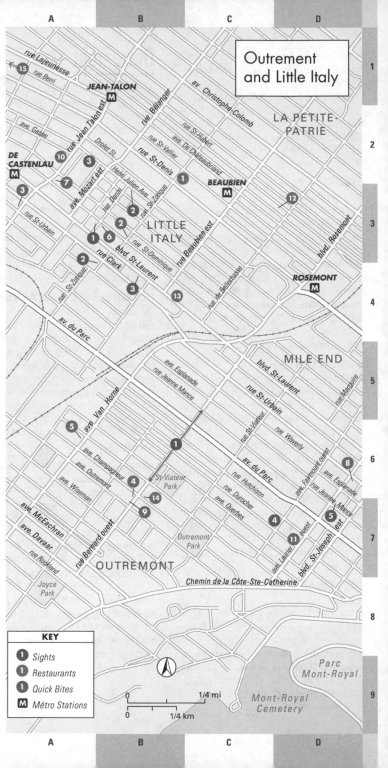

Sights

★ Avenue Bernard

STREET | If your taste runs to the chic and fashionable, then there is simply no better street than rue Bernard, west of Avenue Querbes, for people-watching. Its wide sidewalks and shady trees make it ideal for the kind of outdoor cafés and restaurants that attract the bright and the beautiful. ✉ *Outremont* Ⓜ *Outremont.*

🍴 Restaurants

Outremont caters to affluent French-speaking professionals with restaurants that look as good as the food being served. There are plenty of charming outdoor terraces in the warm months.

Brasserie Les Enfants Terribles

$$$ | **CANADIAN** | With its cavernous corner spot on Outremont's trendy avenue Bernard, sophisticated yet playful décor, and artfully prepared comfort food, this brasserie is always a good bet for quality food and excellent people-watching. The menu at Les Enfants Terribles is a mix of high end cuisine and comfort food favorites, from salmon tartare, grilled oyster mushroom salad, to spaghetti Bolognese, fish-and-chips, and mac 'n' cheese. **Known for:** elevated comfort food; pouding chômeur cake; after-theater crowd. Ⓢ *Average main: C$28* ✉ *1257 av. Bernard Ouest, Outremont* ☎ *514/759–9918* ⊕ *www.jesuisunenfantterrible.com* ⊗ *Closed Mon. No lunch Tues. and Wed.* Ⓜ *Outremont.*

Damas

$$$$ | **MIDDLE EASTERN** | Colorful and cozy, with dishes that are perfect for sharing, this Syrian restaurant is a treat. Try *fatta* (yogurt, tahini, pita, pistachios, pine nuts, and herbs), hummus with lamb, or the *moujaddaraa* (braised lentils with bulgur and caramelized onions, tomato salsa and yogurt mint sauce). **Known for:** hummus with lamb; Mediterranean wines; authentic Syrian cuisine. Ⓢ *Average main: C$36* ✉ *1201 av. Van Horne, Outremont* ☎ *514/439–5435* ⊕ *www.restaurant-damas.com* ⊗ *Closed Mon. and Tues. No lunch* Ⓜ *Outremont.*

La Chronique

$$$$ | **FRENCH** | Although La Chronique is indeed an elegant place with white walls and high ceilings flooded with light, people don't come here for the setting; they come for the excellent food. Without fuss or fanfare, La Chronique has remained one of the best French restaurants in town since it opened in 1995. **Known for:** excellent French cuisine; tasting menu; seared foie gras. Ⓢ *Average main: C$125* ✉ *104 av. Laurier Ouest, Outremont* ☎ *514/271–3095* ⊕ *www.lachronique. qc.ca* ⊗ *Closed Sun.–Tues. No lunch* ☞ *Tasting menu only* Ⓜ *Laurier.*

Le Glacier Bilboquet

$ | **ICE CREAM** | **FAMILY** | Families and couples with dogs congregate here on warm summer nights, where the artisanal ice-cream recipes are prepared by hand. Real cream and real milk are the star ingredients, while the sorbets are 80% fruit puree. **Known for:** late hours in summer; cranberry sorbet; maple taffy ice cream. Ⓢ *Average main: C$8* ✉ *1311 rue Bernard Ouest, Outremont* ☎ *514/276–0414* ⊕ *www.bilboquet.ca* ⊟ *No credit cards* Ⓜ *Outremont.*

★ Leméac

$$$$ | **BISTRO** | Open since 2001, this sophisticated French bistro pleases Montréalers with its flawless classics and its heated wraparound outdoor terrace. Regulars gravitate toward dishes such as the beef or salmon tartare, grilled Cornish hen, asparagus and wild mushroom risotto, mushroom ravioli, and hanger steak— all served with ceremonial aplomb on white linen tablecloths. **Known for:** pain perdu; being busy; salmon tartare. Ⓢ *Average main: C$44* ✉ *1045 av. Laurier Ouest, Outremont* ☎ *514/270–0999* ⊕ *www.restaurantlemeac.com* ⊗ *Closed Sun. and Mon.* Ⓜ *Outremont.*

★ **Pizzeria 900**

$$ | **PIZZA** | No one does pizza quite like these pizzaiolos; they are, after all, legally certified by the Associazione Vera Pizza Napolitana in Italy. Using all-natural and non-processed ingredients, and adhering to traditional pizza-making methods (like using a 900-degree oven), Pizzeria 900 on Bernard is one of the most sought-after pizza spots in town with one of the most popular patios. **Known for:** stylish space; 900 degree oven; Neapolitan-style pizza. [$] *Average main: C$15* ✉ *1248 rue Bernard Ouest, Outremont* ☎ *438/386–0900* 🌐 *no900.com* [M] *Outremont.*

Coffee and Quick Bites

★ **La Croissanterie Figaro**

$$ | **BISTRO** | **FAMILY** | The self-proclaimed "un coin perdu de Paris" is famous for its wraparound patio, Parisian vibe, an 100-year-old corner building featuring stained glass and woodwork, an art deco chandelier, and an art nouveau bar. Although this is a full bistro serving three meals every day of the week, it shines brightest in the morning. **Known for:** opens early and closes late; charming setting; croissant with almond paste. [$] *Average main: C$13* ✉ *5200 rue Hutchison, Outremont* ☎ *514/278–6567* 🌐 *www.lacroissanteriefigaro.com* [M] *Outremont.*

Toi Moi et Café

$$ | **BISTRO** | Film producers and poets congregate at this corner café-bistro, sitting on the terrace to sip award-winning espresso. Although there's a hearty lunch and dinner menu of tofu salads and grilled meat, brunch is the big draw. **Known for:** exclusive blends like baklava coffee; single-origin specialty coffees; student and artist crowd. [$] *Average main: C$13* ✉ *244 av. Laurier Ouest, Outremont* ☎ *514/279–9599* 🌐 *www.toimoicafe.com* [M] *Laurier.*

Performing Arts

CLASSICAL MUSIC

Salle Claude-Champagne

MUSIC | This beautiful concert hall hosts more than 150 symphonic and operatic performances every year by the music faculty of the Université de Montréal. The repertoire includes both classic and contemporary works. ✉ *220 av. Vincent-d'Indy, Outremont* ☎ *514/343–6427* 🌐 *www.musique.uMontréal.ca* [M] *Édouard-Monpetit.*

THEATER

Théâtre Outremont

CONCERTS | Inaugurated in 1929, this gorgeous art deco theater rapidly became a local favorite and had its heyday in the '70s before it fell into disarray. After reopening its doors in the early '90s, the theater has regained much of its steam with mostly theater and live music acts. ✉ *1248 av. Bernard O., Outremont* ☎ *514/495–9944* 🌐 *www.theatreoutremont.ca* [M] *Outremont.*

Shopping

Avenue Laurier in Outremont is a good destination for those in pursuit of a little luxury.

CLOTHING

Billie

WOMEN'S CLOTHING | One of Montréal's favorite boutiques, Billie has rows of bookcases, drawers, and shelves that give the feeling of raiding your best friend's closet. Look for chic dresses and blouses from Velvet, cozy sweaters from 360 Cashmere, and eclectic shoes by Inuikii. If you are shopping for kid sizes, visit Billie le Kid at 1001 avenue Laurier Ouest. ✉ *1012 av. Laurier Ouest, Outremont* ☎ *514/270–5415* 🌐 *www.billieboutique.com* [M] *Laurier.*

★ Lyla

LINGERIE | Helping women feel their best since 1982, this lovely shop carries some of the finest lingerie in the city—including brands like Eres and La Perla. The staff is extremely helpful in finding what fits and flatters. Two other reasons to stop and shop: exquisite fashions from Europe and a great selection of swimsuits and darling cover-ups. ✉ *400 av. Laurier Ouest, Outremont* ☎ *514/271–0763* ⊕ *www.lyla. ca* ⊗ *Closed Sun.* Ⓜ *Laurier.*

Mimi & Coco

WOMEN'S CLOTHING | You'll want to snap up several of the locally designed T-shirts at Mimi & Coco, perhaps pairing them with luxe knitwear from Italy. Beautiful floor-to-ceiling windows create a bright, inviting interior, even on cloudy days. The shop also sells dog collars and leashes, with profits going to a nonprofit foundation that works to promote animal rescue and adoption. Come at lunchtime and sample one of Mandy's gourmet salads from the in-store counter. ✉ *201 av. Laurier Ouest, Outremont* ☎ *514/906–0349* ⊕ *www. mimicoco.com* Ⓜ *Laurier.*

FOOD

Gourmet Laurier

FOOD | Acres of chocolate and candy and the best coffee beans in town draw well-heeled shoppers to this Outremont shop. The colossal assortment of fine cheeses, charcuterie, and other local and imported goodies add to the appeal. ✉ *1042 av. Laurier Ouest, Outremont* ☎ *514/274–5601* ⊕ *www.gourmetlaurier. ca* Ⓜ *Laurier.*

Yannick Fromagerie

FOOD | This gourmet cheese shop is the go-to destination for the city's top chefs and cheese aficionados. Yannick Achim carries 400 varieties, buying from local dairies and stocking an astonishing international selection. You'll find Pikauba cheese from Québec beside pecorino made with raw sheep's milk and laced with black truffles. Cheese lovers here eagerly trade advice on building the perfect after-dinner cheese plate. ✉ *1218 rue Bernard O., Outremont* ☎ *514/279–9376* ⊕ *www.yannickfromagerie.ca* Ⓜ *Outremont.*

Little Italy

Farther north is **Little Italy,** which is still home base to Montréal's sizable Italian community of nearly a quarter of a million people. While families of Italian descent now live all over the greater Montréal area, many come back here every week or so to shop, eat out, or visit family and friends, and the 30-odd blocks bounded by rues Jean-Talon, St-Zotique, Marconi, and Drolet remain its heart and soul. You'll know you've reached Little Italy when the gardens have tomato plants and grapevines, there are sausages and cans of olive oil in store windows, and the heady smell of espresso emanates from cafés.

GETTING HERE AND AROUND

You can take both the Orange and Blue lines to get to Little Italy: get off at Jean-Talon station and walk six short blocks to get to boulevard St-Laurent. Bus 55, which runs north along St-Laurent, will also get you here fairly quickly from Downtown, or you could just take a BIXI bike and get here in roughly 20 minutes. Once here, you can stop for produce and cheese at the Marché Jean-Talon, and you might just see a wedding party outside the Madonna della Difesa church.

◉ Sights

Chiesa della Madonna della Difesa

CHURCH | If you look up at the cupola behind the main altar of Little Italy's most famous church, you'll spot Montréal's most infamous piece of ecclesiastical portraiture. Yes, indeed, that lantern-jaw fellow on horseback who looks so pleased with himself is Benito Mussolini, the dictator who led Italy into World War

It's well worth the métro ride up to Little Italy's busy Marché Jean-Talon to see French Canadian farmers sell their local produce and prepared food.

II—on the wrong side. The mural, by Guido Nincheri (1885–1973), was completed long before the war and commemorates the signing of the Lateran Pact with Pope Pius XI, one of Il Duce's few lasting achievements. The controversy shouldn't distract you from the beauties of the rest of the richly decorated church. ⊠ *6800 av. Henri-Julien, Little Italy* ☎ *514/277–6522* ⊕ *www.facebook.com/MadonnadellaDifesaMTL* ✉ *Free* ☯ *Closed Sat. and Sun.* Ⓜ *Beaubien or Jean-Talon.*

★ Marché Jean-Talon

MARKET | The smells of roasting chestnuts and fresh pastries at this market will surely excite your olfactory system. To further delight your senses there are dozens of tiny shops full of Québec cheeses, Lebanese sweets, country pâtés, local wines, and handmade chocolates. Less threatening to the waistline but a feast for the eyes are the huge mounds of peas, beans, apples, carrots, pears, garlic, and other produce on sale at the open-air stands. Visit on weekends during the warm summer months, and it will feel as if all of Montréal has come out to shop. ■TIP→ **During the holiday season there is a Christmas market, which runs from late November until the 23rd of December.** ⊠ *7070 rue Henri-Julien, Little Italy* ☎ *514/277–1588* ⊕ *www.marchespublics-mtl.com* Ⓜ *Jean-Talon.*

🍴 Restaurants

Little Italy offers a nostalgic look back at what La Bella Italia used to be 40 or 50 years ago, as old men congregate in front of their favorite café and chat about politics and last night's soccer game. With its location just steps away from Jean-Talon Market, it's only fitting that historic Piccola Italia would go on to become the sought-after dining destination that it is today. It's now neighbored by the trendsetting Mile-Ex and Rosemont area, where chefs, moving away from Old Montréal and Downtown's expensive rents, benefit from splendid spaces and eager locals, which include young professionals and diners hungry for new experiences.

Beaufort Bistro

$$$ | SCANDINAVIAN | FAMILY | The only Norwegian-inspired eatery in Montréal, Beaufort Bistro has admittedly received a lot of attention. Part-time restaurant, part-time busy café (complete with freelancers and students on a deadline), this white-washed cozy space serves the only authentic open-faced sandwiches—smørrebrød—this side of the pond, as well as a variety of mains, like *Rösti* (potato galettes), tartares, and, of course, *blinis* and *gravlax* (this is a Scandi café, after all). **Known for:** great coffee; authentic smørrebrød—open-faced sandwiches; tartares. [$] *Average main: C$28* ✉ *414 rue St-Zotique Est, Rosemont* ☎ *514/274–6969* 🌐 *www.beaufortbistro.ca* 🕒 *Closed Sun. and Mon. No lunch* [M] *Beaubien.*

Bottega Pizzeria

$$ | PIZZA | FAMILY | Nobody questions the authenticity of the Neapolitan-style pizza here, seeing as there's a nearly four-ton wood-burning pizza oven made from Vesuvian rock in the kitchen which cooks pizza in 90 seconds flat, at 500 degrees Celsius (932 °F). There are just a few toppings available, but all are fabulously flavorsome, like fresh tomatoes, vegetables, and top-quality salumi. **Known for:** panozzi, calzoni, and tronchetti; excellent gelato to-go; authentic Neapolitan-style pizza. [$] *Average main: C$20* ✉ *65 rue St-Zotique Est, Little Italy* ☎ *514/277–8104* 🌐 *www.bottega.ca* 🕒 *Closed Mon. No lunch Sat.–Wed.* [M] *Beaubien.*

★ Brasserie Harricana

$$ | MODERN CANADIAN | FAMILY | Instagram-famous for its dusty pink chairs and pleasing, contemporary space, this seriously cool brasserie is home to 41 home-brews—sold by the bottle at the boutique upstairs—and a solid menu that includes monkfish burgers, beer-can roast chicken, and a hearty rib eye. In 2021, a new, larger brewhouse was opened. **Known for:** beer-can roast chicken; beer pairings; architectural space. [$] *Average main: C$20* ✉ *95 rue Jean-Talon Ouest, Little Italy* ☎ *514/303–3039* 🌐 *www.brasserieharricana.com* 🕒 *Closed Mon. and Tues. No lunch Sat.* [M] *De Castelnau.*

★ Impasto

$$$ | MODERN ITALIAN | This unpretentious, industrial-chic Little Italy restaurant has garnered a great reputation, thanks in part to its celebrity-chef owners, Stefano Faita and Michele Forgione. Start by sharing the artisanal salumi platter, move on to a primi of some of the best fresh pasta dishes in town, like the mushroom tortelli with a demi-glace vegetable and hazelnut sauce, the melt-in-your-mouth ricotta gnocchi, or the *porchetta del nonno* (grandpa's pork roast), a must-order if it's on the menu. **Known for:** Grandpa's pork roast; modern Italian fare; stylish decor. [$] *Average main: C$30* ✉ *48 rue Dante, Little Italy* ☎ *514/508–6508* 🌐 *www.impastomtl.ca* 🕒 *Closed Sun. and Mon. No lunch* [M] *Jean-Talon.*

Kitchen Galerie

$$$$ | BISTRO | With its small ingredient-based menu, this homey bistro is an example of excellence through simplicity. The chefs do everything—the shopping, the chopping, the cooking, the greeting, and the serving, and the focus is on meats, fish, and vegetable dishes all inspired by what local farmers bring to the adjacent Jean-Talon market that morning. **Known for:** communal seating; gnocchi with lobster, garlic cream confit, mozzarella, and cherry tomatoes; market cuisine. [$] *Average main: C$40* ✉ *Marché Jean-Talon, 60 rue Jean-Talon Est, Little Italy* ☎ *514/315–8994* 🌐 *www.kitchen-galerie.com* 🕒 *Closed Sun.–Wed. No lunch* [M] *Jean-Talon.*

Le Petit Alep

$$ | MIDDLE EASTERN | FAMILY | This casual Middle Eastern spot is comfortable and homey but still has style, with music, ivy, exposed-stone walls, and a lovely terrace come summer. The menu is perfect for grazing, and excellent sharing options include the *mouhamara* (pomegranate-and-walnut spread), *sabanegh* (spinach, coriander, and onion pies), *fattouche* (a salad with pita chips and mint), and *yalandji* (vine leaves stuffed with rice, chickpeas, walnuts, and tomatoes). **Known for:** daily specials; Syrian and Armenian cuisine; atmospheric decor. [$] *Average main: C$16* ✉ *191 rue Jean-Talon Est, Rosemont* ☎ *514/270–9361* 🌐 *www.petitalep.com* 🕓 *Closed Sun.–Tues. No lunch Wed. and Sat.* [M] *Jean-Talon.*

Montréal Plaza

$$$$ | MODERN CANADIAN | You won't see anything too familiar on the menu at this fresh, light-filled restaurant with its high ceilings, clean white walls and tablecloths, and modern mix of wood, glass, and sliding industrial windows that open to outdoor seating in summer. You *will* find whimsical yet unpretentious dishes that surprise and delight—just be sure to order a side of deep-fried Brussels sprouts no matter your main dish. **Known for:** desserts; affordable wines; creative menu. [$] *Average main: C$34* ✉ *6230 rue St-Hubert, Rosemont* ☎ *514/903–6230* 🌐 *Montréalplaza.com* 🕓 *Closed Mon. and Tues. No lunch* [M] *Beaubien.*

Pastaga

$$$ | CANADIAN | Don't be fooled by the name: Pastaga is not a pasta joint; the name is a slang term for alcoholic drinks composed of anise, specifically pastis. Although famous for its signature dish of crispy pork belly marinated in brown sugar (or maple when in season) and inventive chopped liver *à la juive* (creamy chopped liver, hard-boiled egg, crunchy bagel chips, and tart-marinated onions), Pastaga is best known for its all-natural wine list, which is certain to yield uncommon finds. **Known for:** natural wines; local celebrity chef; maple crispy pork belly. [$] *Average main: C$25* ✉ *6389 boul. St-Laurent, Rosemont* ☎ *438/381–6389* 🌐 *www.pastaga.ca* 🕓 *Closed Mon. No lunch* [M] *Beaubien.*

Tapeo

$$ | TAPAS | Bringing tapas uptown, this Spanish-inspired eatery is a chic yet casual place to drink imported wines and share a few small plates. The Tapeo version of the classic *patatas bravas* served with a spicy tomato sauce and aioli is always a good choice, as are the roasted vine tomatoes and the grilled chorizo. **Known for:** house churros; patatas bravas; chef's table. [$] *Average main: C$17* ✉ *511 rue Villeray, Villeray* ☎ *514/495–1999* 🌐 *www.restotapeo.com* 🕓 *Closed Mon. No lunch Sat. and Sun.* [M] *Jarry.*

Coffee and Quick Bites

Caffè San Simeon

$ | CAFÉ | In the heart of Little Italy, this historic coffee shop filled with regulars chatting away in Italian, is one of the city's best nonhipster places to get some excellent brew, be it an espresso, latte, or cappuccino. There also are a few pastries available. **Known for:** opens at 6 am; old-school Italian café; Malibu coffee. [$] *Average main: C$5* ✉ *39 rue Dante, Little Italy* ☎ *514/272–7386* 🌐 *www.facebook.com/caffe.sansimeon* 💳 *No credit cards* [M] *Jean-Talon.*

★ Dinette Triple Crown

$$ | SOUTHERN | Dinette Triple Crown is relatively small (a counter with just eight stools), but the real draw here is not indoor dining but taking the comfort food to go. Locals know to ask for a picnic basket (fully equipped with cutlery, dishes, and a tablecloth) that will be enjoyed in Little Italy Park across the street. **Known for:** fried chicken and other Southern fare; large selection of bourbon; weekly menus. [$] *Average main: C$18* ✉ *6704 rue Clark, Little Italy* ☎ *514/272–2617* 🌐 *www.dinettetriplecrown.com* 🕓 *Closed Mon.–Wed.* [M] *Beaubien.*

Did You Know?

An artifical basin fitted on a former swamp on Mont-Royal, Beaver Lake is named for an old beaver dam discovered during the work.

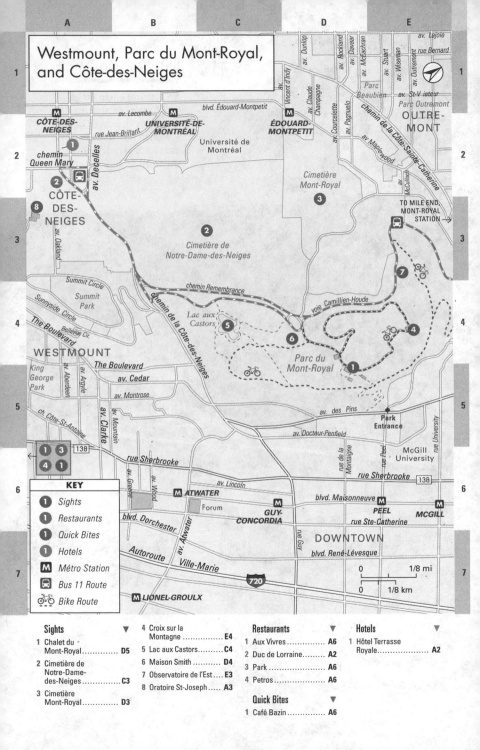

Westmount, Parc du Mont-Royal, and Côte-des-Neiges

La Cornetteria

$ | BAKERY | This lovely little bakery, which magically transports its patrons (or at least, their tastebuds) to Italy, specializes in the cornetto, the Italian version of the croissant. Freshly baked every morning, these delightful pastries are available plain or filled with Nutella, ricotta cream, or almond paste. **Known for:** stracchino sandwiches; nutella cornetto; traditional cannoli. $ Average main: C$5 ⊠ 6528 boul. St-Laurent, Little Italy ☎ 514/277–8030 ⊕ www.lacornetteria.com ⊟ No credit cards ⊗ Closed Mon. Ⓜ Beaubien.

🛍 Shopping

FOOD

★ Marché Milano

FOOD | A huge expansion in 2013 made this local favorite, in business since 1954, even more popular with customers, who form long lines for prepared foods at the takeout counter. There's a vast selection of cheeses, oils, vinegars, and baked goods. For some elbow room, go during the week. ⊠ 6862 boul. St-Laurent, Little Italy ☎ 514/273–8558 ⊕ www.milanofruiterie.com ⊗ Closed Mon. Ⓜ De Castelnau or Jean-Talon.

Parc du Mont-Royal

In geological terms, Mont-Royal is just a bump of basaltlike rock worn down by several ice ages to a mere 760 feet. But in the affections of Montréalers it's a Matterhorn. Without a trace of irony, they call it simply *la Montagne* or "the Mountain," and it's easy to see why it's so well loved.

For Montréalers it's a refuge, a slightly tamed wilderness within the city. It's where you go to get away from it all. And even when you can't get away, you can see the mountain glimmering beyond the skyscrapers and the high-rises—green in summer, gray and white in winter, and gold and crimson in fall.

The nearly 500 acres of forests and meadows were laid out by Frederick Law Olmsted (1822–1903), the man responsible for New York City's Central Park. Olmsted believed that communion with nature could cure body and soul, so much of the park has been left as wild as possible, with narrow paths meandering through tall stands of maples and red oaks. In summer, it's full of picnicking families; in winter, cross-country skiers and snowshoers take over, while families skate at Lac aux Castors and ride sleds and inner tubes down groomed slopes. The nonprofit organization Les amis de la montagne (⊕ *lemontroyal.qc.ca/en*) offers year-round outdoor and educational activities for locals and visitors, like rowboat rentals, mountain clean-ups, and guided walks in summer and guided snowshoeing excursions followed by a bone-warming hot chocolate or mulled wine in winter.

GETTING HERE AND AROUND

If you're in good shape, you can walk, uphill all the way, from Downtown. Climb rue Peel to the entrance to Parc du Mont-Royal and then up the steep stairway to the top of the mountain. Or you can simply take the métro to the Mont-Royal station and catch Bus 11. If you have a car, there's good parking in Parc du Mont-Royal and at the Oratoire St-Joseph (the latter asks for a contribution of C$5 per vehicle Monday to Saturday for anyone not attending a service or coming to pray). Biking up the mountain will test your endurance, but the park has an extensive network of scenic trails.

TIMING

Depending on your interest, you could spend anywhere from a few hours—if you simply just want to see the view—to the entire day here. If you're here for the afternoon, there's a cafeteria at the Beaver Lake pavilion and a café at Smith House, or you can pick up picnic provisions before you set out.

◉ Sights

Chalet du Mont-Royal
VIEWPOINT | No trip to Montréal is complete without a visit to the terrace in front of the Chalet du Mont-Royal. It's not the only place to get an overview of the city, the river, and the countryside beyond, but it's the most spectacular. On clear days you can see not only the Downtown skyscrapers, but also Mont-Royal's sister mountains—Monts St-Bruno, St-Hilaire, and St-Grégoire. These isolated peaks, called the Montérégies, or Mountains of the King, rise up from the flat countryside. Be sure to take a look inside the chalet, especially at the murals depicting scenes from Canadian history. ⊠ Off voie Camillien-Houde, Parc du Mont-Royal ☎ 514/843–8240, ext. 0 for Les amis de la montagnes ⊕ www.lemontroyal.qc.ca/ en ☑ Free Ⓜ Mont-Royal, then Bus 11 westbound.

★ Croix sur la Montagne
(Cross atop Mont-Royal)
OTHER ATTRACTION | Visible from up to 50 miles away on a clear day, the 98-foot-high steel cross at the top of Mont-Royal has been a city landmark since it was erected in 1924, largely with money raised through the efforts of 85,000 high-school students. Once upon a time, it took four hours and the labor of three to replace the 249 electric bulbs used to light the cross; today, the iconic cross is illuminated via a high-tech remote-control LED system. ⊠ Parc du Mont-Royal ⊕ www.lemontroyal.qc.ca.

Lac aux Castors (Beaver Lake)
CITY PARK | FAMILY | Mont-Royal's single body of water, actually a reclaimed bog, is a great place for kids (and parents) to float model boats or rent a rowboat in the summertime. In winter, the lake's frozen surface attracts whole families of skaters, and nearby there's a groomed slope where kids of all ages can ride inner tubes. The glass-fronted Beaver Lake Pavilion is a pleasant bistro that serves lunch and dinner. Skate and cross-country-ski rentals are available downstairs. In summer, rowboat rentals are available. ⊠ Off chemin Remembrance, Parc du Mont-Royal ⊕ www.lemontroyal.qc.ca Ⓜ Mont-Royal, then Bus 11 westbound.

Maison Smith
OTHER MUSEUM | If you need a map of Mont-Royal's extensive hiking trails or want to know about the animals and more than 180 kinds of birds here, the former park keeper's residence is the place to go. It's also a good spot for getting a snack, drink, or souvenir. The pretty little stone house—built in 1858—is the headquarters of Les amis de la montagne (The Friends of the Mountain), a non-profit organization that offers various guided walks—including moonlight snowshoe excursions and cross-country ski lessons in winter around the mountain and in nearby areas. ⊠ 1260 chemin Remembrance, Parc du Mont-Royal ☎ 514/843–8240 ⊕ www. lemontroyal.qc.ca Ⓜ Mont-Royal, then bus 11 westbound.

Observatoire de l'Est
VIEWPOINT | If you're just driving across Mont-Royal, be sure to stop for a few moments at its eastern lookout for a view of the Stade Olympique and the east end of the city. Tourists enjoy the location as it's a great photo spot. ⊠ Voie Camillien-Houde, Parc du Mont-Royal Ⓜ Mont-Royal.

Côte-des-Neiges

Not too many tourists venture north and east of Parc du Mont-Royal, but the primarily residential neighborhood of Côte-des-Neiges has much to offer.

One of Montréal's most-visited sights—the Oratoire St-Joseph (St. Joseph's Oratory)—sits atop the northern slope of Mont-Royal, dominating the surrounding neighborhood of Côte-des-Neiges. More than 2 million people of all faiths visit

Saint Joseph's Oratory is Canada's largest church and claims to have one of the largest domes in the world.

the shrine every year. The most devout pilgrims climb the staircase leading to the main door on their knees, pausing on each of its 99 steps to pray.

Even without the Oratoire (as well as the Cimetière de Notre-Dame-des-Neiges, another site worth seeing), Côte-des-Neiges is a district worth visiting. It's also an area where the dominant languages are neither English nor French.

It's largely working-class immigrants who live here—Filipino, Latin American, Southeast and South Asian, West Indian, Arab, Jewish, Chinese, Haitian, and most recently people from Eastern Europe and Africa. It's also home to a sizable number of students, many of whom attend the Université de Montréal, as well as other smaller surrounding colleges and universities.

As a result, if you're looking for inexpensive, authentic world cuisine, there's no better place in Montréal to come to than Côte-des-Neiges. It's teeming with ethnic shops and restaurants—Thai, Russian,

Korean, Indian, Peruvian, Filipino, and more. You're as likely to find a falafel joint as a Vietnamese noodle eatery or Haitian street food.

GETTING HERE AND AROUND

Côte-des-Neiges is bordered by avenue Decelles to the north and the Cimetière de Notre-Dame-des-Neiges to the south. It's easy to get here by public transit, either the métro to the Côte-des-Neiges station or the 166 Bus from the Guy-Concordia métro station to chemin Queen-Mary. If you take a car—which is not a bad idea if you plan to visit the Parc du Mont-Royal as well—it's usually easy to get a parking space at the Oratoire St-Joseph (a contribution of C\$5 per vehicle is requested Monday to Saturday, except for those attending services or coming to the Oratoire to pray).

TIMING

Côte-des-Neiges bustles during the day, but is a little quieter at night.

◉ Sights

Cimetière de Notre-Dame-des-Neiges

(Our Lady of the Snows Cemetery)
CEMETERY | At 343 acres, Canada's largest cemetery is not much smaller than the neighboring Parc du Mont-Royal, and, as long as you just count the living, it's usually a lot less crowded. You don't have to be morbid to wander the graveyard's 55 km (34 miles) of tree-shaded paths and roadways past the tombs of hundreds of prominent artists, poets, intellectuals, politicians, and clerics. Among them is Calixa Lavallée (1842–91), who wrote "O Canada," the country's national anthem. ■**TIP**➜ **The cemetery offers some guided tours in summer. Phone ahead for details.** ✉ *4601 chemin de la Côte-des-Neiges, Côte-des-Neiges* ☎ *514/735–1361* ⊕ *www.cimetierenotredamedesneiges. ca* Ⓜ *Côte-des-Neiges, then Bus 165 southbound.*

★ Cimetière Mont-Royal

CEMETERY | If you find yourself humming "Getting to Know You" as you explore Mont-Royal Cemetery's 165 acres, blame it on the graveyard's most famous permanent guest, Anna Leonowens (1834–1915). She was the real-life model for the heroine of the Rodgers and Hammerstein musical *The King and I.* The cemetery—established in 1852 by the Anglican, Presbyterian, Unitarian, and Baptist churches—is laid out like a terraced garden, with footpaths that meander between crab-apple trees and past Japanese lilacs. If you're lucky, you may spot a fox sunbathing on one of the tombstones in winter. ✉ *1297 chemin de la Forêt, Côte-des-Neiges* ☎ *514/279–7358* ⊕ *www.mountroyalcem.com* Ⓜ *Mont-Royal, then Bus 11 westbound.*

★ Oratoire St-Joseph

(St. Joseph's Oratory)
RELIGIOUS BUILDING | Each year some 2 million people from all over North America and beyond visit St. Joseph's Oratory. The most devout Catholics climb the 99

Free Church Tours ◉

Nearly all of Montréal's numerous historic churches offer free admission, and some, like St. Joseph's Oratory, one of the world's most visited shrines, offer guided tours. The cost for a guided tour of St. Joseph's Oratory, held at 1:30 and 3 in summer; by appointment only in winter) is C$6 per person.

steps to its front door on their knees. It is the world's largest and most popular shrine dedicated to the earthly father of Jesus (Canada's patron saint), and it's all the work of a man named Brother André Besette (1845–1937).

By worldly standards Brother André didn't have much going for him, but he had a deep devotion to St. Joseph and an iron will. In 1870 he joined the Holy Cross religious order and was assigned to work as a doorkeeper at the college the order operated just north of Mont-Royal. In 1904 he began building a chapel on the mountainside across the road to honor his favorite saint, and the rest is history. Thanks to reports of miraculous cures attributed to St. Joseph's intercession, donations started to pour in, and Brother André was able to start work replacing his modest shrine with something more substantial. The result, which wasn't completed until after his death, is one of the most triumphal pieces of church architecture in North America.

The oratory and its gardens dominate Mont-Royal's northwestern slope. Its copper dome—one of the largest in the world—can be seen from miles away. The interior of the main church is equally grand, although it's also quite austere. The best time to visit it is on Sunday for the 11 am solemn mass, when the sanctuary is brightly lit and the sweet voices of Les Petits Chanteurs de Mont-Royal—the city's best boys' choir—fill the nave with music.

The crypt is shabbier than its big brother upstairs but more welcoming. In a long, narrow room behind the crypt, 10,000 votive candles glitter before a dozen carved murals extolling the virtues of St. Joseph; the walls are hung with crutches discarded by those said to have been cured. Just beyond is the simple tomb of Brother André, who was canonized a saint in 2010. His preserved heart is displayed in a glass case in one of several galleries between the crypt and the main church.

High on the mountain, east of the main church, is a garden commemorating the Passion of Christ, with life-size representations of the 14 stations of the cross. On the west side of the church is Brother André's original chapel, with pressed-tin ceilings and plaster saints that is, in many ways, more moving than the church that overshadows it. Note: the oratoire operates a shuttle bus for visitors who aren't up to the steep climb from the main parking lot to the entrance of the crypt church. The main church is several stories above that, but escalators and two elevators ease the ascent. **■TIP→ A major renovation and expansion project is underway, so expect some potential disruption during your visit.** ✉ *3800 chemin Queen Mary, Côte-des-Neiges* ☎ *514/733–8211, 877/672–8647* 🌐 *www.saint-joseph.org* 🎟 *Free. Parking: contribution of $C5 per vehicle requested (except for those attending services or coming to pray). C$3 for museum.* [M] *Côte-des-Neiges.*

🍴 Restaurants

Duc de Lorraine

$$$ | **CAFÉ** | A light croissant or rich pastry from the city's oldest patisserie makes for a nice break after visiting the Parc Mont-Royal or Oratoire St-Joseph. For lunch, try the quiche du jour, the onion soup, or the mushroom risotto followed by a *tartelette aux abricots* (apricot tart). **Known for:** almond paste croissant (rouleau); Parisian-style pastry shop and bistro; ample patio. [$] *Average main: C$25* ✉ *5002 Côte-des-Neiges, Côte-des-Neiges* ☎ *514/731–4128* 🌐 *www.ducdelorraine.ca* [M] *Côte-des-Neiges.*

🎟 Performing Arts

Segal Centre for the Performing Arts

THEATER | English-language favorites like *Harvey, Inherit the Wind,* and *Joseph and the Amazing Technicolor Dreamcoat* get frequent billing at this Côte-des-Neiges venue, along with locally written works. The center is best known, however, as the home to the **Dora Wasserman Yiddish Theatre,** which presents such musical works as *The Jazz Singer* and *The Pirates of Penzance* in Yiddish. ✉ *5170 chemin de la Côte-Ste-Catherine, Côte-des-Neiges* ☎ *514/739–7944* 🌐 *www.segalcentre.org* [M] *Côte-Ste-Catherine.*

Hochelaga-Maisonneuve

The neighborhood of Hochelaga-Maisonneuve, aka **HoMa,** is one of the best spots to go if you're craving green space, plus it has one of Montréal's top markets. In fact, it's worth the trip on the métro's Green Line just to see the four institutions that make up Montréal's Espace your la Vie, (Space for Life), an innovative natural science museum complex—the first in the world to link humans with nature. It includes the Jardin Botanique (Botanical Garden); the Insectarium, which houses the world's largest collection of bugs (closed for renovations until 2022); the Biosphère, a great place to experience different ecosystems under one roof; and the stunning Rio Tinto Alcan Planetarium.

Parc Maisonneuve is a lovely green area, and an ideal place for a stroll or a picnic.

The leaning tower that supports the roof of the Stade Olympique (Olympic Stadium), which played host to the 1976 Summer Olympics, dominates the skyline here. The area is largely working-class residential, but it's becoming a *quartier branché*, or hip 'hood, with some good restaurants and little shops along rue Ontario Est.

Until 1918, when it was annexed by Montréal, the east-end district of Maisonneuve was a city unto itself, a booming, prosperous industrial center full of factories making everything from shoes to cheese. The neighborhood was also packed with houses for the almost entirely French-Canadian workforce, who kept the whole machine humming.

Maisonneuve was also the site of one of Canada's earliest experiments in urban planning. The Dufresne brothers, a pair of prosperous shoe manufacturers, built a series of grand civic buildings along rue Morgan—many of which still stand—including a theater, public baths, and a bustling market, as well as Parc Maisonneuve. All this was supposed to make working-class life more bearable, but World War I put an end to the brothers' plans and Maisonneuve became part of Montréal, twinned with the east-end district of Hochelaga.

GETTING HERE AND AROUND

It's not necessary to drive to the area, as the Pie-IX and Viau métro stops on the Green Line provide easy access to all the sites, including the Insectarium and the Jardin Botanique. For bikers, it's a straight shot across the path on rue Rachel.

TIMING

If traveling with kids, you'll probably want to dedicate more time to exploring the area to see the sights. One of the city's major markets—Marché Maisonneuve—is on the corner of rue Ontario and avenue Bennett, and is well worth a stop.

⊙ Sights

Château Dufresne

HISTORIC HOME | The adjoining homes of a pair of shoe manufacturers, Oscar and Marius Dufresne, provide a glimpse into the lives of Montréal's francophone bourgeoisie in the early 20th century. The brothers built their beaux arts palace in 1916 along the lines of the Petit-Trianon in Paris, and lived in it with their families—Oscar in the eastern half and Marius in the western half.

Worth searching out are the domestic scenes on the walls of the Petit Salon, where Oscar's wife entertained friends. Her brother-in-law relaxed with his friends in a smoking room decked out like a Turkish lounge. During the house's incarnation as a boys' school in the 1950s, the Eudist priests who ran it covered the room's frieze of nymphs and satyrs with a modest curtain that their charges lifted at every opportunity. ■ TIP→ **A digital tour by tablet is available.** ✉ *2929 rue Jeanne-d'Arc, Hochelaga-Maisonneuve* ☎ *514/259–9201* ⊕ *www.chateaudufresne.com* ◫ *C$14* ⊙ *Closed Mon. and Tues.* Ⓜ *Pie-IX.*

★ Jardin Botanique (*Botanical Garden*)

GARDEN | FAMILY | Creating one of the world's great botanical gardens in a city with a winter as harsh as Montréal's was no mean feat, and the result is that no matter how brutal it gets in January there's one corner of the city where it's always summer. With 181 acres of plantings in summer and 10 greenhouses open all year, Montréal's Jardin Botanique is the second-largest attraction of its kind in the world (after England's Kew Gardens). It grows more than 26,000 species of plants, and among its 30 thematic gardens are a rose garden, an alpine garden, and—a favorite with the kids—a poisonous-plant garden.

You can attend traditional tea ceremonies in the Japanese Garden, which has one of the best bonsai collections

A 100 yards · 100 meters

av. du Mont-Royal

blvd. Pie-IX · rue Sherbrooke

2 Parc de Maisonneuve

rue Rachel · 138 · Tour Olympique · 4 Parc Olympique

rue Sherbrooke · 1 · Stade Olympique · 5

PIE-IX Ⓜ · av. Pierre de Coubertin · **VIAU** Ⓜ

rue Aylwin · av. d'Orléans · rue Nicolet

HOCHELAGA

TO DOWNTOWN ←

rue Hochelaga · rue Hochelaga

JOLIETTE Ⓜ · Parc Lalancette

rue de Ville-Marie · blvd. Viau · rue St-Clément

138 · rue Aylwin · rue de Chambly · rue Nicolet · av. Yabis · av. Bourbonnière · av. d'Orléans · av. Jeanne-d'Arc · blvd. Pie-IX · av. Desjardins · av. de Lasalle · av. Létourneux · av. Bennett · av. Aird · rue Shand · rue Leclaire · rue Théodore

rue de Rouen · Place Marché Maisonneuve

3 **Maisonneuve**

rue Ontario · **MAISONNEUVE** · Parc St-Clément

TO DOWNTOWN ← · rue La Fontaine · rue La Fontaine · Saint-Clément de Viauville

rue Cuvillier · rue Adam · av. Morgan · av. William-David · rue Adam · rue Vimont

KEY · rue Ste-Catherine · 125 · Parc Morgan

1 Sights

Ⓜ Métro Stations

⛗ Bike Route

rue notre-Dame

Hochelaga-Maisonneuve

---

in the West, or wander among the native birches and maples of the Jardin des Premières-Nations (First Nations Garden). The Jardin de Chine (Chinese Garden), with its pagoda and waterfall, will transport you back to the Ming dynasty. In the fall, all three cultural gardens host magical mixes of light, color, plant life, and sculpture during the annual Gardens of Light spectacle. ✉ *4101 rue Sherbrooke Est, Hochelaga-Maisonneuve* ☎ *514/872–1400* ⊕ *www.espacepourlavie.ca* ✉ *C$21.50 or C$80 for an Espace pour la vie Passport* ☉ *Closed Mon., except during holiday season* Ⓜ *Pie-IX or Viau.*

Maisonneuve

HISTORIC DISTRICT | World War I and the Depression killed early 20th-century plans to turn this industrial center into a model city with broad boulevards, grand public buildings, and fine homes, but just three blocks south of the Olympic site a few fragments of that dream have survived the passage of time.

A magnificent beaux arts building, site of the old public market, which has a 20-foot-tall bronze statue of a farm woman, stands at the northern end of tree-lined avenue Morgan. Farmers and butchers have moved into the modern building next door that houses the **Marché Maisonneuve**, which has become one of the city's major markets, along with Marché Jean-Talon and Marché Atwater. The old market is now a community center and the site of summer shows and concerts.

Monumental staircases and a heroic roof-top sculpture embellish the public baths across the street. The **Théâtre Denise Pelletier,** at the corner of rues Ste-Catherine

Est and Morgan, has a lavish Italianate interior; **Fire Station No. 1**, at 4300 rue Notre-Dame Est, was inspired by Frank Lloyd Wright's Unity Temple in suburban Chicago; and the sumptuously decorated **Église Très-Saint-Nom-de-Jésus**, has one of the most powerful organs in North America. The 198-acre **Parc Maisonneuve**, stretching north of the botanical garden, is a lovely place for a stroll. ⊠ *Hochelaga-Maisonneuve* Ⓜ *Pie-IX or Viau.*

Rio Tinto Alcan Planetarium

OBSERVATORY | FAMILY | In early 2013, Montréal got a new, ultramodern, C$48 million planetarium, one of only a handful of planetariums worldwide to have two circular theaters—one for astronomy exhibits and the other a high-tech multimedia venue. Part of the Espace pour la vie complex, this state-of-the-art facility delivers a futuristic experience unlike any other. The permanent exhibit, lets the whole family have fun exploring life on Earth and (perhaps) in the universe through interactive and hands-on stations. ■TIP➜ **Hours vary seasonally.** ⊠ *4801 av. Pierre-de-Coubertin, Hochelaga-Maisonneuve* ☎ *514/868–3000* ⊕ *www.espacepourlavie.ca/en/planetarium* ✆ *C$21.50 or C$80 for an Espace pour la vie passport* ⊘ *Closed Mon., except for holiday season and in summer* Ⓜ *Viau.*

🎭 Performing Arts

Théâtre Denise Pelletier

THEATER | With an objective to introduce younger audiences to theater, the Pelletier, which celebrated its 50th year in 2014, puts on French-language productions in a beautifully restored Italianate hall. It's a 15-minute walk from the métro station. ⊠ *4353 rue Ste-Catherine Est, Hochelaga-Maisonneuve* ☎ *514/253–8974* ⊕ *www.denise-pelletier.qc.ca* Ⓜ *Joliette or Pie-IX.*

🛍 Shopping

TOYS

Franc Jeu

TOYS | FAMILY | The antithesis of the big-box toy store, this shop carries Corolle dolls from France, as well as educational toys from Québec's Jouets Boom and Gladius lines. ⊠ *Place Versailles, 7275 rue Sherbrooke Est, Hochelaga-Maisonneuve* ☎ *514/352–1771* ⊕ *www.francjeuMontréal.com* Ⓜ *Radisson.*

The Islands

The two islands just east of the city in the St. Lawrence River—Île Ste-Hélène, formed by nature, and Île Notre-Dame, created with the stone rubble excavated from the construction of Montréal's métro—are now used for Montréal's indoor-outdoor playground, Parc Jean-Drapeau.

Expo '67, the World's Fair staged to celebrate the centennial of the Canadian federation, was brought here by the city's then-mayor, Jean Drapeau. It was the biggest party in Montréal's history, firmly placing the city on the international map and marking a defining moment in its evolution as a modern metropolis.

The spirit of coming here for excitement and thrills lives on. La Ronde, a major amusement park that has the world's highest double wooden roller coaster, is on Île Ste-Hélène. On Île Notre-Dame, there's Casino de Montréal, which includes gaming tables and more than 3,200 slot machines. The casino might be the only vestige of nightlife on the islands.

For a different kind of thrill, there's much to learn about the Islands' history. At the Stewart Museum at the Old Fort, kids will love watching soldiers in colonial uniforms hold flag-raising ceremonies twice a day, rehearse maneuvers, and even practice drills and fire muskets.

Did You Know?

With its magical Gardens of Light festival and temporary exhibits on all things botanical, from miniature trees to giant botanical sculptures, Jardin Botanique is one of the city's top attractions.

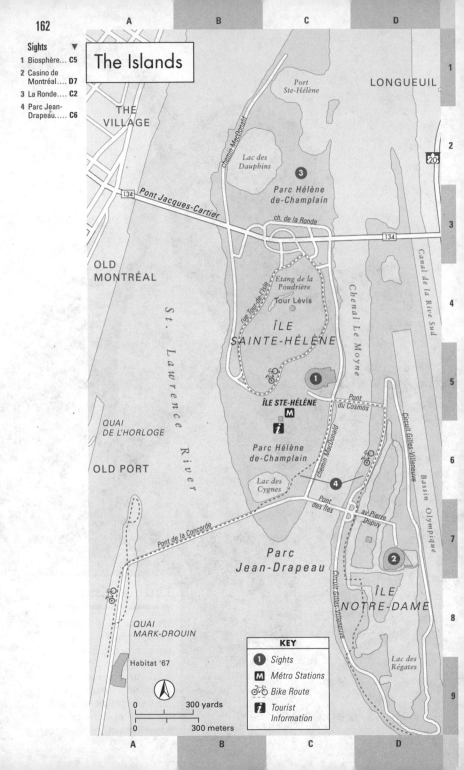

The Islands

LONGUEUIL

Port
Ste-Hélène

THE
VILLAGE

Chemin MacDonald

Lac des
Dauphins

❸

Parc Hélène
de-Champlain

20

134 Pont Jacques-Cartier

ch. de la Ronde

134

OLD
MONTRÉAL

Canal de la Rive Sud

Étang de la
Poudrière
Tour Lévis

rue Tour-de-l'Isle

ÎLE
SAINTE-HÉLÈNE

Chenal Le Moyne

St. Lawrence River

❶

ÎLE STE-HÉLÈNE
M
i

Pont
du Cosmos

QUAI
DE L'HORLOGE

Parc Hélène
de-Champlain

chemin du Tour-de-l'Isle

Circuit Gilles-Villeneuve

OLD PORT

Lac des
Cygnes

❹

Bassin Olympique

Pont
des Îles

av. Pierre
Dupuy

Pont de la Concorde

Parc
Jean-Drapeau

❷

Circuit Gilles-Villeneuve

ÎLE
NOTRE-DAME

QUAI
MARK-DROUIN

Habitat '67

Lac des
Régates

KEY
❶ *Sights*
M *Métro Stations*
🚲 *Bike Route*
i *Tourist
 Information*

0   300 yards

0   300 meters

Lovers of sports and the outdoors enjoy walking the park's 25-plus kilometers of trails, swimming at the aquatic complex or practicing open water swimming in the lake off Île Notre-Dame. In winter, visitors can enjoy skiing, ice-skating, and tobogganing. Nature enthusiasts and photographers love the local wildlife, which includes more than 240 species of birds, as well as groundhogs, squirrels, raccoons, and even red foxes.

GETTING HERE AND AROUND
Both Île Ste-Hélène and Île Notre-Dame are very accessible. You can drive to them via the Pont de la Concorde or the Pont Jacques-Cartier, take the ferry from the Old Port to Île Ste-Hélène (seasonal), or take the métro from the Berri-UQAM station to Jean-Drapeau.

TIMING
If you're traveling with kids, there's enough here to keep them occupied for a full day, especially in nice weather. Because the Islands are so easy to get to with the ferry, visiting can be tacked on to time spent in Old Montréal.

⊙ Sights

Biosphère
SCIENCE MUSEUM | FAMILY | Nothing captures the exuberance of Expo '67 better than the geodesic dome designed by Buckminster Fuller (1895–1983) as the American Pavilion. It's only a skeleton now—the polymer panels that protected the U.S. exhibits from the elements were burned out in a fire long ago—but it's still an eye-catching sight, like something plucked from a science-fiction movie.

Science of a nonfictional kind, however, is explored in the special environmental center the federal government has built in the middle of the dome. It focuses on the challenges of preserving the Great Lakes and St. Lawrence River system, but it has lively and interactive exhibits on climate change, sustainable energy, and air pollution. Kids and others can use

games and interactive displays arranged around a large model of the waterway to explore how shipping, tourism, water supplies, and hydroelectric power are affected. ■TIP→ The Biosphere is now managed by Espace pour la vie. ⊠ Île Ste-Hélène, 160 chemin Tour-de-l'Îsle, The Islands 🕾 514/496–8435 ⊕ espacepourlavie.ca/en/biosphere ⊠ C$21.50 or C$80 for an Espace pour la vie passport ⊘ Closed Mon., except during holiday season Ⓜ Jean-Drapeau.

Casino de Montréal
CASINO | You have to be at least 18 to visit Montréal's government-owned casino, but you don't have to be a gambler. The casino is currently home to three bars and four restaurants, ranging from deli style to gourmet. You can even come just to look at the architecture—the main building was the French pavilion at Expo '67. But if you do want to risk the family fortune, there are more than 3,000 slot machines, a keno lounge, a high-stakes gaming area, and 120 tables for playing blackjack, baccarat, roulette, craps, and various types of poker. There is also music, including cabaret. ⊠ 1 av. du Casino, Île Notre-Dame, The Islands 🕾 514/392–2746, 800/665–2274 ⊕ www.casino-de-Montréal.com ⊠ Free Ⓜ Jean-Drapeau, then Bus 167.

La Ronde
AMUSEMENT PARK/CARNIVAL | FAMILY | Every year, it seems, this amusement park, at the eastern end of Île Ste-Hélène, adds some new and monstrous way to scare the living daylights (and maybe even your lunch) out of you. The most recent additions include Vipère, a free-fly roller coaster that lifts you 107 feet up and subjects you to unexpected drops, vertical free-falls and 360-degree somersaults; Chaos, a single loop that takes you forward, backward, and upside down while sitting face-to-face with other riders; and Titan, a giant swaying pendulum that will have you—or the kids—soaring and spinning 148 feet above the park,

traveling at speeds up to 70 miles per hour. Demon, an extreme ride, will—at high speed (of course)—twist you, twirl you, and turn you upside down, then douse you with water jets. The park also aims to terrify with such stomach-turning champions as the Endor, the Goliath, the Vampire, Monstre, and Vol Ultime. For the less daring, there are Ferris wheels, boat rides, and kiddie rides. The popular International Fireworks Competition is held here on Saturdays and Wednesdays in late June and July. ✉ *22 chemin Macdonald, Île Ste-Hélène* ☎ *514/397–2000* ⊕ *www.sixflags.com/larondeen* ✉ *from C$52 when purchased online at least one day before your visit* ☻ *Hours vary seasonally* Ⓜ *Jean-Drapeau.*

★ Parc Jean-Drapeau

CITY PARK | FAMILY | Île Ste-Hélène and Île Notre-Dame now constitute a single park named, fittingly enough, for Jean Drapeau (1916–99), the visionary (and spendthrift) mayor who built the métro and brought the city both the 1967 World's Fair and the 1976 Olympics. The park includes La Ronde (a major amusement park), acres of flower gardens, a beach with filtered water, the Formula 1 Grand Prix Circuit Gilles Villeneuve, performance spaces, and the Casino de Montréal. There's history, too, at the Old Fort, where soldiers in colonial uniforms display the military methods used in ancient wars. In winter, you can skate on the old Olympic rowing basin or slide down iced trails on an inner tube. ✉ *The Islands* ☎ *514/872–6120* ⊕ *www.parcjeandrapeau.com* Ⓜ *Jean-Drapeau.*

🏃 Activities

RACING

Grand Prix

AUTO RACING | In early June you can join the glitterati of Europe and North America in the grandstand to watch million-dollar Formula One cars shriek around the the Gilles Villeneuve Circuit, a 4.3-km (2.7-mile) track—if you're lucky enough

and rich enough to get a ticket, that is. This is the kind of crowd that uses Perrier to mop up caviar stains from the refreshment tables. During the off season, the track is accessible to everyone. Locals spend sunny summer weekends cycling, rollerblading, and taking walks around this world-famous circuit.

Tickets start at C$90 for general admission (one day) and from C$200 for grandstand tickets (three days). Be sure to book your room early for that entire week, as hotels operate at maximum capacity (and maximum cost). ✉ *Parc Jean Drapeau, 222 Circuit Gilles Villeneuve, The Islands* ☎ *514/350–0000, 855/227–4212 toll-free* ⊕ *gpcanada.ca.*

SWIMMING

Parc-Plage l'Île Notre-Dame (*Plage Jean-Doré*)

SWIMMING | The city's man-made beach on the west side of Île Notre-Dame probably has the cleanest water (tested and monitored) in Montréal. The dress code at the neighboring casino might ban camisoles and strapless tops, but here anything seems to go on hot summer days, when the beach is a sea of oiled bodies. You get the distinct impression that swimming is not uppermost on the minds of many of the scantily clad hordes. If you do want to go in, however, the water is filtered and closely monitored for contamination, and there are lifeguards on duty. A shop rents swimming and boating paraphernalia, and there's a restaurant and picnic areas. ✉ *The Islands* ☎ *514/872–6120* ⊕ *www.parcjeandrapeau.com* ✉ *C$9, C$5.50 after 4pm* Ⓜ *Jean-Drapeau, then Bus 167.*

Sud-Ouest and Lachine

Lower rents and proximity to Downtown make the Sud-Ouest, a historically industrial and poor, working-class area, an appealing alternative. The area consists of Verdun, Saint-Henri, Griffintown, and

Did You Know?

A relic of Canada's World's Fair Exposition in 1967, the massive Biosphère has withstood fire and ice storms to become a museum devoted to the environment.

La petite Bourgogne (aka Little Burgundy). The latter three form what has officially become known as Les Quartiers du Canal, or the Canal Neighborhoods, a gentrifying area lining the Lachine Canal that was once home to factory workers, railway workers, and jazz musicians. These days, the area is better known for its small chef-owned restaurants, design boutiques, antiques shops, and condos populated by young professionals and creatives. Take the time to explore the Griffintown Design District, spanning rues Peel, Ann, Wellington, William, and Notre-Dame O., to get a taste of its 50 or so creative furniture design stores, art galleries, architects' ateliers, and trendy cafés and restaurants. The bilingual Design District booklet can be uploaded from ⊕ *lesquartiersducanal.com/en/ griffintowndesigndistrict.*

If you want to work up an appetite for lunch—or just get some exercise—rent a bike on rue de la Commune, in Old Montréal, and ride west along the 14-km (9-mile) Lachine Canal through what used to be Montréal's industrial heartland to the shores of Lac St-Louis. You could stop at the Marché Atwater to pick up some cheese, bread, wine, and fruit for a picnic in the lakefront park at the end of the trail. If pedaling sounds too energetic, hop aboard an excursion boat and dine more formally in one of the century-old homes that line the waterfront in Lachine, the historic city borough at the western end of the canal that was once the staging point for the lucrative fur trade.

⊙ Sights

Fur Trade at Lachine National Historic Site
HISTORY MUSEUM | Located in the waterfront park at the end of the Lachine Canal, on the shores of Lac St. Louis, this 1803 stone warehouse has been converted into a museum that commemorates the industry that dominated Canada's early history. ⊠ *1255 boul. St-Joseph,*

Lachine ☎ *888/773–8888, 514/637–7433* ⊕ *pc.gc.ca/en/lhn-nhs/qc/lachine* ⊠ *C$4* ⊘ *Closed Oct.–May.*

Lachine Canal National Historic Site
TRAIL | FAMILY | The canal is all about leisure—biking, rollerblading, strolls along the water, and picnicking—but it wasn't always so. Built in 1825 to get boats and cargo around the treacherous Lachine Rapids, it quickly became a magnet for all sorts of industries. But when the St. Lawrence Seaway opened in 1959, allowing large cargo ships to sail straight from the Atlantic to the Great Lakes without stopping in Montréal, the canal closed to navigation and became an illicit dumping ground for old cars and the bodies of victims of underworld killings. The area around it degenerated into an industrial slum.

A federal agency rescued the site in 1978, planting lawns and trees along the old canal, transforming it into a long, narrow park, or *parc linéaire.* Some of the abandoned canneries, sugar refineries, and steelworks have since been converted into desirable residential and commercial condominiums. The bicycle path is the first link in the more than 97 km (60 miles) of bike trails that make up the Pôle des Rapides (☎ *514/364–4490*).

Two permanent exhibits at the Lachine Canal Visitor Services Centre, at the western end of the canal, explain its history and construction. The center also has a shop and lookout terrace. ⊠ *Lachine* ☎ *514/283–6054* ⊕ *pc.gc.ca/ en/lhn-nhs/qc/canallachine/visit* ⊠ *Free* Ⓜ *Angrignon, then bus 195.*

⊙ Restaurants

Blackstrap BBQ
$$ | SOUTHERN | FAMILY | Memphis-style barbecue is the name of the game at this popular, self-serve spot owned and operated by a champion pit master honing his skill behind the smoker and Missouri-imported barbecue pits. Pork, brisket,

Golfing in Montréal

Teeing up in Montréal

Montréal golf enthusiasts have several excellent golf courses available to them, many less than a half-hour drive from Downtown. If you're willing to trek a bit farther (about 45 minutes), you'll find some of the best golfing in the province. For a complete listing of the many golf courses in the area, Tourisme Québec (⊕ *bonjourquebec.com/en-ca*) is the best place to start.

Club de Golf Métropolitain Anjou (Anjou Metropolitan Golf Club). One of the longest courses in the province, the Championship course features an undulating landscape with five lakes and some tricky bunkers, all calling for accurate shots. Beginners and improvers can hone their skills on the short Executive course. A clubhouse featuring a restaurant, several banquet halls, a pro shop with an indoor practice range (winter only), and an outdoor driving range all serve to make this a top-notch facility. A dress code is in effect. The club is in Anjou, a 20-minute drive from Downtown Montréal. ✉ *9555 boul. du Golf, Montréal* ☎ *514/353–5353* ⊕ *www.golfmetropolitainanjou.com* ⌨ *Championship Course, C$27–C$45* ⚑ *Championship Course: 18 holes, 7005 yards, par 3, 4, and 5; Executive Course: 6 holes, 1022 yards, par 3* ☞ *Facilities: Driving range, golf carts, restaurant* Ⓜ *Honoré-Beaugrand.*

The Falcon. Designed by Graham Cooke, this course winds through a verdant, well-wooded landscape dotted with water hazards and sand traps, and offers an exciting challenge. Five sets of tees accommodate different skill levels. It's 25 minutes west of Downtown in the picturesque and largely anglophone village of Hudson (which is worth a visit in itself). ✉ *59 rue Cambridge, Hudson* ☎ *450450/458–1997* ⊕ *www.falcongolf. ca* ⌨ *C$22–C$60 weekdays, C$22–C$76 weekends and holidays* ⚑ *18 holes, 7096 yards, par 72* ☞ *Facilities: Driving range, putting green, golf carts, rental clubs, lessons, restaurant, clubhouse, practice facilities.*

Golf Dorval. The two original courses here, designed by Graham Cooke, were combined into a single challenging par-72 golf course with a rolling parkland setting. There are four levels of difficulty, finishing with a long, narrow par-4 18th hole with a slope up to the green. There's a dress code. The course is a 20-minute drive from downtown Montréal. ■TIP→ **Reserve a weekday morning three days in advance and get two tickets and one cart for C$98–C$106.** ✉ *2000 av. Reverchon, Dorval* ☎ *514/631–4653* ⊕ *www.golfdorval.com* ⌨ *C$20–C$78 weekdays; C$20–C$82 weekends* ⚑ *18 holes, 6643 yards, par 72* ☞ *Facilities: Driving range, putting green, golf carts, rental clubs, lessons, snack bar.*

Golf Ste-Rose. With lovely views of the Rivière des Mille-Îles, hardwood forests, and myriad ponds, this course may be the most beautiful in Québec. It's a short hop over the bridge to the island of Laval. The course features four sets of tees to accommodate different skill levels. The 18-hole course was designed by John Watson, one of the great names of Canadian golf course architecture. ✉ *1400 boul. Mattawa, Ste-Rose* ☎ *450/628–6072, 450/628–3573* ⊕ *www.golfsterose.com* ⌨ *C$30–C$55* ⚑ *18 holes, 6134 yards, par 70* ☞ *Facilities: Driving range, golf carts, rental clubs, restaurant, bar.*

168

Sights ▼

1 Fur Trade at Lachine National Historic Site **B9**

2 Lachine Canal National Historic Site **B9**

Restaurants ▼

1 Blackstrap BBQ **C8**

2 Da Emma ... **D1**

3 Joe Beef **B3**

4 Le Vin Papillon **B3**

5 Nora Gray... **C1**

6 Restaurant le H4C **A4**

7 Satay Brothers **A4**

Quick Bites ▼

1 Patrice Pâtissier **B3**

Hotels ▼

1 ALT Montréal Griffintown . **D1**

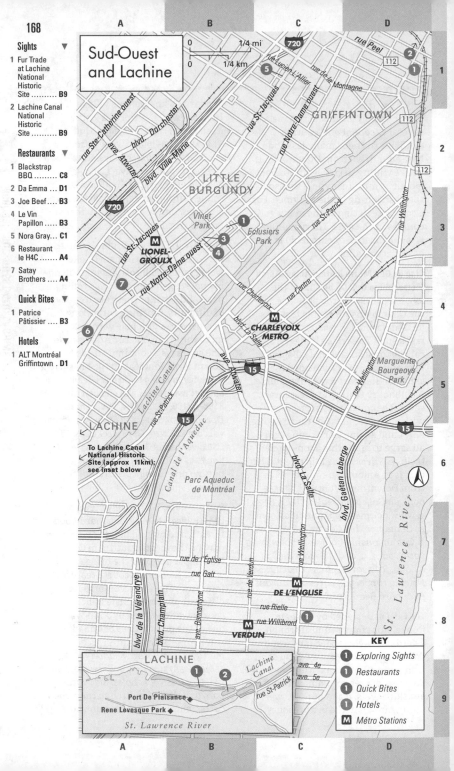

Sud-Ouest and Lachine

KEY

1 Exploring Sights
1 Restaurants
1 Quick Bites
1 Hotels
M Métro Stations

chicken, and ribs all get a secret-rub treatment and are then cooked slowly for up to 16 hours. **Known for:** locally sourced meat; "burnt ends" poutine; Memphis-style barbecue. [$] *Average main: C$19* ✉ *4436 rue Wellington, Verdun* ☎ *514/507–6772* 🌐 *www.blackstrapbbq.ca* 🕒 *Closed Sun. and Mon.* [M] *De l'Église.*

Da Emma

$$$$ | ITALIAN | The cellar of what used to be Montréal's first women's prison hardly sounds like the ideal setting for an Italian eatery, but grandma Emma's cooking hushes any bad vibes from the 1800s. Stone walls and heavy beams serve as backdrop for Roman dishes like roasted lamb, fettuccine *con funghi porcini* and pasta *al vongole*, which have all foregone fussy presentation to focus on superior fixings. **Known for:** rustic, authentic Roman dishes; 300-year-old stone walls; friendly ambience. [$] *Average main: C$36* ✉ *777 rue de la Commune Ouest, Old Montréal* ☎ *514/392–1568* 🕒 *Closed Sun. No lunch* [M] *Square-Victoria.*

★ Joe Beef

$$$$ | MODERN CANADIAN | Eating out at this establishment in the St. Henri/ Little Burgundy neighborhood is a little like being invited to a dinner party by a couple of friends who just happen to be top-notch chefs. Everything written on the chalkboard menu is simple, hearty, and just delicious, from the fresh oysters to the organic rib steak and the now famous lobster spaghetti. **Known for:** celebrity chef; lobster spaghetti; leafy patio. [$] *Average main: C$40* ✉ *2491 rue Notre-Dame Ouest, Verdun* ☎ *514/935–6504* 🌐 *www.joebeef.ca* 🕒 *Closed Sun. and Mon. No lunch* [M] *Lionel-Groulx.*

Restaurant le H4C

$$$$ | CANADIAN | Housed inside a stately former bank topped by a clock tower, this well-worth-the-trek restaurant uses the bank's old vault as a walk-in cellar, while the dining room features stone walls and elegant leather chairs. Main dishes are hard to predict because of the product-driven cuisine, but regularly features local and seasonal ingredients such as snow crab, Québec halibut, asparagus, and fiddleheads—but one thing that indeed does not change is the dedication and resourcefulness of the chef. **Known for:** delicious brunch menu; seasonal tasting menus only; old bank building. [$] *Average main: C$85* ✉ *538 pl. St-Henri, Verdun* ☎ *514/316–7234* 🌐 *leh4c.com* 🕒 *Closed Mon.–Wed. No dinner Sun.* [M] *Place St-Henri.*

★ Le Vin Papillon

$$ | MODERN ITALIAN | First and foremost a wine bar, this atmospheric 30-seat spot also dishes out delicious vegetable-centric, market-based cuisine. The cuisine features local and seasonal ingredients, and the flavors are simple enough to go well with the stars of the show: the many wines on offer. **Known for:** extensive wine list; Italian tapas; Brussels sprouts *à la plancha.* [$] *Average main: C$20* ✉ *2519 rue Notre-Dame Ouest, Verdun* 🌐 *vinpapillon.com* 🕒 *Closed Sun. and Mon.* [M] *Lionel-Groulx.*

Nora Gray

$$$$ | SOUTHERN ITALIAN | The crowd that fills this casual and lively spot nightly is hip, and the simple, modern Southern Italian comfort food and impeccable service keeps them coming back. Start your meal with the roasted cauliflower frittata or the Dungeness crab salad with confit Meyer lemon and deer carpaccio. **Known for:** classic old-world wine list; Southern Italian cuisine; celery root Marsala, mixed mushrooms and hazelnuts. [$] *Average main: C$35* ✉ *1391 rue St-Jacques, Verdun* ☎ *514/419–6672* 🌐 *noragray.com* 🕒 *Closed Sun. and Mon.* [M] *Lucien L'Allier.*

Satay Brothers

$$ | ASIAN | Bringing southeast Asia to southwest Montréal, Satay Brothers is operated by two brothers obsessed with the street food found in Singapore, Malaysia, Thailand, and Cambodia. The eclectic and oddly charming space—think red walls, illuminated Chinese

Under the Big Tent

Montréal's reinvention of the ancient art of the circus began in the 1980s, when two street performers, Guy Laliberté and Daniel Gauthier, founded the now world-famous Cirque du Soleil. But it didn't stop there. The city is also home to a huge complex, out beyond Mont-Royal in the St-Michel district, housing Canada's National Circus School, En Piste (Circus Arts National Network), and Cirque du Soleil's head office. The school attracts budding acrobats and clowns from all over the world, as well as several other smaller schools, and puts on several performances throughout the year at the complex's performance venue, TOHU Cité des Arts du Cirque (⊕ tohu.ca). Montréal has become so synonymous with the circus arts that for 10 days each July, since 2010, the city plays host to Montréal Complètement Cirque (⊕ Montréalcompletementcirque.com), a circus festival that transforms theaters, city streets, parks, and sidewalks into stages showcasing high-flying acrobatic performances by talented artists from around the world.

Cirque du Soleil. This amazing circus is one of Montréal's great success stories. The company—founded in 1984 by a pair of street performers—has completely changed people's idea of what a circus can do. Its shows, now an international phenomenon, use no animals. Instead, colorful acrobatics flirt with the absurd through the use of music, humor, dance, and glorious (and often risqué) costumes.

The Cirque has companies in Las Vegas and one each in Orlando and Los Angeles—but none in Montréal (though its HQ and a circus school are located in the northern part of the city). Nevertheless, every couple of years one of its international touring companies returns to where it all began, the Old Port, and sets up the familiar blue-and-yellow tent for a summer of sold-out shows. ⊠ Montréal ☎ 514/790–1245, 800/361–4595 ⊕ www. cirquedusoleil.com.

Cirque Éloize. This award-winning troop has been touring the globe since 1993, and with well over 4,000 performances under its belt, shows no signs of slowing down. Constantly evolving, Cirque Éloize uses artistic mediums like video and music to bring the circus arts to the masses. ⊠ Montréal ☎ 514/596–3838 ⊕ www.cirque-eloize. com.

Les 7 doigts de la main. Literally translated as "the seven fingers of the hand," the name is a play on a French expression about working collectively toward a common goal, and these seven fingers—the seven founding partners of the circus—have done just that, building up a world-renowned circus troop over the past two decades. Combining acrobatics, theater, and dance, they've performed at special events across the globe, including a Royal Variety Performance for Queen Elizabeth II and at the Olympics in Turin and Vancouver. They even made an appearance on America's Got Talent. ⊠ Montréal ☎ 514/521–4477 ⊕ www.7doigts.com.

Cirque du Soleil is Montréal's hometown circus, founded here in 1984. Today there are several troupes across several countries that perform hundreds of shows per year.

lanterns, a mishmash of Asian patterns and décor—features communal seating and a long bar facing the kitchen, which fires out steamed pork buns, *laksa* soup, papaya salad and, of course, satays to keep the constant and lively crowd fed. **Known for:** long lines; festive ambience; papaya salad. [$] *Average main: C$14* ✉ *3721 Notre-Dame rue O., Verdun* ☎ *514/933–3507* 🌐 *www.sataybrothers.com* [M] *Lionel-Groulx.*

Coffee and Quick Bites

Patrice Pâtissier

$ | BAKERY | FAMILY | Pick up a pastry to go at the counter or choose one of the plated desserts to enjoy on-site at Patrice Pâtissier, a beautifully designed pastry shop and lunch spot, overseen by one of Québec's most renowned pastry chefs. The almond cream with seasonal fruits is luscious and will certainly please those following a gluten-free and/or vegan diet. **Known for:** celebrity chef; frozen pistachio and passion fruit "lollipops" in summer; kouign amann. [$] *Average main: C$5* ✉ *2360 rue Notre-Dame Ouest, Local 104, Verdun* ☎ *514/439–5434* 🌐 *patricepatissier.ca* 🕒 *Closed Mon.–Wed.* [M] *Lionel-Groulx.*

Hotels

ALT Montréal Griffintown

$ | HOTEL | FAMILY | This stylish, tech-savvy Griffintown hotel appeals for its affordable set rates, modular loft-style rooms, partially open 7th floor terrace, light ecofootprint, and the ultimate luxury of no set checkout time. **Pros:** underground parking with Tesla charging stations available; no set checkout time; close to Downtown. **Cons:** a bit of a walk to the métro; no restaurant; minimalist service may not suit those who want more pampering. [$] *Rooms from: C$199* ✉ *120 rue Peel, Verdun* ☎ *514/375–0220, 855/823–8120* 🌐 *www.althotels.com/en/Montréal* 🛏 *154 rooms* 🍴 *No Meals* [M] *Bonaventure, then bus 107.*

☮ Nightlife

Burgundy Lion

PUBS | This British pub in St-Henri serves food that's a notch above the usual. Scotch eggs and the ploughman's lunch are paired with an English take on Québec's beloved poutine—with Stilton cheese and caramelized onions—though it's the fish-and-chips that really shine. Be sure to grab a pint of the Burgundy Lion Ale, or any of the many other beers on draft. Two patios are open in the summer for alfresco drinking. Note that it can get loud in the evenings. ✉ *2496 rue Notre-Dame Ouest, Downtown* ☎ *514/934–0888* ⊕ *www.burgundylion. com* Ⓜ *Lionel-Groulx.*

🎭 Performing Arts

Théâtre Corona

CONCERTS | Built in 1912, this exquisite former cinema and vaudeville theater in the heart of St-Henri has proudly preserved its small stage for the maneuvering of scenery, the artists' lodges under the stage, and the orchestra pit in the foreground. It is the only vintage movie theater in Montréal whose exterior façade and interior have remained almost unchanged. Today the Corona serves as a concert venue for artists like Milk & Bone, Bobby Bazini, Tom Odell, and Rumours of Fleetwood Mac. ✉ *2490 rue Notre Dame Ouest, Westmount* ☎ *855/310–2525* ⊕ *www.theatrecorona. ca/en* Ⓜ *Lionel-Groulx.*

👜 Shopping

CLOTHING

Harricana

SECOND-HAND | Yesterday's old fur coats and stoles are transformed into everything from car coats and ski jackets to baby wraps and throw pillows at this designer shop. For summer, vintage scarves become flirty little tops. The recycled furs, leather, silks, and woolen items are sold at dozens of shops, but the best place to see what's available is this combination atelier and boutique. ✉ *3697 rue Wellington, Verdun* ☎ *514/282–1616 ext. 2221* ⊕ *www.harricana.qc.ca* Ⓜ *De l'Église.*

SIDE TRIPS FROM MONTRÉAL

4

Updated by
Chris Barry

👁 **Sights**
★★★★★

🍴 **Restaurants**
★★★★★

🛏 **Hotels**
★★★★★

🛍 **Shopping**
★★★★☆

🍸 **Nightlife**
★★★★★

WELCOME TO
SIDE TRIPS FROM MONTRÉAL

TOP REASONS TO GO

★ **Ski at Mont-Tremblant:** Heading 150 km (90 miles) north of Montréal takes you to some of the best skiing east of the Rockies, as well as fine hotels and restaurants, a lively ski village, and great golf courses.

★ **Take a driving tour of Eastern Townships wineries:** The vineyards here resemble those in the Niagara Region and Okanagan Valley.

★ **Visit Abbaye St-Benoit-du-Lac:** The Benedictine monks built this splendid church—with its fairy-tale castle bell tower—on the shores of Lake Memphrémagog.

★ **Spend a night among wolves in Parc Omega:** Go with an experienced guide to explore the lives of these great predators in their natural habitat—the magnificent Outaouais region.

★ **Go leaf-peeping ... anywhere:** From mid-September through mid-October the entire Laurentians, Eastern Townships, and Outaouais are ablaze with spectacular fall foliage.

1 Oka. Oka is most famous for its abbey and provincial park, which also features one of Montréal's only nearby nude beaches.

2 St-Sauveur-des-Monts. The unofficial gateway to the Laurentians.

3 Morin Heights. A small, primarily Anglophone hamlet that's home to the popular Ski Morin Heights recreational center.

4 Ste-Adèle. With numerous nearby ski hills and dozens of restaurants and hotels, this is the largest village in the Laurentians.

5 Val-David. Home to the largest farmers' market in the Laurentians and the hugely successful 1001 Pots ceramics exhibition/workshop.

6 Ste-Agathe-des-Monts. Best known for its ski hills and winter activities, Ste-Agathe also plays home to some of the best beaches in the Laurentians.

7 Mont-Tremblant. Consistently ranked one of the top ski centers in eastern North America.

8 Montebello. Best known for its historic Le Château Montebello, a spectacular hotel that's also the largest log cabin in the world.

9 Gatineau. Directly across the water from Ottawa, the nation's capital, Gatineau is a large town that's home to the Canadian Museum of History.

10 Bromont. An all-season recreational center offering the only night skiing in the Townships.

11 Knowlton (Lac Brome). The quintessential Eastern Townships resort town.

12 Abbaye St-Benoît-du-Lac. Located on spectacular grounds bordering Lac Memphrémagog, this impressive abbey operates a quaint shop where you can purchase their own sparkling apple wine and outstanding local cheese.

13 Parc du Mont-Orford. One of the top ski centers in the Townships, in addition to being a nature reserve.

14 Magog. A bustling little town located on the banks of Lac Memphrémagog, Magog has one of the nicest beaches in the Townships.

15 North Hatley. One of eastern Québec's prettiest villages.

16 Sherbrooke. his is the Townships' premier "big city," with trendy restaurants and boutiques lining Wellington street in the downtown core.

17 Notre-Dame-des-Bois. n the shadow of Mont-Megantic with a world-renowned observatory.

In the minds of many who live here, one of Montréal's greatest attributes is its proximity to the sheer physical beauty of the surrounding countryside. From Downtown Montréal you can head in pretty much any direction and within an hour or so, you'll be, if not in the wilderness, then at least in the thick of cottage country. The three most popular side-trip destinations from Montréal are the Laurentians, the Eastern Townships, and the Outaouais—each possessing its own distinct characteristics and flavor.

Most people traveling to this region do so by car, making it easy to spend as much or as little time in any given area as desired. Nevertheless, Québec has created the Route Verte (Green Route), a 5,000-km (3,100-mile) network of bike trails in the southern part of the province. Many of the trails are currently open for access.

MAJOR REGIONS

The Laurentians (les Laurentides) range is a delightful year-round destination for getting outdoors, whether it's for golf and white-water rafting in the summer or skiing and dog sledding in the winter. Along with its stunning natural beauty, it's also known for its authentic Québec food—all of this to be found in little towns like **Oka**, less than an hour's drive from Downtown Montréal, traffic allowing. The main tourist region, which actually encompasses only a small part of the Laurentian mountain range, is divided into two major regions: the Lower Laurentians (les Basses Laurentides) and the Upper Laurentians (les Hautes Laurentides). But don't be fooled by the designations; they don't signify great driving distances. The rocky hills here are relatively low, but many are eminently skiable, with a few peaks above 2,500 feet. Mont-Tremblant, at 3,150 feet, is the region's highest. The resort area begins at **St-Sauveur-des-Monts** (Exit 60 on Autoroute 15) and extends north to **Mont-Tremblant**. Beyond, the region turns into a wilderness of lakes and forests best visited with an outfitter. Fishing guides are concentrated around Parc du Mont-Tremblant. To the first-time visitor, the hilly areas around St-Sauveur, **Ste-Adèle**, **Morin Heights**, Val-Morin, and **Val-David** up to **Ste-Agathe-des-Monts** form a pleasant hodgepodge of villages, hotels, and inns that seem to blend one into another. Tourisme Laurentides in Mirabel provides information and offers a daily lodging-booking service. Its main information center is at the Porte du Nord complex at Exit 51 on Autoroute 15.

The Outaouais. First settled in the mid-19th century and long known for its logging, the Outaouais (pronounced: ewt–away) region is now a nature lover's paradise as well, with 20,000 lakes, countless rivers, 400 km (249 miles) of hiking trails, and 2,730 km (1,696 miles) of snowmobile trails. To fully experience the majesty of the Outaouais wilderness you could spend close to a week here, but simply driving to any of the region's major provincial parks is a good one-day journey. **Montebello**, a little country village on the banks of the Ottawa River, is only a 1½-hour drive from Montréal, and is where you'll find Le Château Montebello, the largest log structure ever built. From there you can find excursions to take you to the surrounding countryside, or if you'd prefer, you can simply take in nearby Omega Park, a safari adventure where you'll bear witness to many of the region's creatures interacting within their natural environment. It encompasses an enormous body of land located in the southwest corner of the province. **Gatineau**, just about two hours outside Montréal, is in another quaint area of Outaouais. Bordering Ontario, and just across the river from Ottawa, this region contains the vast and gorgeous Gatineau Park.

The Eastern Townships (also known as les Cantons de l'Est, and formerly as l'Estrie) refers to the southeast corner of the province of Québec, which borders Vermont, New Hampshire, and Maine, and is known for its mountains, spas, lush forests, and many vineyards. In winter, the Townships are the place to be for serious ski and snowboard enthusiasts, boasting many of the province's highest peaks and most challenging trails. In summer, boating, swimming, sailing, golfing, in-line skating, hiking, and bicycling take over. And every fall the inns are booked solid with visitors eager to take in the brilliant foliage. Fall is also a good time to visit the wineries (although most are open all year). Because of its mild microclimate, the Townships area has become one of the more prominent wine regions in Canada, with a dozen of Québec's 33 commercial wineries.

Planning

When to Go

The Laurentians are a big skiing destination in winter, but the other seasons all have their own charms: you can drive up from Montréal to enjoy the fall foliage; to hike, bike, play golf, camp, or fish; or to engage in spring skiing—and still get back to the city before dark. The only slow periods are early November (aka "mud season"), when there isn't much to do, and June, when the area has plenty to offer but is plagued by black flies. Control programs have improved the situation somewhat.

The Outaouais region is beautiful at any time of year, but unless you're looking to spend several days there it's best to go in summer and stay in the lower region, around Montebello. Making your way up to the provincial parks in the north is a lengthy journey at best, but in winter, potentially hazardous road conditions could well add several more hours to your trip.

The Eastern Townships are best in fall, when the foliage is at its peak; the region borders Vermont and has the same dramatic colors. It's possible to visit wineries at this time, but you should call ahead, since harvest is a busy time.

Getting Here and Around

The Laurentians: Autoroute 15 is the fastest and most direct route from Montréal to the most in-demand spots in the Laurentians. This limited access highway peters out at Ste-Agathe and morphs into Autoroute 117, which runs all the way to Rouyn-Noranda. Exit numbers on Autoroute 15 reflect the distance from Montréal. Autoroute 15 starts at the New York–Québec border where it connects to Interstate 87, so it's also the most direct route for most visitors from the United States. The highway crosses into Montréal on the Champlain Bridge and follows the Décarie and Metropolitan expressways across the island. Visitors arriving from Boston and points east on Interstate 91 can follow Autoroute 55 from the border north to Autoroute 10 (the Autoroute des Cantons de l'Est) and then drive west until it merges with Autoroute 15 at the Champlain Bridge.

The Outaouais: To get to the Outaouais take Autoroute 15 North roughly 40 km (25 miles) until you get to Autoroute 50 West heading toward Lachute. Drive another 70 km (43 miles) past Lachute and you'll soon be in Montebello. Continue on another 15 km (9 miles) to reach Gatineau.

The Eastern Townships: For the Eastern Townships, take Autoroute 10 Est (the Autoroute des Cantons de l'Est) from Montréal, or U.S. 91 from New England, which becomes Autoroute 55 as it crosses the border into the Eastern Townships.

Visitor Information

THE LAURENTIANS Tourisme Laurentides (Porte du Nord). ⊠ 1000 autoroute des Laurentides, St-Jérôme. ☎ 445/224–7007 from Montréal area; 800/561–6673 from rest of North America ⊕ www.laurentides.com.

THE OUTAOUAIS Tourisme Outaouais. ⊠ 103 rue Laurier, Gatineau ☎ 819/778–2222, 800/265–7822 ⊕ www.tourismeoutaouais.com.

THE EASTERN TOWNSHIPS Tourisme Cantons-de-l'Est. ⊠ 20 rue Don-Bosco Sud, Sherbrooke ☎ 819/820–2020, 800/355–5755 ⊕ www.easterntownships.org.

Oka

40 km (25 miles) west of Montréal.

If you like apples and delicious cheese, Oka is sure to be a highlight of your trip. It was once the home of Cistercian monks, but the urban sprawl has driven them from their abbey, on the shores of Lac des Deux-Montagnes, to seek solace farther north in St-Jean-de-Matha in the Lanaudière region, but the cheese they made famous is still produced by a private firm here and is available in local shops. The rolling hills around the little town of Oka are where you'll find many of the apple orchards. If you love cider, follow the Route des Vergers, stopping at various properties along this "Orchard Route" to sample the local wares.

GETTING HERE AND AROUND
To get from Montréal to Oka, take Autoroute 15 North to Autoroute 640 West.

◉ Sights

Hudson
TOWN | A quick detour on the ferry (C$12 one-way) across Lac des Deux-Montagnes brings you to this small town with old houses now used for art galleries, boutiques, and Christmas shops. In winter there's an "ice bridge": basically a plowed path across a well-frozen lake. Taking a walk across the bridge is a singular experience. If you happen to visit on a Saturday from May to October, make a stop at the popular **Finnegan's Market**. Open from 9 to 4, the flea market sells

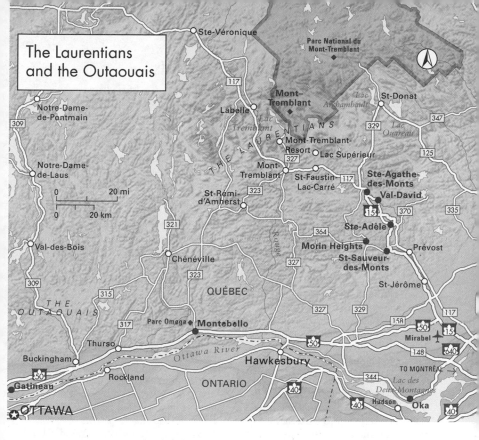

The Laurentians
and the Outaouais

antiques, jewelry, crafts, and preserves, among other goods. ✉ *Hudson* ⊕ *hudson.Québec/en.*

Parc d'Oka (*Oka National Park*)
NATURE SIGHT | Beautifully surrounded by low hills, this park has a lake fringed by a sandy beach and plenty of opportunities for outdoor sports, including hiking and biking trails, kayaking, canoeing, fishing, and, in winter, snowshoeing and cross-country skiing. Locals also consider it to be one of the top camping destinations. Administered by the province along environmentally conscious lines—they implemented the Ecological Integrity Monitoring Program (EIMO) in 2004—it has nearly 900 campsites, and you can rent bicycles, cross-country skis, snowshoes, canoes, and kayaks

from the office. Note that the strip at the far eastern end of the beach is "clothing optional," or, in effect, "clothing nonexistent." ✉ *2020 chemin Oka, Oka* ☎ *450/479–8365, 800/665–6527 activities* ⊕ *www.sepaq.com* ✉ *C$9.*

🛍 Shopping

★ Magasin de l'Abbaye d'Oka
OTHER SPECIALTY STORE | This shop offers a wide variety of local products, not the least being the abbey's famous Oka cheese. They also have a small dining area where you can dine on Oka cheese poutine and other tasty sundries. ✉ *Magasin de l'Abbaye d'Oka, 1600 Oka Road, Oka* ☎ *450/479–6170* ⊕ *www.abbayeoka.ca.*

St-Sauveur-des-Monts

85 km (53 miles) north of Oka, 63 km (39 miles) north of Montréal.

Just a 45-minute drive from Montréal (or 90 minutes when the traffic's heavy, as it frequently is), St-Sauveur is probably the busiest little town in Québec, especially on weekends. Its rue Principale (basically, main street) bristles with bars and restaurants that serve everything from lamb brochettes and spicy Thai stir-fries to steaks and burgers. On summer weekends, the street is so jammed with cars and the sidewalks so packed with visitors that it's sometimes called Crescent Street North after the action-filled street in Montréal. Despite the glitz and the sea of condos that surround it, the town has managed to retain a bit of rural charm in its fine old church and veranda-fronted clapboard homes.

St-Sauveur in winter is no less busy. The "mountains" surrounding the town hardly qualify as Alpine—none has a vertical drop of more than 700 feet—but they're close to Montréal, well serviced by lifts, and lit at night, so the winter sports scene here is very lively. Whether you ski or not, the après-ski scene in St-Sauveur is worth sampling.

GETTING HERE AND AROUND

Take Highway 15 north from Montréal and get off at Exit 60. The best way to explore the main street is to find a parking lot and walk around. Driving through town is difficult in winter, impossible in summer.

VISITOR INFORMATION

CONTACT Tourist Welcome Bureau of Pays-d'en-Haut. ✉ *1014 rue Valiquette, Ste-Adèle* ☎ *450/229–6637* 🌐 *www.lespaysdenhaut.com.*

Sights

Mont-St-Sauveur Water Park
WATER PARK | FAMILY | Slides, a giant wave pool, a wading pool, and snack bars will all keep the kids occupied here. The river rafting attracts an older, braver crowd; the nine-minute ride follows the natural contours of steep hills. On the tandem slides, plumes of water flow through figure-eight tubes and make for a great time. But if you'd rather stay dry, take an adventure through the trees on their zip line or enjoy a fast ride with the Viking Alpine Coaster. ✉ *350 rue St-Denis, St-Sauveur-des-Monts* ☎ *450/227–4671* 🌐 *www.sommets.com/en* 🎟 *C$49.99.*

Musée du ski des Laurentides
OTHER MUSEUM | The Laurentians are one of the oldest ski regions in North America, and ski buffs will enjoy this little museum tracing the long history of this area with great photos, artifacts, and some interesting models of early ski lifts. It also houses the Temple de la Renomée du ski (the Ski Hall of Fame). ✉ *30 rue Filion, St-Sauveur-des-Monts* ☎ *877/227–2564* 🌐 *museeduski.com* 🎟 *Free, though donation of C$3 suggested.*

Hotels

Relais St-Denis
$ | B&B/INN | Once a wartime refuge for well-heeled English children and their governesses, this inn and spa now offers everyone a refuge from everyday stress, with a fireplace and a whirlpool bath in every room and a year-round outdoor heated pool and steam room. **Pros:** walking distance to restaurants, outlet shopping, and activities; variety of spa services and in-room massage packages; kitchenette in all rooms and suites. **Cons:** Wi-Fi can be slow; decor is basic and could use updating; no restaurant on site. [$] *Rooms from: C$139* ✉ *61 rue St-Denis, St-Sauveur-des-Monts* ☎ *450/227–4766, 888/997–4766* 🌐 *www.relaisstdenis.com* 🛏 *42 rooms* 🍴 *No Meals.*

One of the most popular times to visit the region is in fall, when the mountains are splashed with a spectrum of warm yellows, oranges, and reds.

🛍 Shopping

SHOPPING CENTERS

Rue Principale

NEIGHBORHOODS | Small fashion boutiques, restaurant terraces, and cute gift shops in old French-Canadian and Victorian homes adorned with bright awnings and flowers line this popular tree-lined shopping street. ✉ *St-Sauveur-des-Monts.*

🏃 Activities

SKIING

Sommet St-Sauveur

SKIING & SNOWBOARDING | The hills surrounding St-Sauveur might be relatively low, but this vibrant ski resort is long-established and perennially popular for good reason. It has an extensive skiable area, good snow-making and lift capacity, and many trails that are lit at night, making it possible for energetic Montrealers to drive up after work for a couple of hours of skiing. There are several other hills in the area, but Mont-St-Sauveur is the largest, with a 700-foot vertical drop

and 142 acres of skiable terrain. Seventeen of its 38 trails are for beginners and intermediates, 16 are for experts, and five are rated extreme. Mont-Avila has 13 trails (two beginner, three intermediate, five difficult, three extremely difficult), a snow park, a fun tubing park, and the Viking, a tobaggan-style ride in a cart that twists and turns on a track through the forest. ✉ *350 av. St-Denis, St-Sauveur* ☎ *450/227–4671* ⊕ *www.sommets.com.*

Station de Ski Mont-Habitant

SKIING & SNOWBOARDING | More than 60 years in operation, Mont-Habitant is one of the last of the independent ski operations in St-Sauveur. This mountain has always been a favorite with families and with beginner and intermediate skiers because the vertical drop is just 600 feet and the 10 trails are relatively gentle. Mont-Habitant also has St-Sauveur's only beach, which makes it very popular in summer. ✉ *12 chemin des Skieurs, St-Sauveur-des-Monts* ☎ *450/227–2637, 866/887–2637* ⊕ *www.monthabitant.com* 🎟 *C$55 day pass.*

Morin Heights

10 km (6 miles) west of St-Sauveur-des-Monts, 73 km (45 miles) northwest of Montréal.

If St-Sauveur is too busy and overdeveloped for your liking, Morin Heights is a great alternative, with plenty of restaurants, bookstores, boutiques, and craft shops to explore free from the crowds. The town's British architecture and population reflect its settlers' heritage; most residents here speak English.

In summer, windsurfing, swimming, and canoeing on the area's two lakes—Claude and Lafontaine—are popular. In fall and winter, come for the foliage and the Alpine and Nordic skiing.

GETTING HERE AND AROUND

From Montréal to Morin Heights, take Autoroute 15 North, then take Exit 60.

Hotels

Morin Heights is true cottage country, and thus options for accommodation are slim. Your best bet might be to rent a cottage, or as they're known by French-speaking locals, a *chalet*. The Montréal pages for and are full of posts advertising private chalet rentals in the Laurentians. If you'd prefer to go through a third party, most area real estate agents broker short- and long-term cottage and chalet rentals as well; try Remax Laurentides (☎ *450/227–8411*).

Hotel Alila

$ | **B&B/INN** | This auberge by the main road is one of the best-equipped spa destinations in the area, and its outdoor terrace is a pleasant place to relax. **Pros:** garden has cold-water pools; some rooms have beautiful views of the Rivière du Nord; whirlpool baths and fireplaces in some units. **Cons:** breakfast not included; close to highway; isolated from village. [$] *Rooms from: C$108* ✉ *500 Rte. 364, Morin Heights* ☎ *450/644–0168* 🌐 *www.alila.ca* 🛏 *29 rooms* 🍴 *No Meals.*

Shopping

CRAFTS

Créations d'Aujourd'hui

CRAFTS | Specializing in decorative accessories, unique jewelry, candles, soaps, and natural perfumes, most created by local artists and artisans, many of the items on sale here have been transformed and repurposed by the shop's owner to give them a distinctive second life. ✉ *Créations d'Aujourd'hui, 910, chemin du Village, Morin Heights* ☎ *450/644–0089* 🌐 *creationsdaujourdhui.weebly.com.*

Activities

SPAS

Amerispa Spa Nordique

SPAS | Only 45 minutes outside Montréal, this is a great place to escape and unwind. Hidden in a Laurentian forest of maples, firs, and birches is a beautifully rustic pavilion housing a spa with hot tubs and cold pools, eucalyptus-scented steam baths, and thermal and Nordic waterfalls. The Elixir Ice Cider Massage with companion body wrap is a must. ✉ *160 rue Watchorn, Morin Heights* ☎ *450/226–7722, 866/263–7477* 🌐 *www.amerispa.ca.*

SKIING

Ski Morin Heights

SKIING & SNOWBOARDING | **FAMILY** | This small, family-oriented ski center with 32 trails (for all levels) offers a warm and friendly place to enjoy winter sports. Downhill and cross-country skiing, snowboarding, and snowshoeing are available and free daycare is offered to skiers. ✉ *231 rue Bennett, Morin Heights* ☎ *450/227–2020* 🌐 *www.sommets.com/en/ski-mountains/sommet-morin-heights* 🎫 *C$64 ski pass for the day.*

Ste-Adèle

12 km (7 miles) north of Morin Heights, 85 km (53 miles) north of Montréal.

Although Ste-Adèle is not as pretty as St-Sauveur, this town has a lot to offer, with attractions and activities to please families, outdoors enthusiasts, and visitors who want to experience something of the local culture. With a permanent population of more than 10,000, it's the largest community in the lower part of the Laurentians, and has good boutiques, restaurants, summer theater (performed in French), and art galleries. Active types can find horseback riding, golf, and lengthy bike trails in summer and skiing in winter.

GETTING HERE AND AROUND

From Montréal to Ste-Adèle, take Autoroute 15 North and then take Exit 67.

VISITOR INFORMATION

CONTACT Tourist Welcome Bureau of Pays-d'en-Haut. ✉ *1014, rue Valiquette, Ste-Adèle* ☎ *450/229–6637* 🌐 *www.lespaysdenhaut.com.*

Sights

Au Pays des Merveilles

AMUSEMENT PARK/CARNIVAL | FAMILY | Fairy tale characters such as Snow White, Little Red Riding Hood, and Alice in Wonderland wander the grounds, playing games with children. Small fry may also enjoy the petting zoo, amusement rides, wading pool, and puppet show. A ride called Le Petit Train des Merveilles (the Little Train of Wonders) is a nod to the historic train that launched the tourism industry in the Laurentians. There are 45 activities, enough to occupy those aged two to eight for about half a day. Check the website for discount coupons. The theme park is completely accessible to strollers and wheelchairs. ✉ *3795 Chemin de la Savane, Ste-Adèle* ☎ *450/229–3141* 🌐 *www.paysmerveilles.com* 🎟 *C$24.*

Restaurants

Nickels

$$ | SANDWICHES | FAMILY | One of the last surviving franchises of Celine Dion's formerly ubiquitous Nickels chain, large portions of reasonably priced smoked meat, barbecued chicken, and other classic deli fare are on the menu at this family restaurant. **Known for:** classic deli; smoked meat; affordable. [$] *Average main: C$15* ✉ *480, boul. Sainte-Adèle, St-Adèle* ☎ *450/229–9553* 🌐 *nickelsdeli.com.*

Hotels

Auberge & Spa Beaux Rêves

$ | B&B/INN | With a year-round Nordic spa and outdoor hot tub, hammocks hung all around the property, and a waterfall, relaxation is the order of the day at this rustic riverside retreat. **Pros:** all about "unplugging"; personalized packages tailored to meet specific needs; all rooms overlook the river and have balconies or walk-out terraces. **Cons:** no pool; no phone or television in rooms; can be noisy due to close proximity to the road. [$] *Rooms from: C$158* ✉ *2310 boul. Ste-Adèle, Ste-Adèle* ☎ *450/229–9226, 800/279–7679, 514/316–7808 From Montréal* 🌐 *www.beauxreves.com* 🛏 *9 rooms, 1 loft* 🍴 *Free Breakfast.*

Hôtel Mont-Gabriel

$ | HOTEL | FAMILY | At this 1,200-acre resort you can relax in a contemporary room with a valley view or commune with nature in a rustic-style cabin with a fireplace, and there are activities aplenty. **Pros:** reasonable packages on offer; beautiful grounds; ski-out from many rooms. **Cons:** some complaints of poor service; can be noisy; rooms are on the small side. [$] *Rooms from: C$139* ✉ *1699 chemin du Mont-Gabriel, Ste-Adèle* ☎ *450/229–3547, 800/668–5253* 🌐 *www.montgabriel.com* 🛏 *132 rooms* 🍴 *No Meals.*

🏃 Activities

GOLF

Club de Golf Chantecler

GOLF | Every hole here will provide panoramic views of the surrounding Laurentian scenery. Opened in 1950, this semiprivate club offers a mountainside course with long and narrow fairways and three sets of tees for different skill levels. Just one hour from Montréal, it's easy and convenient for a day trip. ⊠ *2520 chemin du Club, Ste-Adèle* ☎ *450/476–1339, 450/229–3742* ⊕ *www. groupebeaudet.com* ⊠ *C$25–C$40* 🏌 *18 holes, 6120 yards, par 72* ⛳ *Facilities: Putting green, golf carts, pull carts, rental clubs, pro shop, restaurant, bar.*

SKIING

Ski Mont-Gabriel

SKIING & SNOWBOARDING | Part of Les Sommets chain of ski resorts, Mont Gabriel has five lifts, 18 superb downhill trails, which are primarily for intermediate and advanced skiers, and a vertical drop of 656 feet. It's about 19 km (12 miles) northeast of Ste-Adèle. ⊠ *1501 chemin du Mont-Gabriel, Ste-Adèle* ⊕ *www. sommets.com/en/ski-mountains/sommet-gabriel* ⊠ *C$48 day ski pass.*

Val-David

33 km (20 miles) west of Ste-Adèle, 82 km (51 miles) north of Montréal.

Val-David is a major destination for mountain climbers, hikers, and campers. It's also a place that many Québec artists and artisans call home, a fact suggested by the several galleries and marvelous art shops in town.

GETTING HERE AND AROUND

The village is just a couple of kilometers east of Exit N6 on Autoroute 15, making it easy to get to by car, but it's also accessible by bicycle: Le P'tit Train du Nord cycling trail runs right through town.

VISITOR INFORMATION

CONTACT Tourist Bureau of Val-David. ⊠ *2525 rue de l'Église, Val-David* ☎ *888/322–7030, 819/324–5678* ⊕ *www. valdavid.com.*

👁 Sights

Village du Père Noël (*Santa Claus Village*)

OTHER ATTRACTION | FAMILY | Santa is not just for Christmas here. In his summer residence kids can sit on his knee and speak to him in French or English, then have fun in the grounds, which contain bumper boats; a petting zoo with goats, sheep, horses, and colorful birds; games; and a large outdoor pool in the summer. There is a snack bar, but visitors are encouraged to bring their own food (there are numerous picnic tables). During the cold winter months, the park transforms into a winter wonderland with skating rinks and tubing fun for the kids. ⊠ *987 rue Morin, Val-David* ☎ *819/322–2146, 800/287–6635* ⊕ *www.noel.qc.ca* ⊠ *C$23.49.*

🍽 Restaurants

★ Au Petit Poucet

$$ | CANADIAN | FAMILY | For a true Québécois treat, stop by this rustic cabin for breakfast or lunch. Founded in 1945, it's a big draw with tourists and locals alike. **Known for:** fresh baked country bread; generous portions; good variety of breakfast options. $ *Average main: C$20* ⊠ *1030 Rte. 117, Val-David* ☎ *819/322–2246, 888/334–2246* ⊕ *www.aupetitpoucet.com* ☾ *No dinner.*

🛏 Hotels

★ La Maison de Bavière

$ | B&B/INN | Walking into this charming B&B is like being transported to a cozy Bavarian mountain inn. **Pros:** lovely backyard facing the rushing Rivière du Nord; directly across from the P'tit Train du Nord cycling and cross-country ski trail;

two-minute walk to the village of Val-David. **Cons:** the bedroom of the efficiency/studio apartment is only accessible by a short ladder; common area is small and right off the bedrooms, so guests need to keep voices down; only four rooms. [$] *Rooms from: C$140* ✉ *1470 chemin de la Rivière, Val-David* ☎ *819/322–3528, 866/322–3528* 🌐 *www.maisondebaviere.com* 🛏 *6 rooms* 🍴 *Free Breakfast.*

Performing Arts

★ Le Centre d'exposition de Val-David
ARTS CENTERS | Showcasing the work of regional and international artists, the nonprofit Le Centre d'exposition de Val-David is the largest art gallery and exhibition hall in the area. Admission is free. ✉ *Le Centre d'exposition de Val-David, 2495 de l'Eglise, Val-David* ☎ *819/322–7474* 🌐 *centreexpositionvaldavid.com.*

Shopping

CERAMICS

1001 Pots
CERAMICS | One of the most interesting events in Val-David is this ceramic exhibition, held from July through mid-August, which started in 1988. On view is the Japanese-style pottery of 1001 Pots' founder Kinya Ishikawa—as well as pieces by up to 100 other ceramists. Ishikawa's studio also displays work by his wife, Marie-Andrée Benoît, who makes fish-shaped bowls with a texture derived from pressing canvas on the clay. There are workshops for adults and children throughout the exhibition, and there is always at least one artisan on-site. While you're there, take the time to enjoy tea in one of the three beautiful gardens and learn the art of the Japanese tea ceremony. ✉ *2435 rue de l'Église, Val-David* ☎ *819/322–6868* 🌐 *www.1001pots.com* ☞ *C$3 admission.*

HOUSEHOLD

Atelier Bernard Chaudron, Inc.
HOUSEWARES | If you're looking for an interesting conversation piece to bring back home with you, check out master craftsman Bernard Chaudron's hand-forged, lead-free pewter household objects that include oil lamps, hammered-silver beer mugs, pitchers, candleholders, and animal-themed knife rests. ✉ *2347 rue de l'Église, Val-David* ☎ *819/322–3944, 888/322–3944* 🌐 *www.chaudron.ca.*

Activities

SKIING

Centre de Ski Vallée-Bleue
SKIING & SNOWBOARDING | Family-run and family-focused, this ski hill suits everyone, from beginners to advanced level skiers and snowboarders, with 19 trails, three lifts, and a vertical drop of 365 feet. ✉ *1418 chemin Vallée-Bleue, Val-David* ☎ *819/322–3427, 866/322–3427* 🌐 *www.valleebleue.com* 🎟 *Ski pass from C$30.*

Ste-Agathe-des-Monts

5 km (3 miles) north of Val-David, 96 km (60 miles) northwest of Montréal.

The wide, sandy beaches of Lac des Sables are the most surprising feature of Ste-Agathe-des-Monts, a tourist town best known for its ski hills. Water activities include canoeing, kayaking, swimming, and fishing. Ste-Agathe is also a stopover point on the Linear Park, the bike trail between St-Jérôme and Mont-Laurier.

GETTING HERE AND AROUND

From Montréal to Ste-Agathe-des-Monts, take Autoroute 15 North. Take Exit 89 to reach QC–329 South, and then take QC–117.

VISITOR INFORMATION

CONTACT Tourist Bureau of Ste-Agathe-des-Monts. ✉ *24 rue St-Paul est, Ste-Agathe-des-Monts* ☎ *819/326–3731, 888/326–0457* 🌐 *ville.sainte-agathe-des-monts.qc.ca/visiteurs/bureau-daccueil-touristique.*

Beaches

Major Beach

SWIMMING | FAMILY | The biggest, most popular municipal beach in Ste-Agathe. Full-day admission is C$12. **Amenities:** lifeguards; parking (free); showers; water sports. **Best for:** swimming. ✉ *Major Beach, 1 Chemin du Lac des Sables, Ste-Agathe-des-Monts* ☎ *819/326–3731, 888/326–0457* 🌐 *ville.sainte-agathe-des-monts.qc.ca/citoyens/activites/plages-municipales.*

Hotels

Hôtel Spa Watel

$$ | HOTEL | If you're looking for a room with a double-size Jacuzzi, a fireplace, and a balcony with a superb view of Lac des Sables, try this white-painted, lodge-style hotel, which is also convenient for the boutiques and cultural activities in Ste-Agathe. **Pros:** year-round outdoor spas; adjacent to three beaches; indoor and outdoor pools and Jacuzzis. **Cons:** the facilities could stand to benefit from a little updating; some lake-view rooms are off an enclosed glass balcony, motel style, so they don't receive direct air from outside; not all rooms have a Jacuzzi, fireplace, and lake view. [$] *Rooms from: C$160* ✉ *250 rue St-Venant, Ste-Agathe-des-Monts* ☎ *819/326–7016, 800/363–6478* 🌐 *www.hotelspawatel.com* 🛏 *31 rooms* 🍴 *Free Breakfast.*

Camping

In the woods near a lively resort area, Camping Ste-Agathe-des-Monts has activities for all age groups, from sport competitions to outings for the kids. There's a sandy beach where you can rent canoes and kayaks and launch your boat from the town's marina. Reservations for this campground (open mid-May through September) are recommended. ✉ *2 chemin du Lac-des-Sables, Ste-Agathe-des-Monts 819/324–0482 or 800/561–7360* 🌐 *www.campingsteagathe.com.*

Activities

BOAT TOURS

Alouette V and VI

BOATING | These sightseeing boats offer guided 50-minute tours of Lac des Sables. They run at least seven times a day from mid-June to mid-August and five times a day from mid-August to mid-October. The first boat leaves the dock at 11:30 am. ✉ *Municipal Dock, rue Principale, Ste-Agathe-des-Monts* ☎ *819/326–3656, 866/326–3656* 🌐 *www.croisierealouette.com* 🎟 *C$21.75 for 50-minute cruise.*

Mont-Tremblant

25 km (16 miles) north of Ste-Agathe-des-Monts, 100 km (62 miles) north of Montréal.

At more than 3,000 feet, Mont-Tremblant is one of the highest peaks in the Laurentians and a major draw for skiers. The resort area at the foot of the mountain (called simply Tremblant) is spread around 14-km (9-mile)-long Lac Tremblant and is consistently—and

Renting a Ski Chalet in Mont-Tremblant 🛏

If you think you'd like to spend more than a few days in the Laurentians you might want to consider renting a chalet from a private owner. There are generally plenty to choose from, and not only is a private rental often less expensive than staying at a hotel, it's a lot homier as well, especially if you are traveling with children. And even with the many restaurants in Mont-Tremblant, every once in a while it's nice to buy groceries and come home to cook your own dinner.

Options range from cozy little cottages for four to multibedroom properties where you could have a real house party with family and friends. If you fill a place to capacity the cost can be very competitive, particularly if you don't mind being outside the main hub of the resort or out of the peak season. Some places offer weekend rates as well as renting by the week. Very good sources for chalet rentals in this part of the province are the websites and the Montréal pages are full of posts advertising private chalet rentals in the Laurentians. If you'd prefer to go through a third party, most area real estate agents broker short- and long-term cottage and chalet rentals as well. Try Remax Laurentides at 286 Principal in St-Sauveur (☎ 450/227–8411) for starters.

justifiably—ranked among the top ski resorts in eastern North America.

The hub of the resort is a pedestrians-only village that gives an architectural nod to the style of New France, with dormer windows and colorful steep roofs on buildings that house pubs, restaurants, boutiques, sports shops, a movie theater, self-catering condominiums, and hotels. A historical town this is not: built for the resort, it may strike you as a bit of Disney in the mountains.

GETTING HERE AND AROUND
The easiest way to get here is by car. Drive north on Autoroute 15 until it ends just beyond Ste-Agathe-des-Monts and then continue on Route 117 (a four-lane highway) for another 30 km (18 miles) to the Mont-Tremblant exit (Exit 119). The resort's parking lots are vast, but they fill up quickly. A shuttle bus links them to the main resort and ski area. Mont-Tremblant has two tourist offices, one in the village and one in the downtown area.

VISITOR INFORMATION
CONTACT Tourisme Mont-Tremblant.
✉ 5080 Montée Ryan, Mont-Tremblant ☎ 877/425–2434, 819/425–2434 ⊕ www.mont-tremblant.ca.

◉ Sights

La Diable Vistors' Centre
VISITOR CENTER | The park entrance closest to Mont-Tremblant is at La Diable Vistors' Centre, just beyond the village of Lac-Supérieur and about a half-hour drive from the resort. ✉ 3824 chemin du Lac Supérieur, Lac Supérieur ☎ 819/688–2281 visitor center, 800/665–6527 Sépaq (government national park agency) ⊕ www.sepaq.com/pq/mot.

★ Parc National du Mont-Tremblant
NATIONAL PARK | **FAMILY** | This vast wildlife sanctuary has more than 400 lakes and rivers and is home to nearly 200 species of birds and animals, so it's great for wildlife watching. Cross-country skiers, snowshoers, and snowmobilers enjoy the park's trails in winter and camping, fishing, canoeing, and hiking are the

Did You Know?

With summer activities like festivals, hiking, biking, zip-lining, and a luge trail, Mont-Tremblant's Alpine pedestrian village is well worth a visit outside ski-season.

popular summer activities. The park was once the home of the Algonquins, who called this area Manitonga Soutana, meaning "mountain of the spirits." ✉ *Mont-Tremblant* ☎ *800/665–6527* 🌐 *www.sepaq.com* 🎫 *C$9 per day.*

Hotels

★ Fairmont Tremblant

$$$$ | **HOTEL** | **FAMILY** | The centerpiece of the Tremblant resort area takes its cues from the grand 19th-century railroad "castle hotels" scattered throughout Canada. **Pros:** easy access to ski hills and the village; poolside barbecue during the summer; dogs (under 50 lbs.) allowed. **Cons:** public parking (fees may apply) is a 10-minute walk away; valet parking C$25 plus tax; it's in the fairly busy village rather than more scenic grounds. [$] *Rooms from: C$320* ✉ *3045 chemin de la Chapelle, Mont-Tremblant* ☎ *819/681–7000, 800/257–7544* 🌐 *www.fairmont.com/tremblant* 🛏 *314 rooms* 🍴 *Free Breakfast.*

Le Grand Lodge

$$ | **HOTEL** | **FAMILY** | At this Scandinavian-style log-cabin hotel, on 13½ acres on the shore of Lac Ouimet, you'll find great year-round amenities and activities for families and sports lovers and a resort-style feel that survives its busy conference trade schedule. **Pros:** private beach; peaceful environment amid woods and walking trails; ice rink and ice path in winter. **Cons:** fireplaces are gas, not wood-burning; narrow swimming pool; rooms and suites not very stylish. [$] *Rooms from: C$170* ✉ *2396 rue Labelle, Mont-Tremblant* ☎ *819/425–2734, 800/567–6763* 🌐 *www.legrandlodge.com* 🛏 *112 rooms* 🍴 *Free Breakfast.*

Quintessence

$$$$ | **HOTEL** | There are spectacular views of Lac Tremblant from every room of this quiet, chic, boutique hotel near the ski slopes. **Pros:** lovely garden; very large, elegant rooms ranging from 700 to 1,200 square feet; massages in your suite; concierge can provide firewood. **Cons:** offer of babysitting service for guests but not all sitters satisfactory; furnishings could be of better quality; very expensive. [$] *Rooms from: C$510* ✉ *3004 chemin de la Chapelle, Mont-Tremblant* ☎ *819/425–3400, 866/425–3400* 🌐 *www.hotelquintessence.com* 🛏 *31 suites* 🍴 *Free Breakfast.*

Performing Arts

Festi Jazz

FESTIVALS | Tons of fun and completely free, the very popular five-day jazz festival in early August draws in at least 15,000 tourists and locals to Mont-Tremblant. The concerts take place under the stars on two outdoor stages and in at least 10 restaurants, bars, and hotels in the Village or St-Jovite (downtown area). ✉ *Mont-Tremblant* 🌐 *www.jazzmttremblant.com.*

Festival International du Blues de Tremblant

(*Tremblant International Blues Festival*)

CONCERTS | People don't just flock to Mont-Tremblant for outdoor fun. This place is becoming a music lovers' paradise, especially for 10 days in July when the Blues Festival takes place with more than 130 shows. Artists such as Otis Taylor, JJ Grey & Mofro, and Thornetta Davis entertain fans on outdoor stages and in intimate clubs right in the village. ✉ *Mont-Tremblant* ☎ *819/681–3000 #46643* 🌐 *blues.tremblant.ca/en.*

Activities

GOLF

Mont-Tremblant

GOLF | The same company that operates the ski resort also runs two of the most challenging and popular championship golf courses in Québec. **Le Géant** (the Giant) was designed by Thomas McBroom to take full advantage of the fantastic scenery. **Le Diable** (the

Devil), with long narrow fairways and strategically placed red sand bunkers, was designed by Michael Hurdzan and Dana Fry. Also at Le Diable, you can find the reputable Tremblant Golf Academy. ⊠ *Mont-Tremblant* ☎ *866/356–2233, 866/783–5634* ⊕ *www.tremblant.ca* ⬛ *C$129* ⫣. *Le Diable, 18 holes, 7056 yards, par 71; Le Géant, 18 holes, 6836 yards, par 72* ☞ *Facilities: Le Diable: Driving range, putting green, golf carts, caddies (digital/GPS), rental clubs, pro shop, golf academy/lessons, restaurant, bar; Le Géant: Driving range, putting green, golf carts, rental clubs, pro shop, gold academy/lessons, restaurant, bar.*

SKIING
Mont-Tremblant
SKIING & SNOWBOARDING | With a 2,116-foot vertical drop, 654 acres of skiable terrain, 95 trails, 18 acres of ramps and jumps for snowboarders, and enough state-of-the-art snowmaking equipment to blanket a small city, Mont-Tremblant is truly one of the great ski resorts of North America, arguably the best east of the Rockies. Its 14 lifts—including two heated gondolas and five high-speed, four-passenger chairlifts—can handle 27,230 skiers an hour. It has some of the toughest expert runs on the continent, but it also has long, gentle runs like the 6-km (3.7-mile) Nansen and dozens of exciting trails for intermediate skiers. Its altitude and location, as well as all that snowmaking equipment, gives it some of eastern Canada's most reliable ski conditions, especially now that winters are getting warmer. All this doesn't come cheap, mind you. A day lift ticket costs C$119 on weekends, but for serious skiers there is no better mountain in Québec. ⊠ *1000 chemin des Voyageurs, Mont-Tremblant* ☎ *866/356–2233, 819/681–3000* ⊕ *www.tremblant.ca* ⬛ *One-day lift ticket C$119.*

Montebello

130 km (80 miles) west of Montréal.

Located on the banks of the Ottawa River, this little village is best known for the Fairmont Le Château Montebello, a spectacular hotel touted as the largest log cabin in the world. Given the town's relative proximity to Ottawa, the nation's capital, more than a few world leaders and dignitaries have visited Montebello for one of the many international summits hosted by the Château since it was built in 1930. The Outaouais in general is well-known for the rugged beauty of its wilderness, and even in this more populated southern section of the region there's still excellent fishing, hunting, canoeing, hiking, and wildlife-spotting, with a series of hiking paths starting right beside the Château Montebello. Even if an expedition into the bush isn't quite your thing, you can still get up close to the local wildlife in a more controlled environment at Parc Omega, home to a wide variety of indigenous species and domestic animals.

GETTING HERE AND AROUND
From Montréal, take Autoroute 50 West for 130 km (80 miles); it's about a 90-minute trip.

VISITOR INFORMATION
CONTACT Montebello Tourist Information Office. ⊠ *Gare de Montebello, 502-A rue Notre-Dame, Montebello* ☎ *819/423–5602* ⊕ *www.tourismeoutaouais.com.*

⊙ Sights

Parc Omega
NATURE PRESERVE | FAMILY | In the 1,800 acres of hills, valleys, rivers, and streams that make up the park, visitors drive along designated trails to view wild animals roaming free in their beautiful natural environment. These include bear, Alpine ibexes, buffalo, wolves, elk, and more. There are also walking trails among

nonaggressive species like white-tailed deer, with caged golf-cart rental available in summer to save the legwork. Also in summer, you can visit farm animals in the restored 19th-century Léopold's Farm and see a birds of prey show. ✉ *399 Rte. 323 N, Montebello* ☎ *819/423–5487* 🌐 *www.parcomega.ca* 🎟 *C$33.*

🍴 Restaurants

Le Napoleon

$$$ | **ITALIAN** | In what is basically a one-street town, this restaurant's reputation for serving outstanding food at affordable prices stands out, and the knowledgeable, personable waitstaff does, too. Though the cuisine is primarily Italian, some Mediterranean, French, and Québécois influences are also in evidence, backed up by a fairly extensive and reasonably priced wine list. **Known for:** beautiful quiet area; great wine list; good food at reasonable prices. [$] *Average main: C$26* ✉ *489 rue Notre-Dame, Montebello* ☎ *819/423–5555* 💳 *No credit cards* 🕒 *No lunch.*

🛏 Hotels

★ Fairmont Le Château Montebello

$$$$ | **HOTEL** | **FAMILY** | On a bank of the Ottawa River, with its own marina, this grand log-built hotel provides rustic luxury, local flavor, beautiful grounds, great views, and heaps of activities—no wonder it's an annual family destination for many well-heeled Canadians. **Pros:** beautiful pool and spa; great place to bring children; state-of-the-art conference facility. **Cons:** carpeting in some rooms looks a bit worn as does some of the furniture in the lounge; pricey, and a C$35 per-room, per-night resort fee is added to your bill at checkout; no nearby restaurants of note. [$] *Rooms from: C$419* ✉ *392 rue Notre-Dame, Montebello* ☎ *819/423–6341, 866/540–4462* 🌐 *www.fairmont.com/montebello* 🛏 *211 rooms* 🍽 *No Meals.*

Gatineau

205 km (127 miles) west of Montréal.

This town on the northern edge of the Ottawa River is best known for the nearby Gatineau Park and the many outdoor activities that can be done here. For more history, visit the Canadian Museum of History, which emphasizes the changes the country has undergone, from the prehistoric past to the present day. From Gatineau, it's a short walk over the Alexandra Bridge to visit Ottawa, the nation's capital. The view from either side of the river is stunning.

GETTING HERE AND AROUND

From Montréal, take Autoroute 50 west for 205 km (127 miles); it's about a two-hour trip.

VISITOR INFORMATION

CONTACT Gatineau Tourist Information Office. ✉ *103 rue Laurier, Gatineau* ☎ *819/778–2222; 800/265–7822* 🌐 *www.tourismeoutaouais.com.*

👁 Sights

Canadian Museum of History

HISTORY MUSEUM | **FAMILY** | Formerly known as the Canadian Museum of Civilization, this superb institution officially changed its name in 2013 when it received C$25 million in funding from the Canadian government in order to renovate and expand. More than 50,000 square feet of the existing museum has been renovated, and a Canadian History Hall showcasing the people and events that have shaped Canada over the last 15,000 years. Other highlights include the First Peoples Hall, which has some 2,000 objects on display, and the Children's Museum. ✉ *100 rue Laurier, Gatineau* ☎ *819/776–7000, 800/555–5621* 🌐 *www.historymuseum.ca* 🎟 *C$20.*

Gatineau Park

NATIONAL PARK | **FAMILY** | This massive park—nearly 364 square km (140 square miles)—brings nature lovers from all over throughout the year. You can hike up King Mountain on a challenging trail that takes you 300 meters (980 feet) above the Ottawa Valley, explore Lusk Cave, go camping, view the Luskville Falls, or swim at one of the six beaches here (there are also 50 lakes). In winter, the cross-country skiing trails cover approximately 200 km (125 miles) of the park. From June to mid-October, you can use the park's south entrance on Taché Boulevard; stop at the reception center for visitor information. ✉ *Gatineau* ☎ *819/827–2020* 🌐 *www.ncc-ccn.gc.ca/places/gatineau-park* 🎟 *Free admission but C$13 per vehicle (parking).*

🍴 Restaurants

★ Edgar

$$$ | **CANADIAN** | Wonderful homemade pastries such as pear-and-almond tarts, lemon-curd doughnuts, and chai scones have brought renown to this little place (only 11 seats), but there's more to it than that. Breakfast and lunch are always busy, and weekend brunch, served until 2 pm, brings a line out the door. **Known for:** cute terrace; weekend brunch; homemade pastries. [$] *Average main: C$23* ✉ *60 rue Bégin, Gatineau* ☎ *819/205–1110* 🌐 *www.chezedgar.ca* 🕒 *Closed Mon. No dinner.*

🛏 Hotels

Moulin Wakefield Mill Hotel and Spa

$$$$ | **HOTEL** | Part heritage mill with original features, part modern environmentally friendly building, this waterside hotel and spa on the edge of Gatineau Park has lots of character, wonderful views of the MacLaren Falls, and plenty of pampering on offer. **Pros:** pets allowed; walking distance to Gatineau Park; great views. **Cons:** hardwood floors in rooms in the main building are in need of refinishing; expensive; hotel caters mostly to adults. [$] *Rooms from: C$292* ✉ *60 chemin Mill, Gatineau* ☎ *888/567–1838, 819/459–1838* 🌐 *www.wakefieldmill.com* 🛏 *42 rooms* 🍽 *Free Breakfast.*

Bromont

78 km (48 miles) east of Montréal.

The boating, camping, golf, horseback riding, swimming, tennis, biking, canoeing, fishing, hiking, cross-country and downhill skiing, and snowshoeing available here make this a place for all seasons. Bromont has the only night skiing in the Eastern Townships—and there's even a slope-side disco, Le Bromontais. The town also has more than 100 km (62 miles) of maintained trails for mountain bikers.

GETTING HERE AND AROUND

Bromont is about one hour from Montréal on Autoroute 10. Get off at Exit 78.

VISITOR INFORMATION

CONTACT Bromont Tourism Office. ✉ *15 boul. de Bromont, Bromont* ☎ *877/276–6668, 450/534–2006* 🌐 *www.tourisme-bromont.com.*

👁 Sights

★ Route des Vins (*Wine Route*)

WINERY | Make sure you bring along a designated driver for this Wine Route, which includes 22 wineries. Map out your chosen stops then travel from one to the next to learn about their history, local products and, best of all, sample the wine. Most wineries have an area outdoors where you can enjoy a picnic. **■ TIP→ Call for hours as they may change from one season to the next.** ✉ *Bromont* ☎ *888/811–4928* 🌐 *www.laroutedesvins.ca/en.*

Did You Know?

Warm summer days and cool nights make this region ideal for producing wine; travelers can visit several vineyards along the Route des Vins in and around the town of Dunham.

Vignoble de l'Orpailleur
WINERY | Established in 1982, this vineyard produces 11 wines, including its Double Gold medal-winning ice wine at the Finger Lakes International competition. Guided tours (in French) cost C$10 and are given three times a day during the summer. You can also stop by the museum, where you'll learn about the history and production of wine, from the cultivation of the vines to the bottling process. Guided tours given in English need to be reserved two weeks in advance. The patio restaurant is a nice place to take a break. ✉ *1086 rue Bruce (Rte. 202), Dunham* ☎ *450/295–2763* 🌐 *www.orpailleur.ca.*

Vignoble Domaine Côtes d'Ardoise
WINERY | This winery, opened in 1980, was one of the first to set up shop in the area, and is considered to be the oldest vineyard still in operation in Québec. On nearly 30 acres of land, 50,000 vines go to produce some award-winning reds, whites, rosés, and ice wines. Visit for a tasting and enjoy a picnic on the grounds. From July through October, a sculpture garden showcases the works of more than 80 artists, primarily from the area. ✉ *879 rue Bruce (Rte. 202), Dunham* ☎ *450/295–2020* 🌐 *www.cotesdardoise.com.*

Vignoble Les Trois Clochers
WINERY | This lovely winery is another great stop along the wine route. It produces a dry, fruity white from Seyval grapes as well as several other white, red, and ice wines. In addition to the tastings, you can take a tour of the grounds (reservations required), stroll along the trails, and stop for a picnic before you move on to the next stop. ✉ *341 chemin Bruce (Rte. 202), Dunham* ☎ *450/295–2034* 🌐 *www.3clochers.com.*

Hotels

Auberge Château Bromont
$ | HOTEL | Among the rolling hills of the Townships and with great views of the local countryside from every room, this modern hotel is part of the Domaine Château-Bromont complex, and well priced, considering all the amenities available. **Pros:** close to ski hill and golf course; outstanding views from each room; friendly staff. **Cons:** some rooms still need to be renovated; the décor is somewhat dated; lack of an elevator makes it difficult for guests on the upper floors, especially those with ski equipment. [$] *Rooms from: C$135* ✉ *95 rue de Montmorency, Bromont* ☎ *888/276-6668* 🌐 *www.chateaubromont.com* 🛏 *40 rooms* 🍴 *No Meals.*

Hôtel Château Bromont
$$ | HOTEL | Massages, algae wraps, and aromatherapy are just a few of the services at this European-style resort, which also includes a large, Turkish-style *hammam* (steam room) and the Château Bromont Golf Course. **Pros:** scenic mountain views; outdoor hot tubs; Turkish-style hammam. **Cons:** some rooms are dated; windows facing the interior courtyard/indoor swimming pool do not open; some rooms are small. [$] *Rooms from: C$160* ✉ *90 rue Stanstead, Bromont* ☎ *450/534-3433, 888/276-6668* 🌐 *www.chateaubromont.com* 🛏 *166 rooms* 🍴 *No Meals.*

Shopping

MARKETS

★ Bromont Five-Star Flea Market
MARKET | The gigantic sign on Autoroute 10 is hard to miss. Take Exit 78 to explore more than 1,000 vendors at this indoor flea market. T-shirts, household gadgets, and much, much more. Weekends (9–5) from April to the end of October. Shoppers come from as far away as Vermont. ✉ *16 rue Lafontaine, Bromont* ☎ *450/534-0440* 🌐 *www.mapbromont.com.*

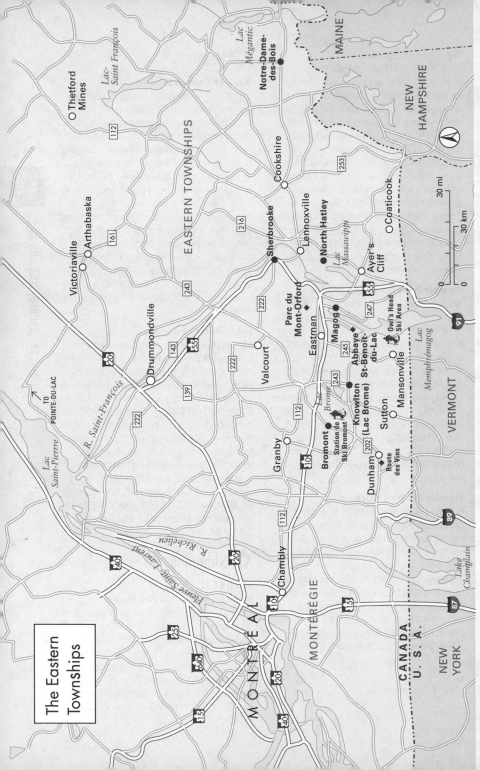

The Eastern Townships

Activities

GOLF
Royal Bromont

GOLF | Designed by Graham Cooke, one of the most reputable golf course architects, the Royal Bromont was built in 1992 and is located in the center of Bromont. All 18 holes provide wonderful views of the surrounding mountains and, from novice to expert, this golf course is considered to be one of the top places to play. In 1994, the Royal Bromont hosted the Canadian PGA Championships. ☒ *400 chemin Compton, Bromont* ☎ *450/534–4653, 888/281–0017* ⊕ *www.royalbromont.com* ✉ *C$30–C$60* ⚑ *18 holes, 7036 yards, par 72* ⚐ *Facilities: driving range, putting green, golf carts, pull carts, rental clubs, pro shop, golf lessons, restaurant, bar.*

SHOW JUMPING
Parc Équestre Olympique Bromont

SPORTS VENUE | If you love horses and competitions, the Bromont Equestrian Center is the place to visit. Once an Olympic site, it hosts show jumping, dressage, and pony club events, and, in late July, the annual International-al Bromont Equestrian competition. ☒ *450 chemin de Gaspé, Bromont* ☎ *819/437–5548.*

SKIING
★ **Station de Ski Bromont**

SKIING & SNOWBOARDING | FAMILY | Not many metropolises in eastern North America can boast a 1,300-foot ski mountain within an hour's drive of Downtown. That height and proximity has made Bromont very popular with Montréal day-trippers and weekenders. But Bromont's 156 trails (102 of them lighted at night) and nine lifts can handle the crowds quite comfortably. Like many other ski hills, Bromont operates as a year-round resort. In summer and early fall, you can take a mountain bike to the summit aboard a chairlift and test your nerves on one of 19 downhill trails, two

of which are labeled "easy"—the rest are "hard" to "extreme." Part of the ski hill is converted into the **Bromont Aquatic Park** in summer, with a 24,000-square-foot wave pool and 25 rides and slides. ☒ *150 rue Champlain, Bromont* ☎ *450/534–2200, 866/276–6668* ⊕ *www.skibromont.com* ✉ *Skiing C$39–C$69; aquatic park C$41; mountain biking C$49 per day.*

SPAS
Balnea Réserve Thermale

SPAS | Tucked away in a forest and overlooking a lake, this strikingly contemporary spa takes advantage of its location with air beds that float among lily pads, and tiers of sundecks with gorgeous views. In addition to steam rooms, saunas, and baths, Balnea also has 30 body treatments: you can bliss out with the misra herbs and green-tea wrap, a chocolate and grape-seed massage, or yoga by the lake. Full- and half-day spa packages are available. During the summer, Balnea plays host to Summer of Chefs, a gourmet cooking competition that takes places over 10 Sundays and features 10 of Québec's best chefs who take over the kitchen and create their own menu inspired by ingredients available at the nature reserve. ☒ *319 chemin du Lac Gale, Bromont* ☎ *866/734–2110, 450/534–0604* ⊕ *www.balnea.ca.*

Knowlton (Lac Brome)

49 km (29 miles) northeast of Bromont, 101 km (63 miles) southeast of Montréal.

Knowlton is the quintessential Eastern Townships resort town, with Loyalist-era buildings, old inns, great antiques shops, and enticing pastry shops. Fortunately, it's managed to retain its particular identity, with a main street full of stores selling antiques, art, clothes, and gifts. Interesting little restaurants have taken residence in renovated clapboard houses painted every color of the rainbow. A frequent feature on most menus here is

Brome Lake duck, served in many different ways. These internationally renowned birds are raised at a farm on the shores of Brome Lake just a few miles outside town. The main regional tourist office is in Foster, one of the other old villages that constitute Lac Brome, but walking maps of Knowlton are available from many local businesses.

GETTING HERE AND AROUND

To get from Montréal to Knowlton, take Autoroute 10 Est, head toward Autoroute 15 Sud, and take Exit 90 for QC–243.

VISITOR INFORMATION

CONTACT Lac Brome Tourism Office. ✉ *696 rue Lakeside, Lac Brome* ☎ *450/243–1221* 🌐 *www.tourismelacbrome.com.*

Sights

★ **Brome Country Historical Museum**

HISTORY MUSEUM | FAMILY | Here's a wonderful opportunity to learn about the Loyalists who settled the area after fleeing the American Revolution. Several buildings, including the former county courthouse dating back to 1859, the old firehall (fire station), and a former school, house an eclectic collection that include 19th-century farm tools, Native Canadian arrowheads, and a military collection that includes uniforms and a World War I Fokker aircraft. The museum also maintains the Tibbits Hill Pioneer School, a stone schoolhouse built in 1834 to serve rural families—kids can find out what education was like in the mid-19th century. ✉ *130 chemin Lakeside, Knowlton* ☎ *450/243–6782* 🎟 *C$8* 🕒 *Closed Sun. and Mon.*

Restaurants

Knowlton Pub

$$ | CANADIAN | Serving traditional pub fare, the Knowlton Pub has been around since time immemorial and is one of the best-known establishments in the Eastern Townships. The service is friendly but diners have been known to wait a little longer than they'd like for their food to be served, particularly on dinner theater nights. **Known for:** local institution; hearty burgers; unrushed service. [$] *Average main: C$16* ✉ *267 Chemin Knowlton, Knowlton* ☎ *450/242–6862* 🌐 *www.facebook.com/theknowltonpub* 🕒 *Closed Wed. and Thurs.*

Hotels

★ **Auberge Knowlton**

$ | B&B/INN | A local landmark since 1849, when it was first a stagecoach stop, and later a railway stop, this rustic inn is a special-occasion venue for locals and a delightful option for visitors who relish period style and good regional cuisine. **Pros:** atmospheric restaurant serving good food; within walking distance of Knowlton's main attractions; storage, repair kits, and so on, for bicycles. **Cons:** dark, natural light blocked due to veranda roof on second floor; no elevator; on the main road through town, so not the most scenic location. [$] *Rooms from: C$135* ✉ *286 chemin Knowlton, Lac Brome, Knowlton* ☎ *450/242–6886* 🌐 *www.aubergeknowlton.ca* 🕒 *Closed Tues. and Wed.* 🛏 *12 rooms* 🍴 *No Meals.*

Domaine Jolivent

$ | B&B/INN | Somewhat hidden away, in the Bondville section of Lac Brome, and on 112 acres of sheer bucolic splendor, is Domaine Jolivent, one of the best kept secrets in the Eastern Townships. **Pros:** excellent location; gorgeous common areas; plenty of outdoor activities year-round. **Cons:** might be noisy from other rooms; no coffee machines in rooms; rooms can be small. [$] *Rooms from: C$130* ✉ *667 Bondville, Lac Brome* ☎ *866/525–4272, 450/243–4272* 🌐 *jolivent.ca* 🛏 *12 rooms* 🍴 *No Meals.*

🎭 Performing Arts

Théâtre Lac Brome

THEATER | This local theater company stages high quality productions in both English and French. Under the leadership of executive artistic director Ellen David, TLB is now open year round and showcases work by local artists in their new lobby. They aim to offer as much and as varied entertainment as possible while reflecting national and regional talent and content. The 175-seat, air-conditioned theater is located behind the Townships' institution, the Knowlton Pub. ⊠ *9 chemin Mont-Echo, Knowlton* ☎ *450/242–2270 tickets* ⊕ *www.theatrelacbrome.ca.*

🛍 Shopping

ANTIQUES

Camlen

ANTIQUES & COLLECTIBLES | Cameron and Helen Brown (get it? Cam + len) import gorgeous antiques from China and eastern Europe, create reproductions using old wood, and sell antique Canadian pieces. Their passion for, and dedication to, the art of furniture making is reflected in the high standard of their merchandise. ⊠ *110 Lakeside Rd., Knowlton* ☎ *450/243–5785* ⊕ *www.camlenfurniture.ca.*

CLOTHING

Rococo Designer Factory Outlet

MIXED CLOTHING | Owners Carla Hadlock and Anita Laurent—the latter a former model—know fashion and style, and have many contacts in the business, so their collection of clothing and accessories includes many items obtained straight from manufacturers. You'll love the prices, too, which are a fraction of what you'd pay in a large retail store. ⊠ *293 Knowlton Rd., Knowlton* ☎ *450/243–6948* ⊕ *www.facebook.com/rococodesignerfactoryoutlet.*

Abbaye St-Benoît-du-Lac

132 km (82 miles) southeast of Montréal.

At this impressive abbey, a bell juts above the trees like a fairy-tale castle. Combine its calm and peaceful surroundings with the chance to pick up some of the products sold here, including sparkling apple wine and some of the best cheese in Québec, and you have an expedition that makes for a very memorable experience.

GETTING HERE AND AROUND

To get to the abbey from Magog, take Route 112 and follow the signs for the side road (Rural Route 2, or rue des Pères) to the abbey.

👁 Sights

★ **Abbaye St-Benoît-du-Lac**

CHURCH | Built by the Benedictines in 1912 on a wooded peninsula on Lac Memphrémagog, the abbey is home to over 50 monks. They sell apples and sparkling apple wine from their orchards, as well as cheeses: Ermite (which means "hermit"), St-Benoît, and ricotta. Gregorian prayers are sung daily, and some masses are open to the public; call for the schedule. Dress modestly if you plan to attend vespers or other rituals, and avoid shorts. If you wish to experience a few days of retreat, there are guesthouses for both men and women. Reserve well in advance. Overnight visits cost C$65–C$70 per night, which includes three meals. Guided tours of the abbey cost C$12. ⊠ *1 rue Principale, St-Benoît-du-Lac* ☎ *819/843–4080, 819/843–2861 store* ⊕ *www.abbaye.ca* ⊙ *Closed major holidays and on July 11th, aka the Feast of Saint Benedict, there are no guided tours.*

Parc du Mont-Orford

19 km (12 miles) north of Abbaye St-Benoît-du-Lac, 115 km (72 miles) east of Montréal.

In addition to a multitude of year-round outdoor activities, such as hiking, camping, fishing, and snowmobiling, the provincial park here also serves as a nature reserve.

The annual music performances that make up the Festival Orford always draw crowds to the foot of Mont-Orford.

GETTING HERE AND AROUND

From Montréal, go east on Highway 10 (Autoroute des Cantons de l'Est), take Exit 115 onto QC–112 and go north onto QC–141 (chemin du Mont-Orford). Coming from the east, leave Highway 10 at Exit 118 and go north on QC–141.

Sights

Parc du Mont-Orford

NATURE SIGHT | FAMILY | The amount of activities seems almost endless at this 58-square-km (22-square-mile) park. Summertime sees hikers, campers, beach lovers, and canoers enjoying the grounds and in winter, showshoers and cross-country skiers take over. White-tailed deer and blue herons share the park with tourists. The scenery in the fall is spectacular, with vibrant orange, yellow, and red hues spreading across the landscape. ✉ *3321 chemin du Parc, Orford* ☎ *819/843–9855, 800/665–6527* 🌐 *www.sepaq.com/pq/mor* 🎟 *C$9 a day.*

Hotels

Estrimont Suites & Spa

$$ | HOTEL | With a Nordic shower, Scandinavian baths, and relaxation yurt, plus nearby golf courses, riding stables, and ski hills, this attractive complex fits the bill for an active or relaxing break. **Pros:** two outdoor hot tubs in scenic surroundings; very reasonably priced spa packages; excellent place for conferences or business retreats. **Cons:** children not allowed in spa yet children were there and noisy; rooms appear dated; only one suite is wheelchair accessible. [$] *Rooms from: C$190* ✉ *44 av. de l'Auberge (Rte. 141 Nord), Orford* ☎ *800/567–7320, 819/843–1616* 🌐 *www.estrimont.ca* 🛏 *95 suites* 🍴 *Free Breakfast.*

Performing Arts

Festival Orford

MUSIC FESTIVALS | Every summer, from the end of June to mid-August, a celebration of music and art brings classical music, jazz, and chamber orchestra concerts to Parc du Mont-Orford. It's organized by the Orford Arts Centre, which has been teaching students the art of classical music and performance since 1951. ✉ *3165 chemin du Parc, Orford* ☎ *819/843–3981 tickets, 800/567–6155 in Canada* 🌐 *www.orford.mu/en.*

Magog

11 km (6 miles) south of Parc du Mont-Orford, 118 km (74 miles) east of Montréal.

This bustling town is at the northern tip of Lac Memphrémagog, a large body of water that stretches into northern Vermont. Its sandy beaches are a draw, and it's also a good place for boating, bird-watching, sailboarding, horseback riding, dog sledding, in-line skating, golfing, bass fishing, and snowmobiling. You might even see Memphré, the lake's mythical sea dragon, on one of the many lake cruises—there have been more than 100 sightings since 1816.

In recent years this formerly depressed textile town has enjoyed something of an economic and cultural rebirth, partially due to the substantial number of artists who have chosen to relocate to this welcoming, and relatively inexpensive, region of the province. The streets downtown are lined with century-old houses that have been converted into boutiques, stores, and eateries.

GETTING HERE AND AROUND

From Montréal to Magog, take Autoroute 10 Est, keep left toward Autoroute 15 Sud, and then take Exit 118 for QC–141.

VISITOR INFORMATION

CONTACT Memphrémagog Tourism Office. ✉ *2911 chemin Milletta, Magog* ☎ *819/843–2744; 800/267–2744* 🌐 *www.tourisme-memphremagog.com.*

Sights

Le Cep d'Argent

WINERY | The Scieur brothers, Jean-Paul and François, are sixth generation winemakers originally from France, who have created their own "Champagne universe" in Québec. Their Selection range of wines includes sparkling, white, and rosé. Red, fortified, flavored, and ice wines are also available. From mid-June to end-October, they offer the Bubbles, Wines, and Champagne guided tour (but only in French due to the extensive vocabulary of the subject) as well as a la carte tastings of over 10 of their finest wines all for the price of a C$5 souvenir glass. Visitors may also tour the Traditional Method Interpretation Center to learn about the history of the Scieur brothers or just wander the vineyard and experience a little bit of France in Québec. ✉ *1257 chemin de la Rivière, Magog* ☎ *819/864–4441, 877/864–4441* 🌐 *www.cepdargent.com* 🎫 *C$28 for the Bubbles, Wine, and Champagne tour* ✍ *Reservations are essential and should be made well in advance to guarantee a spot as space is limited.*

Hotels

Ripplecove Lakefront Hotel and Spa

$$$$ | B&B/INN | The accommodations, service, and food at the Ripplecove, 11 km (7 miles) south of Magog, are good enough reason to make the detour. **Pros:** spectacular grounds; beautiful lakeside setting; first-class dining. **Cons:** reports of rude hotel staff; absence of privacy due to thin walls; expensive and a little stuffy. [$] *Rooms from: C$350* ✉ *700 rue Ripplecove, Ayer's Cliff* ☎ *800/668–4296, 819/838–4296* 🌐 *www.ripplecove.com* 🛏 *37 rooms* 🍴 *Free Breakfast.*

Spa Eastman

$$$$ | HOTEL | The oldest spa in Québec, once a simple health center, has evolved into a bucolic haven for anyone seeking rest and therapeutic treatments, including lifestyle and weight-management counseling. **Pros:** wheelchair-accessible rooms; dinner included in room rate; stunning surroundings. **Cons:** very pricey; limited dining selection; no phone or TV might prove too isolating for some. [$] *Rooms from: C$525* ✉ *895 chemin des Diligences, Eastman* ☎ *450/297–3009, 800/665–5272* 🌐 *www.spa-eastman.com* 🛏 *44 rooms* 🍴 *Free Breakfast.*

Nightlife

Auberge Orford

BARS | Come by boat and you can moor right alongside this patio bar that overlooks the Magog River. Sometimes there's live entertainment, but when musicians aren't around, the flocks of ducks lining up alongside the café to beg crumbs from patrons' plates keep patrons entertained. ✉ *20 rue Merry Sud, Magog* ☎ *819/843–9361* 🌐 *www.auberge-orford.com.*

Café St-Michel

CAFÉS | In a century-old building, this pub, outfitted in shades of charcoal and ebony, serves Tex-Mex food, pasta, fish-and-chips and local beers. Its patio bar, at Magog's main intersection, may not be peaceful, but it's a great spot to watch the world go by. *Chansonniers* (singers) belt out popular hits for a full house on Friday and Saturday evening starting at 6 pm. ⊠ *503 rue Principale Ouest, Magog* ☎ *819/868–1062* ⊕ *www.cafestmichel. com* ☾ *Closed Mon. and Tues.*

Microbrasserie La Memphré

PUBS | Named after the monster said to lurk in Lake Memphrémagog, La Memphré dates back to the 1800s, when it belonged to Magog's first mayor, Alvin H. Moore. Now a British-style gastropub, it offers up three styles of cheese fondue alongside Bavarian onion soup, burgers, and all manner of modern pub fare in a non-pub setting. All selections are best accompanied by a cold one of whatever other tempting refreshments are on offer. Making your selection is that much more fun ⊠ the beautifully presented menu provides not only mouthwatering descriptions of the food and beverages but also historical information and more! ⊠ *12 rue Merry Sud, Magog* ☎ *819/843–3405* ⊕ *lamemphre.com.*

🎭 Performing Arts

Le Vieux Clocher de Magog

MUSIC | Originally built in 1881 as a Methodist church, and converted into a theater by local impresario Bernard Caza 100 years later, this theater headlines well-known francophone comedians and singers such as Claude Dubois and Gilles Vigneault. Most, if not all, performances are in French. ⊠ *64 rue Merry Nord, Magog* ☎ *819/847–0470* ⊕ *www.vieux-clocher.com.*

🏃 Activities

GOLF

Golf Owl's Head

GOLF | This course, close to the Vermont border, has some spectacular views. Laid out with undulating fairways, bent-grass greens, and 64 sand bunkers, Golf Owl's Head, designed by Graham Cooke, is surrounded by peaceful sloping mountains and evergreens. The clubhouse, a stunning timber-and-fieldstone structure with five fireplaces and 45-foot-high ceilings, is a popular watering hole. ⊠ *181 chemin Owl's Head, Mansonville* ☎ *450/292–3342, 800/363–3342* ⊕ *www. owlshead.com* 💲 *C$45 weekdays, C$54 weekends* 🏌 *18 holes, 6710 yards, par 72* ☞ *Facilities: driving range, putting green, pitching area, golf carts, pull carts, rental clubs, pro shop, golf lessons, restaurant, bar.*

Manoir des Sables Golf Course

GOLF | Between Mont-Orford and Lake Memphrémagog, this resort course comes with some of the best scenery in the Eastern Townships and has been voted a clear favorite in Québec. The best views are from the second, third, and fourth holes. Several water hazards are dotted around the course, with streams cutting across more than half the fairways and ponds calling for accuracy on certain greens. ⊠ *90 av. des Jardins, Orford* ☎ *819/847–4299, 866/656–4747* ⊕ *manoirdessables.com* 💲 *C$41 weekdays, C$40 weekends* 🏌 *18 holes, 6352 yards, par 71.*

Mont-Orford Golf Club

GOLF | This venerable course in the heart of the national park winds through forested land, with the peak of Mont-Orford visible from many of its greens. There are some tricky holes—look out for the pond to the right of the fairway and an uphill putt on the 5th, the two streams cutting across the 8th, and the sharp dog-leg on the 13th. All in all, it's a satisfying challenge and an exceptionally scenic course

to play. ✉ *3074 chemin du Parc, Magog*
☎ *819/843–5688, 866/673–6731* ⊕ *www.*
orford.com ✉ *C$42 weekdays, C$45*
weekends ⚑ *18 holes, 6095 yards, par*
72 ☞ *Facilities: golf carts, rental clubs,*
pro shop, lessons, restaurant.

SKIING
★ Owl's Head Ski Area
SKIING & SNOWBOARDING | On the Knowlton Landing side of Lake Memphrémagog, Owl's Head is great for skiers seeking sparser crowds—and the views from its peak are truly exceptional. It has eight lifts, a 1,772-foot vertical drop, and 50 trails, including a 4-km (2½-mile) intermediate run, the longest such run in the Eastern Townships. For decades, it was one of the least expensive hills in the Townships, but the price of lift tickets have been increasing as the hill grows progressively swankier. Under new management since 2017, the facility has been privy to many recent upgrades, and there are millions more pledged to further modernize the facility throughout 2021. ✉ *40 chemin du Mont-Owl's Head, Magog* ☎ *450/292–3342, 800/363–3342* ⊕ *www. owlshead.com* ✉ *C$73 day ski pass.*

North Hatley

10 km (6 miles) east of Magog, 133 km (83 miles) east of Montréal.

Along with Frelighsburg and Knowlton, North Hatley is undoubtedly one of Québec's prettiest villages. The small resort town on the tip of Lac Massawippi has a theater as well as some excellent inns and restaurants. Set among hills and farms, it was discovered by rich vacationers in the early 1900s, and has been drawing visitors ever since. It was particularly popular with magnates from the American South who were looking for a cool summer refuge that wasn't controlled by the Yankees. The result is that some of the village's most majestic buildings are more reminiscent of Georgia than Vermont.

GETTING HERE AND AROUND
From Montréal to North Hatley, take Autoroute 10 Est to Autoroute 15 Sud, and then take Exit 121 to get onto Autoroute 55 Sud. Take Exit 29 for QC–108.

🍽 Restaurants

Pilsen Pub
$$$ | **AMERICAN** | Massawippi pale and brown ales and a vast selection of microbrews and imports are all on tap here. Pub food is served both in the upstairs dining room and in the tavern. **Known for:** lively, welcoming atmosphere; a vast selection of microbrews and imports on tap; burgers and homemade soups. 💲 *Average main: C$21* ✉ *55 Main Street, North Hatley* ☎ *819/842–2971* ⊕ *www. pilsen.ca.*

🛏 Hotels

★ Manoir Hovey
$$$$ | **HOTEL** | Overlooking Lac Massawippi, with a private beach, this elegant retreat feels rather like a private estate, with many activities, such as tennis, boating, and bicycling, included in the room rate. **Pros:** wheelchair accessible; secluded, lakeside setting; historic buildings. **Cons:** 10% tax added to Saturday-night room rate; grounds often taken over by weddings on weekends; main restaurant overpriced. 💲 *Rooms from: C$460* ✉ *575 chemin Hovey, North Hatley* ☎ *819/842–2421, 800/661–2421* ⊕ *www.manoirhovey.com* ⊃ *36 rooms* ❢⊙❢ *Free Breakfast.*

🎭 Performing Arts

★ Piggery
THEATER | Enriching the Townships' cultural landscape since 1965, this theater, in a former pig barn in the mountains, is known for showcasing English-language plays, with a focus on Canadian playwrights. Concerts, magic shows, and

comedy acts also feature in a season that runs mid-May through October. ⊠ *215 chemin Simard, North Hatley* ☏ *819/842–2431* ⊕ *www.piggery.com.*

Sherbrooke

21 km (12 miles) northeast of North Hatley, 130 km (81 miles) east of Montréal.

Sherbrooke bills itself as the *Reine des Cantons de l'Est* (Queen of the Eastern Townships), and with a population of more than 160,000, it's the region's largest and most important city. The Loyalists who founded the city in the 1790s and who named it for Sir John Coape Sherbrooke, one of Canada's pre-Confederation governors-general, used the power of the Rivière St-François to build a strong industrial base. Though the city's economic importance has waned, it still has significant manufacturing and textile plants, and Wellington Street, in the downtown area, is experiencing a significant face-lift, with trendy restaurants, bars, and clubs now occupying once vacant lots.

A highlight of the town is the many beautifully painted murals on the sides of downtown buildings, and you can follow a self-guiding 6-km (4-mile) tour of them, starting from the tourist office on rue King.

GETTING HERE AND AROUND

Sherbrooke is easy to get to by car via Autoroute 10. From the United States, it's an easy stop on the way to Montréal if you cross the border via Interstate 91 and take Autoroute 55. There are also frequent bus connections between Montréal and Sherbrooke. The city is large and quite hilly, so getting around on foot can be difficult. But there's a well-developed bus system.

VISITOR INFORMATION

CONTACT Sherbrooke Tourism Office. ⊠ *785 rue King Ouest, Sherbrooke* ☏ *819/821–1919, 800/561–8331* ⊕ *www. destinationsherbrooke.com.*

◉ Sights

Musée de la Nature et des Sciences

SCIENCE MUSEUM | FAMILY | Fun and educational for the whole family, this natural history museum utilizes imaginative multisensory displays with state-of-the-art light and sound effects—the buzzing of mosquitoes may be *too* lifelike—and hands-on displays to enhance the experience. Long-running exhibits include Terra Mutantes, a geological experience portraying the birth of the Appalachian Mountains, and AlterAnima, a mythical forest featuring hundreds of animals and providing viewers a unique perspective on the world as these animals see and experience it, showing us that it's not always what you see, but what you don't. ⊠ *225 rue Frontenac, Sherbrooke* ☏ *819/564–3200, 877/434–3200* ⊕ *mns2. ca* ⊠ *C$13.*

Musée des Beaux-Arts de Sherbrooke

ART MUSEUM | This fine-arts museum has a permanent exhibit on the history of art in the region from 1800 to the present. More than 10 exhibits per year are staged in its three galleries, with an emphasis on artists from the Eastern Townships. ⊠ *241 rue Dufferin, Sherbrooke* ☏ *819/821–2115* ⊕ *www.mbas.qc.ca* ⊠ *C$10* ⊙ *Closed Mon. and Tues.*

⑪ Restaurants

Auguste

$$$$ | BISTRO | FAMILY | Auguste placed Sherbrooke on the foodie map when it opened in 2008, and it continues to impress. Local ingredients take pride of place in this minimalist bistro-style restaurant, which features dishes like mushroom risotto or sweet potato ravioli. **Known for:** providing a true gastronomic

The Mont Mégantic Observatory provides the best views of the beautifully wild and mountainous area that became the first-ever International Dark Sky Reserve.

experience; *pouding chômeur* (poor man's pudding) drenched in maple syrup; free children's dinner menu Sun.–Wed. [$] *Average main: C$34* ✉ *82 rue Wellington N, Sherbrooke* ☎ *819/565–9559* 🌐 *www.auguste-restaurant.com* 🕒 *No brunch weekdays.*

Performing Arts

Centennial Theatre

THEATER | On the campus of Bishop's University, this 600-seat theater presents a roster of jazz, classical, and rock concerts, as well as opera, dance, mime, and children's theater. ✉ *2600 rue College, Sherbrooke* ☎ *819/822–9692* 🌐 *www.centennialtheatre.ca* 🕒 *Closed Sat. and Sun.*

Le Vieux Clocher de l'Université de Sherbrooke

MUSIC | Le Vieux Clocher de l'Université de Sherbrooke presents music, from classical to jazz, and a variety of theater and comedy shows. ✉ *1590 rue Galt ouest, Sherbrooke* ☎ *819/822–2102* 🌐 *www.centreculturedudes.ca.*

Shopping

La Centrale Métiers d'Art

CRAFTS | Stop into this charming little shop filled with crafts, jewelry, kitchenware, and clothing made by artists from the Eastern Townships. ✉ *210 Wellington nord, Sherbrooke* ☎ *819/823–0221* 🌐 *www.metiersdartestrie.com* 🕒 *Closed Mon. and Tues.*

Notre-Dame-des-Bois

72 km (43 miles) east of Sherbrooke, 204 km (127 miles) east of Montréal.

Notre-Dame-des-Bois is a sleepy little one-street village just north of the Maine border. It sits in the shadow of one of the region's tallest and steepest mountains—Mont-Mégantic, which soars 576 meters (1,890 feet) above the surrounding plain, with a height of 3,601 feet above sea level. In 2007, the Mont-Mégantic Observatory area was declared the first International Dark Sky Reserve, in recognition of the lack of light pollution that provides some of the clearest night skies in Québec, a quality that attracts stargazers, both professional and amateur.

GETTING HERE AND AROUND

Count on a three-hour journey from Montréal, some of it over paved but bumpy secondary roads. To get here, follow Autoroute 10 east past Sherbrooke to its end near Ascot Corner, then follow Route 112 to East Angus, then Route 253 to Cookshire, and finally Route 212 through L'Avenir to Notre-Dame-des-Bois. If you want to make the journey comfortably, plan to stay overnight somewhere rather than just coming for the day.

Sights

Astrolab du Mont-Mégantic (*Mont-Mégantic's Observatory*)

OBSERVATORY | Both amateur stargazers and serious astronomers head to this observatory, located in a beautifully wild and mountainous area that in 2007 became the first-ever International Dark Sky Reserve. The observatory is at the summit of the Townships' second-highest mountain (3,601 feet above sea level and 1,890 feet above the surrounding landscape), whose northern face records annual snowfalls rivaling any in North America. A joint venture of the University of Montréal and Laval University, the observatory has a powerful telescope, the largest on the East Coast. In the Astrolab's welcome center at the mountain's base, there is an exhibition and multimedia display to provide visitors with information about the night sky. ■ **TIP→ Hours vary depending on the season, so check the website for updated information.** ✉ *Parc Mégantic, 189 Rte. du Parc, Notre-Dame-des-Bois* ☎ *819/888–2941, 888/665–6527* 🌐 *www.astrolab-parc-national-mont-megantic.org* 🎫 *Observatory and Astrolab: C$19.75 daytime, C$22–C$25.75 at night. Free for visitors 17 and under. Additional fee of C$9 charged to enter Parc Mégantic* ✍ *Reservations essential.*

Parc du Mont-Mégantic

NATURE SIGHT | If you're short on time or don't feel like a hike you can take a shuttle bus to the top of Mont-Mégantic for spectacular views of Québec, Maine, New Hampshire, and on really clear days, Vermont. But if you want the full experience, make the trek by foot. The park has 50 km (31 miles) of hiking trails that are also open in winter to snowshoers and cross-country skiers. For a real adventure, you can stay overnight in one of the park's rustic shelters. ✉ *189 Rte. du Parc, Notre-Dame-des-Bois* ☎ *819/888–2941, 800/665–6527* 🌐 *www.sepaq.com/pq/mme* 🎫 *C$9.*

Hotels

★ Aux Berges de l'Aurore

$ | **B&B/INN** | From its lofty perch, this delightful century-old inn has spectacular views day and night—it's within the International Dark Sky Reserve—and is less than a minute's drive from Mont Mégantic National Park and the Astrolab. **Pros:** hiking trails on the property; close to area activities; delicious breakfasts. **Cons:** some bathrooms have musty odor; no shampoo or conditioner provided; minimum two-night stay holiday weekends and some other times. [$] *Rooms from: C$140* ✉ *139 Rte. du Parc, Notre-Dame-des-Bois* ☎ *819/888–2715, 514/232–0703* 🌐 *www.auberge-aurore.qc.ca* 🛏 *5 rooms* 🍴 *Free Breakfast.*

Chapter 5

QUÉBEC CITY

Updated by
Marie-Ève Vallières

👁 **Sights**   🍴 **Restaurants**   🛏 **Hotels**   🛍 **Shopping**   🍸 **Nightlife**

★★★★★   ★★★★☆   ★★★★★   ★★★☆☆   ★★★★☆

WELCOME TO QUÉBEC CITY

TOP REASONS TO GO

★ **See the Château Frontenac:** Even if you're not staying at Québec City's most famous landmark, make sure to pop into one of the world's legendary hotels and admire its French Renaissance architecture.

★ **Dine at world-class restaurants:** High-end bistros, hip cafés, amazing breweries, and wine bars: Québec City has it all.

★ **Explore La Citadelle:** Québec City's pièce de résistance is the largest fortified base in North America and site of the daily Changing of the Guard in summer.

★ **Play on the Plains of Abraham:** This massive waterfront park is a popular place for outdoor fun, from cross-country skiing and sledding in winter to picnicking and concerts in summer.

★ **Get festive:** For three weekends in February, the city hosts one of the biggest winter festivals in the world. In July, up to 80,000 people cheer some of the biggest rock and pop stars at the open-air Summer Festival.

1 Upper Town. Crowning Cap Diamant and partially surrounded by the Fortifications, Upper Town hosts the city's main attractions, including the Château Frontenac and La Citadelle. The sweeping views of the St. Lawrence River, the Laurentian Mountains to the north, and the Appalachians to the south are all enchanting.

2 Lower Town. A maze of cobblestone streets with tucked-away cafés, boutique hotels, antique shops, and art galleries characterizes Lower Town.

3 Outside the Old City. Rue St-Jean, St-Roch district, avenue Cartier, and the Grande-Allée all have restaurants, shops, and nightlife worth checking out.

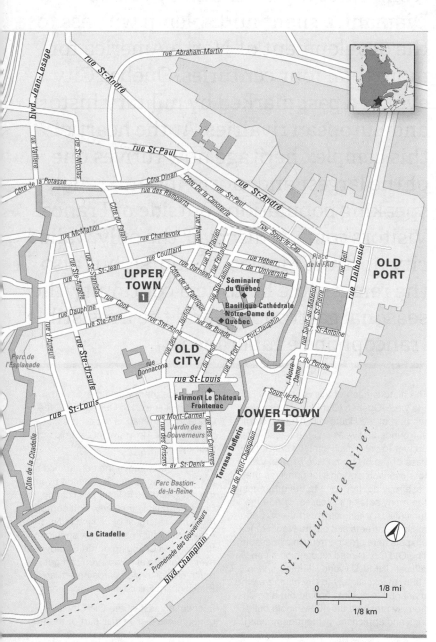

Overlooking the St. Lawrence River from the rocky promontory of Cap Diamant, a silent and solemn witness to the development of North America for more than four centuries, Québec City evokes a past marked by military history and European rivalries. At the heart of this complex heritage now thrives one of the largest and most vibrant French-speaking populations outside of France. Visitors come to discover the only walled city north of Mexico, of course, but also the remarkable historical continuity, the seasonal gastronomy, and the irresistible francophone exuberance.

The historic heart of this community is the Vieux-Québec (Old City), comprising the part of the Haute-Ville (Upper Town) surrounded by walls and the Basse-Ville (Lower Town), which spreads out at the base of the hill from Place Royale. Visitors can walk downhill (or uphill, as the case may be) from one to the other using the many sets of staircases, or ride the funicular that runs between them. Cobblestone streets and ornate New France chapels here are charming in all seasons. The Old City earned recognition as an official UNESCO World Heritage site in 1985, thanks largely to city planners who managed to not just update but also fiercely preserve the 400-year-old buildings and attractions without destroying what made them worth preserving. The most familiar icon of Québec City, the Château Frontenac, is set on the highest point in Upper Town, where it holds court over the entire city.

Sitting proudly above the confluence of the St. Lawrence and St. Charles rivers, the city's famous military fortification, La Citadelle, built in the early 19th century, remains the largest of its kind in North America. In summer, visitors should try to catch the Changing of the Guard, held every morning at 10 am; you can get much closer to the guards here than at Buckingham Palace in London.

Enchanting as it is, the Old City is nonetheless just a small part of the true

Québec City experience. Think outside the walls and explore St-Roch's hipster microbreweries, award-winning restaurants, designer boutiques, and third-wave cafés. Meander down the Grande-Allée and avenue Cartier to find a livelier part of town dotted with nightclubs and fun, casual eateries. Or while away the hours in St-Jean-Baptiste, a neighborhood with strong literary vibes and colorful architecture.

Planning

When to Go

Winter can be formidable, but the city stays alive—especially during the popular Winter Carnival. Spring is short and sweet with the *cabanes à sucre* (sugar shacks) bringing fresh maple goodies. In summer, the city's terraces and courtyards open and everyone comes out to enjoy the sunshine. In late September and early October, the region's foliage blazes with color.

Getting Here and Around

The Funiculaire du Vieux-Québec, a small elevator up the side of the steep embankment, travels between Upper and Lower towns. Another option, and a good workout, is to take one of the sets of stairs that start in Upper Town and end at the Quartier du Petit Champlain in Lower Town. Renting a car isn't recommended (parking can be a real issue) unless you're taking day trips outside the city.

AIR

If you're flying in, Jean-Lesage International Airport is about 19 km (12 miles) northwest of Downtown. Driving into town, take Route 540 (Autoroute Duplessis) to Route 175 (boulevard Laurier). The ride takes about 30 minutes. Taxis are available immediately outside the airport exit near the baggage-claim area. A ride into the city costs C$35.10.

BUS

Bus service in Québec City is an effective way to go from the Vieux-Québec to other parts of the city, particularly using the Metrobus lines (those with an 800 number). It is C$8.85 for a one-day ticket or C$3.50 for a one-way trip.

CAR

Montréal and Québec City are linked by Autoroute 20 on the south shore of the St. Lawrence River and by Autoroute 40 on the north shore. On both highways, the ride between the two cities is about 240 km (150 miles) and takes about three hours. U.S. I–87 in New York, U.S. I–89 in Vermont, and U.S. I–91 in New Hampshire connect with Autoroute 20, as does Highway 401 from Toronto. Driving northeast out of Montréal on Autoroute 20, follow signs for Pierre Laporte Bridge (Pont Pierre-Laporte) as you approach Québec City. After you've crossed the bridge, take the exit to boulevard Laurier (Route 175), which becomes the Grande-Allée.

TRAIN

VIA Rail, Canada's passenger rail service, has service between Montréal and Québec City. The trip takes less than three hours. One-way tickets cost C$89, but early reservation rates can be as low as C$29. A taxi from the Gare du Palais train station to the Château Frontenac is about C$8.

Restaurants

Bistros, sidewalk cafés, and chic, cutting-edge restaurants make up the dining scene in Québec City. "Grab and go" is more the exception than the rule; be prepared to eat at a leisurely pace. Québec's culinary scene offers variety, including modern international cuisine and inventive farm-to-table bistros, traditional French dishes like foie gras and escargot; distinctly French-Canadian specialties such as *tourtière* (meat pie); and local fare such as ice cider, poutine, and maple sugar pie.

With so many options, choosing where to go can be difficult. Many establishments post their *menu du jour* outside, so you can stroll along and let your cravings guide the way. But bear in mind that reservations are a must at most restaurants during holidays, Winter Carnival, and in the summer months, when the coveted outdoor terraces open. When ordering, remember that in this French-speaking province, an *entrée* is an appetizer and the *plat principal* is the main course. Plan to tip at least 15% of the bill.

WHAT IT COSTS in Canadian Dollars			
$	$$	$$$	$$$$
RESTAURANTS			
under C$12	C$12–C$20	C$21–C$30	over C$30

Hotels

There are over 35 hotels in the Old City alone, with everything from family-run B&Bs to household hospitality brands. There truly is something for every taste: modern high-rises outside the ramparts to wake up to spectacular views of Québec City or old-fashioned inns where no two rooms are alike to fully experience the city's historic charm.

In any case, be sure to book well in advance if you plan on visiting during peak season (May through September) or the Winter Carnival (early February) as hotel rates may rise by up to 30%. On the other hand, many lodgings offer weekend discounts and other promotions from November through April.

WHAT IT COSTS in Canadian Dollars			
$	$$	$$$	$$$$
HOTELS			
under C$160	C$160–C$200	C$201–C$250	over C$250

Nightlife

In winter, nightlife activity grows livelier as the week nears its end, beginning on Wednesday. As warmer temperatures set in, the café-terrace crowd emerges, and bars are active just about every night. Most bars and clubs stay open until 3 am.

Performing Arts

Québec City has a good variety of cultural institutions for a city of its size, thanks to its renowned symphony orchestra and its many charming venues that welcome (mainly French-speaking) music, theater, comedy, and dance acts.

Shopping

On the fashionable streets of Vieux-Québec, shopping has a European tinge. The boutiques and specialty shops clustered along narrow streets such as rue du Petit-Champlain and rues de Buade and St-Jean are especially traditional. For designer brands and curated collections, rue St-Joseph down in the St-Roch neighborhood is the place to be.

Stores are generally open Monday through Wednesday from 9:30 to 5:30, Thursday and Friday until 9, Saturday until 5, and Sunday noon to 5. In summer, most shops have later evening hours.

Visitor Information

CONTACT Québec City Tourist Information. ✉ *12 rue Sainte-Anne, Upper Town* ☎ *418/641–6290, 877/266–5687* ⊕ *www. Québec-cite.com/en.*

Upper Town

No other place in Canada has so much history squeezed into such a small area. Upper Town was a barren, windswept cape when Samuel de Champlain decided to build a fort here over 400 years ago. Now it's a major tourist destination surrounded by cannon-studded stone ramparts.

Home to the city's most famous sites, Upper Town's Old City offers a dramatic view of the St. Lawrence River and the countryside, especially while walking along the Terrasse Dufferin, in front of the Château Frontenac. Historic buildings that house bars, cafés, shops, and hotels line the neighborhood's winding streets. A 3-mile-long wall neatly splices off this section of the city with entrances on rues St-Jean and St-Louis, Vieux-Québec's two main thoroughfares. The wall itself is a national historic monument. It began as a series of earthworks and wooden palisades built by French military engineers to protect the Upper Town from an inland attack following the siege of the city by Admiral Phipps in 1690. Over the next century, the French expended much time, energy, and money to strengthen the city's fortifications. After the fall of New France, the British were equally concerned about strengthening the city's defenses and built an earth-and-wood citadel atop Cap Diamant. Slowly, the British replaced the palisades that surrounded the city with the massive cut-stone wall that has become the city's trademark attraction. The crowning touch came after the War of 1812, with the construction of the cut-stone, star-shaped citadel, perched high on Cap Diamant.

Like La Citadelle, most of the homes that line the narrow streets in Upper Town are made of granite cut from nearby quarries in the 1800s. The stone walls, copper roofs, and heavy wooden doors on the government buildings and high-steepled churches in the area also reflect the Upper Town's place as the political, educational, and religious nerve center of both the province and the country during much of the past four centuries.

GETTING HERE AND AROUND

Many people begin their tours in Upper Town, taking in the spectacular hilltop views as well as the Château Frontenac, which is probably Québec City's top site. The Fortifications border this section of the city. Walk along rue d'Auteuil, between rues St-Louis and St-Jean, to get a good sense of where the wall divides the Old City.

If you're coming from Lower Town, take the funicular (C$3.50), or brave one of the many staircases that connect the top of the hill to the bottom. Shops and restaurants provide an opportunity for a quick rest along the way uphill.

TIMING

Plan to spend a whole day visiting the many sights and shops clustered around the Château Frontenac. Rue St-Jean offers many lunch options, or do as the locals do and grab a sandwich and head to a bench in one of the area's parks.

Allot at least a half day for walking the walls of La Citadelle. Set out early in the morning to catch the Changing of the Guard (10 am in summer). Afterward, picnic on the Plains, or one of the terraces on the Grande Allée and avenue Cartier.

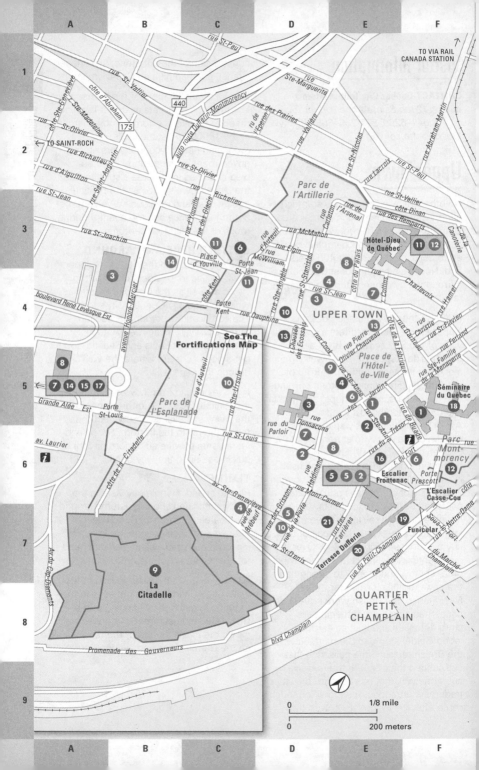

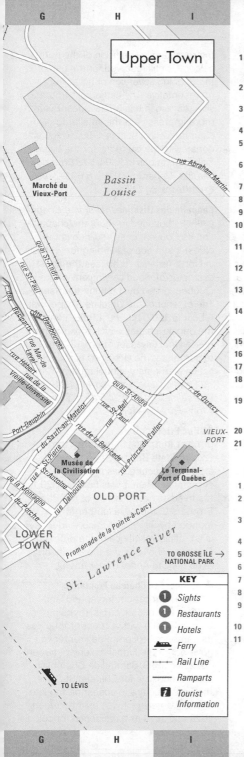

Upper Town

Marché du Vieux-Port

Bassin Louise

rue Abraham-Martin

quai St-Antoine

rue St-André

r. des Remparts

rue St-Paul

côte Dambourges

rue Mar-de Lever

rue Hébert

rue de la Vieille-Université

Port-Dauphin

r. du Sault-au-Matelot

rue St-Pierre

rue St-Paul

rue St-Bell

rue de la Barricade

rue Prince-de-Galles

r. de Quercy

quai St-André

Musée de la Civilisation

rue St-Antoine

rue Dalhousie

de la Montagne

du Porche

OLD PORT

Le Terminal-Port of Québec

VIEUX-PORT

LOWER TOWN

Promenade de la Pointe-à-Carcy

St. Lawrence River

TO GROSSE ÎLE →
NATIONAL PARK

TO LÉVIS

KEY

1 Sights
1 Restaurants
1 Hotels
Ferry
Rail Line
Ramparts
Tourist Information

Sights ▼

1 Basilique Cathédrale Notre-Dame de Québec **F5**
2 Cathedral of the Holy Trinity **E6**
3 Chapelle des Ursulines **D5**
4 Édifice Price **E5**
5 Fairmont Le Château Frontenac **E6**
6 Fortifications of Québec National Historic Site.... **C3**
7 Henry Stuart House **A5**
8 Hôtel du Parlement..... **A5**
9 La Citadelle **B7**
10 Maison de la Littérature **D4**
11 Monastère des Augustines **F4**
12 Montmorency Park National Historic Site.... **F6**
13 Morrin Cultural Centre **D4**
14 Musée National des Beaux-Arts du Québec **A5**
15 Parc Jeanne d'Arc **A5**
16 Place d'Armes **E6**
17 Plains of Abraham...... **A5**
18 Séminaire de Québec.................. **F5**
19 St-Louis Forts and Châteaux National Historic Site **F7**
20 Terrasse Dufferin **E7**
21 Wolfe-Montcalm Monument.............. **D7**

Restaurants ▼

1 Alphonse................. **E5**
2 Aux Anciens Canadiens **D6**
3 Café-Boulangerie Paillard.................. **D4**
4 Chez Boulay **D4**
5 Le Champlain............. **E6**
6 Le Chic Shack........... **F6**
7 Le Clan **D6**
8 Le Continental........... **E6**
9 L'Entrecôte St-Jean **D4**
10 Le St-Amour............. **C5**
11 Sapristi................... **C4**

Hotels ▼

1 Auberge Place d'Armes **E5**
2 Fairmont Le Château Frontenac **E6**
3 Hilton Québec........... **B4**
4 Hôtel Cap Diamant....... **C7**
5 Hôtel Château Bellevue **D7**
6 Hôtel Clarendon.......... **E5**
7 Hôtel du Vieux-Québec............ **E4**
8 Hôtel Manoir Victoria ... **E3**
9 Hôtel Marie Rollet **D5**
10 Hôtel Nomad **D7**
11 Le Capitole Hôtel......... **C3**
12 Le Monastère des Augustines **F4**
13 Monsieur Jean........... **E4**
14 Québec City Marriott Downtown **B3**

◉ Sights

Basilique Cathédrale Notre-Dame de Québec (*Our Lady of Québec Basilica Cathedral*)

CHURCH | François de Laval, the first bishop of New France and founder of Canada's Catholic Church, once ruled a diocese that stretched to the Gulf of Mexico. Videos and pictures astutely illustrate his life throughout the visit.

Laval's original cathedral burned down and has been rebuilt several times, but the current basilica still has a chancel lamp that was a gift from Louis XIV, the Sun King. The church's interior includes a canopy dais over the Episcopal throne, a ceiling of painted clouds decorated with gold leaf, and richly colored stained-glass windows. A "holy door" was added to the church in 2014. The large crypt was Québec City's first cemetery; more than 900 bodies are interred here, including, perhaps, Samuel de Champlain; archaeologists have been searching for his tomb since 1950. Guided tours of the cathedral and crypt are available (by appointment only). ⊠ *16 rue de Buade, Upper Town* ☎ *418/692–2533* ⊕ *notre-dame-de-Québec.org* ✉ *C$5.*

Cathedral of the Holy Trinity

CHURCH | The first Anglican cathedral outside the British Isles was erected in the heart of Québec City's Upper Town between 1800 and 1804. Its simple, dignified façade is reminiscent of London's St. Martin-in-the-Fields, and the pediment, archway, and Ionic pilasters introduced Palladian architecture to Canada. The land on which the cathedral was built was originally given to the Récollets (Franciscan monks from France) in 1681 by the king of France for a church and monastery. When Québec came under British rule, the Récollets made the church available to the Anglicans for services. Later, King George III ordered construction of the present cathedral, with an area set aside for members of the royal family. A portion of the north balcony is still reserved for the use of the reigning sovereign or his or her representative. The cathedral's impressive rear organ has 3,058 pipes. Even more impressive is the smaller English chamber organ, built in 1790, which was donated to the cathedral for the bicentennial celebrations in 2004. ⊠ *31 rue des Jardins, Upper Town* ☎ *418/692–2193* ⊕ *cathedral.ca* ✉ *Free.*

Chapelle des Ursulines (*Ursuline Chapel*)

CHURCH | Founded in 1639, the chapel and its Couvent des Ursulines is the oldest institution of learning for women in North America. It houses the finest examples of wood carving anywhere in Québec, gilded by the nuns themselves. The exterior of the Ursuline Chapel was rebuilt in 1902, but the interior contains the original chapel, which took sculptor Pierre-Noël Levasseur from 1726 to 1736 to complete. The Ursulines is still an active elementary school today. ⊠ *2 rue du Parloir, Upper Town* ☎ *418/694–0694* ⊕ *ursulines-uc.com* ✉ *Free* ۞ *Closed Mon.–Fri. Nov.–Apr.*

Édifice Price

NOTABLE BUILDING | Styled after the Empire State Building, this 17-story, art deco structure was the city's first skyscraper when it was built in 1929. It served as headquarters of the Price Brothers Company, a lumber firm founded by Sir William Price, and today is an official residence of the premier of Québec, who uses the top two floors. ⊠ *65 rue Ste-Anne, Upper Town.*

★ Fairmont Le Château Frontenac

HOTEL | The most photographed landmark in Québec City. This imposing turreted castle with a copper roof owes its name to the Comte de Frontenac, governor of the French colony between 1672 and 1698. Samuel de Champlain was responsible for Château St-Louis, the first structure to appear on the site of the Frontenac; it was built between 1620 and 1624 as a residence for colonial

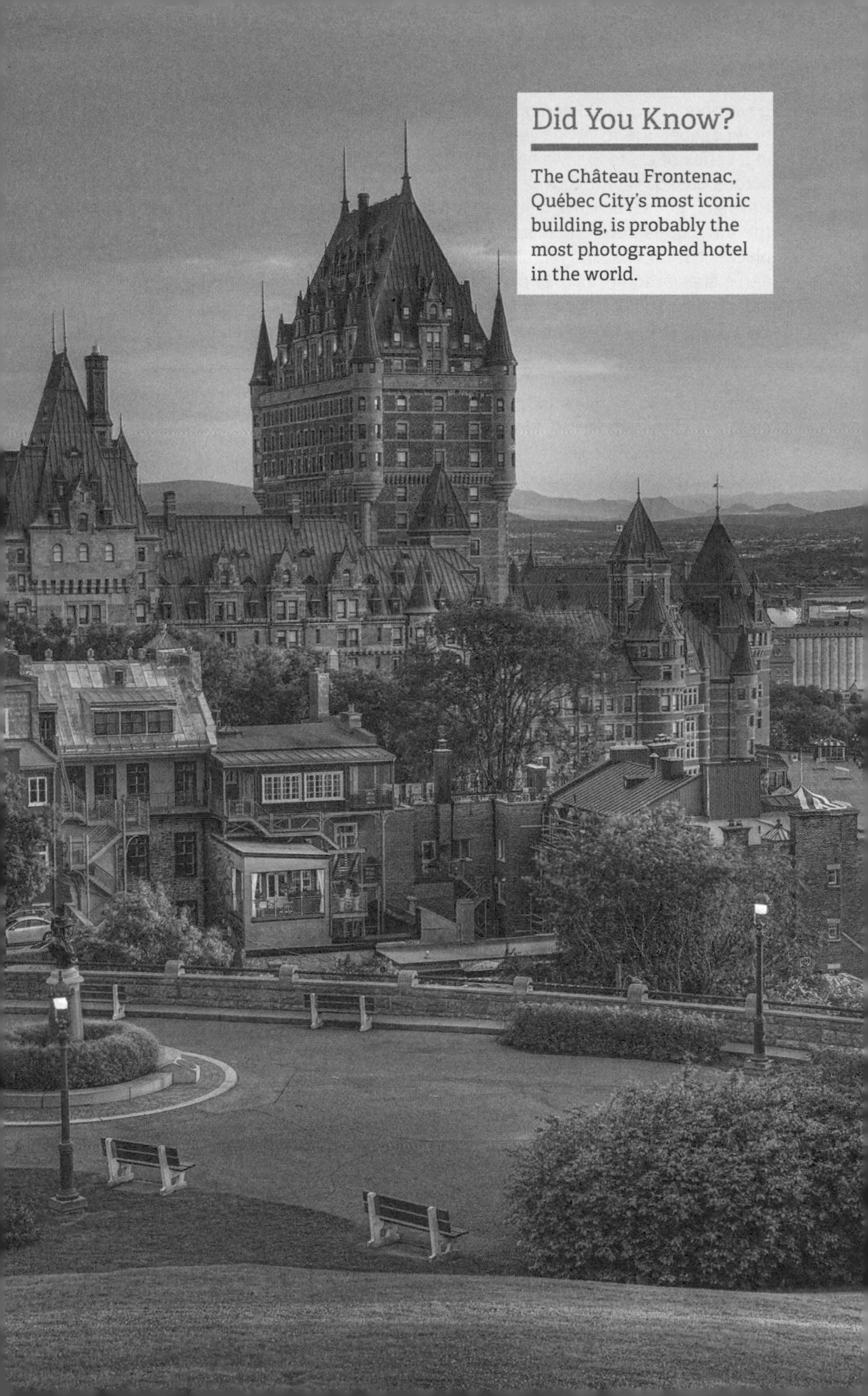

Did You Know?

The Château Frontenac, Québec City's most iconic building, is probably the most photographed hotel in the world.

governors. The original portions of the hotel opened the following year, one in a series of château-style hotels built across Canada to attract wealthy railroad travelers. It was remarkably luxurious for the time: guest rooms contained fireplaces, bathrooms, and marble fixtures, and a special commissioner purchased antiques for the establishment. The hotel was designed by New York architect Bruce Price, who also worked on Québec City's train station, Gare du Palais. The addition of a 20-story central tower in 1924 completed the hotel. Since then the Château, as it's called by locals, has accumulated a star-studded guest roster, including Prince William and Kate Middleton, Queen Elizabeth II, Princess Grace of Monaco, Alfred Hitchcock, and Ronald Reagan, as well as Franklin Roosevelt and Winston Churchill, who met here in 1943 and 1944 for two wartime conferences.

Visitors who can spend the night can book a guided visit of the hotel and learn more about its many secrets. ☒ *1 rue des Carrières, Upper Town* ☎ *418/692–3861* ⊕ *fairmont.com/frontenac-Québec.*

Fortifications of Québec National Historic Site

MILITARY SIGHT | Thick stone walls stretching for 5 kilometers (3 miles), connected by four gates, and adjoined by forts, bastions, and even a citadel: with such a special and unique landmark, it's not difficult to understand why the Historic District of Old Québec is a UNESCO World Heritage Site. These nearly intact ramparts, virtually the only ones of their kind in North America, recall the complex history of the French and British regimes in Québec City. French colonists began building ramparts along the city's cliffs as early as 1690 to protect themselves from the British, but they had trouble convincing the French government to take the threat of invasion seriously. And when the British did invade in 1759, the walls

were unsurprisingly still incomplete. The British, despite attacks by the Americans during the American Revolution and the War of 1812, took over a century to finish them—and they never saw armed conflict.

From June to September, two guided tours are offered: one starts at Artillery Park and focuses on the social and architectural heritage of the ramparts, while the other is more military-focused and begins at Terrasse Dufferin. Either way, the Dauphine Redoubt in Artillery Park on the northern end of the fortifications should not be missed; it's one of the oldest military buildings in the Americas. The four gates—Saint-Jean, Saint-Louis, Kent and the more modern Prescott—are well worth a stop, too. ☒ *2 rue d'Auteuil, Upper Town* ⊕ *pc.gc.ca/fortifications* ☒ *C$8.50* ☉ *Closed Oct.–May.*

Henry Stuart House

HISTORIC HOME | If you want to get a firsthand look at how the well-to-do English residents of Québec City lived in a bygone era, this is the place. Built in 1849 by the wife of wealthy businessman William Henry, the Regency-style cottage was bought in 1918 by the sisters Adèle and Mary Stuart. Active in such philanthropic organizations as the Red Cross and the Historical and Literary Society, the sisters were pillars of Québec City's English-speaking community. They also maintained an English-style garden behind the house. The home has since been classified a historic site for its immaculate physical condition and the museum-like quality of its furnishings, almost all of them Victorian. Guided tours of the house and garden start on the hour and include a cup of tea and piece of lemon cake. ☒ *82 Grande Allée Ouest, Montcalm* ☎ *418/647–4347* ⊕ *maisonhenrystuart. qc.ca* ☒ *C$8* ☉ *Closed Sun. and Mon. and Sept.–late June.*

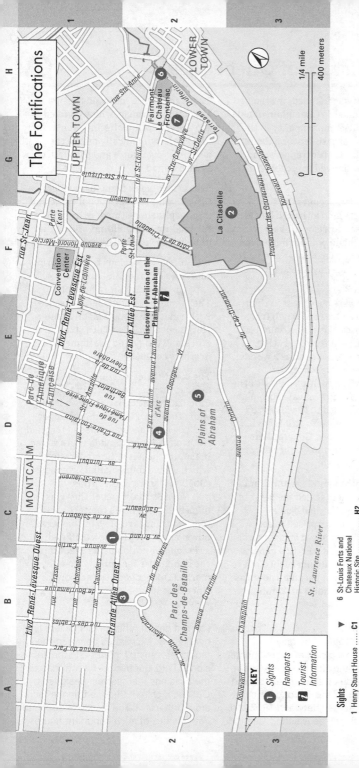

The Fortifications

UPPER TOWN

LOWER TOWN

La Citadelle

MONTCALM

Parc de
l'Amérique
Française

Convention
Center

Discovery Pavilion of the
Plains of Abraham

Plains of
Abraham

Parc des
Champs-de-Bataille

St. Lawrence River

Fairmont
Le Château
Frontenac

1/4 mile

400 meters

0

0

KEY

● Sights ▶

— Ramparts

ℹ Tourist
Information

Sights

1 Henry Stuart House **C1**

2 La Citadelle **F3**

3 Musée National des
Beaux-Arts
du Québec **B2**

4 Parc Jeanne d'Arc **D2**

5 Plains of Abraham **D2**

6 St-Louis Forts and
Chateaux National
Historic Site **H2**

7 Wolfe-Montcalm
Monument **G2**

The History of Québec City

Québec City was founded by French explorer Samuel de Champlain in 1608 and is the oldest municipality in the province. In the 17th century, the first French explorers, fur trappers, and missionaries arrived to establish a colony.

French explorer Jacques Cartier arrived in 1535, and although he did attempt to set up a (short-lived) colony, it was Champlain who founded "New France" some 70 years later and built a fort (called Place Royale today) on the banks of the St. Lawrence.

The British were persistent in their efforts to dislodge the French from North America, but the colonists of New France built forts and other military structures, such as a wooden palisade (defensive fence) that reinforced their position on top of the cliff. It was Britain's naval supremacy that ultimately led to New France's demise. After capturing all French forts east of Québec, General James Wolfe led his army to Québec City in the summer of 1759.

After a months long siege, thousands of British soldiers scaled the heights along a narrow cow path on a moonless night. Surprised to see British soldiers massed on a farmer's field so near the city, French general Louis-Joseph Montcalm rushed out to meet them in what became known as the Battle of the Plains of Abraham.

The French were routed in the 20-minute skirmish, which claimed the lives of both Wolfe and Montcalm. The battle symbolically marks the death of New France and the birth of British Canada.

British rule was a boon for Québec City. Thanks to more robust trade and large capital investments, the fishing, fur-trading, shipbuilding, and timber industries expanded rapidly.

Wary of new invasions from its former American colonies, the British also expanded the city's fortifications. They replaced the wooden palisades with a massive stone wall and built a star-shaped fortress. Both structures still stand today, and are named Fortifications de Québec.

The constitution of 1791 established Québec City as the capital of Lower Canada, a position it held until 1840, when the Act of Union united Upper and Lower Canada and made Montréal the capital. When Canada was created in 1867 by the Act of Confederation, which united four colonial provinces (Québec, Ontario, New Brunswick, and Nova Scotia), Québec City was named the province's capital city, a role it continues to play. In Québec; however, the city is known officially as *la capitale nationale*, a reflection of the nationalist sentiments that have marked Québec society and politics since the 1960s.

Hôtel du Parlement

GOVERNMENT BUILDING | The only French-speaking legislature in continental North America, the 125-member Assemblée Nationale du Québec meets behind the stately walls of this Second Empire-style building erected between 1877 and 1886. If the Assemblée is sitting, see if you can get into the visitors gallery to hear heated exchanges between the federalist-leaning Liberals and the secessionist Parti Québécois. Failing that, the buildings themselves, designed by Québec architect Eugène-Étienne Taché, are worth a visit. The facade is decorated with statues of such important figures

Kids will love watching the Royal 22nd Regiment's Changing of the Guard every summer day at 10 am, from June 24 until the first Monday in September.

of Québec history as Cartier, Champlain, Frontenac, Wolfe, and Montcalm. A 30-minute tour (in English, French, or Spanish) takes in the President's Gallery, the Parlementaire restaurant, the Legislative Council Chamber, and the National Assembly Chamber. Tours may be restricted during legislative sessions. Outdoor tours of the gardens and statues are also available during summer. ⊠ *1045 rue des Parlementaires, Upper Town* ☎ *866/337–8837* ⊕ *assnat.qc.ca* ⊡ *Free* ☉ *Closed Sat. and Sun.* ⌂ *Reservations are mandatory.*

★ La Citadelle

MILITARY SIGHT | Built at the city's highest point, on Cap Diamant, the Citadelle is the largest fortified base in North America still occupied by troops. The 25-building fortress is, quite literally, the star of the Fortifications of Québec National Historic Site. It was intended to protect the port, prevent the enemy from taking up a position on the Plains of Abraham, and provide a refuge in case of an attack.

Since 1920, the Citadelle has served as a base for Canada's most storied French-speaking military formation, the Royal 22e Régiment, known across Canada as the Van Doos, from the French "vingt-deux" (22). Firearms, uniforms, and decorations from as far back as the 17th century are displayed in the Musée du Royal 22e Régiment in the former powder magazine, built in 1750. Watch the Changing of the Guard, a ceremony in which troops parade before the Citadelle in red coats and black fur hats while a band plays. The regiment's mascot, a well-behaved goat, watches along. The queen's representative in Canada, the governor-general, has a residence in the Citadelle, and it's open for tours in summer. You must take a tour to access the Citadelle, since it's a military base. ■**TIP**➔ **The location—set high above the St. Lawrence river with stunning views of the city and surrounding countryside—is worth a visit even if you don't want to pay (or wait) to take a tour.** ⊠ *Côte de la Citadelle, Upper Town* ☎ *418/694–2815*

⊕ *lacitadelle.qc.ca* ✉ *C$18* ☞ *Changing of the Guard at 10 am in summer.*

★ Maison de la Littérature

LIBRARY | Well worth a stop for design, architecture, and book lovers alike, this stunning library houses permanent exhibitions on French Canadian literature. Set in a former 19th century Methodist church, the now white-washed, design-heavy building was completely revamped a few years ago, winning international acclaim and architecture awards in the process. ✉ *40 rue St-Stanislas, Upper Town* ☎ *418/641–6797* ⊕ *maisondelalitterature.qc.ca* ☽ *Closed Mon.*

★ Monastère des Augustines (*Augustinian Monastery and Museum*)

RELIGIOUS BUILDING | Augustinian nuns arrived from Dieppe, France, in 1639 with a mission to care for the sick in the new colony. They established the first hospital north of Mexico, the Hôtel-Dieu, the large building west of the monastery. The complex underwent a complete renovation and expansion, in 2015, and now includes a quiet, health-conscious restaurant (with silent breakfast!), as well as accommodations—both contemporary en-suite rooms and dorm-like rooms with antique furniture—for those looking for a calm retreat. The museum houses an extensive collection of liturgical and medical artifacts of all kinds, and it's also worth visiting the richly decorated chapel designed by artist Thomas Baillairgé, as well as the vaults, which date to 1659 and were used by the nuns as shelter from British bombardments. There is still a small order of nuns living in a section of the monastery. ✉ *32 rue Charlevoix, Upper Town* ☎ *418/692–2492* ⊕ *monastere.ca* ✉ *C$11.50, C$16 for guided tours* ☽ *Closed Mon. and statutory holidays.*

Montmorency Park National Historic Site

CITY PARK | Seemingly floating between Upper and Lower Town, Montmorency Park is a must-see for visitors walking up (or down) Côte de la Montagne. The leafy park was home to Parliaments of Lower Canada, Canada East, and Québec from 1791 to 1883; while virtually zero surface structure remains to illustrate this role, it's now a national historic site filled with centenary trees and walkways describing the significance of the site. Along the southeastern edge are the ramparts and defensive walls, from which visitors will find a beautiful panoramic view of the Lower Town and the river. ✉ *Côte de la Montagne, Upper Town.*

★ Morrin Cultural Centre

ARTS CENTER | This stately gray-stone building has served many purposes, from imprisoning and executing criminals to storing the national archives. Built between 1808 and 1813, it was the first modern prison in Canada and was converted into Morrin College, one of the city's first private schools, in 1868. That was also when the Literary and Historical Society of Québec, forerunner of Canada's National Archives, moved in. Historical and cultural talks are held in English, and tours of the building, including two blocks of prison cells, the Victorian-era library, and College Hall, are also available. Children and families particularly enjoy this space. ✉ *44 Chaussée des Écossais, Upper Town* ☎ *418/694–9147* ⊕ *morrin.org* ✉ *Library free; guided tours C$8* ☽ *Closed Mon. and Tues.*

★ Musée National des Beaux-Arts du Québec (*National Museum of Fine Arts of Québec*)

ART MUSEUM | Situated on the city's liveliest avenue, the Grand Allée, this neoclassical museum in the park with a slick and modern wing is a remarkable steel-and-glass setting for its collection of 22,000 traditional and contemporary pieces of Québec art. Designed by starchitects Rem Koolhaas and Shohei Shigematsu, the Lassonde Pavilion, added in 2016, features three stacked, cascading galleries; a grand stairwell that spirals dramatically from the top floor to the basement, where a rising almost-mile-long tunnel connects to the museum's three other wings; and views of the neighboring neo-Gothic church from both the rooftop terrace and courtyard.

MNBAQ houses works by loçal legends Jean-Paul Riopelle, Jean-Paul Lemieux, Alfred Pellan, Fernand Leduc, and Horatio Walker that are particularly notable, as well as temporary exhibits by international artists such as Turner, Miro, and Giacometti. The original museum building in Parc des Champs-de-Bataille is part of an abandoned prison dating from 1867; a hallway of cells, with the iron bars and courtyard, has been preserved as part of a permanent exhibition on the prison's history. ✉ *Parc des Champs-de-Bataille, Upper Town* ☎ *418/643–2150* ⊕ *mnbaq.org* ⊠ *C$16 for permanent collection; C$25 for temporary exhibits* ⊘ *Closed Mon. Sept.–May.*

★ Parc Jeanne d'Arc

CITY PARK | Bright with colorful flowers in summer, this urban park is lined with stunning 19th-century mansions and is often adorned with seasonal decorations. It makes for a lovely place to rest between museums. The focus of the park is an equestrian statue of Joan of Arc. A symbol of military courage and of France itself, the statue stands in tribute to the heroes of 1759 near the place where New France was lost to the British. The park also commemorates the Canadian national anthem, "O Canada"; it was played here for the first time on June 24, 1880. ✉ *Avenue Wilfrid-Laurier, Upper Town.*

Place d'Armes

PLAZA/SQUARE | For centuries, this wide square was used for parades and military events; today, it's mostly strollers, buskers, and visitors enjoying restaurant terraces. On its west side stands the majestic **Ancien Palais de Justice** (Old Courthouse), a Renaissance-style building from 1887. The plaza is on land that was occupied by a church and convent of the Récollet missionaries (Franciscan monks), who in 1615 were the first order of priests to arrive in New France. The Gothic-style **fountain** in the center pays

tribute to their arrival. ✉ *Rues St-Louis and du Fort, Upper Town.*

★ Plains of Abraham

HISTORIC SIGHT | This park, named after Abraham Martin, who used the plains as a pasture for his cows, is the site of the famous battle on September 13, 1759, that decided New France's fate as part of the acrimonious Seven Years' War. On that date, British soldiers under the command of General Wolfe climbed the steep cliff under the cover of darkness, ultimately defeating the French through a single deadly volley of musket fire, causing the battle to be over within 30 minutes. At the Museum of the Plains of Abraham, check out the multimedia display, which depicts Canada's history, as well as the numerous family-friendly activities at Martello Towers.

Nowadays, locals come here to cross-country ski and admire the relentless St. Lawrence River even as it freezes over in winter; in July, the Summer Festival takes over with tens of thousands of concertgoers. ✉ *Parc des Champs-de-Bataille, Upper Town* ☎ *418/649–6157* ⊕ *ccbn-nbc.gc.ca* ⊠ *C$17.75 for museum admission.*

Séminaire de Québec

HISTORIC SIGHT | Behind iron gates, next to the Notre-Dame-de-Québec cathedral, lies a tranquil courtyard surrounded by austere stone buildings with rising steeples, structures that have housed classrooms and student residences since 1663. François de Montmorency Laval, the first bishop of New France, founded the Québec Seminary to train priests in the new colony. In 1852 the seminary gave birth to Université Laval, the first francophone university in North America.

Today priests still live on the premises, and Québec City's architecture school occupies part of the building. The small Second Empire–style Chapelle Extérieure, at the west entrance of the seminary, was built in 1888 after fire destroyed the 1750

Québec City's Best Walking Tours 👁

Ghost Tours of Québec. Costumed actors lead ghoulish 90-minute evening tours of Québec City murders, executions, and ghost sightings. The tours (C$22) are available in English or French, from May through October. After the walk, you can buy a copy of *Ghost Stories of Québec*, which has stories not told on the tours. ✉ *34 boul. Champlain, Lower Town* ☎ *855/692–9770* ⊕ *www.ghosttoursof-Québec.com.*

Tours Voir Québec. This tour company offers English- and French-language (and Spanish from June to September) walking tours of the Old City, starting at C$25. Other tours include a "Bury Your Dead" murder mystery tour based on the novels of Louise Penny, as well as a popular food tour with tastings at various establishments for C$55. Self-guided audio tours are also available. ✉ *12 rue St-Anne, Upper Town* ☎ *418/694–2001, 866/694–2001* ⊕ *www.toursvoirQuébec.com.*

original; its interior is patterned after that of the Église de la Trinité in Paris. ✉ *1 côte de la Fabrique, Upper Town* ☎ *418/692–2843* ۞ *Closed Sat. and Sun.*

St-Louis Forts and Châteaux National Historic Site

RUINS | Venture under the Terrasse Dufferin to see archaeological treasures from the official residence and power base of the French and British governors. Massive excavations unearthed artifacts from the first château, built under the direction of Governor Montmagny, to the time the Château St-Louis burned in 1834. Wine bottles, kitchenware—even remains of walls and door frames—give clues to the luxurious life of the governors, who were among the most powerful men in the nation. Don't miss the guided tours and activities. History buffs might consider attending one of the in-depth archaeology conferences held here. ✉ *Terrasse Dufferin, Upper Town* ☎ *418/648–7016* ⊕ *pc.gc.ca/en/lhn-nhs/qc/saintlouisforts* ▨ *C$3.90* ۞ *Closed mid-Oct.–June.*

★ Terrasse Dufferin

VIEWPOINT | This wide boardwalk with an intricate wrought-iron guardrail has a panoramic view of the St. Lawrence River, the city of Lévis on the opposite shore, Île d'Orléans, the Laurentian Mountains

to the north, and the edge of the Appalachians to the south. It was named for Lord Dufferin, governor of Canada between 1872 and 1878, who had this walkway constructed in 1878. Château St-Louis, whose remains can be seen under the walkway, was home to every governor from 1626 to 1834, when it was destroyed by fire. There are 90-minute tours of the fortifications that leave from here. The Promenade des Gouverneurs begins at the boardwalk's western end; the path skirts the cliff and leads up to Québec's highest point, Cap Diamant, and also to the Citadelle. ✉ *Terrasse Dufferin, Upper Town.*

Wolfe-Montcalm Monument

MONUMENT | Surrounded by a leafy, small park right next to the Château Frontenac, this 50-foot-tall obelisk pays tribute to both a winning (English) and a losing (French) general. More specifically, it marks the place where the British general James Wolfe and French marquis Louis-Joseph Montcalm died during the Battle of Québec in September 1759. Wolfe landed his troops about 3 km (2 miles) from the city's walls; 4,500 English soldiers scaled the cliff and began fighting on the Plains of Abraham. Wolfe was mortally wounded in battle and was carried behind the lines to this spot. Montcalm, who had been famous for winning four major battles in North America, was also fatally injured; he was carried into the walled city, where he died the next morning, essentially marking the end of the French regime in Québec City.

On the south side of the park is avenue Ste-Geneviève, lined with well-preserved Victorian houses dating from 1850 to 1900. Many have been converted to inns, B&Bs, and hotels. ✉ *rue des Carrières, Montcalm.*

🍴 Restaurants

In addition to quick to-go *boulangeries* (bakeries), cafés, and diners, Upper Town also has its share of legendary, white-tablecloth restaurants (albeit more popular with tourists than locals) known for market-fresh ingredients and legions of creative chefs and sommeliers.

Poutine Stop 🍴

As far as fast food goes, nothing is more Québécois than poutine, that rough-and-ready dish made of fries, cheese curds, and gravy. In Québec City, regional chain Chez Ashton, founded in 1969, is the local favorite for hurried lunchers and late-night snackers. Also well worth trying here is a hot-dog du lac, a "steamie" (steamed hot dog) with mayo, cabbage, and a few fries on top. ✉ *54 Côte du Palais, Upper Town chezashton.ca*

Alphonse

$$$ | MODERN CANADIAN | Sun-drenched, open-space corner bistro, complete with black and dark wood accents for a profoundly Parisian flair, serves local fare in a relaxed yet refined atmosphere. From game meat to seafood (try the gin sauce scallops), from fresh pasta to revisited classics (try the Brussel sprouts Ceasal), along with a string of vegan options, Alphonse certainly aims to please. **Known for:** beautiful space; vegan menu; wonderful cocktails. [$] *Average main: C$28* ✉ *19 rue des Jardins, Upper Town* ☎ *418/694–0707* 🌐 *alphonse.ca* 🕒 *Closed Mon.; lunch Wed.–Fri. only.*

Aux Anciens Canadiens

$$$ | CANADIAN | Named for a 19th-century book by Philippe-Aubert de Gaspé, who once resided in the 1675 house, this establishment has a modern menu and a good wine list, but most people come for the authentic French-Canadian cooking. Servers are dressed in period costume and each of the five dining rooms has a different theme, such as the bright and cheerful *vaisselier* (dish room), featuring colorful antique dishes and a fireplace. **Known for:** historical setting; tourtière (meat pie); maple syrup pie. [$] *Average main: C$29* ✉ *34 rue St-Louis, Upper Town* ☎ *418/692–1627* 🌐 *auxancienscanadiens.qc.ca.*

Café-Boulangerie Paillard

$ | BAKERY | FAMILY | Owned by Yves Simard and his wife, Rebecca, this bakery, pastry counter, sandwich bar, pizza shop (summer only), and ice-cream parlor is known for its selection of nouvelle French pastries, whole grain breads, gourmet sandwiches, and artisanal gelato. Long wooden tables, designed to get customers talking to each other, create a convivial atmosphere. **Known for:** efficient service; communal tables; delicious sandwiches and pastries. [$] *Average main: C$10* ✉ *1097 rue St-Jean, Upper Town* ☎ *418/692–1221* 🌐 *paillard.ca.*

★ Chez Boulay

$$$$ | CANADIAN | Chefs Jean-Luc Boulay and Arnaud Marchand, who are both revered in this town, delight patrons with elegant interpretations of cuisine inspired by northern Québec and made entirely from local ingredients, including reinvented classic desserts, such as iced nougat with cloudberries. A mix of locals celebrating special occasions and tourists fresh from shopping rue St-Jean dine in this elegant dining room on bison tartare, braised beef ravioli with candied red cabbage, and salmon in a flavorful cranberry glaze. **Known for:** vegetarian menu; signature brunch on weekends; excellent wine list. $ Average main: C$35 ⊠ 1110 rue St-Jean, Upper Town ☎ 418/380–8166 ⊕ chezboulay.com ⊘ Closed Mon. and Tues. No lunch.

★ Le Champlain

$$$$ | MODERN CANADIAN | Inside the most romantic dining room at Fairmont Château Frontenac, chef Hugo Coudurier has made this one of the city's top gastronomical tables, showcasing unexpected combinations, delicious flavors, Nordic-inspired ingredients (such as wild hare and even Lapland reindeer), and whimsical presentations. Although service can be a bit stiff, the food is anything but, and the rewards on the plate are definitely worth any formality. **Known for:** C$119 tasting menu; creative gastronomy; in the classic landmark, Fairmont Château Frontenac. $ Average main: C$45 ⊠ Fairmont Le Château Frontenac, 1 rue des Carrières, Upper Town ☎ 418/692–3861 ⊕ fairmont. com/frontenac-Québec/dining/champlain ⊘ Closed Mon. and Tues. No dinner on Sun.

Le Chic Shack

$ | FAST FOOD | FAMILY | At this refreshing alternative to the Old City's ubiquitous white-linen bistros, you can get fast food that's also high quality. Burgers made from grass-fed cattle served on soft artisanal brioche buns make this a prime locale for lunch goers. **Known for:** delicious milkshakes; great burgers; quality fast food. $ Average main: C$11 ⊠ 15 rue du Fort, Upper Town ☎ 418/692–1485 ⊕ lechicshack.ca.

Le Clan

$$$$ | MODERN CANADIAN | The premise already has foodies salivating: "anthropomorphic universe" of local and organic cuisine. Chef Stéphane Modat, whose fame on this side of the pond is largely due to his masterful time in the kitchen of the Fairmont Château Frontenac, surrounds himself with precious collaborators (the name of the restaurant, "the clan," is by no means a coincidence) and brings his characterful verve to boreal gastronomy. **Known for:** local organic cuisine; French savoir-faire; C$125 tasting menu. $ Average main: C$40 ⊠ 44 rue des Jardins, Upper Town ☎ 418/692–0333 ⊕ restaurantleclan.com ⊘ Closed Tues. and Wed.

Le Continental

$$$$ | EUROPEAN | If Québec City had a dining hall of fame, Le Continental would be there among the best. Since 1956 this historic spot, steps from the Château Frontenac, has been serving solid, traditionally gourmet dishes, such as tableside-prepared orange duckling and filet mignon, which is flambéed in a cognac sauce and then luxuriously covered in a gravy seasoned with mustard and sage. **Known for:** old-school excellence; classic gastronomy; tableside "guéridon" service. $ Average main: C$60 ⊠ 26 rue St-Louis, Upper Town ☎ 418/694–9995 ⊕ restaurantlecontinental.com ⊘ No lunch.

L'Entrecôte St-Jean

$$$ | FRENCH | Steak frites (steak with fries) is on menus everywhere in Québec City and in lots of other places throughout the world, but this popular and lively establishment has a 30-year reputation as the master of the dish—L'entrecôte is a particular sirloin cut, usually long and relatively thin. Diners at this red-and-blue-trimmed house choose between three steak sizes, and each comes smothered in the restaurant's signature peppery sauce with a heaping pile of crispy fries. **Known for:** great patio; steak frites and signature sauce; simple and well executed menu. $ Average main: C$27 ⊠ 1080 rue St-Jean, Upper Town

☎ *418/694–0234* 🌐 *entrecotesaintjean.com* 🕒 *No lunch Sat.–Sun.*

Le St-Amour
$$$$ | FRENCH | At one of the city's most romantic and treasured restaurants, chef Jean-Luc Boulay entices diners with such creations as the Foie Gras experience (with five variations of this French delicacy) and Arctic char with buttermilk sauce and lemon vervain oil. For dessert, try their seasonal hazelnut chocolate crème brûlée. They are also famous for their robust wine cellar, which contains over 15,000 bottles from around the world making it one of the largest in Canada. **Known for:** art nouveau-inspired decor; foie gras; curated wine list. [$] *Average main: C$50* ✉ *48 rue Ste-Ursule, Upper Town* ☎ *418/694–0667* 🌐 *saint-amour.com* 🕒 *Closed Sun.–Tues.*

Sapristi
$$ | ITALIAN | FAMILY | The menu at this Italian-leaning restaurant with an industrial-cool feel is satisfying, with a number of imaginative pizzas, pastas, salads, and such. Try the fried mozzarella or the chef's risotto, which changes daily. **Known for:** gluten-free options; creative pizzas; great patio. [$] *Average main: C$18* ✉ *1001 rue St-Jean, Upper Town* ☎ *418/692–2030* 🌐 *sapristi.ca.*

Hotels

Upper Town, inside the Old City's walls, is famous for its accommodations in historic buildings, decorated with antique furnishings and heavy fabrics. Few have restaurants, but there are lots of places to eat nearby.

Auberge Place d'Armes
$$$ | B&B/INN | Old Québec charm meets modern convenience at this property near the Château Frontenac, which attracts a mix of couples and businesspeople staying on expense accounts. **Pros:** central location; comfortable, well-equipped rooms; good restaurant on premises, Chez Jules. **Cons:** no elevator means working off breakfast on the stairs; traditional furniture may not be for everyone; no on-site parking. [$] *Rooms from: C$235* ✉ *24 rue Ste-Anne, Upper Town* ☎ *418/694–9485* 🌐 *aubergeplacedarmes.com* 🛏 *33 rooms* 🍴 *Free Breakfast.*

★ Le Capitole Hôtel
$$$$ | HOTEL | Freshly renovated, this turn-of-the-20th-century structure just outside the St-Jean Gate and the fortifications is a fancy hotel, dining destination, and 1920s cabaret-style dinner theater (the Théâtre Capitole) all rolled into one. **Pros:** rain shower; luxurious bedding; rooftop garden with views. **Cons:** some rooms are small; limited room service; theater-hotel complex not very peaceful. [$] *Rooms from: C$300* ✉ *972 rue St-Jean, Upper Town* ☎ *800/363–4040* 🌐 *lecapitole.com* 🛏 *39 rooms, 1 suite* 🍴 *No Meals.*

★ Fairmont Le Château Frontenac
$$$$ | HOTEL | In this landmark building, perked up with some sleek and well-integrated modern touches, the public rooms—from the cozy and elegant Bar 1608 to the 700-seat ballroom reminiscent of the Hall of Mirrors at Versailles—are all opulent; guest rooms are just as elegantly furnished, like minichâteaux, with cream, gold, and green touches. **Pros:** Le Labo toiletries; top historic attraction; river views. **Cons:** some guest rooms inferior to Deluxe category are not renovated; rooms are small for the price; busy lobby. [$] *Rooms from: C$259* ✉ *1 rue des Carrières, Upper Town* ☎ *418/692–3861* 🌐 *fairmont.com/frontenac-Québec* 🛏 *648 rooms* 🍴 *No Meals.*

Hilton Québec
$$ | HOTEL | Next to Parliament Hill, this hotel may be all business (as in, it caters primarily to a corporate clientele) but it has chic and contemporary rooms with views of Vieux-Québec or the Laurentian Mountains to the north. **Pros:** great city views; direct access to the convention center; amazing executive lounge. **Cons:**

lacks Old Québec charm; can be businesslike; blocky exterior. $ *Rooms from: C$199 ⊠ 1100 boul. René-Lévesque Est, Upper Town ☎ 800/447–2411 ⊕ hilton-Québec.com ⟡ 571 rooms* ❍❘ *No Meals.*

Hôtel Cap Diamant

$$ | B&B/INN | An eclectic collection of vintage furniture and ecclesiastical accents—stained glass from a church, a confessional door, an angel or two—complement the decorative marble fireplaces, stone walls, and hardwood floors at this hotel. **Pros:** some rooms have private balconies; Victorian style and charm; a four-season veranda. **Cons:** outdated furniture; poor soundproofing; stairs to third-floor rooms are a bit steep. $ *Rooms from: C$190 ⊠ 39 avenue Ste-Geneviève, Upper Town ☎ 888/694–0313 ⊕ hotelcapdiamant.com ⟡ 12 rooms* ❍❘ *Free Breakfast.*

Hôtel Château Bellevue

$$ | HOTEL | Behind the Château Frontenac, facing a pleasant park, this 1898 hotel occupies four heritage houses with the same green roofing, and offers modern rooms with standard hotel furnishings in a good location, often with views of the St. Lawrence River. **Pros:** river views; distinctive package deals; good continental breakfast. **Cons:** décor can be eclectic; no pool or spa; poor soundproofing. $ *Rooms from: C$199 ⊠ 16 rue de la Porte, Upper Town ☎ 800/463–2617 ⊕ hoteloldQuébec.com ⟡ 49 rooms* ❍❘ *Free Breakfast.*

Hôtel Clarendon

$$ | HOTEL | This is the oldest operating hotel in Québec City; half of its rooms have excellent views over Old Québec, and the others overlook a courtyard. **Pros:** some rooms have Old-Québec views; the piano in the lounge attracts merrymakers; valet service. **Cons:** rooms on the lower floors can be noisy; some rooms feel dark and small; décor can feel a bit bare. $ *Rooms from: C$164 ⊠ 57 rue Ste-Anne, Upper Town ☎ 888/554–6001 ⊕ hotelclarendon.com ⟡ 143 rooms* ❍❘ *No Meals.*

Hôtel du Vieux-Québec

$$ | HOTEL | Nicely situated at the end of rue St-Jean, surrounded by stores and restaurants, this eco-friendly spot has rooms spread over three floors, including a suite with a king bed and huge flat-screen television, and a "superior room" with two queen beds and an exposed brick wall. **Pros:** carbon neutral; amazing staff; lively location. **Cons:** dim lighting; off-site parking; can be noisy. $ *Rooms from: C$180 ⊠ 1190 rue St-Jean, Upper Town ☎ 800/361–7787 ⊕ hvq.com ⟡ 45 rooms* ❍❘ *No Meals.*

Hôtel Manoir Victoria

$$ | HOTEL | The recent renovations at this European-style hotel, with a discreet entrance on Côte du Palais, include the elegantly simple rooms with hardwood furnishings and white bedding. **Pros:** heated bathroom floors; indoor parking; great location. **Cons:** not the best cleaning service; lots of stairs at the entrance; lobby can get busy with restaurant or convention crowds. $ *Rooms from: C$175 ⊠ 44 côte du Palais, Upper Town ☎ 800/463–6283 ⊕ manoir-victoria.com ⟡ 156 rooms* ❍❘ *No Meals.*

Hôtel Marie Rollet

$ | B&B/INN | Located on a charming street corner at the heart of Vieux-Québec, this intimate inn built in 1876 by the Ursuline order has quaint décor and antiques and sometimes small but warm rooms, some with exposed brick. **Pros:** free coffee in the morning; central location; rooftop terrace with garden view. **Cons:** very small bathrooms; steep stairs; no elevator. $ *Rooms from: C$129 ⊠ 81 rue Ste-Anne, Upper Town ☎ 800/275–0338 ⊕ hotelmarierollet.com ⟡ 11 rooms* ❍❘ *No Meals.*

Hôtel Nomad

$ | HOTEL | At Hôtel Nomad, each of the six rooms has a story to tell and a personality all of its own. **Pros:** great views of Old Québec landmarks; charming, design-oriented rooms; spa-and-meals packages available. **Cons:** limited amenities in rooms; no elevator; some rooms are tiny. [$] *Rooms from: C$100* ✉ *15 avenue Ste-Geneviève, Upper Town* ☎ *418/694–1884* 🌐 *hotelnomad.ca* 🛏 *6 rooms* 🍴 *No Meals.*

★ Le Monastère des Augustines
$ | B&B/INN | Stay in a 17th-century monastery—and the birthplace of the first hospital in North America—that's been transformed into a contemporary holistic retreat. **Pros:** free access to museum; historical building; modern, design-oriented rooms. **Cons:** en-suite in contemporary rooms only; not the best staff; mum's the word at this silent retreat. [$] *Rooms from: C$95* ✉ *77 rue des Remparts, Upper Town* ☎ *844/694–1639* 🌐 *monastere.ca* 🛏 *65 rooms* 🍴 *Free Breakfast.*

Monsieur Jean
$$$$ | HOTEL | Quirky and whimsical, close to all the historical and culinary attractions of Old Québec, Monsieur Jean's suites will appeal to travelers who love Louis XIV luxury in its most contemporary expression. **Pros:** excellent views from rooms; impeccably appointed rooms; central location. **Cons:** parking is expensive; front desk not always open; street can get busy. [$] *Rooms from: C$300* ✉ *2 rue Pierre-Olivier-Chauveau, Upper Town* ☎ *418/977–7777* 🌐 *monsieurjean.ca* 🛏 *49 rooms* 🍴 *No Meals.*

Québec City Marriott Downtown
$$ | HOTEL | This former bank building exudes a quiet elegance, with modern guest rooms with wood furniture and stained-glass windows, two fireplaces, and a tiny wood-lined corner bar in the lobby. **Pros:** central location; 24/7 fitness center; helpful staff. **Cons:** street can be busy; rooms are not sound-proofed; lacks Old Québec charm. [$] *Rooms from: C$199* ✉ *850 place d'Youville, Upper Town* ☎ *866/694–4004* 🌐 *marriott.com* 🛏 *111 rooms* 🍴 *No Meals.*

🍸 Nightlife

BARS AND LOUNGES

★ Bar 1608
COCKTAIL LOUNGES | One of the city's most romantic spots is the Fairmont Château Frontenac's bar, which boasts the most interesting cocktail menu in town. You can also have some wine, a bit of charcuterie and cheese, and relax while looking at the St. Lawrence River or the two fireplaces. ✉ *1 rue des Carrières, Upper Town* ☎ *418/266–3906* 🌐 *fairmont.com/frontenac-Québec.*

L'Atelier
COCKTAIL LOUNGES | Doubling up as a restaurant that notably serves all kinds of tartares, L'Atelier is a Québec City hot spot dedicated to libations of all kinds. The chief mixologist is notorious for his creative, audacious cocktails; case in point, the Kentucky Lime (bourbon, lime juice, bitters, and maple syrup). ✉ *624 Grande-Allée Est, Upper Town* ☎ *418/522–2225* 🌐 *bistrolatelier.com.*

Les Voûtes Napoléon
LIVE MUSIC | The brick walls and wine cellar–like atmosphere help make Les Voûtes a popular place to listen to live Québécois music. Much of the beer here is from local microbreweries. ✉ *680 Grande-Allée Est, Montcalm* ☎ *418/640–9388* 🌐 *voutesdenapoleon.com.*

BREWPUBS

Bar Le Sacrilège
BREWPUBS | Across the street from Église St-Jean-Baptiste, this place bears its name well, with a couple of church pews and religious icons. Le Sacrilège has local microbrews like Boréale and Trou du Diable in bottles and on tap, and the special changes daily. It also has the best terrace in the city, an enclosed garden that's constantly full in summer. Live music or DJs play on a regular basis. ✉ *447 rue St-Jean, Upper Town* ☎ *418/649–1985* 🌐 *lesacrilege.com.*

L'Inox

BREWPUBS | A popular Upper Town brewpub, L'Inox serves beers that have been brewed on-site, like Trouble-Fête and Coulée-Douce, as well as a rotating list of limited-edition brews. Inside are billiard tables and excellent European-style hot dogs (featuring long, tasty sausages served on a baguette); outside there's a summer terrace. ⊠ *655 Grande-Allée Est, Montcalm* ☎ *418/692–2877* ⊕ *brasserieinox.com.*

Le Pub Saint-Alexandre

BREWPUBS | This popular English-style pub offers dozens of single-malt scotch and more than 200 kinds of beer, 30 of which are on tap, and many of which are exclusive imports. ⊠ *1087 rue St-Jean, Upper Town* ☎ *418/694–0015* ⊕ *pubstalexandre.com.*

🎭 Performing Arts

Art is everywhere in Québec City—from theater and chic galleries to accordion-playing street performers and statue mimes in the parks. From September through May, a steady stream of concerts, plays, and performances is presented in theaters and halls. In summer, many indoor theaters close, and outdoor shows of all kinds appear, most of them free.

★ **Orchestre symphonique de Québec**

(*Québec Symphony Orchestra*)

MUSIC | Canada's oldest symphony orchestra, directed by the dynamic French conductor Fabien Gabel, performs mainly at Louis-Fréchette Hall in the Grand Théâtre de Québec. ⊠ *269 boul. René-Lévesque Est, St-Jean-Baptiste* ☎ *418/643–8486* ⊕ *osq.org* 🎫 *From C\$45.*

Théâtre Capitole

MUSIC | This cabaret-style theater schedules pop music and musical comedy shows by the most famous French-speaking artists in Québec. ⊠ *972 rue St-Jean, Upper Town* ☎ *418/694–4444* ⊕ *lecapitole.com.*

Le Diamant

ARTS CENTERS | Multi-disciplinary space that welcomes the world's most prestigious contemporary creations to its strikingly modern stage in the heart of Old Québec. It is also the home of EX MACHINA, the production company of Robert Lepage, director and author known worldwide for his large-scale projects (including the *Image Mill*, the largest architectural projection ever created). At Le Diamant, dance, theater, and opera productions are enhanced by new technologies, continuously pushing the limits of the imagination. ⊠ *966 rue St-Jean, Upper Town* ☎ *418/692–5353* ⊕ *lediamant.ca.*

WINTER CARNIVAL

For three weekends in January and February, Québec City throws one of the biggest winter parties in the world. Each year, an Ice Palace is built as the center of the festivities, which include dog sled races, two parades, and events on several city streets. Ice bars are plentiful on the Grande Allée, and the streets fill with families and visitors singing songs and blowing into trumpets.

★ **Carnaval de Québec**

FESTIVALS | **FAMILY** | A flurry of activity, mainly on the Plains of Abraham but also on several of the city's main drags, surrounds Carnaval de Québec, which occurs over three weekends every January and February. Snow and ice sculpture contests, dog sled relays, and canoe races on the icy St. Lawrence River chase away winter doldrums. Visitors brave the cold to get a glimpse of Bonhomme, the friendly Carnival Master, and tour his Ice Palace, which is rebuilt each year. Caribou, a strong mixture of red wine, hard liquor, and maple syrup, is a popular libation during the festivities. ⊠ *Québec City* ⊕ *carnaval.qc.ca.*

Did You Know?

If you visit Québec City during the Carnaval de Québec, you'll have the opportunity to tour Bonhomme's Ice Palace.

Le fromage du Québec ⬤

It used to be that all good cheese in Québec City was imported from France—not anymore. During the last several decades there's been an impressive and still-growing cheese movement in La Belle Province. Regional cheese makers long produced award-winning aged cheddar, but that's been joined by a wealth of specialty cheeses, including *lait cru* (unpasteurized) cheeses that you'll want to sample before going home. There are more than 400 original varieties made here.

Luckily, there are enough cheese shops to keep you cheese shop–hopping all afternoon. Smile, and say "fromage"!

Aux petits délices. In the market at Les Halles du Petit Quartier, Aux Petits Délices has a large selection of specialty cheeses, along with crackers, charcuterie, and condiments for a picnic on the Plains.
✉ *1191 avenue Cartier, Montcalm* ☎ *418/522–5154.*

Épicerie Européenne. Stop by the Épicerie Européenne in the St-Jean-Baptiste quarter, and let the knowledgeable consultants help you choose from their excellent selection of cheeses.
✉ *560 rue St-Jean, St-Jean-Baptiste* ☎ *418/529–4847.*

Épicerie J.A. Moisan. This is the oldest continuously operating grocery store in Québec City, stocked with a great selection of charcuterie, cheese, fruit and vegetables, local beers, specialty sodas, spices, and much more.
✉ *699 rue St-Jean, St-Jean-Baptiste* ☎ *418/522–0685.*

Some good cheeses to watch out for at local shops include Bleu Bénédictin from St-Benoît Abbey, Île aux-Grues four-year-old cheddar, Le Migneron de Charlevoix, and Le Louis d'Or, made in Central Québec. There's also a *chèvre noire*, a raw, goat "cheddar" by Fromagerie Tournevent—wrapped in black wax—that's not to be missed. If Gouda is your thing, try a piece from Fromagerie Bergeron.

👜 Shopping

ART GALLERIES

★ Galerie Art Inuit Brousseau
ART GALLERIES | Inuit art is the specialty of this large, well-known gallery. The gallery director, Jean-Francois Brousseau, selects works by artists represented by the North Canadian Inuit cooperatives, and the gallery receives much praise for improving life in the Canadian Arctic. ✉ *35 rue St-Louis, Upper Town* ☎ *418/694–1828* ⊕ *artinuitbrousseau.ca.*

Galerie Michel Guimont
ART GALLERIES | Located in the Old Port area, this is probably the most sought-after gallery for contemporary art in Québec City, with solid exhibits of paintings, drawings, and prints from emerging and well-established artists. ✉ *273 rue St-Paul, Lower Town* ☎ *418/692–1188* ⊕ *galeriemichelguimont.com* ⊘ *Closed Mon.–Wed.*

CLOTHING

Ça va de soi
MIXED CLOTHING | "Montréal-based knitwear"; the *raison d'être* alone evokes a feeling of respect for the material and the kind of luxury that's usually reserved for products crafted with great care. Founded in 1991 by Odile and Antoine Nasri with the desire to democratize access to slow fashion and responsibly produced clothing, Ça va de soi is a ready-to-wear boutique focused on natural fibers. Sweaters, scarves,

socks, all the essentials of snow fashion are there. ⊠ *1154 rue St-Jean, Upper Town* ☎ *418/692–0077* ⊕ *cavadesoi.com* ⊘ *Closed Sat. and Sun.*

GIFTS AND SOUVENIRS

★ **Artisans Canada**

SOUVENIRS | The Racine family has been operating a family boutique on this site since 1946; formerly of handmade furniture, now of objects by more than 200 nearby artisans. The current owners, Sara and Thomas, handpick their collaborators with great care and sell clothing, jewelry, leather goods, skin care products, and home décor in a historic building in Old Québec. The right address for quality souvenirs. ⊠ *30 Côte de la Fabrique, Upper Town* ☎ *418/692–2109* ⊕ *artisanscanada.com.*

DEPARTMENT STORES

La Maison Simons

DEPARTMENT STORE | This growing Canadian chain store started here in Québec City in the 19th century, and is still owned by its founding family. The store carries affordable women and menswear, designer brands, linens, and other household items. ⊠ *20 côte de la Fabrique, Upper Town* ☎ *418/692–3630* ⊕ *simons.ca.*

🏃 Activities

ICE-SKATING

Ice-skating in Québec City is a popular pastime for locals and visitors alike.

★ Place d'Youville

ICE-SKATING | FAMILY | This well-known outdoor rink, just outside St-Jean Gate, is open daily November through the end of March, from noon to 9 pm. Skate rental is C$10, and skating itself is free. A locker will run you C$1. ⊠ *Place d'Youville, Upper Town* ☎ *418/641–6256.*

Plains of Abraham

ICE-SKATING | FAMILY | The sports field at the western end of Battlefields park features a large skating rink open from December to March, complete with music and fire pits. ⊠ *Anneau de glace des plaines d'Abraham, Montcalm* ☜ *Free. Skate rental C$8 for 2 hrs.*

SKIING

Plains of Abraham (*Battlefields Park*)

SKIING & SNOWBOARDING | FAMILY | This park is a must for winter sports! In addition to its ice-skating facilities, it also has 10 kilometers (6 miles) of marked and groomed cross-country ski trails for beginner, intermediate, and expert skiers. There are also trails for snowshoeing. Moreover, skis and snowshoes can be rented at the Plains of Abraham Museum, on the northeast side of the park. ⊠ *Plaines d'Abraham, Montcalm.*

SNOW SLIDES

The snow slide from Dufferin Terrace is easily one of the most exciting winter activities in Québec.

★ Glissade de la Terrasse

SNOW SPORTS | FAMILY | A wooden toboggan takes you down a 270-foot-high snow slide that's adjacent to the Château Frontenac at 43 miles per hour! Four rides cost C$10. Open every day from 10 am to 6 pm, December to March. ⊠ *Terrasse Dufferin, Upper Town* ☎ *418/829–9898* ⊕ *au1884.ca* ☜ *C$10.*

SPAS

Strøm Spa Nordique

SPAS | Designed by a local star-architect firm, this Nordic-oriented spa—a branch of the Montréal-based upscale spa company—has a panoramic view of the St. Lawrence River. Enjoy outdoor whirlpools, thermal and Nordic baths, a Finnish sauna, a eucalyptus steam bath, and thermal and Nordic waterfalls. ⊠ *515 boul. Champlain, Lower Town* ☎ *418/425–2772* ⊕ *stromspa.com* ☜ *From C$54.*

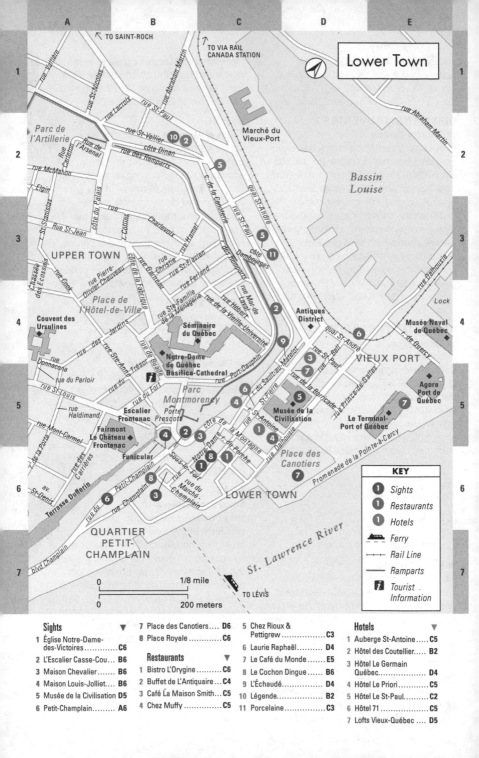

Lower Town

KEY

- **1** Sights
- **1** Restaurants
- **1** Hotels
- Ferry
- Rail Line
- Ramparts
- **i** Tourist Information

Sights ▼

1. Église Notre-Dame-des-Victoires..............**C6**
2. L'Escalier Casse-Cou... **B6**
3. Maison Chevalier........**B6**
4. Maison Louis-Jolliet....**B6**
5. Musée de la Civilisation **D5**
6. Petit-Champlain.........**A6**
7. Place des Canotiers....**D6**
8. Place Royale **C6**

Restaurants ▼

1. Bistro L'Orygine **C6**
2. Buffet de L'Antiquaire ...**C4**
3. Café La Maison Smith....**C5**
4. Chez Muffy **C5**
5. Chez Rioux & Pettigrew **C3**
6. Laurie Raphaël...........**D4**
7. Le Café du Monde.......**E5**
8. Le Cochon Dingue **B6**
9. L'Échaudé................**D4**
10. Légende.................**B2**
11. Porcelaine................**C3**

Hotels ▼

1. Auberge St-Antoine **C5**
2. Hôtel des Coutellier.....**B2**
3. Hôtel Le Germain Québec...................**D4**
4. Hôtel Le Priori............**C5**
5. Hôtel Le St-Paul.........**C2**
6. Hôtel 71 ....**C5**
7. Lofts Vieux-Québec **D5**

Lower Town

Seeing all the bustle and upscale commerce here, it's hard to imagine that 40 years ago, this area was run-down and looking for a new lease on life. Today, after exploring Place Royale and its cobblestone streets, you can walk along the edge of the St. Lawrence River and watch the sailboats and ships go by, shop at the market, or kick back on a *terrasse* (patio) with a local craft beer. Rue Petit-Champlain also has charming places to stop and listen to street musicians, and the scene near the Old Port starts buzzing as soon as the sun goes down.

If there's a cradle of French civilization in North America, you're standing in it when you visit Lower Town. In 1608, Champlain chose this narrow, U-shaped spit of land sandwiched between the frigid waters of the St. Lawrence River and the craggy heights of Cap Diamant as the site for his settlement. Champlain later abandoned the fortified habitation at the foot of Cap Diamant and relocated to the more easily defendable Upper Town.

Nevertheless, the area continued to flourish as a bustling port and trading center for French merchants, fur traders, and *coureurs des bois* (woodsmen), and France's Native American allies. It was also the base from which dozens of military campaigns and fact-finding missions were launched into the heart of the continent. A bust of France's Sun King, Louis XIV, was erected in the main square, Place du Marché, which was renamed Place Royale in 1686. Destroyed by British cannons that were set up on the opposite shore during the siege of 1759, the port and buildings were rebuilt by the British, and the area quickly regained its role as Canada's leading commercial and business center.

Lower Town went into an economic tailspin in the late 1800s, becoming a slum whose narrow streets were lined with pawnshops, rough-and-tumble taverns, and smoky brothels that catered to sailors and lumberjacks. This lasted until the 1960s, when it received a multimillion-dollar face-lift that remade it into a sanitized version of its 1700s self. Today, once-dilapidated houses and warehouses contain busy boutique hotels, stylish shops, art galleries, and popular restaurants and bars. Lower Town, home to approximately 850 people, is bounded by the Dufferin-Montmorency Highway to the west, the St. Charles River to the north, the St. Lawrence River to the east, and Petit Champlain shopping area to the south.

GETTING HERE AND AROUND

Because Lower Town is the oldest part of the city, many prefer to see it first to get a sense of how the city developed chronologically. If coming from Upper Town, head down L'Escalier Casse-Cou, a stairway steep enough to earn that name, which means "Breakneck Stairs." Have your camera ready; you'll get that quintessential Petit-Champlain photo at the top of the staircase.

TIMING

You'll need one full day to see the area surrounding two of the city's most famous squares, Place Royale and Place de Paris. Pause for lunch before touring the Musée de la Civilisation and the antiques district.

◉ Sights

★ **Église Notre-Dame-des-Victoires**
(*Our Lady of Victory Church*)
CHURCH | Welcome to the oldest stone church in North America! The fortress shape of the altar is no accident; this small, but beautiful stone church on Place Royale is linked to a bellicose past. Grateful French colonists named it in honor of the Virgin Mary, whom they credited with helping French forces defeat two British invasions: one in 1690 by Admiral William Phipps and the other by Sir Hovendon Walker in 1711. The

church itself was built in 1688, making it the city's oldest—it has been restored twice since then. Several interesting paintings decorate the walls, and a model of *Le Brezé*, the boat that transported French soldiers to New France in 1664, hangs from the ceiling. The side chapel is dedicated to Ste. Geneviève, the patron saint of Paris. ⊠ *32 rue Sous-le-Fort, Lower Town* ☎ *418/692–1650* ⊕ *notre-dame-de-Québec.org* ⌨ *C$5 for guided tours.*

★ L'Escalier Casse-Cou

VIEWPOINT | Often regarded as one of the most iconic attractions in the Old City due to its location and stunning views of the neighborhood. But the steepness of the city's first iron stairway, an ambitious 1893 design by city architect and engineer Charles Baillairgé, is ample evidence of how it got its name: Breakneck Steps. No serious injuries have been reported on the stairs, despite their ominous name! Still, those 59 steps were quite an improvement on the original wooden stairway, built in the 17th century, that linked the Upper Town and Lower Town. ⊠ *Escalier Casse-Cou, Lower Town.*

Maison Chevalier

NOTABLE BUILDING | This graded stone house (which is actually three houses brought together) was built in 1752 for the shipowner Jean-Baptiste Chevalier. This location near the docks was popular with import-export merchants and, later, with innkeepers. The architecture is quintessential New France, with its mansards and scarlet roof. Although the building is not open to visitors, it's well worth a look from the outside. ⊠ *50 rue du Marché-Champlain, Lower Town.*

Maison Louis-Jolliet

NOTABLE BUILDING | Louis Jolliet, the first European to see the Mississippi River, and his fellow explorers used this 1683 house as a base for westward journeys. Today it's the lower station of the funicular. A monument commemorating Jolliet's 1672 trip to the Mississippi stands in the small park next to the house, which

---

A View From the Water 👁

Crossing the St. Lawrence River on the Québec–Lévis Ferry will reward you with a striking view of the Québec City skyline, with the Château Frontenac in plain view, which is even more impressive at night. Ferries generally run every 20 or 30 minutes from 6 am until 6 pm, and then every hour until 2:20 am; there are additional ferries from April through November. ⊠ *10 rue des Traversiers, 1 block south of pl. de Paris traversiers. com C$3.75 each way (pedestrians, cyclists, car passengers).*

---

is at the foot of the Escalier Casse-Cou (Breakneck Staircase). ⊠ *16 rue du Petit-Champlain, Lower Town.*

★ Musée de la Civilisation
(*Museum of Civilization*)

HISTORY MUSEUM | **FAMILY** | Wedged between narrow streets at the foot of the cliff, this spacious museum with a striking limestone-and-glass facade was designed by architect Moshe Safdie to blend into the landscape. Its bell tower echoes the shape of the city's church steeples. Two excellent permanent exhibits examine Québec's history. *People of Québec, Now and Then* engagingly synthesizes 400 years of social and political history—including the role of the Catholic church and the rise of the Québec nationalist movement—with artifacts, time lines, original films and interviews, and news clips. It's a great introduction to the issues that face the province today. *This Is Our Story* looks at the 11 aboriginal nations that inhabit Québec. The temporary exhibits here are also always worth a visit. ⊠ *85 rue Dalhousie, Lower Town* ☎ *866/710–8031* ⊕ *mcq.org* ⌨ *C$25* ⊙ *Closed Mon.*

One of Lower Town's top sights is the Place Royale, also one of the oldest public squares in the country.

Place des Canotiers

CITY PARK | What used to be a vast parking lot across from the Museum of Civilization has been replaced by an elegant and modern park that provides great views of Upper Town and improves access to the river for locals who now linger and stroll here, and also for the cruise ships that often moor here. Even the new multistory parking garage has been dressed up in an elegant wooden façade that gives the area extra character. ⊠ *Place des Canotiers, Lower Town.*

★ Place Royale

PLAZA/SQUARE | Place Royale is where Samuel de Champlain founded the City of Québec in 1608; more than 400 years and several iterations later, this cobblestone square is still considered to be the cradle of French-speaking North America. Flanked on one side by the oldest stone church in North America, Église Notre-Dame-des-Victoires, and on the other by houses with steep Normandy-style roofs, dormer windows, and chimneys, once the homes of wealthy merchants, Place

Royale is the epicenter of Old Québec. Until 1686 the area was called Place du Marché, but its name changed when a bust of Louis XIV was placed at its center. During the late 1600s and early 1700s, when Place Royale was continually under threat of British attack, the colonists moved progressively higher to safer quarters atop the cliff in Upper Town. After the French colony fell to British rule in 1759, Place Royale flourished again with shipbuilding, logging, fishing, and fur trading. The *Fresque des Québécois,* a 4,665-square-foot trompe-l'oeil mural depicting 400 years of Québec's history, is to the east of the square, at the corner of rue Notre-Dame and côte de la Montagne. ⊠ *Place Royale, Lower Town.*

★ Petit-Champlain

NEIGHBORHOOD | Rue du Petit-Champlain, the oldest street in the city, was once the main thoroughfare of a harbor village, with trading posts and the homes of rich merchants. Today it has pleasant boutiques, art galleries, and cafés, and on summer days the street is packed with

Did You Know?

You'll find some of the best buys of Inuit carvings, hand-painted silks, and enameled copper crafts on touristy rue du Petit-Champlain.

tourists. Natural-fiber weaving, Inuit carvings, hand-painted silks, local designers, and enameled copper crafts are among local specialties for sale here. If you're coming from Upper Town, take the Escalier Casse-Cou (Breakneck Steps) down, and the funicular back up (or round-trip): both deliver you to the start of this busy, unique street. ✉ *Rue du Petit-Champlain, Lower Town* 🌐 *quartierpetitchamplain.com.*

🍴 Restaurants

Lower Town has its fair share of renowned eateries, and you'll find some of the best terraces in town. Dine after the sun goes down under twinkling lights at L'Échaudé, discover the best of Québécois savoir-faire with Laurie Raphaël's tasting menu, or for impeccable wines, go to L'Orygine.

Bistro L'Orygine
$$$ | **MODERN CANADIAN** | One hundred percent organic—that is the promise of L'Orygine, a brand-new bistro in the heart of the Lower Town. With an emphasis on freshness and local flavors, the chef prepares seasonal and shareable plates that are (almost) guilt-free, such as lobster cavatelli and a creative mix of duck and eggplant. **Known for:** small plates to share; vegetarian menu; vast patio. [$] *Average main: C$25* ✉ *36 1/2 rue St-Pierre, Lower Town* ☎ *418/872–4386* 🌐 *lorygine.com* 🕒 *Closed Sun.–Tues.*

Buffet de L'Antiquaire
$$ | **CANADIAN** | Hearty home cooking, generous portions, and rock-bottom prices have made this no-frills, diner-style eatery in the heart of the antiques district, a Lower Town institution. It's a good place to sample traditional Québécois dishes such as pea soup and *cipaille* (a deep-dish layered pie using poultry, meat, or seafood), and the homemade and delicious sugar pie, crepes, and other desserts. **Known for:** Québec City institution; traditional dishes; gluten-free options. [$] *Average main: C$15* ✉ *95 rue St-Paul, Lower Town* ☎ *418/692–2661* 🌐 *lebuffetdelantiquaire.com* 🕒 *No dinner Sun.–Wed.*

Le Café du Monde
$$$ | **BISTRO** | Next to the cruise terminal in the Old Port, this massive, Parisian-bistro-style restaurant with etched-glass dividers and palm trees has a spectacular view. The outdoor terrace in front overlooks the St. Lawrence River, while the side *verrière* (glass atrium) looks onto l'Agora amphitheater and the old stone Customs House. **Known for:** delicious seafood; lively scene; great views. [$] *Average main: C$30* ✉ *84 rue Dalhousie, Suite 140, Lower Town* ☎ *418/692–4455* 🌐 *lecafedumonde.com* 🕒 *No dinner Sun. Closed Mon. and Tues.*

Café La Maison Smith
$ | **CAFÉ** | This casual and attractive café right on the corner of scenic Place Royale is a great place to stop for an afternoon pick-me-up, be it coffee or various indulgent sweets. For a light lunch, there are yummy sandwiches, quiches, and soups. **Known for:** coffee roasted on-site; outdoor seating; great sandwiches. [$] *Average main: C$9* ✉ *23 rue Notre-Dame, Lower Town* ☎ *581/742–6777* 🌐 *smithcafe.com.*

Chez Muffy
$$$$ | **MODERN CANADIAN** | At this restaurant, inside the museum-like Auberge Saint-Antoine, dishes change with the seasons, but fresh, locally sourced ingredients are at the core of the classic prix-fixe (C$85 per person) menu. The space has stone walls, attractive wooden floors, and exposed beams from the building's warehouse days, in the early 1800s. **Known for:** prix-fixe menu; historic setting; Sunday brunch. [$] *Average main: C$85* ✉ *10 rue St-Antoine, Lower Town* ☎ *418/692–1022* 🌐 *saint-antoine.com/chez-muffy* 🕒 *No lunch; closed Mon. and Tues.*

Did You Know?

Many of the chairs found at cafés along the rue du Petit-Champlain are styled after those of famous cafés found in Paris.

★ **Chez Rioux & Pettigrew**

$$$ | MODERN CANADIAN | This is the place to go for the freshest flavors of Canadian cuisine (think seafood, terroir vegetables, game meat) without the white tablecloth fuss. Chez Rioux & Pettigrew is a casual dining experience in a convivial, inviting venue with exposed brick. **Known for:** Sunday brunch; local, seasonal ingredients; C$75 tasting menu. $ Average main: C$25 ⊠ 160 rue St-Paul, Lower Town ☎ 418/694–4448 ⊕ chezriouxetpettigrew.com.

★ **Laurie Raphaël**

$$$$ | MODERN CANADIAN | Local and regional products are emphasized here, and the food is among the best gastronomical offerings in Québec. Among local celebrity chef Daniel Vézina's creations are crystallized foie gras with truffle snow, and venison tartare. **Known for:** tasting menus; smart, high-end gastronomy; elegant setting. $ Average main: C$145 ⊠ 117 rue Dalhousie, Lower Town ☎ 418/692–4555 ⊕ laurieraphael.com ☉ Closed Sun.–Tues.

Le Cochon Dingue

$$ | CAFÉ | FAMILY | The café dishes at this cheerful chain, whose name translates into the Crazy Pig, include delicious tartares, steak with fries, hearty soups, a selection of international dishes like satays and "général Dingue" chicken, as well as substantial desserts like sugar pie with vanilla cream. Sidewalk tables and indoor dining rooms artfully blend the chic and the antique; black-and-white checkerboard floors contrast with ancient stone walls. **Known for:** good people-watching; often long waits for a table; affordable bistro. $ Average main: C$16 ⊠ 46 boul. Champlain, Lower Town ☎ 418/692–2013 ⊕ cochondingue.com ☉ No dinner Mon.–Wed.

★ **L'Échaudé**

$$$ | FRENCH | A mix of businesspeople and tourists having been frequenting L'Échaudé for the past 30 years because of its location between the nearby business and antiques districts. For lunch, the flank steak with shallots is a classic, and every day there's excellent fish, tartares, and pasta on the menu. **Known for:** three-course brunch; French-inspired dishes; cheese plate. $ Average main: C$22 ⊠ 73 rue Sault-au-Matelot, Lower Town ☎ 418/692–1299 ⊕ echaude.com.

Légende

$$$ | MODERN CANADIAN | Set on the ground floor of the Hôtel des Coutellier, in the Old Port area, Légende is set in a large wood and stone room with plush banquettes and an elegant bar. There are a lot of sharing plates—the smartly prepared fish and seafood board (including things like salmon rillettes and welk salad) is particularly delightful. **Known for:** vegetarian menu available; local ingredients, served creatively; vast patio in summer. $ Average main: C$28 ⊠ 255 rue St-Paul, Lower Town ☎ 418/614–2555 ⊕ restaurantlegende.com ☉ Closed Mon. and Tues.

Porcelaine

$$$ | SEAFOOD | The most recent project of neighboring restaurant Chez Rioux & Pettigrew is a casual oyster bar that's quickly become the place to go for happy hour or a lengthy, relaxed dinner. You can either pop in for a few oysters and a drink before going to a concert, or you can sit back and enjoy the vintage furnishings, get to know the friendly waiters, and cut your gluttony some slack by ordering another glass of wine, and perhaps even dessert. **Known for:** reasonable prices; fresh oysters; relaxed, intimate atmosphere. $ Average main: C$25 ⊠ 160 rue St-Paul, Lower Town ☎ 418/694–4448 ☉ Closed Mon.–Wed.

Hotels

Many visitors insist on staying near the water, among the quays, warehouses, and cobblestone squares—as well as many boutique hotels, inspired eateries, and impressive entertainment venues.

★ Auberge St-Antoine

$$$$ | **HOTEL** | This elegant hotel incorporates the historic stone walls of a 19th-century warehouse along with artifacts dating to the 1600s, many of which were found during an expansion and are now in glass displays in the public areas and guest rooms. **Pros:** excellent restaurant; unique architectural accents and exhibits; some rooms have fireplaces and terraces. **Cons:** not all terraces have nice views; the eclectic décor doesn't always match the price; low vacancy means guests must plan well in advance. [$] *Rooms from: C$349* ✉ *8 rue St-Antoine, Lower Town* ☎ *888/692–2211* 🌐 *saint-antoine.com* 🛏 *95 rooms* 🍴 *No Meals.*

Hôtel des Coutellier

$$$ | **HOTEL** | Charming details like buttery croissants delivered to the room each morning, exposed brick walls, and lush linens make this boutique hotel a popular base for demanding travelers. **Pros:** old-world charm; an elevator (a rarity in this part of town); breakfast delivered each morning. **Cons:** a bit of a climb to Upper Town attractions; in-room temperature controls aren't intuitive; small and open-plan bathrooms. [$] *Rooms from: C$205* ✉ *253 rue St-Paul, Lower Town* ☎ *888/523–9696* 🌐 *hoteldescoutellier.com* 🛏 *24 rooms* 🍴 *Free Breakfast.*

★ Hôtel Le Germain Québec

$$$$ | **HOTEL** | Sophistication and attention to every detail prevails in the modern rooms of this chic boutique hotel—from the custom-designed swing-out night tables to the white goose-down duvets and custom umbrellas. **Pros:** pets welcome; deluxe continental breakfast; higher floors have views of the St. Lawrence River or the Old City. **Cons:** not all rooms have separate bath and shower; lacks Old Québec spirit; minimal interior is not for everyone. [$] *Rooms from: C$295* ✉ *126 rue St-Pierre, Lower Town* ☎ *888/833–5253* 🌐 *germainhotels.com/en/le-germain-hotel/Québec* 🛏 *60 rooms* 🍴 *No Meals.*

Hôtel Le Priori

$$ | **HOTEL** | Housed in a 300-year-old building with stone and brick walls, this boutique hotel has a rigorously modern décor, with custom leather beds, stainless steel sinks, slate floors, and three-head shower jets. **Pros:** unbeatable Old Québec location; outdoor terrace; breakfast box delivered to the room. **Cons:** high-occupancy rates mean that you'll need to reserve some time ahead; some rooms are small; suites are in a separate building. [$] *Rooms from: C$199* ✉ *15 rue Sault-au-Matelot, Lower Town* ☎ *800/351–3992* 🌐 *hotellepriori.com* 🛏 *28 rooms* 🍴 *Free Breakfast.*

Hôtel Le St-Paul

$$$ | **HOTEL** | Perched at the edge of the antiques district, this four-story hotel inside what was once a 19th-century office building, is near art galleries, trendy restaurants, and the train station. **Pros:** convenient location; charming vintage details; modern bathrooms. **Cons:** ambient street noise; not all rooms are renovated; mostly no frills. [$] *Rooms from: C$209* ✉ *229 rue St-Paul, Lower Town* ☎ *888/794–4414* 🌐 *lesaintpaul.qc.ca* 🛏 *26 rooms* 🍴 *No Meals.*

★ Hôtel 71

$$$ | **HOTEL** | Guest rooms at this luxury hotel, inside the city's first National Bank of Canada office, have 12-foot-high ceilings, excellent amenities, and stunning views of Old Québec. **Pros:** boxed breakfast delivered to the room; decadent and modern; luxurious packages. **Cons:** poor soundproofing; valet service is steep; chic interiors not kid-friendly. [$] *Rooms from: C$209* ✉ *71 rue St-Pierre, Lower*

Québec Summer Festival

Festival d'été de Québec (Québec City Summer Festival). An annual highlight in the first half of July is this exuberant Summer Festival, over seven days of rock, folk, hip-hop, and world music. The main concerts take place each evening on three outdoor stages in or near the Old City, including one holding up to 80,000 people on the Plains of Abraham. A pass (C$115) grants admission to all events throughout the festival. Some concerts at indoor theaters cost extra, but free music and activities, such as family concerts and street performers during the day, are also plentiful. At night rue St-Jean near the city gate turns into a free street theater, with drummers, dancers, and skits. Book accommodation several months in advance if you plan to attend. ✉ *Québec City* ☎ *888/992–5200* 🌐 *feq.ca.*

Town ☎ *888/692–1171* 🌐 *hotel71.ca* 🛏 *69 rooms* 🍴 *No Meals.*

★ Lofts Vieux-Québec
$$ | APARTMENT | This collection of lofts, located in some of the Lower Town's most historic buildings (although not all), offers travelers the chance to live like locals, at their own pace. **Pros:** feels like a home, not a hotel; tons of character; full kitchens. **Cons:** some apartments lack sunlight; some are 21+; not all are in historic buildings. [$] *Rooms from: C$195* ✉ *Various locations, Lower Town* ☎ *418/431–9905* 🌐 *loftsvieuxQuébec.com* 🛏 *13 properties* 🍴 *No Meals.*

Nightlife

Justine
COCKTAIL LOUNGES | Just across the Gare du Palais, Justine is a classic speakeasy that's just mysterious enough, with a décor that takes us back to the days of prohibition. Thick black velvet curtains, no visible sign outside. A hushed atmosphere and emblematic cocktails from the 1920s are on the menu, alongside nice platters of gourmet charcuteries and cheeses. ✉ *303 rue Saint-Paul, Lower Town* ☎ *418/914–5637* ⏲ *Closed Mon.–Wed.*

Performing Arts

Théâtre Petit-Champlain
CONCERTS | The charming and intimate Théâtre Petit-Champlain is a fine spot to hear contemporary francophone music and comedy acts during the year and take in a play in summer. ✉ *68 rue du Petit-Champlain, Lower Town* ☎ *418/692–2631* 🌐 *theatrepetitchamplain.com.*

Shopping

ANTIQUES

French-Canadian, Victorian and art deco furniture, clocks, silverware, and porcelain are some of the rare collectibles found here, mainly on quaint and historic rue St-Paul street. Be aware, however, that authentic Québec pine furniture, characterized by simple forms and lines, is rare—and pricey.

Antiquités Bolduc
ANTIQUES & COLLECTIBLES | The largest antiques store on rue St-Paul sells furniture, household items, old paintings, and knickknacks from the 19th and 20th centuries. ✉ *89 rue St-Paul, Lower Town* ☎ *418/694–9558* 🌐 *lesantiquitesbolduc.com* ⏲ *Closed Sun.*

Gérard Bourguet Antiquaire

ANTIQUES & COLLECTIBLES | You're not likely to find any bargains here, but this shop has a very good selection of authentic 18th- and 19th-century Québec pine furniture. ⊠ *97 rue St-Paul, Lower Town* ☎ *418/694–0896.*

L'Héritage Antiquité

ANTIQUES & COLLECTIBLES | This is probably the best place in the antiques district to find good Québécois furniture, clocks, oil lamps, porcelain, and ceramics. It's a very welcoming store as well. ⊠ *109 rue St-Paul, Lower Town* ☎ *418/692–1681.*

ART GALLERIES

Lacerte Art Contemporain

ART GALLERIES | Head to this well-established gallery in an old car-repair garage for contemporary art and sculpture. ⊠ *39 côte de la Canoterie, Lower Town* ☎ *418/692–1566* ⊕ *galerielacerte.com* ⊘ *Closed Sat. and Sun.*

CLOTHING

Charlevoix Pure Laine

MIXED CLOTHING | Discover the beautiful Charlevoix sheep wool at this lovely boutique. Passionate craftswomen (and craftsmen, too!) work tirelessly to upcycle and recycle this regional wool, transforming it into stockings, *toques*, throws, and soles. ⊠ *61 rue du Petit-Champlain, Lower Town* ☎ *418/692–7272* ⊕ *charlevoixpurelaine.ca.*

★ Lowell

LEATHER GOODS | The official Québec City outpost for a Montréal-based company (where the goods are designed and made), this boutique offers distinctive, durable, and well-designed leather goods, sleek computer bags, and colorful messenger bags with an old-school vibe. ⊠ *66 boul. Champlain, Lower Town* ☎ *418/614–0851* ⊕ *lowellmtl.ca.*

les ptits mosüs

CHILDREN'S CLOTHING | FAMILY | The name says it all: "les ptits mosüs" means "the naughty kids" in Québécois, so it's only logical that this lovely boutique is dedicated to the little ones. Expect a highly curated selection of local designers with items ranging from clothing to toys, and from books to tableware. ⊠ *88 1/2 rue du Petit Champlain, Lower Town* ☎ *418/914–5838* ⊕ *lesptitsmosus.com* ⊘ *Closed Tues.*

CRAFTS

Boutique des métiers d'art du Québec

CRAFTS | This boutique, run by the Conseil des métiers d'art, a coordinating body that oversees all kinds of arts and crafts disciplines and organizes annual fairs, features the best from Québec in glass art, porcelain, jewelry, woodworking, and much more, most with a stylish, contemporary feel. ⊠ *29 rue Notre-Dame, Lower Town* ☎ *418/694–0267* ⊕ *www.metiersdart.ca.*

Le Packwood

CRAFTS | Charming little café-boutique home to the products of more than 50 artisans from across Québec. Everything here is preciously handpicked by the owner for its originality. Candles, jams, toys, jewelry, stationery, soaps, everything is there! The store also serves as a café: enjoy homemade sandwiches or salads at a good price and excellent specialty coffees. ⊠ *152 rue St-Paul, Lower Town* ☎ *418/694–3066* ⊕ *lepackwood.ca* ⊘ *Closed Mon.*

Outside the Old City

Venture outside the walls for a glimpse of the real Québec City. Grande-Allée and avenue Cartier, in the Montcalm neighborhood, buzz with clubs and bars inside Queen Anne–style mansions. Cafés, galleries, and good restaurants are popping up regularly in St-Roch, the city's urban core. If you do have a car, it's a beautiful drive on boulevard Champlain, which runs from Lower Town all around the southern edge of Québec City, following the St. Lawrence River: you might want to take a stroll along the Promenade Samuel-de-Champlain, a stunning, modern linear park created in 2008 for the city's 400th anniversary. Above are the cliffs that lead to the Plains of Abraham, and farther on are the Sillery Coves. Any one of the steep hills will take you back toward the main roads that run east–west or the highways that cross north–south: Duplessis, the farthest west; Henri IV; Robert-Bourassa; and Dufferin-Montmorency.

GETTING HERE AND AROUND
It's a breezy and lovely 15-minute walk from the Old City to avenue Cartier in the Montcalm neighborhood, but the bus system is excellent here and easy to use. There are many bus stops throughout Upper Town, and a number of lines run up and down boulevard René-Lévesque and Grande Allée from place d'Youville. If you do choose to walk, take a detour to avenue Laurier or avenue Georges VI for a tour through leafy green streets with gorgeous homes.

St-Roch, on the other hand, is just down the hill from Place d'Youville if you're in Upper Town; it can also easily be reached by bus from the Lower Town and Petit-Champlain.

When in doubt, just catch a cab, which aren't hard to find, to take you there and back. But with increasing attractiveness and atmosphere of both neighborhoods, it's a no-brainer.

TIMING
There's no need to dedicate more than half a day to see the area around Grande-Allée or the St-Roch neighborhood. Both are great destinations for lunch, an afternoon browsing in the shops, or an evening out at a restaurant or bar.

◉ Sights

Aquarium du Québec
AQUARIUM | FAMILY | Breakfast with the walruses, lunch (carefully) with the polar bears, and spend the afternoon watching the seals do their tricks at this clifftop aquarium overlooking the St. Lawrence and Québec City's two main bridges. When you tire of the mammals, check out the thousands of species of fresh and saltwater fish in the aquarium's massive, three-level aquatic gallery, or have some hands-on experiences with mollusks, starfish, and stingrays. Don't miss the jellyfish ballet or seahorse tanks. This is the only aquarium in North America with examples of all five species of cold-water seals. ⊠ *1675 avenue des Hôtels, Outside the Old City* ☏ *866/659–5264* ⊕ *sepaq.com/ct/paq* ⊠ *C$21.50.*

Avenue Cartier
STREET | The mix of reasonably priced restaurants and bars, groceries and specialty food shops, and boutiques makes avenue Cartier a favorite lunchtime and after-work stop for many local residents. After business hours the street hums with locals running errands or soaking up the sun on patios. When darkness falls, the avenue's patrons get noticeably younger. The attraction? A half-dozen nightclubs and pubs that offer everything from wine and quiet conversation to Latin music and earsplitting dance tunes. ⊠ *Montcalm.*

Grande-Allée
STREET | One of the city's oldest streets, the Grande Allée was the route people took from outlying areas to come sell their furs in town. In the 19th century, the wealthy built neo-Gothic and Queen Anne–style mansions here, which now house trendy cafés, clubs, and restaurants. The street actually has four names: inside the city walls it's rue St-Louis; outside the walls, Grande Allée Est; farther west, Grande Allée Ouest; then finally, boulevard Laurier. ⊠ *Grande-Allée, Montcalm.*

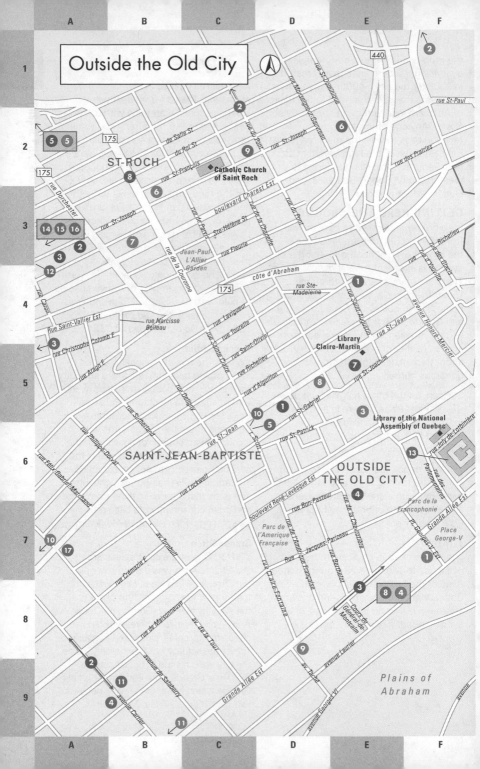

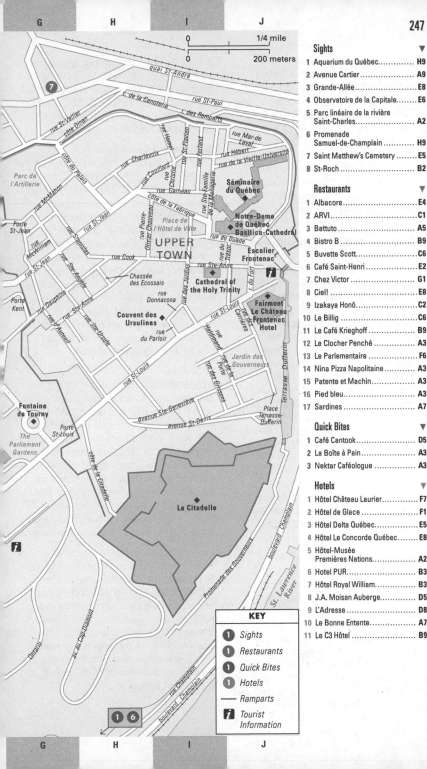

Sights ▼

Restaurants ▼

Quick Bites ▼

Hotels ▼

KEY

1 Sights
1 Restaurants
1 Quick Bites
1 Hotels
— Ramparts
🛈 Tourist Information

★ **Observatoire de la Capitale**
VIEWPOINT | Located atop the Édifice Marie-Guyart, the city's tallest building, Observatoire de la Capitale offers a spectacular panorama of Québec City from 31 stories up. The site features an overview of the city's history with 3-D imagery, audiovisual displays in both French and English, and a time-travel theme with a 1960s twist. ✉ *1037 rue de la Chevrotière, St-Jean-Baptiste* ☎ *888/497–4322* ⊕ *observatoire-capitale.com* 🏷 *C$14.75* ◷ *Closed on Mon. Oct.–Feb.*

Parc linéaire de la rivière Saint-Charles (*St Charles River Linear Park*)
CITY PARK | This 32-km (20-mile) stretch of trails and walkways follows the St. Charles River from its source at Lake St. Charles, to the northwest (which supplies a large part of Québec City's drinking water), all the way to the Bassin Louise Marina, in the Vieux-Port. Many sections are in quiet stretches of forests, or run along wetlands and meadows. The trails immediately west of the harbor offer a green oasis at the heart of the city. The recently-reimagined Cartier-Brébeuf National Historic Site in Limoilou is particularly lovely and explains the various ways Jacques Cartier helped shape the city as we see it today. It's also possible to rent kayaks and paddle over 11 km (6.5 miles) of the northernmost part of the river. ✉ *Maison Dorion-Coulombe, Outside the Old City* ☎ *418/691– 4710* ⊕ *societerivierestcharles.qc.ca.*

Promenade Samuel-de-Champlain
PROMENADE | This 4-km (2.5-mile) park along the St. Lawrence River is a local favorite, with an amazing view of the river and the two bridges that cross it to the west, as well as some smart, whimsical, and modern landscape design. On a sunny summer day, the place is busy with strollers, bikers, and in-line skaters, as well as kids playing in the fountains and on the lawns. You will find a café and observation tower toward the western end of the park. In summer, special buses will take you from Lower Town to the promenade. ✉ *Boul. Champlain, Outside the Old City* ☎ *418/528–0773* ⊕ *capitale. gouv.qc.ca/sites-de-la-capitale/parcs/ promenade-samuel-de-champlain.*

St. Matthew's Cemetery
CEMETERY | The burial place of many of the earliest English settlers in Canada was established in 1771 and is the oldest cemetery remaining in Québec City. Also buried here is Robert Wood, the disavowed half-brother of Queen Victoria. Closed in 1860, the cemetery has been turned into a park. Next door is **St. Matthew's Anglican Church,** now a recently renovated public library. It has a book listing most of the original tombstone inscriptions, including those on tombstones removed to make way for the city's modern convention center. ✉ *755 rue St-Jean, St-Jean-Baptiste.*

★ **St-Roch**
NEIGHBORHOOD | Hip bars and trendy shops pepper St-Roch, once an industrial area and now a technology hub. With so little locals living in the old part of town, St-Roch is a great place to mingle with residents. New spots are popping up constantly. The "main drags" of the neighborhood are boulevard Charest and rue Saint-Joseph, which offer a mix of office buildings, modern lunch spots, and afterwork hangouts. Jardins Saint-Roch, a large square, provides good people-watching.

Look for Église St-Roch, a massive stone church, and you'll quickly find rue St-Joseph, the district's other major thoroughfare, known for trendy shops and third-wave cafés. Shop for new duds here and walk west to go dine in one of the neighborhood's sleek new bistros. The popularity of the area has spawned many new restaurants. When it comes time for an after-dinner drink, there's a plethora of pubs and terraces.

Art abounds in the neighborhood, from the famed street-art-covered viaduct (right by rue Saint-Paul) and modern sculptures to outdoor theater and circus acts.

St-Roch is a long, but downhill jaunt from the Old City and walkable if you have the time. If you're not in the mood for exercise, the best way to reach this neighborhood is by cab. Plan to spend about C$9 each way. There are usually plenty of cabs available for the reverse trip. Taking the bus (800 or 801) is also an option. ⊠ St-Roch ⊕ Québec-cite.com/en/ neighbourhoods-Québec-city/saint-roch.

🍴 Restaurants

There are many cute cafés and fine eateries within the walls of the Old City, but don't miss the thriving culinary scene beyond them. Le Clocher Penché is arguably the bistro with the friendliest service, and it gives you an excuse to visit trendy St-Roch. Or if you're looking for a little more luxury, head to Le Parlementaire for lunch to nibble on trendy dishes while playing "spot the politico."

Work up a good appetite by wandering through the streets—and climbing those steep stairs. For something to nibble on for a picnic in the park, pop into one of the city's little out-of-the-way patisseries for buttery croissants and heavenly brioches.

★ Albacore

$$$ | SEAFOOD | Seafood lovers, rejoice: Québec City now has its very own ocean-based restaurant, and a great one at that. Helmed by a team of seasoned chefs, this gourmet restaurant provides diners with flavorful, flawless, and generously sized dishes of anything from scallops to clams and marlin tatakis, all nicely complemented by delicate side dishes such as lentils, sorbet (yes, ice cream for dinner!), and edible flowers. **Known for:** beautiful décor; mandatory reservations; imaginative seafood. ⓢ *Average main: C$25* ⊠ *819 Côte d'Abraham,*

St-Jean-Baptiste ☎ 418/914–6441 ⊕ albacore.business.site ⊗ Closed Mon. and Tues. No lunch.

ARVI

$$$ | MODERN CANADIAN | The trek to Limoilou is worth it, if it's to dine at ARVI. Local critics have deemed ARVI an unforgettable gourmet experience, and it was selected as one of Canada's 35 top restaurants by Air Canada's in-flight magazine. **Known for:** delicate, creative plates; vegetarian menu; wine pairings for meals. ⓢ *Average main: C$30* ⊠ *519 3e avenue, Limoilou* ☎ 581/742–4202 ⊕ *restaurantarvi.ca* ⊗ Closed Sun. and Mon. No lunch.

★ Battuto

$$$ | MODERN ITALIAN | Chef Guillaume Saint-Pierre's love for authentic Italian cuisine led him to open this popular 25-seat restaurant, located off the main Saint-Roch thoroughfares, where he can fully concentrate on that passion with gusto and skill. Italian tradition (there's arancini and *vitello tonatto*) blend with local flair (there's *cacio e pepe* with Swiss chard, and scallop crudo). **Known for:** tiramisu for two; perfect fresh pasta; a blend of local flair and Italian know-how. ⓢ *Average main: C$24* ⊠ *527 boul. Langelier, St-Roch* ☎ 418/614–4414 ⊕ *battuto.ca* ⊗ Closed Sun.–Tues. No lunch.

Bistro B

$$$$ | BISTRO | Behind the success of city hot spot Chez Muffy (formerly Panache), Chef François Blais decided on a more casual approach, including having a simple interior, when he opened his own restaurant on avenue Cartier. The "market cuisine" is straight to the point and well executed, and the whole menu fits on a blackboard, with a handful of appetizers, main courses, and desserts that change daily. **Known for:** popular with locals; open kitchen; upbeat atmosphere. ⓢ *Average main: C$35* ⊠ *1144 avenue Cartier, Montcalm* ☎ 418/614–5444 ⊕ *bistrob.ca* ⊗ Closed Mon.–Tues. No lunch weekends.

Buvette Scott

$$ | **MODERN CANADIAN** | La Buvette Scott is an unpretentious address that pleasantly surprises with its attractive menu and impeccable service. Located in the heart of St-Jean-Baptiste, it's quickly been adopted by locals who have made this place their favorite neighborhood hangout. **Known for:** unfussy, convivial atmosphere; affordable plates to share; vast selection of local microbreweries. [$] *Average main: C$18* ✉ *821 rue Scott, St-Jean-Baptiste* ☎ *581/741–4464* 🌐 *buvettescott.com* 🕒 *Closed Sun. and Mon. No lunch.*

★ Café Saint-Henri

$ | **CAFÉ** | Expect the usual crowd of students, freelancers, and others toting laptops at this third-wave café that has thoughtfully selected beans roasted on-site. Even so, the contemporary, all-white café is a welcome respite from the cold in wintertime—and the doughnuts alone are worth a visit. **Known for:** beans roasted on the premises; delicious artisan doughnuts; architectural highlight. [$] *Average main: C$5* ✉ *849 rue St-Joseph Est, St-Roch* ☎ *581/300–7211* 🌐 *sainthenri.ca* 🕒 *No dinner.*

Chez Victor

$$ | **BURGER** | This cozy burger joint with brick-and-stone walls has a wide range of topping combinations, daily special burgers, and French fries are served with a dollop of homemade mayonnaise (there are five varieties available) and poppy seeds. Salads, sandwiches, and a daily dessert made fresh by the pastry chef are also available. **Known for:** poutine; hearty burgers; good selection of local beers. [$] *Average main: C$17* ✉ *145 rue St-Jean, St-Jean-Baptiste* ☎ *418/529–7702* 🌐 *chezvictorburger.com* 🕒 *Closed Sun.*

Ciel!

$$$ | **MODERN CANADIAN** | Spectacular views of the whole city are not the only reason to climb up to this rotating restaurant with unobstructed, panoramic views. The service here is friendly and well-managed, and the food is unfussy, creative, and delicious—try the roasted Arctic char with lemon gnocchi and shiitakes or something from the solid brunch menu (on weekends). **Known for:** tasty farm-to-table dishes; 360-degree view of the city; weekend brunch. [$] *Average main: C$30* ✉ *1225 cours du General Montcalm, St-Jean-Baptiste* ☎ *418/640–5802* 🌐 *cielbistrobar.com.*

Izakaya Honō

$$ | **JAPANESE** | Small dishes served in the purest tradition of *izakayas* (Japanese taverns) in a venue that's flooded with light and minimally decorated with birch and green plants. On the menu, just classics: *yakotori* (mini skewers), sashimi, *okonomiyaki*, and dumplings, as well as a tataki that changes daily. **Known for:** creative cocktails; popular with locals; excellent, classic Japanese small plates. [$] *Average main: C$15* ✉ *670 rue St-Joseph Est, St-Roch* ☎ *418/524–2888* 🌐 *honoizakaya.com* 🕒 *Closed Tues. No lunch.*

Le Billig

$$ | **CANADIAN** | **FAMILY** | At this lovely crepe shop, buckwheat flour crepes are filled with simple ham and cheese, or fancier combos like duck confit with onion marmalade, while a wheat crepe with salted caramel and sweet Chantilly cream makes a good dessert. The large shop also has bistro items like cod beignets, charcuterie plates, and cassoulet, and there's a nice selection of ciders and beers. **Known for:** gluten-free items; great crepes, often original; ciders. [$] *Average main: C$16* ✉ *481 rue St-Jean, St-Jean-Baptiste* ☎ *418/524–8341* 🕒 *No lunch Mon.–Wed.*

Le Café Krieghoff

$$ | **BISTRO** | This busy, noisy Paris-like bistro featuring artwork by its namesake Canadian painter and patios in front and back has been around for more than 40 years and is a big local literary hangout, with a selection of great coffee, tea, and desserts. Open every day from early

morning to late evening, Krieghoff serves specialties that include salmon, quiche, *la Toulouse* (a big French sausage with sauerkraut), steak with French fries, *boudin* (pig-blood sausage), and *la Bavette* (hanger steak). **Known for:** good place to people-watch or study; big bowls of hot chocolate; simple, flavorful dishes. [$] *Average main: C$15* ✉ *1089 avenue Cartier, Montcalm* ☎ *418/522–3711* 🌐 *cafekrieghoff.qc.ca.*

★ Le Clocher Penché

$$$ | **MODERN CANADIAN** | The high ceilings and imposing vault door give away the fact that this was once a bank, but an amiable staff and inventive bistro cuisine (without pretentious fluff) make this establishment a local favorite who munch on well-prepared shareable plates of seasonal, creative, flavorful shareable plates like smoked aubergine with romesco sauce or veal tartare with lemon and fiddleheads. **■ TIP→ Wine lovers, this restaurant recently hired the best sommelier in Québec City.** **Known for:** beautiful, inviting decor; changing menu using fresh, regional ingredients; on-site sommelier. [$] *Average main: C$27* ✉ *203 rue St-Joseph Est, St-Roch* ☎ *418/640–0597* 🌐 *clocherpenche.ca* 🕒 *Closed Sun. and Mon. No lunch.*

Le Parlementaire

$$ | **CANADIAN** | Despite its magnificent beaux arts interior and its reasonable prices, the National Assembly's restaurant remains one of the best-kept secrets in town. Chef Martin Gagné prepares contemporary cuisine with products from Québec's various regions, such as mini-fondues made with Charlevoix cheese to ravioli made from lobster caught in the Gaspé to pork from the Beauce region, trout from the Magdalen Islands, or candied-duck salad. **Known for:** only open for lunch; elegant, historic decor; tasty regional dishes. [$] *Average main: C$24* ✉ *1045 rue des Parlementaires, Upper Town* ☎ *418/643–6640* 🌐 *assnat.qc.ca* 🕒 *Closed Sat. and Sun. No dinner.*

★ Nina Pizza Napolitaine

$$ | **ITALIAN** | Specializing in Neapolitan-style pizza and antipasti, this stylish pizzeria has been on everyone's lips ever since it opened (thanks to crowdfunding!). Its beast of an oven weighs 2.5 tons and was imported straight from Italy—and it's worth it: the thin-crust pizzas are cooked in just 90 seconds at 900 degrees. **Known for:** Aperol spritz; wood-fired pizzas; charcuteries plate. [$] *Average main: C$16* ✉ *410 rue St-Anselme, St-Roch* ☎ *581/742–2012* 🌐 *ninapizzanapolitaine.ca* 🕒 *Closed Mon.–Wed. No lunch Sun.*

Patente et Machin

$$$ | **ECLECTIC** | This fun and friendly place has a menu with terrific meats, grilled cheese, and whimsical ideas, like the use of guinea fowl wings in lieu of chicken wings. The food here has personality, humor, and … lots of butter. **Known for:** great wine selection; playful dishes; pleasantly chaotic service. [$] *Average main: C$25* ✉ *82 rue St-Joseph Ouest, St-Roch* ☎ *581/981–3999* 🕒 *Closed Sun.–Tues.*

★ Pied bleu

$$$$ | **BISTRO** | It's worth heading to the outskirts of the St-Roch Downtown district for this unique dining experience, inspired by the French *bouchons* (as bistros are called in the city of Lyon). "In the pig, everything is good": so goes the French adage that advocates responsible, farm-to-table gastronomy. This is precisely what drives Pied Bleu: every week, the chefs receive a whole pig and come up with proven, creative ways to serve it (the charcuterie plate is a must). **Known for:** Lyon-style restaurant; prix-fixe tasting menu; charcuterie plate. [$] *Average main: C$35* ✉ *179 rue St-Vallier Ouest, St-Roch* ☎ *418/914–3554* 🌐 *piedbleu.com* 🕒 *No lunch Tues.–Sat., brunch only Fri.–Sun.*

Sardines

$$ | **MODERN CANADIAN** | A living metaphor for a can of sardines, with its small, cozy space (only about 20 seats) and its explosion of flavors, Sardines is a must stop for foodie travelers. Upon entering, the display case features the chef's bakery creations, including his famous baguette. **Known for:** creative small plates; good beer selection; reservations recommended. [$] *Average main: C$18* ✉ *1 rue St-Jean, Montcalm* ☎ *581/300–9449* 🌐 *spoursardines.ca* 🕒 *Closed Sun.–Tues.*

Coffee and Quick Bites

Café Cantook

$ | **CAFÉ** | One of the newer additions to the St-Jean-Baptiste neighborhood, Cantook is a micro-roaster that is more traditional than trendy, but no less excellent. Visit for a cappuccino, a good conversation with the owner, maybe even both. **Known for:** popular with locals; friendly staff; fuss-free atmosphere. [$] *Average main: C$5* ✉ *575 rue St-Jean, St-Jean-Baptiste* ☎ *418/529–4769* 🌐 *cantookcafe.com.*

★ La Boîte à Pain

$ | **BAKERY** | La Boîte à Pain makes it a point of honor to serve fresh products prepared on site every day. In a convivial atmosphere, this European-inspired bakery has been making gourmet and artisanal products for more than 20 years. **Known for:** intricate, affordable pastries; large coffee selection; on-site daily baking. [$] *Average main: C$10* ✉ *289 rue St-Joseph Est, St-Roch* ☎ *418/647–3666* 🌐 *boiteapain.com.*

Nektar Caféologue

$ | **CAFÉ** | Another five-star coffee shop to visit in St-Roch, either for a roasting lesson or a warm macchiato respite from the Québec winter. Known for its ecological and humanist approach, Nektar works closely with its fair trade producers in Brazil to produce their Para Ela blend, which means "for her" and is harvested by hand and processed exclusively by women who are paid 50% more than the regional average. **Known for:** fair trade coffee; several flavors to choose from; vegan milk. [$] *Average main: C$5* ✉ *235 rue St-Joseph Est, St-Roch* ☎ *418/977–9236* 🌐 *nektar.ca.*

Hotels

Booking a room outside the walled city puts you in a mixed area of student housing, convention hotels, and chains, although there are still a few inns and B&Bs to choose from. Many of the options are within easy proximity to the Plains of Abraham, the restaurants of Avenue Cartier, and museums such as the Musée des Beaux-Arts du Québec.

L'Adresse

$$ | **APARTMENT** | Built in 1899 at the request of an influent bourgeois family, this historic red brick residence exudes refinement, authenticity, and commands attention. **Pros:** kitchenettes; private parking; historic stay, minus the dated amenities. **Cons:** no lobby; some lofts can feel small; décor can feel impersonal, almost bare. [$] *Rooms from: C$175* ✉ *401 Grande Allée Est, Upper Town* ☎ *877/515–2730* 🌐 *ladresse.ca* 🛏 *14 lofts* 🍴 *No Meals.*

Le Bonne Entente

$$ | **HOTEL** | Twenty minutes from Downtown, the 11-acre Château Bonne Entente offers tasteful simplicity at its finest, with classic rooms featuring white duvets, marble bathrooms (toiletries by The White Company), and refinished wood furniture. **Pros:** free shuttle to Old Québec and Downtown; country-club feel; chic, relaxing atmosphere. **Cons:** shuttle not available fall through spring; not the best room service; golf is 20 minutes away. [$] *Rooms from: C$199* ✉ *3400 chemin Ste-Foy, Outside the Old City* ☎ *800/463–4390* 🌐 *lebonneentente.com* 🛏 *165 rooms* 🍴 *No Meals.*

Le C3 Hôtel

$$ | **HOTEL** | Located right across the street from Musée national des beaux-arts du Québec and within minutes from some of the best bars and restaurants in the city. **Pros:** easy access to Montcalm and St-Jean-Baptiste nightlife; modern furniture and linens; beautiful building. **Cons:** limited parking; rooms in the Creative category are in the basement; 10-minute walk from the Old City. [$] *Rooms from: C$200* ✉ *170 Grande Allée Ouest, Montcalm* ☎ *418/525–9726* 🌐 *lec3hotel.com* 🛏 *24 rooms* 🍴 *No Meals.*

Hôtel Château Laurier

$$ | **HOTEL** | Brown leather sofas and wrought-iron chandeliers fill the spacious lobby of this former private house. **Pros:** some rooms for budget travelers; professional and helpful staff; convenient to Grande-Allée. **Cons:** some ambient noise; hotel a bit of a maze; not all rooms are renovated. [$] *Rooms from: C$199* ✉ *1220 place George V Ouest, Upper Town* ☎ *888/522–8108* 🌐 *hotelchateaulaurier.com* 🛏 *289 rooms* 🍴 *No Meals.*

Hôtel Delta Québec

$$ | **HOTEL** | This recently renovated hotel with large, functional rooms is an excellent and stylish option for business and budget-minded travelers. **Pros:** four-season outdoor pool; kid-friendly environment; some rooms are adapted for people with limited mobility. **Cons:** drab lobby; attracts convention groups; building is uninspiring. [$] *Rooms from: C$215* ✉ *690 boul. René-Lévesque Est, St-Jean-Baptiste* ☎ *888/884–7777* 🌐 *marriott.com/hotels/travel/yqbdr-delta-hotels-Québec* 🛏 *377 rooms* 🍴 *No Meals.*

Hôtel Le Concorde Québec

$$ | **HOTEL** | Built in 1974, this 29-story concrete high-rise with an excellent location on Grande Allée offers larger-than-average rooms with Keurig coffeemakers, huge windows, and good views of Battlefields Park and the St. Lawrence River. **Pros:** heated pool; central location; revolving rooftop restaurant. **Cons:** décor is dated; pool is open only in summer; high-traffic hotel. [$] *Rooms from: C$130* ✉ *1225 cours du Général-de-Montcalm, Upper Town* ☎ *800/463–5256* 🌐 *hotelleconcordeQuébec.com* 🛏 *406 rooms* 🍴 *No Meals.*

★ **Hôtel-Musée Premières Nations**

$$$ | **HOTEL** | **FAMILY** | Welcome to one of Canada's premier aboriginal tourism destinations, where visitors can experience warm First Nation hospitality. **Pros:** excellent restaurant; luxury rural escape; spa features Nordic pools, heated sidewalks, a fire pit, and yurt. **Cons:** 20-minute drive from the Old City; pet fee; rustic style might not appeal to animal lovers. [$] *Rooms from: C$200* ✉ *5 place de la Rencontre, Outside the Old City* ☎ *418/847–2222* 🌐 *hotelpremieresnations.ca* 🛏 *55 rooms* 🍴 *No Meals.*

★ **Hotel PUR**

$$$ | **HOTEL** | Travelers with a preference for minimal and modern design will appreciate this slick boutique hotel (part of Tribute Portfolio/Marriott alliance) with its light-filled rooms, great views, and location in an interesting neighborhood. **Pros:** in bustling St-Roch district; clean, modern design; great dining room doubles as a bar late evenings. **Cons:** a bit of a trek from Old Québec on foot; customer service can vary in quality; minimal design doesn't work for everyone. [$] *Rooms from: C$200* ✉ *395 rue de la Couronne, St-Roch* ☎ *888/627–8397* 🌐 *marriott.com/hotels/travel/yqbpu-hotel-pur-Québec-a-tribute-portfolio-hotel* 🛏 *242 rooms* 🍴 *No Meals.*

Hôtel Royal William

$$ | **HOTEL** | **FAMILY** | Like its namesake, the first Canadian steamship to cross the Atlantic (in 1833), the Royal William embodies the spirit of technology and innovation. **Pros:** spacious rooms with kitchenettes; friendly staff; convenient location in a hip area. **Cons:** far from Québec City center; parking is a little far; practical but nothing exceptional.

Hôtel de Glace—North America's first ice hotel—rebuilt each winter, is only 15 minutes from Québec City by car, and worth a tour even if you don't spend the night.

[$] *Rooms from: C$160* ⊠ *360 boul. Charest Est, St-Roch* ☎ *888/541–0405* ⊕ *royalwilliam.com* 🛏 *44 rooms* ❚❍❚ *No Meals.*

★ Hôtel de Glace

$$$$ | HOTEL | The first of its kind in North America, this hotel, open from the first week in January to the end of March at Village Vacances Valcartier, is built entirely from ice and snow each year. **Pros:** unique experience; spectacular engineering feat and design; festive atmosphere. **Cons:** 30-minute drive from Downtown Québec City; can get cold; limited availability. [$] *Rooms from: C$389* ⊠ *Village Vacances Valcartier, 1860, boul. Valcartier, Outside the Old City* ☎ *888/384–5524* ⊕ *valcartier.com* 🛏 *24 rooms* ❚❍❚ *No Meals.*

J.A. Moisan Auberge

$$$ | B&B/INN | Exceptional B&B in one of Québec City's most iconic buildings: right above the famous renowned J.A. Moisan fine grocery store, which was founded in 1871. **Pros:** excellent breakfast; within walking distance of the Old City; like stepping back in time. **Cons:** Victorian style isn't for everyone; some may not like staying above a grocery store; rooms are very small. [$] *Rooms from: C$205* ⊠ *695 rue St-Jean, St-Jean-Baptiste* ☎ *418/914–3777* ⊕ *jamoisan.com* 🛏 *4 rooms* ❚❍❚ *Free Breakfast.*

ⓨ Nightlife

BARS AND LOUNGES

Korrigane Brasserie Artisanale

BREWPUBS | A popular after-work spot with the locals, this brewery crafts high-quality beer and tapas-inspired pub fare. A friendly vibe and ample seating make Korrigane the ideal spot for a *cinq à sept* or a low-key night out. In addition to the house brews, there's a good selection of other local options. ⊠ *380 rue Dorchester, St-Roch* ☎ *418/614–0932* ⊕ *korrigane.ca.*

Le Projet

BREWPUBS | With 30 beer and cider lines (a great way to discover Québec's brewery scene), Le Projet is a 65-seat bistro-pub specializing in Québec micro-brewery beers and ciders in a beautiful 112-year-old building—a former bank—where the architecture is reminiscent of the quintessential English pub. The cozy façade and the imposing ceiling moldings contribute to the welcoming atmosphere that makes the food (and beer) even tastier. ✉ *399 rue St-Jean, St-Jean-Baptiste* ☎ *418/914–5322* ⊕ *publeprojet.com.*

★ **Noctem Artisans Brasseurs**
BREWPUBS | A great selection of beers, brewed on premises or coming from some of the best microbreweries in Québec, attract diners here, along with the smart menu of reinvented pub fare (fish and waffle, blood sausage pie, braised pork belly with chimichurri sauce and parsley root chips, for example). The décor, with raw plywood and exposed structures, is modern and trendy. ✉ *438 rue du Parvis, St-Roch* ☎ *581/742–7979* ⊕ *noctem.ca* ⊘ *No lunch Mon.–Wed.*

⊕ Performing Arts

Centre Vidéotron
MUSIC | This state-of-the-art arena opened in the fall of 2015, with the hope of attracting a National Hockey League franchise. For now, the hockey is from a junior league, but there are world-class concerts and popular acts playing here regularly. ✉ *Parc de l'Expocité, 250 boul. Wilfrid-Hamel, Outside the Old City* ☎ *855/790–1245* ⊕ *lecentrevideotron.ca.*

Carrefour international de théâtre de Québec
THEATER | This international theatrical festival takes over several spaces in late May and early June: the Salle Albert-Rousseau, the Grand Théâtre de Québec, the Théâtre Périscope (near avenue Cartier), and Complexe Méduse. There are usually at least one or two productions in English or with English subtitles, and an outdoor show that takes over different parts of the Downtown area. ✉ *Québec City* ☎ *888/529–1996* ⊕ *carrefourtheatre.qc.ca.*

Coopérative Méduse
THEATER | This multidisciplinary arts center, built in a row of historic houses mixed with new structures, is a hub for local artists and presents edgy installations and live shows, including a modern dance series. ✉ *650 côte d'Abraham, St-Roch* ☎ *418/640–9218* ⊕ *meduse.org.*

École de Cirque
CIRCUSES | For two weeks every June, students of this circus school and others take to the trapeze to promote their art form through the Circus Days festival. Throughout the year, students and teachers put on various shows, training camps, and workshops, including a Christmas Cabaret, in the former church that now houses their school. ✉ *750 2e avenue, Outside the Old City* ☎ *418/525–0101* ⊕ *ecoledecirque.com.*

Grand Théâtre de Québec
ARTS CENTERS | Québec City's main theater has two stages for symphonic concerts, opera, plays, and touring companies of all sorts. The Grand Théâtre also presents a dance series with Canadian and international companies. Inside, a three-wall mural by the Québec sculptor Jordi Bonet depicts death, life, and liberty. Bonet wrote "La Liberté" on one wall to bring attention to the Québécois struggle for freedom and cultural distinction. ✉ *269 boul. René-Lévesque Est, St-Jean-Baptiste* ☎ *418/643–8131* ⊕ *grandtheatre.qc.ca.*

★ Orchestre symphonique de Québec
(*Québec Symphony Orchestra*)
MUSIC | Canada's oldest symphony orchestra, directed by the dynamic French conductor Fabien Gabel, performs mainly at Louis-Fréchette Hall in the Grand Théâtre de Québec. ✉ *269 boul. René-Lévesque Est, St-Jean-Baptiste* ☎ *418/643–8486* ⊕ *osq.org* ▣ *From C$45.*

Salle Albert-Rousseau

THEATER | A diverse repertoire, from classical music to comedy, is staged here. ⊠ *2410 chemin Ste-Foy, Ste-Foy* ☎ *418/659–6710* ⊕ *sallealbertrousseau.com.*

Théâtre Périscope

THEATER | This multipurpose theater hosts about a dozen different productions a year, staged by several different theater companies. New creations and experimental productions are always a strong part of the mix. ⊠ *2 rue Crémazie Est, St-Jean-Baptiste* ☎ *418/529–2183* ⊕ *theatreperiscope.qc.ca.*

🛍 Shopping

CLOTHING

Ivy

WOMEN'S CLOTHING | The mother-daughter duo at the helm of this charming boutique selects the trendiest clothing pieces from both local and international brands, in addition to second-hand accessories, jewelry from local artisans, delicate undergarments, leather bags, and even candles. ⊠ *3B boul. René-Lévesque Est, Montcalm* ☎ *418/353–2371* ⊕ *ivyboutique.ca.*

★ Jupon pressé

WOMEN'S CLOTHING | Lovers of fashion with a penchant for retro, the two friendly owners of this boho-chic boutique, Sylvie and Josiane, curate each season a selection of women's outfits from more than 60 trendy brands. You can also find all kinds of accessories, jewelry, bags, and even vegan body products. ⊠ *790 rue St-Jean, Montcalm* ☎ *418/704–7114* ⊕ *juponpresse.com* ☉ *Closed Sun.*

Latulippe

SPORTING GOODS | Latulippe is an outdoor equipment and clothing store, a true institution in Québec City operated by the same family since 1940. Visitors will find quality winter coats, boots, and various accessories from the most trusted brands (including a few local ones), just

---

Stop and Shop 🛍

Les Halles Cartier is a small but busy food mall on avenue Cartier. It has restaurants and shops that sell fish, flowers, pastries, breads, vegetables, fresh coffee, candies, and some excellent local cheeses, as well as a few Italian and other European specialties. There's no fast food here, but if you're looking for picnic snacks for a day trip to the Plains of Abraham, plan to fill your basket here before you head to the park. ⊕ *hallescartier.ca.*

---

in case they've seriously under-packed and came underprepared for the harsh, sometimes unpredictable Québec climate. The store is slightly outside the core downtown area; hailing a cab is the best way to get there and back. ⊠ *637 rue St-Vallier Ouest, Outside the Old City* ☎ *877/529–0024* ⊕ *latulippe.com.*

FOOD

Camellia Sinensis Maison de Thé

FOOD | This modern and elegant space stocks 150 different teas from China, Japan, Africa, and beyond, most of them imported by the owners themselves. You can sign up for a number of tea-tasting sessions and workshops, or just sip some tea on premises. ⊠ *624 rue St-Joseph Est, St-Roch* ☎ *418/525–0247* ⊕ *camellia-sinensis.com.*

La Boîte à Pain

FOOD | Baker Patrick Nisot offers a selection of baguettes, multigrain breads (pumpernickel, rye), special flavors (olive, tomato and pesto, Sicilian), and dessert breads. Even something as common as a date square has a special and delicious twist to it. Sandwiches and salads are also available for lunch. No credit cards are accepted. Two more locations are available in Sainte-Foy and in the quaint Limoilou neighborhood. ⊠ *289 rue*

St-Joseph Est, St-Roch ☎ 418/647–3666 ⊕ boiteapain.com.

Fromagerie des Grondines

FOOD | La Fromagerie des Grondines is an entirely organic cheese factory in Portneuf County, not far from Québec City, specializing in the artisanal production of organic raw milk cheeses from cows, goats, and sheep. It recently opened a tasting counter in the heart of the St-Roch district, where it sells its own cheeses as well as products from other Québec artisans. Their 12-month Le Closdes-Roches is an absolute delight. ☒ 199 rue St-Joseph Est, St-Roch ☎ 581/742–4866 ⊕ fromageriedesgrondines.com.

Le Grand Marché

FOOD | Québec City's answer to Paris's Le Bon Marché, this shop is a must for gourmet-loving travelers. Expect tons of artisan-made goods, such as upscale jams, honeys, ciders, cheeses, chocolate, beers, and maple—all locally made. It's a bit further out in the suburbs of Québec City, but there is easy and regular bus service on route 801. ☒ 250-M boul. Wilfrid-Hamel, Outside the Old City ☎ 418/692–2517 ⊕ www.legrandmarchedeQuébec.com.

★ Maison J.A. Moisan

FOOD | Founded in 1871 by Jean-Alfred Moisan, this place claims the title of the oldest continuously operating grocery store in North America. The original display cases, woodwork, and tin ceilings preserve the old-time feel. The store sells hard-to-find products from various regions of Québec, including cheeses, charcuterie, and some outstanding local ales. The original owner's upstairs home has now been turned into a classic B&B with all the trimmings. ☒ 699 rue St-Jean, St-Jean-Baptiste ☎ 418/522–0685 ⊕ jamoisan.com.

La société des cafés

FOOD | In a light-filled location on a street known for its gourmet side, the one-of-a-kind boutique in Québec City spills the beans on more than 50 Canadian roasters, each with its own set of particularities and colorful packaging. They also aim to educate consumers on roasting methods, sourcing beans and crafting the perfect espresso. Their mission is noble, yet simple: "coffee, simply made" by democratizing specialty coffee and its various iterations, as well as by helping local roasters to share their know-how and passion. Also on sale are a wide variety of coffee accessories such as grinders, filters, and beautiful reusable cups, as well as gift boxes for the most pleasant of travel souvenirs. ☒ 1024 avenue Cartier, Québec City ☎ 581/814–2233 ⊕ societedescafes.com.

GIFTS

Zone

HOUSEWARES | Design oriented, whimsical yet practical objects abound in this popular store, which features tons of modern décor, tableware, and accessories for the home and office. From the latest cooking implement to lovely decorative objects and fancy clocks, there's something for just about everyone. ☒ 999 avenue Cartier, Montcalm ☎ 418/522–7373 ⊕ zonemaison.com.

PERFUME/COSMETICS

Aliksir

OTHER HEALTH & BEAUTY | This small boutique is packed with essential oils and natural beauty products of all kinds, from skin care to dental care products, mostly organic and largely produced just outside of Québec City. ☒ 89 rue St-Joseph Est, St-Roch ☎ 418/977–3715 ⊕ aliksir.com.

SHOPPING MALLS

Galeries de la Capitale

MALL | **FAMILY** | Thirty-five restaurants, some 280 shops, an IMAX theater, and an adjacent indoor amusement park make this recently and extensively renovated mall ideal for a whole day of family retail therapy. ☒ 5401 boul. des Galeries, Lebourgneuf, Outside the Old City ☎ 418/627–5800 ⊕ galeriesdelacapitale.com.

Laurier Québec

MALL | There are more than 300 stores in Québec City's busiest mall, with everything from fashion and electronics to children's toys and books. Easily accessible by bus or (from some downtown hotels) shuttle, it's next door to Place de la Cité and Place Sainte-Foy. Together, the three malls form the largest stretch of shopping in the city. ⊠ *2700 boul. Laurier, Ste-Foy* ☎ *418/651–5000* ⊕ *laurierQuébec.com.*

TOYS/GAMES

Benjo

TOYS | **FAMILY** | Whimsy runs wild at Benjo. This store features games and toys, kids' clothes, a large café with thrones for little princes and princesses, an ample bookstore filled with French storybooks (and some English), and even an electric train you can ride around the store. ⊠ *550 boul. Charest Est, St-Roch* ☎ *418/640–0001* ⊕ *benjo.ca.*

🏃 Activities

Scenic rivers and nearby mountains (no more than 30 minutes away by car) make Québec City a great place for exploring the outdoors.

Québec City Tourist Center

Contact the tourist board for information about sports and fitness activities around the city. ⊠ *12 rue Ste-Anne, Upper Town* ☎ *877/266–5687* ⊕ *Québec-cite.com.*

BIKING

There are more than 100 km (60 miles) of fairly flat, well-maintained bike paths on Québec City's side of the St. Lawrence River and a similar amount on the south shore. Detailed route maps are available through tourism offices. The two best and most scenic of the bike paths are the one that follows the old railway bed in Lévis, accessible near the Québec-Lévis ferry terminal, and the one that follows the St. Lawrence River on the north shore, all the way to Montmorency Falls. Many parts of the regional network are now part of the province-wide Route Verte, a government-funded, 4,000-km-long (2,500-mile-long) circuit of long-distance bicycle paths and road routes.

Corridor des Cheminots

BIKING | Ambitious cyclists can embark on the 22-km-long (14-mile-long) trail that runs from Québec City near Old Québec to the town of Shannon. It's a slow uphill on the way out—with the reward of an easier ride back. ⊠ *Outside the Old City.*

Côte-de-Beaupré

BIKING | Paths along the beginning of the Beaupré coast, at the confluence of the St. Charles and St. Lawrence rivers, are especially scenic. Ride along bucolic panoramas and scenic views of the river through New France villages along one of the oldest roads in Canada, Avenue Royale, on the new Marie-Hélène-Prémont cycling route. The 55 km (3 miles) path starts at Montmorency Falls and finishes at Mont-Sainte-Anne. ⊠ *Outside the Old City.*

Mont-Ste-Anne

BIKING | The site of the 1998 world mountain-biking championship and races for the annual World Cup has around 150 km (93 miles) of mountain-bike trails and an extreme-mountain-biking park. ⊠ *Outside the Old City* ☎ *800/463–1568* ⊕ *mont-sainte-anne.com* 🎫 *C$49 unlimited access to ski lift and trails.*

BOATING AND FISHING

Permits are needed for fishing in Québec. Most sporting-goods stores and all Walmart and Canadian Tire stores sell permits. A one-day fishing permit for a nonresident is C$19, a three-day permit is C$33, a seven-day permit is C$50 (and includes all sport fish except Atlantic salmon).

Gesti-faune

FISHING | A corporate fishing outfitter, Gesti-faune has two properties within easy driving distance of Québec City. From May to September, the company's nature guides organize trout-fishing trips that include food and lodging in private wilderness retreats. Three-day trips, organized from May to September for groups of 14, cost from C$900 per person, and include everything, including gourmet cuisine. There are also daily packages starting at C$146 per person. Reservations are required. ✉ *3 route Tewkesbury, Outside the Old City* ☎ *418/848–5424* ⊕ *gestifaune.com.*

Parc nautique de Cap-Rouge

KAYAKING | This park, at the western tip of Québec City on the St. Lawrence River, has canoes and pedal boats to rent. ✉ *4155 chemin de la plage Jacques-Cartier, Outside the Old City* ☎ *418/641–6148.*

Réserve faunique des Laurentides

FISHING | This wildlife reserve has good lakes for fishing. It's approximately 48 km (30 miles) north of Québec City via Route 73. Reserve a boat 48 hours in advance by phone. ✉ *Camp Mercier, Outside the Old City* ☎ *800/665–6527* ⊕ *sepaq.com/ rf/lau.*

DOG SLEDDING

For centuries, dog sledding has been a part of the Canadian winter experience. Outfitters around Québec City generally offer excursions from January through March.

Aventures Nord-Bec Stoneham

LOCAL SPORTS | **FAMILY** | This outfitter will teach you how to mush in the forest. A half-day expedition, which includes a crash course, dog sledding, a guided tour of kennels, and a snack, costs C$145 per person. Overnight camping trips, snowshoeing, and ice fishing are also available. In summer, this location offers fishing, mountain biking, and kennel tours. Transportation between Stoneham (a 30-minute drive from the Old City) and your hotel costs C$45 extra. ✉ *4 chemin des Anémones, Stoneham* ☎ *418/848– 3732* ⊕ *traineaux-chiens.com.*

GOLF

The Québec City region has 18 golf courses, and most are open to the public. Reservations are essential in summer.

Club de Golf Cap-Rouge

GOLF | Established in 1959, this is one of the closest courses to the city center, just 25 minutes by car from Vieux-Québec in a pleasant suburban area. Its 18-hole course is set up with variations for women, men, and advanced players. You're close to the St. Lawrence River, so be careful not to let the wind play tricks on you. ✉ *4600 rue St-Félix, Cap-Rouge* ☎ *418/653–9381* ⊕ *golfcap-rouge.qc.ca* ⚐ *From C$35* ⚑ *18 holes, 6756 yards, par 72.*

Club de Golf de Mont Tourbillon

GOLF | The cooler air of the Laurentian Mountains is quite welcome on a hot summer day, as you play golf and enjoy views of the rolling hillside and Lac Beauport. Mont Tourbillon features three courses and the brand-new, modern clubhouse offers a bistro with a pleasant terrace. It's 25 minutes from the city by car via Route 73 North (take the Lac Beauport exit). In winter, golfing yields the way to long, fun slides. ✉ *55 montée du Golf, Lac-Beauport* ☎ *418/849–4418* ⊕ *monttourbillon.com* ⚐ *From C$40 weekends, from C$35 weekdays* ⚑ *Blue Course: 18 holes, 6090 yards, par 70; White Course: 18 holes, 5590 yards, par 70; Red Course: 18 holes, 4625 yards, par 70.*

Le St-Ferréol

GOLF | Located within sight of the Mont-Sainte-Anne ski slopes, this club has one of the best and best-priced courses in the region—it's been fine-tuned by pro Denis Gagné. The course is a half-hour drive northeast of Québec City, and features a large driving range for practice. ⊠ *1700 boul. les Neiges, St-Ferréol-les-Neiges* ☎ *418/827–3778* ⊕ *golfstferreol.com* ✉ *From C$32* ⅄. *18 holes, 6445 yards, par 72.*

HIKING AND JOGGING

Runners and foot soldiers have a choice of routes in areas like Battlefields Park, Cartier-Brébeuf, and along the waterfront in the city itself.

Bois-de-Coulonge Park

RUNNING | Along with Battlefields Park, Bois-de-Coulonge is one of the most popular places for jogging, with forest trails and river views. ⊠ *1215 Grande Allée Ouest, Outside the Old City* ☎ *418/528–0773.*

ICE-SKATING

In addition to rinks in town, Village Vacances Valcartier (see *Snow Slides* section), just outside Québec City, offers skating trails with lighting and sound systems.

RAFTING

Just outside the city, the Jacques-Cartier River (to the west) and Riviére Malbaie (to the east) both make for an easy white-water rafting day trip. Village Vacances Valcartier (⇨ see *Snow Slides section*) also runs three-hour rafting excursions on the river from May through September.

Excursions Jacques-Cartier

WHITE-WATER RAFTING | This outfitter runs rafting trips on the Jacques-Cartier River, about 48 km (30 miles) northwest of Québec City, from May through October. Tours originate from Tewkesbury, a half-hour drive from Québec City. A half-day trip ranges from C$90 per person, wet suits included. ⊠ *860 av. Jacques-Cartier Nord, Stoneham-et-Tewkesbury* ☎ *418/848–7238* ⊕ *excursionsj-cartier. com.*

SKIING

Skiing is very popular here, whether it's downhill on one of the mountains surrounding the city or cross-country in an urban park. A dynamic landscape, top-notch ski resorts, and lots of fresh powder have helped make this a major training area for some of Canada's top athletes.

⇨ *For more cross-country and downhill skiing options near Québec City, see the Side Trips from Québec City chapter.*

CROSS-COUNTRY

Regroupement des stations de ski de fond

SKIING & SNOWBOARDING | Thirty-seven cross-country ski centers in the Québec area have 2,000 km (1,240 miles) of groomed trails and heated shelters between them; contact this group for more information. Many also offer snowshoeing trails. ⊠ *Québec City* ⊕ *skidefondraquette.com.*

SKI CENTERS

Les Sentiers du Moulin

SKIING & SNOWBOARDING | This center is 19 km (12 miles) north of the city and has more than 20 marked trails covering 48 km (28 miles), overall, with 28 km (17 miles) multitrack. There's even fat-bike and snowshoeing. ⊠ *99 chemin du Moulin, Lac-Beauport* ☎ *418/849–9652* ⊕ *sentiersdumoulin.com* ✉ *C$21.*

Station touristique Duchesnay
SKIING & SNOWBOARDING | Located west of Québec City, this center has 150 km (93 miles) of marked trails, which can be used for snowshoeing and cross-country skiing in the winter. There's a wonderful lakeside inn on-site. ✉ *140 montée de l'Auberge, Ste-Catherine-de-la-Jacques-Cartier* ☎ *866/683–2711* ⊕ *sepaq.com/ct/duc* ✍ *C$16 per adult.*

DOWNHILL
Multiple downhill ski resorts are nearby, and some are barely 30 minutes away from Downtown Québec City. Most have night skiing. ⇨ *For information on Le Massif and Mont-Ste-Anne, see the Côte-de-Beaupré section in Side Trips from Québec City.*

Le Relais
SKIING & SNOWBOARDING | There are 28 trails and a vertical drop of 734 feet at this relatively small, family-friendly ski center, where you can buy lift tickets by the hour. Le Relais is about 20 minutes from Downtown Québec City. ✉ *1084 boul. du Lac, Lac-Beauport* ☎ *418/849–1851* ⊕ *skirelais.com.*

Station Touristique Stoneham
SKIING & SNOWBOARDING | Stoneham is 20 minutes north of Old Québec. The hill has a vertical drop of 1,380 feet, with a number of long, easy slopes and some more challenging runs. It has 42 downhill runs and seven lifts, plus three terrain parks and one super-half-pipe. ✉ *600 chemin du Hibou, Stoneham-et-Tewkesbury* ☎ *800/463–6888,* ⊕ *ski-stoneham.com.*

SNOWMOBILING
Québec is the birthplace of the snowmobile, and with 32,000 km (19,840 miles) of trails, it's one of the best places in the world for the sport. Two major trails, the 2,000-km (1,250-mile) Trans-Québec Snowmobile Trail and the 1,300-km (806-mile) Fur Traders Tour, run just north of Québec City. Trail maps are available at tourist offices.

Nord Expe
SNOW SPORTS | Availability of full-day and half-day introductory snowmobile packages 30 minutes from Québec City, with professional certified snowmobile guides. Access to snowmobile circuits and routes in a safe and natural setting, in the middle of the mountains and the Jacques-Cartier valley. Depending on the duration of the expedition, rates vary from C$200 to C$600. ✉ *354 rue Auclair, Outside the Old City* ☎ *418/825–1772* ⊕ *nordexpe.com.*

SNOW SLIDES
Village Vacances Valcartier
SNOW SPORTS | FAMILY | Hop on an inner tube or carpet and shoot down one of more than 35 snow slides here. Or join 6 to 12 others for a snow-raft ride on one of three groomed trails. You can also take a dizzying ride on the Tornado, a giant inner tube that seats eight and spins down the slopes. Rafting and sliding cost C$45 per day for those taller than 52 inches, C$38 for those between 39 and 52 inches, and free for those under 39 inches. Trails open daily at 10 am; closing times vary. ✉ *1860 boul. Valcartier, St-Gabriel-de-Valcartier* ☎ *888/384–5524* ⊕ *valcartier.com.*

SPAS
Sibéria Spa
SPAS | A 20-minute drive from Vieux-Québec, Siberia Spa offers thermal and cold baths, a eucalyptus steam room, a relaxing yurt, an elegant café set inside a former chapel, and a quiet pavilion where you can sit by a fire and look out to the Jacques Cartier River. Massages and packages run from C$100 to C$300. It's normally adults only, but families are welcome on Sunday mornings (between 9 am and noon) and on regular hours during the holidays and spring break. ✉ *339 rue de Genève, Lac-Beauport* ☎ *855/841–1325* ⊕ *siberiaspa.com* ✍ *C$55; C$37 evenings.*

Nordique Spa Stoneham

SPAS | Located on the banks of the majestic Jacques-Cartier River, Le Nordique offers a Scandinavian-style relaxation concept based on alternating heat and cold. Finnish sauna, Turkish steam bath, outdoor whirlpool, and massage therapy are available. The site also offers the rental of mini-cabins, also Nordic, for two people; access to the spa is included in the price of the night. ✉ *747 Jacques-Cartier Nord, Stoneham-et-Tewkesbury* ☎ *418/848–7727* ⊕ *lenordique.com* ▣ *C$50.*

WATER PARKS

Village Vacances Valcartier

WATER SPORTS | FAMILY | The largest water park in Canada has a wave pool, a 1-km (½-mile) tropical-river adventure called the Amazon, more than 35 waterslides, and a 100-foot accelerating slide on which bathers reach a speed of up to 80 kph (50 mph). The interior Bora Parc, featuring 14 slides, a river, and a wave pool, is open year-round. ✉ *1860 boul. Valcartier, St-Gabriel-de-Valcartier* ☎ *888/384–5524* ⊕ *valcartier.com* ▣ *C$50 per adult; C$43 per child.*

Chapter 6

SIDE TRIPS FROM QUÉBEC CITY

6

Updated by
Chris Barry

👁 **Sights**   🍴 **Restaurants**   🛏 **Hotels**   💼 **Shopping**   🍸 **Nightlife**

★★★★★   ★★★★★   ★★★★★   ★★★★★   ★★★★★

WELCOME TO
SIDE TRIPS FROM QUÉBEC CITY

TOP REASONS TO GO

★ **Ski at Le Massif:** This three-peak ski resort has the largest vertical drop in eastern Canada, at more than 2,500 feet.

★ **Whale-watch in Tadoussac:** About 220 km (137 miles) east of Québec City, you can see small white beluga whales—an endangered species—year-round in the Saguenay River.

★ **Farm-hop on Île d'Orléans:** The "Garden of Québec" is covered with farmland and bed-and-breakfasts, and makes for the perfect day or overnight trip from Québec City.

★ **Take the footbridge across Montmorency Falls:** These waterfalls on the Côte-de-Beaupré are double the height of Niagara Falls. The bridge and stairs, which go over and around them, make for a spectacular stroll.

★ **See Basilique Ste-Anne-de-Beaupré:** More than a million people a year make pilgrimages to this church, named after the patron saint of Québec.

1 **Ste-Pétronille.** Enjoy splendid views of Montmorency Falls and Cap Diamant.

2 **St-Laurent de l'Île d'Orléans.** Farm stands and strawberry fields.

3 **St-Jean.** Find preserved row houses from the 1800s and strawberry farms.

4 **St-François.** A rustic village with an observation tower.

5 **Ste-Famille.** The island's oldest parish.

6 **St-Pierre.** Shop for local specialties at the most populated part of the island.

7 **Côte-de-Beaupré.** Rich landscapes alongside the St. Lawrence River.

8 **Baie-St-Paul.** The cultural capital of the Charlevoix region.

9 **St-Joseph-de-la-Rive.** Board the ferry to the majestic L'Isle-aux-Coudres.

10 **La Malbaie.** Rich in history and natural beauty.

11 **Tadoussac.** One of the best whale-watching centers in Québec.

12 **Port Saguenay.** Famous for Lac Saint-Jean.

13 **Trois-Rivières.** The second-oldest city in Québec.

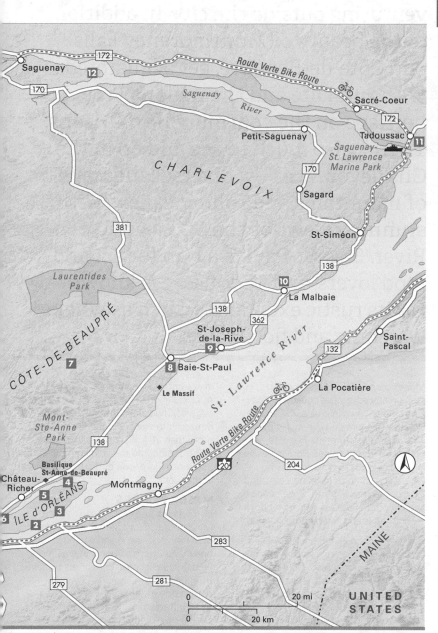

Experience a deeper understanding of this region's history and culture by venturing outside the city. In addition to the beauty of Montmorency Falls and Côte-de-Beaupré, get acquainted with rural life and the region's French heritage on the charming Île d'Orléans. There's also much to see and do in the Charlevoix area—a diverse landscape of mountains and rolling valleys with stunning views of the St. Lawrence River. Baie-St-Paul is a hub for art and food lovers, and Tadoussac is known for its rustic excursions, such as whale-watching and fjord tours.

Montmorency Falls is an excellent first stop on any adventure outside the city. From there, you can cruise up Québec's Côte-de-Beaupré and eventually make your way to Ste-Anne-de-Beaupré, where there's an immense neo-Roman basilica. Or take the bridge to Île d'Orléans, where you can pick fresh berries, sample ice cider fermented from frozen apples, and shop for antiques. A leisurely drive around the island can be done in a day.

Charlevoix, a couple of hours from Québec City, takes more planning and probably an overnight stay, but is well worth the drive. There are plenty of gorgeous villages and picnic spots along the way. Artists of all disciplines draw inspiration from this region, which is steeped in natural beauty and Algonquin history. Approaching Tadoussac, at the eastern edge of Charlevoix, the St. Lawrence River begins to seem like the open sea—it's more than 20 km (12 miles) wide at this point. Slicing into the land is the dramatic Saguenay Fjord, one of the largest fjords in the world.

MAJOR REGIONS

Île d'Orléans. The Algonquins called it Minigo, the "Bewitched Place," and over the years the island's tranquil rural beauty has inspired poets and painters. Île d'Orléans is only 15 minutes by car from Downtown Québec City, but a visit here is one of the best ways to get a feel for traditional life in rural Québec. Centuries-old homes and some of the oldest churches in the region dot the road that rings the island. About 8 km (5 miles) wide and 35 km (22 miles) long, Île d'Orléans is made up of six small villages that have sought over the years to retain their identities: **Ste-Pétronille, St-Laurent de l'Île d'Orléans, St-Jean, St-François, Ste-Famille,** and **St-Pierre.** The bridge to the mainland was built in 1935, and in 1970 the island was declared a historic area to protect it from most sorts of development.

To get to Île d'Orléans, take Route 440 (Autoroute Dufferin–Montmorency) northeast. After a drive of about 10 km (6 miles), take the bridge (Pont de l'Île d'Orléans) to the island. The main road, chemin Royal (Route 368), circles the island, extending 67 km (42 miles) through the island's six villages; the route turns into chemin du Bout de l'Île as it loops around the western tip of the island.

Côte-de-Beaupré. Driving along this coast offers views of Île d'Orléans, as well as Montmorency Falls and the famous pilgrimage site, Ste-Anne-de-Beaupré.

To get to the Côte-de-Beaupré, take Route 440 (Autoroute Dufferin–Montmorency) northeast from Québec City. It's approximately 9.5 km (6 miles) to the exit for the Chutes Montmorency and about 35 km (21 miles) to Ste-Anne-de-Beaupré.

Charlevoix. People refer to Charlevoix as the "Switzerland of Québec" due to its terrain of mountains, valleys, streams, and waterfalls. A couple of hours from Québec City, it takes more planning and probably an overnight stay, but is well worth the drive. Charlevoix's charming villages line the shore of the St. Lawrence River for about 200 km (125 miles). Artists of all disciplines draw inspiration from this region, which is steeped in natural beauty and Algonquin history. Approaching **Tadoussac,** at the eastern edge of Charlevoix, the St. Lawrence River begins to seem like the open sea—it's more than 20 km (12 miles) wide at this point. Winter activities include downhill and cross-country skiing, snowmobiling, ice fishing, dogsledding, and snowshoeing. Charlevoix's many great local food products and restaurants are also a big draw for tourists. Slicing into the land is the dramatic Saguenay Fjord, one of the largest fjords in the world.

To get to Charlevoix from Québec City, take Route 440 (Autoroute Dufferin–Montmorency) northeast and then continue on Route 138 past Côte-de-Beaupré. From there you'll be able to branch out for destinations such as Petite-Rivière-St-François or Baie-St-Paul.

Planning

When to Go

Côte-de-Beaupré, Île d'Orléans, and Charlevoix are spectacular in the fall, when you can leaf-peep and go apple picking. Summer means roadside stands featuring fresh-from-the-farm produce on Île d'Orléans or Côte-de-Beaupré. Artists and art lovers flock to Baie-St-Paul in Charlevoix for festivals and gallery openings. It's also the perfect time to see beluga whales in Tadoussac. In winter, in all regions, there are plenty of cold-weather activities, including cross-country skiing, snowshoeing, and ice fishing. The area's best downhill skiing can be found in Charlevoix, but if you don't want to tackle driving on mountain roads, consider taking a shuttle. Spring has its own magic, when the snow melts and the maple syrup starts to flow.

Getting Here and Around

The best, and in some cases the only way to explore these regions is by car, and this makes it easy to spend as much or as little time as desired in any given area. Start by heading northeast out of Québec City on Route 440 (Autoroute Dufferin–Montmorency) and then Route 138 (Boulevard Ste-Anne).

Another way to explore the exceptional beauty of the region is to hop aboard Le Train du Massif Charlevoix, a train that runs mid-June through mid-October along the shoreline from Parc de la Chute-Montmorency station to Baie-St.-Paul or La Malbaie, with several excursion options. ⇨ For further details, see the Baie-St.-Paul and La Malbaie sections of this chapter.

TRAIN INFORMATION Train de Charlevoix. ☎ 418/240–4124, 844/737–3282 ⊕ www.traindecharlevoix.com.

Québec continues to expand its Route Verte (Green Route), a 5,000-km (3,100-mile) network of bike trails in the southern part of the province.

⇨ For more information on getting here and around, refer to the Travel Smart chapter.

Restaurants

Some of the restaurants on the Côte-de-Beaupré and Île d'Orléans are open only during high season, May to October, so check ahead. But visitors who do arrive in season won't be disappointed. Fast-food or chain outlets are essentially absent from the island, and your best—and most widely available—option is to sample some of the regional cuisine on offer. And while fine dining is the order of the day on Île d'Orléans, those traveling on a budget won't go hungry, as there are some good pubs and family-style restaurants with fairly reasonable prices.

In Charlevoix, the same rules apply—call ahead if you're visiting from June to September or during the Christmas holidays. During summer, Charlevoix is a food lover's haven, with fresh berries and cheeses sold roadside and plenty of bistros in the towns. Pick up a map (available at most hotels and restaurants) of La Route des Saveurs, a route through the region dotted with restaurants and farms, and taste your way to Tadoussac.

Hotels

Reservations at hotels are highly recommended, although off-season it's possible to book a room the same day. B&Bs are the most common lodging options on Île d'Orléans, although there is a handful of inns and one motel. Côte-de-Beaupré, on the other hand, not only has plenty of inns and B&Bs, but several hotels and motels as well.

Given its status as one of Québec's premier summer vacation destinations, the Charlevoix region has lots to offer travelers on almost any budget. Nevertheless, it's wise to book ahead in high season, especially if you're looking for one of the less expensive rooms here, which tend to fill up pretty quickly during the summer months.

Restaurant and hotel reviews have been shortened. For full information, visit Fodors.com.

WHAT IT COSTS in Canadian Dollars			
$	$$	$$$	$$$$
RESTAURANTS			
under C$12	C$12–C$20	C$21–C$30	over C$30
HOTELS			
under C$160	C$160–C$200	C$201–C$250	over C$250

Visitor Information

CONTACTS Association Touristique Régionale de Charlevoix. ✉ *495 boul. de Comporté, C.P. 275, La Malbaie* 🕿 *418/665–4454, 800/667–2276* ⊕ *www. tourisme-charlevoix.com.* **Bureau touristique de l'île d'Orléans.** (*Tourist Information Center Île d'Orléans*) ✉ *490 Côte du Pont, St-Pierre-de-l'Île-d'Orléans* 🕿 *418/828–9411, 866/941–9411.* **Centre d'Interpretation de la Côte-de-Beaupré.** (*Beaupré Coast Interpretation Center*) ✉ *7976 av. Royale, C.P. 40, Château-Richer* 🕿 *418/824–3677, 877/824–3677* ⊕ *www.histoire-cotedebeaupre.org.*

Ste-Pétronille

17 km (10½ miles) northeast of Québec City.

The lovely village of Ste-Pétronille, the first to be settled on Île d'Orléans, is west of the bridge to the island. Founded in 1648, the community was chosen in 1759 by British General James Wolfe for his headquarters. With 40,000 soldiers and a hundred ships, the English bombarded French-occupied Québec City and the surrounding shorelines.

In the late 19th century, the English population of Québec developed Ste-Pétronille into a resort village. This area is considered to be the island's most beautiful, not only because of its spectacular views of Montmorency Falls and Québec City but also for its Regency-style English villas and exquisitely tended gardens.

GETTING HERE AND AROUND

Once across the bridge from the mainland, the Côte du Pont leads to Route 368. Turn right on chemin Royal and drive 4 km (2½ miles) to Ste-Pétronille.

◉ Sights

Maison Gourdeau de Beaulieu

HISTORIC HOME | The island's first home was built in 1648 for Jacques Gourdeau de Beaulieu, who was the first seigneur (a landholder who distributed lots to tenant farmers) of Ste-Pétronille. Remodeled over the years, this white house with blue shutters now incorporates both French and Québec styles. Its thick walls and dormer windows are characteristic of Breton architecture, but its sloping, bell-shaped roof, designed to protect buildings from large amounts of snow, is typical Québec style. The house is not open to the public. ✉ *137 chemin du Bout de l'Île, Ste-Pétronille.*

Plante Family Farm

FARM/RANCH | Pick apples and strawberries (in season) or buy fresh fruits, vegetables, and apple cider at this family farm. In March/April, enjoy maple-sugar treats from the roadside shack. ✉ *20 chemin du Bout de l'Île, Ste-Pétronille* 🕿 *418/828–9603.*

Rue Horatio-Walker

STREET | Art fans might want to explore this tiny street off chemin Royal, named after the early-19th-century painter known for his landscapes of the island. Horatio Walker lived on this street from 1904 until his death in 1938. At Nos. 11 and 13 rue Horatio-Walker are his home and workshop, but neither are open to the public. ✉ *Ste-Pétronille.*

Vignoble de Ste-Pétronille

WINERY | Since they bought it in 2003, Louis Denault and Nathalie Lane have turned this vineyard into one of the best wine producers in Québec. Most of the wine is produced from a hybrid variety called vandal-cliche, which was bred by a Laval University biologist to thrive in the area's climate, along with a growing proportion of vidal. The results are a range of fresh, crisp white wines (still and bubbly), as well as ice wine. The winery has also started producing small amounts of

Riesling, and does some tasty reds. In summer, Panache Mobile, a food cart managed by Panache, one of Québec City's best restaurants, serves delicious lunches on a terrace with a stunning view of the St. Lawrence River and Montmorency Falls. ✉ *1A chemin du Bout de l'Île, Ste-Pétronille* ☎ *418/828–9554* 🌐 *www.vignobleorleans.com* 🎫 *Wed.–Sat.: 1 hour VIP tasting tour C$22.*

Hotels

Auberge La Goéliche

$$$ | B&B/INN | This English-style country manor (rebuilt in 1996–97 following a fire) is steps away from the St. Lawrence River, and the small but elegant rooms, decorated with antiques, all have river views. **Pros:** beautiful views of the river; spectacular location; great base for exploring the island. **Cons:** restaurant has a limited menu; some rooms are quite small; riverfront but no access to the water. [$] *Rooms from: C$245* ✉ *22 chemin du Quai, Ste-Pétronille* ☎ *418/828–2248, 888/511–2248* 🌐 *www.goeliche.ca* 🛏 *16 rooms, 3 suites* 🍴 *Free Breakfast.*

Shopping

FOOD

Chocolaterie de l'Île d'Orléans

CHOCOLATE | Belgian chocolate is combined with local ingredients to produce the handmade confections here: with a maple butter filling, for example, or *framboisette,* made from raspberries. In summer, try the 24 different kinds of ice creams and sherbets, or bring home some chocolate-infused jams. They've also opened a smaller counter in the presbytery of Saint-François, at the other end of the island. ✉ *150 chemin du Bout de l'Île, Ste-Pétronille* ☎ *418/828–2250* 🌐 *www.chocolaterieorleans.com.*

What's in a Name?

Île d'Orléans was discovered in 1935, around the same time as the future site of Québec City. Explorer Jacques Cartier noticed an abundance of vines and called it the Island of Bacchus, after the Greek god of wine. (A couple of vineyards are working hard to earn back that moniker.) In 1536, Cartier renamed the island in honor of the duke of Orléans, son of the French king François I. Its fertile soil and abundant fishing made it so attractive to settlers that in the 17th century there were more people living here than in Québec City.

St-Laurent de l'Île d'Orléans

9 km (5½ miles) east of Ste-Pétronille.

Founded in 1679, St-Laurent is one of the island's maritime villages. Until as late as 1935, residents used boats as their main means of transportation. St-Laurent has a rich history in farming and fishing. Work is underway to help bring back to the island some of the species of fish that were once abundant here.

GETTING HERE AND AROUND

Continue along chemin Royal from Ste-Pétronille, looping around the western end of the island and driving east along the southern shore.

Sights

Église St-Laurent

CHURCH | The tall, inspiring church that stands next to the village marina on chemin Royal was built in 1860 on the site of an 18th-century church that had to be torn down. One of the church's

Tucked away on the far southeastern side of Île d'Orléans, St-Jean is perhaps the most picturesque of all the small villages that pepper the island.

procession chapels is a miniature stone reproduction of the original. ✉ *1532 chemin Royal, St-Laurent* ☎ *418/828–2551* 🎟 *Free.*

La Forge à Pique-Assaut
STORE/MALL | This working forge belongs to the talented local artisan Guy Bel, who has done ironwork restoration for Québec City. He was born in Lyon, France, and studied there at the École des Beaux-Arts. You can watch him and his team at work; his stylish candlesticks, chandeliers, fireplace tools, and other ironwork are for sale. ✉ *2200 chemin Royal, St-Laurent* ☎ *418/828–9300* 🌐 *www.forge-pique-assaut.com.*

Parc Maritime de St-Laurent
CITY PARK | This former boatyard includes the Chalouperie Godbout (Godbout Longboat), which holds a collection of tools used by specialist craftsmen during the golden era of boat-building. You can picnic here and watch fishermen at work, trapping eels in tall nets at low tide. ✉ *120 chemin de la Chalouperie, St-Laurent* ☎ *418/828–9672* 🌐 *www.parcmaritime.ca* 🎟 *C$5.*

🍴 Restaurants

Moulin de St-Laurent
$$$ | CAFÉ | You can dine inside amid old stone walls or outside on the patios at the foot of a tiny, peaceful waterfall at this restaurant, which was converted from an early-18th-century stone mill. Scrumptious snacks, such as quiche and salads, are available on the terrace, and evening dishes include local pork tenderloin and venison stew. **Known for:** pleasant patio; cozy atmosphere; hearty dishes. [$] *Average main: C$28* ✉ *754 chemin Royal, St-Laurent* ☎ *418/829–3888, 888/629–3888* 🌐 *www.moulin-stlaurent.qc.ca* 🕓 *Closed mid-Oct.–May.*

St-Jean

12 km (7 miles) northeast of St-Laurent.

The village of St-Jean used to be occupied by river pilots and navigators. At sea most of the time, the sailors didn't need the large homes and plots of land that the farmers did. Often richer than farmers, they displayed their affluence by building their houses with bricks brought back from Scotland as ballast. Most of St-Jean's small, homogeneous row houses were built between 1840 and 1860.

GETTING HERE AND AROUND

From St-Laurent, continue northeast along chemin Royal.

Sights

Église St-Jean

CHURCH | At the eastern end of the village sits a massive granite structure built in 1749, with large red doors and a towering steeple. The church resembles a ship; it's big, round, and appears to be sitting right on the river. Paintings of the patron saints of seamen line the interior walls. The church's cemetery is also intriguing, especially if you can read French. Back in the 1700s, piloting the St. Lawrence was a dangerous profession; the cemetery tombstones recall the many lives lost in these harsh waters. ✉ *2001 chemin Royal, St-Jean* ☎ *418/828–2551* 🎟 *Free.*

Manoir Mauvide-Genest

HISTORIC HOME | St-Jean's beautiful Normandy-style manor was built in 1734 for Jean Mauvide, the surgeon to Louis XV, and his wife, Marie-Anne Genest. The most notable thing about this house, which still has its original thick walls, ceiling beams, and fireplaces, is the degree to which it has held up over the years. The house serves as an interpretation center of New France's seigneurial regime, with 18th-century furniture, a historic vegetable garden, a multimedia presentation, and tours with guides dressed in 18th-century costumes. ✉ *1451 chemin Royal, St-Jean* ☎ *418/829–2630* 🌐 *www.manoirmauvidegenest.com* 🎟 *C$10 with guided tour. Groups of 20 or more only.*

Restaurants

La Boulange

$$ | **BAKERY** | This excellent, friendly bakery is located in the village of St-Jean's historic rectory, across the street from the church and a promenade along the river. In addition to delicious fresh croissants, pastries, and breads, La Boulange also offers pizzas and other light lunches that you can enjoy on the large covered porch in the summer. **Known for:** covered patio; great pastries; light lunches. [$] *Average main: C$14* ✉ *2001 chemin Royal, St-Jean* ☎ *418/829–3162* 🌐 *laboulange.ca* 💳 *No credit cards* 🕒 *No dinner. Season hours vary.*

St-François

12 km (7 miles) northeast of St-Jean.

Sprawling open fields separate 17th-century farmhouses in St-François, the island's least-toured and most rustic village. At the eastern tip of the island, this community was settled mainly by farmers. St-François is the perfect place to visit one of the island's *cabanes à sucre* (maple-sugaring shacks), found along chemin Royal. Stop at a hut for a tasting tour; sap is gathered from the maple groves and boiled until it's reduced to syrup (it takes 40 gallons of sap to produce one gallon of syrup). Boiled a little more and poured over snow, it becomes a delicious toffee. Maple-syrup season is from mid-March through April.

GETTING HERE AND AROUND

From St-Jean, continue northeast along chemin Royal.

Sights

Église St-François

CHURCH | Built in 1734, St-François is one of eight extant churches in Québec dating from the French regime. At the time the English seized Québec City in 1759, General James Wolfe knew St-François to be a strategic point along the St. Lawrence. Consequently, he stationed British troops here and used the church as a military hospital. In 1988, a car crash set the church on fire, and most of the interior treasures were lost. A separate children's cemetery stands as a silent witness to the difficult life of early residents. ✉ *341 chemin Royal, St-François* ☎ *418/828–2551* 🎫 *Free.*

Observation Tower

VIEWPOINT | This 60-foot-high wooden tower within a picnic area is well sited for viewing the majestic St. Lawrence and the many small islands in the estuary. In spring and fall, wild Canada geese can be seen here. The area is about 2 km (1 mile) north of Eglise St-François on chemin Royal. ✉ *St-François.*

Ste-Famille

14 km (9 miles) west of St-François.

The village of Ste-Famille, founded in 1661, has exquisite scenery, including abundant apple orchards and strawberry fields with views of Côte-de-Beaupré and Mont-Ste-Anne in the distance. But it also has historic charm, with the area's highest concentration of stone houses dating from the French regime.

GETTING HERE AND AROUND

From St-François, chemin Royal cuts north across the eastern tip of the island and continues west along the northern shore.

Sights

Église Ste-Famille

CHURCH | This impressive church, constructed in 1749, is the only one in Québec to have three bell towers at its front. The ceiling was redone in the mid-19th century with elaborate designs in wood and gold. The church also holds a famous painting, *L'Enfant Jésus Voyant la Croix* (Baby Jesus Looking at the Cross); it was done in 1670 by Frère Luc (Brother Luc), who had been sent from France to decorate churches in the area. ✉ *3915 chemin Royal, Ste-Famille* ☎ *418/828–2656* 🎫 *Free.*

Restaurants

Microbrasserie de l'île d'Orléans

$$ | CANADIAN | This is one of the most interesting microbreweries in the Québec City region, producing a colorful range of beers named after historical characters from l'Île d'Orléans. You can taste them all at the adjoining Pub Le Mitan, along with standard pub fare including burgers, pizzas, and fries. **Known for:** river view; great beer; pub fare. [$] *Average main: C$19* ✉ *3885 chemin Royal, Ste-Famille* ☎ *418/203–0588* 🌐 *www.microorleans.com* 🕒 *Closed Mon.–Thurs. mid-Oct.–May.*

St-Pierre

14 km (9 miles) southwest of Ste-Famille.

Established in 1679, this town is set on a plateau that has the island's most fertile land and has long been the center of traditional farming industries. The best products grown here are potatoes, asparagus, and corn. The Espace Félix-Leclerc—an exhibit by day and a *boîte à chansons* (combination coffeehouse and bar with live performances) by night—works to honor the late singer and songwriter, who made St-Pierre his home. The bridge back to the mainland and Route 440 is just west on chemin Royal.

GETTING HERE AND AROUND

From Ste-Famille, continue southwest along chemin Royal. After visiting St-Pierre, the same road will take you back to the bridge to return to the mainland.

Sights

Cassis Monna et filles

STORE/MALL | This family farm has won international awards for its *crème de cassis*, a liqueur made from black currants. In its vast and attractive tasting room and shop, you can taste free samples of the strong, sweet cassis or black currant wines; the tour explains how they are made. In summer, you can sample foods made with cassis at La Monnaguette, the house bistro featuring a terrace overlooking the river. ✉ *726 chemin Royal, St-Pierre-de-l'Île-d'Orléans* ☎ *418/828–1057* 🌐 *www.cassismonna.com* 🎫 *Free; guided tours (upon reservation) for groups only* ✍ *No reservations for La Monnaguette restaurant.*

Église St-Pierre

CHURCH | The oldest church on the island dates from 1717. It's no longer used for worship, but it was restored during the 1960s and is open to visitors. Many original components are still intact, such as benches with compartments below where hot bricks and stones were placed to keep people warm in winter. Félix Leclerc, the first Québécois singer-songwriter to make a mark in Europe, is buried in the cemetery nearby. ✉ *1249 chemin Royal, St-Pierre-de-l'Île-d'Orléans* ☎ *418/828–9824* 🎫 *Free.*

Restaurants

Les Ancetres Auberge Restaurant

$$$$ | **CANADIAN** | If you're in the market for traditional French Canadian food, les Ancetres Auberge is highly unlikely to disappoint. With all dishes created from local ingredients, you can dine on classic Québécois fare like meatballs and pork hock ragout with root vegetables and pickled beats, or try another house specialty, their "famous" Ancetres pea and ham soup. **Known for:** local ingredients; excellent views; Ancetres pea and ham soup. [$] *Average main: C$35* ✉ *1101 Chemin Royal, St-Pierre-de-l'Île-d'Orléans* 🌐 *www.lesancetres.ca/en* 🕒 *Closed Sun–Tues. No lunch.*

Côte-de-Beaupré

25 km (15 miles) east of Québec City.

As legend has it, when explorer Jacques Cartier first caught sight of the north shore of the St. Lawrence River in 1535, he exclaimed, "*Quel beau pré!*" ("What a lovely meadow!"), because the area was the first inviting piece of land he had spotted since leaving France. Today the Côte-de-Beaupré (Beaupré Coast), first settled by French farmers, stretches 40 km (25 miles) east from Québec City to the famous pilgrimage site of Ste-Anne-de-Beaupré. Historic Route 360, or avenue Royale, winds its way from Beauport to St-Joachim, east of Ste-Anne-de-Beaupré. The impressive Chute Montmorency (Montmorency Falls) lie between Québec City and Ste-Anne-de-Beaupré.

GETTING HERE AND AROUND

Route 440 (Autoroute Dufferin–Montmorency) heads northeast from Québec City along the Côte-de-Beaupré. It's approximately 9.5 km (6 miles) to the exit for the Chutes Montmorency and about 35 km (21 miles) to Ste-Anne-de-Beaupré.

Sights

Atelier Paré (Economuseum of Wood Sculpture)

OTHER MUSEUM | Two centuries of wood sculpture tradition are showcased at this "economuseum," a combination workshop and store. Visitors can watch artisans at work, tour an outdoor museum,

Did You Know?

The Basilique Ste-Anne-de-Beaupré draws more than a million pilgrims each year.

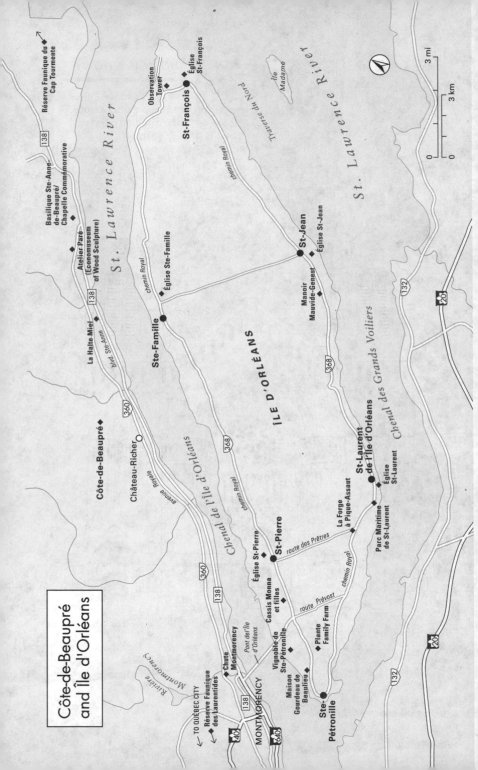

Côte-de-Beaupré and Île d'Orléans

St. Lawrence River

Réserve Faunique du Cap Tourmente

138

Basilique Ste-Anne de-Beaupré/ Chapelle Commémorative

Atelier Paré (Economuseum of Wood Sculpture)

138

La Halte Miel

bivd. Ste-Anne

360

Côte-de-Beaupré

Château-Richer

avenue Royale

138

360

Observation Tower

Église St-François

St-François

Traverse du Nord

Île Madame

chemin Royal

St. Lawrence River

Église Ste-Famille

chemin Royal

Ste-Famille

Église St-Jean

St-Jean

132

20

Manoir Mauvide-Genest

368

Chenal des Grands Voiliers

ÎLE D'ORLÉANS

Chenal de l'île d'Orléans

368

chemin Royal

St-Laurent de l'île d'Orléans

Église St-Laurent

La Forge à Pique-Assaut

route des Prêtres

Parc Maritime de St-Laurent

Église St-Pierre

St-Pierre

Cassis Monna et filles

chemin Royal

route Prévost

Pont de l'île d'Orléans

Vignoble de Ste-Pétronille

Plante Family Farm

Chute Montmorency

Maison Gourdeau de Beaulieu

Ste-Pétronille

Rivière Montmorency

Réserve Faunique des Laurentides

TO QUÉBEC CITY

138

MONTMORENCY

440

640

132

20

3 mi

3 km

see a 13-minute video presentation (in English and French), and learn about key characters in Québec's history and culture through the Legend Theatre Workshop. ⊠ *9269 av. Royale, Ste-Anne-de-Beaupré* ☎ *418/827–3992* ⊕ *www.atelierpare.com* ✉ *Free; guided tour C$5* ◔ *Closed Mon. and Tues. Oct.–May.*

★ **Basilique Ste-Anne-de-Beaupré**
RELIGIOUS BUILDING | Named for Québec's patron saint (the mother of the Virgin Mary), this small town is on Route 138, east of Québec City. It attracts more than a million pilgrims each year who come to visit the region's most famous religious site.

The French brought their devotion to St. Anne (also the patron saint of shipwrecked sailors) when they sailed across the Atlantic to New France. According to local legend, St. Anne was responsible for saving voyagers from shipwrecks in the harsh waters of the St. Lawrence. In 1650, Breton sailors caught in a storm vowed to erect a chapel in honor of this patron saint at the exact spot where they landed.

The present neo-Roman basilica, constructed in 1923, is the fifth to be built on the site where the sailors first touched ground. The original 17th-century wood chapel was built too close to the St. Lawrence and was swept away by river flooding.

The gigantic structure is in the shape of a Latin cross and has two imposing granite steeples. The interior has 22 chapels and 18 altars, as well as rounded arches and numerous ornaments in the Romanesque style. The 214 stained-glass windows, completed in 1949, are by Frenchmen Auguste Labouret and Pierre Chaudière.

Tributes to St. Anne can be seen in the shrine's mosaics, murals, altars, and ceilings. A bas-relief at the entrance depicts St. Anne welcoming her pilgrims, and ceiling mosaics represent her life. Numerous crutches and braces posted on the back pillars have been left by those who have felt the saint's healing

powers. ⊠ *10018 av. Royale, Ste-Anne-de-Beaupré* ☎ *418/827–3781* ⊕ *www.ssadb.qc.ca* ✉ *C$3 suggested donation.*

Chapelle Commémorative (*Memorial Chapel*)
RELIGIOUS BUILDING | Across from Basilique Ste-Anne-de-Beaupré, this chapel was designed by Claude Bailiff and built in 1878. It was constructed on the transept of a church built in 1676, and Bailiff made use of the old stones and foundation. Among the remnants is a white-and-gold-trimmed pulpit designed by François Baillargé in 1807 and adorned with a sculpture depicting Moses and the Ten Commandments.

Scala Santa, a smaller chapel next to this one, resembles a wedding cake. On bended knees, pilgrims climb its replica of the Holy Stairs, representing the steps Jesus climbed to meet Pontius Pilate. ⊠ *10018 av. Royale, Ste-Anne-de-Beaupré* ☎ *418/827–3781* ⊕ *www.sanctuaire-sainteanne.org.*

Chute Montmorency
NATURE SIGHT | The river cascading over a cliff into the St. Lawrence is one of the most beautiful sights in the province—and at 27 stories high, the falls are almost double the height of Niagara's. The Montmorency River was named for Charles de Montmorency, viceroy of New France in the 1620s and explorer Samuel de Champlain's immediate commander. A cable car runs to the top of the falls in Parc de la Chute-Montmorency (Montmorency Falls Park) from late April to late October. During very cold weather the falls' heavy spray freezes and forms a giant loaf-shaped ice cone known to the Québécois as the Pain du Sucre (Sugarloaf); this phenomenon attracts sledders and sliders from Québec City. Summer activities include three via ferrata trails built onto the cliff, as well as a zipline that shoots across the canyon, in front of the falls.

The park also has a history. The British General James Wolfe, on his way to

Montmorency Falls along the Côte-de-Beaupré might not be as wide, but it's nearly twice as tall as Niagara Falls.

conquer New France, camped here in 1759. In 1780, Sir Frederick Haldimand, then the governor of Canada, built a summer home atop the cliff. The structure burned down in 1993, however, and what stands today, Manoir Montmorency, is a re-creation. Offering a stunning view of the falls and river below, it's open year-round, with a restaurant and terrace open in summertime. ⊠ *2490 av. Royale, Beauport* ☎ *418/663–3330* ⊕ *www. sepaq.com/destinations/parc-chute-mont-morency* ⊠ *C$5.22 parking for non-resident; Cable car C$14.57.*

La Halte Miel

STORE/MALL | FAMILY | Things are buzzing at this workshop and store devoted to bees and honey. An exhibit explains every aspect of honey production, and you can taste honey and honey ice creams, chocolates, and snacks made by bees that have fed on different kinds of flowers, including clover and blueberry. It's a 10-minute drive east of Montmorency Falls. ⊠ *8862 boul.*

Ste-Anne, Château-Richer ☎ *418/824– 4411* ⊕ *www.naturoney.com/en/honey-place* ⊠ *Free.*

Réserve Faunique des Laurentides

NATIONAL PARK | The Réserve Faunique des Laurentides wildlife reserve, which incorporates the Parc national de la Jacques-Cartier and hundreds of lakes, is approximately 60 km (37 miles) north of Québec City via Highway 73, which leads to the Saguenay region. It has great hiking trails and camping spots, and good lakes for canoeing and fishing (but you should phone 48 hours in advance to reserve a fishing time.) From July to September, you can join bilingual guides to observe black bears in their natural environment from the safety of the park's observation towers. In winter, the park is a popular venue for sledding, snowshoeing, and cross-country skiing. ☎ *418/528– 6868, 418/890–6527 fishing reservations* ⊕ *www.sepaq.com/rf/lau.*

★ **Réserve Faunique du Cap Tourmente**
(*Cap Tourmente Wildlife Reserve*)
NATURE PRESERVE | FAMILY | Recognized as a Wetland of International Significance, this nature reserve protects a vital habitat for migrating greater snow geese, and sees more than a million fly through every October and May, with tens of thousands of birds present every day. The park harbors hundreds of other kinds of birds and mammals, and more than 700 plant species. This enclave also has 18 km (11 miles) of hiking trails; naturalists give guided tours. It's on the north shore of the St. Lawrence River, about 8 km (5 miles) east of Ste-Anne-de-Beaupré. ✉ *570 chemin du Cap Tourmente, St-Joachim* ☎ *418/827–4591* 🌐 *www.canada.ca/en/environment-climate-change/services/national-wildlife-areas/locations/cap-tourmente.html* 🎫 *C$6 summer. C$4 Winter.*

🍴 Restaurants

★ **Auberge Baker**
$$$$ | CANADIAN | The best of old and new blend at this restaurant in an 1840 French-Canadian farmhouse, built by the owners' ancestors, which lies east of Château-Richer toward Ste-Anne-de-Beaupré. Antiques and old-fashioned woodstoves decorate the dining rooms, where you can sample traditional Québec dishes, from *tourtière* (meat pie) and pork hocks to maple-sugar pie. **Known for:** sugar pies; French Canadian pea soup; tourtière. [$] *Average main: C$30* ✉ *8790 av. Royale, Château-Richer* ☎ *418/824–4478, 866/824–4478* 🌐 *www.aubergebaker.com.*

🏃 Activities

SPAS

Spa des neiges
SPAS | An *inukshuk* (Inuit stone marker) greets you at the entrance to this spa, set in elegant wood buildings right by the St. Lawrence River. Just the view, looking toward Île d'Orléans, is enough to relax anyone, but you can also enjoy the thermal baths (starting at C$40) or get one of many treatments, including massages, body wraps, mani-pedis, exfoliation, and light therapy. ✉ *9480 boul. Ste-Anne, Ste-Anne-de-Beaupré* ☎ *418/702–0631* 🌐 *www.spadesneiges.com.*

SKIING

Mont-Ste-Anne
BIKING | Part of the World Cup downhill circuit, Mont-Ste-Anne is one of the largest resorts in eastern Canada, with a vertical drop of 2,050 feet, 71 downhill trails, two half-pipes for snowboarders, a terrain park, and 13 lifts, including a gondola. The mountain stays active even after the sun goes down, with 19 lighted downhill trails. Cross-country skiing is also a draw here, with 21 trails totaling 224 km (139 miles). When the weather warms, mountain biking becomes the sport of choice. Enthusiasts can choose from 150 km (93 miles) of mountain-bike trails and 14 downhill runs (and a gondola up to the top). Three bike runs are designated "extreme zones." ✉ *2000 boul. du Beau-Pré, Beaupré* ☎ *418/827–4561, 888/827–4579* 🌐 *www.mont-sainte-anne.com* 🎫 *From C$92.*

Le Massif
SKIING & SNOWBOARDING | This three-peak ski resort has Canada's longest vertical drop east of the Rockies—2,526 feet. Owned by Daniel Gauthier, a cofounder of Cirque du Soleil, the resort has two multiservice chalets at the top and bottom. Six lifts and one gondola service the 53 trails, which are divided into runs for different levels; the longest run is 4.8 km (3 miles). There's also a section of expert glades. Non-skiers can go snowshoeing at the top of the mountain, and there is also an exciting, 7½-km (4¾-mile) sled trail. Equipment can be rented on-site, and the resort offers daycare for younger children and shuttles from Québec City, Beaupré, Baie-St-Paul, and the Montréal area. ✉ *1350 rue Principale, Petite-Rivière-St-François* ☎ *418/632–5876, 877/536–2774* 🌐 *www.lemassif.com.*

Baie-St-Paul is a charming small town popular with writers and artists. Each August it hosts a modern art show.

Baie-St-Paul

120 km (72 miles) northeast of Québec City.

Baie-St-Paul, one of the oldest towns in the province, is popular with craftspeople, artists, and foodies. With its centuries-old mansard-roof houses, the village is on the banks of a winding river, on a wide plain encircled by high hills—the crater of a large meteor that crashed to earth 350 million years ago. Boutiques and a handful of commercial galleries line the historic narrow streets in the town center; most have original artwork and crafts for sale. In addition, each August more than a dozen artists from across Canada take part in the Symposium of Modern Art.

GETTING HERE AND AROUND

By road, Baie-St-Paul is approximately 95 km (59 miles) northeast of Québec City via Route 440 and Route 138. Le Massif de Charlevoix train runs day trips from the Chutes-Montmorency station mid-June through early July Thursday through Sunday, then Wednesday through Sunday until mid-October. Departing at 9:10 am and including breakfast en route, it arrives in Baie-St-Paul at 11:45 am; the return journey, including dinner, leaves at 3 pm and arrives back at Chutes-Montmorency station at 4:45 pm. The fare is C$229 round-trip, plus C$60 for a guaranteed riverside seat.

◉ Sights

Maison d'affinage Maurice Dufour

FARM/RANCH | FAMILY | The Dufour family produces some of the best cheese in the region, made from the milk of the herds of sheep and cows that can be seen grazing around the property in the summer. A modern and elegant tasting room allows visitors to discover the various cheeses and find out more about production, and taste the fresh and fun wines that they make from local vines. They've even started distilling vodka and spirits from whey, a fun way to produce something delicious from cheese-making by-products. A restaurant called Les Faux Bergers, featuring lots of wood-fired dishes, is also on the premises. ✉ *1339 boul. Mgr de Laval, Baie-St-Paul* ☎ *418/435–5692* 🌐 *www.famillemigneron.com.*

Maison René Richard

ART GALLERY | Many of Québec's greatest landscape artists, including Jean-Paul Lemieux and Clarence Gagnon, have depicted the area, and a selection of these works is on show here (some are also for sale). The gallery was Gagnon's former studio and also the home of painter René Richard for the last 43 years of his life. Guided tours of the studio are available for groups. ✉ *58 rue St-Jean-Baptiste, Baie-St-Paul* ☎ *418/435–5571* 🌐 *www.grandquebec.com/charlevoix/maison-rene-richard* 🎫 *Free; call for group tour rates.*

Musée d'Art Contemporain de Baie-St-Paul

ART GALLERY | This museum highlights modern and contemporary art created by Charlevoix artists from 1920 to 1970. It also has a robust collection from the province in general, with works from Georges D. Pepper, Kathleen Daly, René Richard, the Bolduc sisters, and others. For more than 30 years, the museum has been organizing a yearly modern art symposium, held in late July and early August. ✉ *23 rue Ambroise-Fafard, Baie-St-Paul* ☎ *418/435–3681* 🌐 *www.macbsp.com* 🎫 *C$10.*

Hotels

Auberge à l'Ancrage

$$$ | **B&B/INN** | A restored 1920s redbrick home with antiques, a maritime theme, a wraparound porch, and a back garden that sits at the edge of the Gouffre River, Auberge à l'Ancrage is run by a charming couple who offer delicious, multicourse breakfasts and eagerly share information about activities and attractions in the area. **Pros:** riverside yard; quiet and privacy; only a few minutes' walk from downtown. **Cons:** pricey; inconsistent customer service; rooms are on the smaller side. [$] *Rooms from: C$229* ✉ *29 rue Ste-Anne, Baie-St-Paul* ☎ *418/240–3264* 🌐 *www.aubergeancrage.com* 🛏 *4 rooms* 🍴 *Free Breakfast.*

★ Hotel Le Germain Charlevoix

$$$$ | **HOTEL** | This stylish and modern hotel, owned by one of the best boutique hotel groups in Canada, consists of five distinct pavilions housing three eateries and rooms in various styles, including lofts and dormitories, all with contemporary finishes and elegant design. **Pros:** convenient location on public square with train station; farm-to-table cuisine in three on-site eateries; contemporary design. **Cons:** layout with multiple pavilions is a bit complicated; some rooms are small; inconsistent service. [$] *Rooms from: C$305* ✉ *50 rue de la Ferme, Baie-St-Paul* ☎ *418/240–4100, 877/536–2774* 🌐 *www.legermainhotels.com/en/charlevoix* 🛏 *152 rooms* 🍴 *No Meals.*

The Scenic Route

From Baie-St-Paul, instead of the faster Route 138 to La Malbaie, drivers can choose the open, scenic coastal drive on Route 362. This section of road has memorable views of charming villages and rolling hills—green, white, or ablaze with fiery hues, depending on the season—meeting the broad expanse of the "sea," as the locals like to call the St. Lawrence estuary.

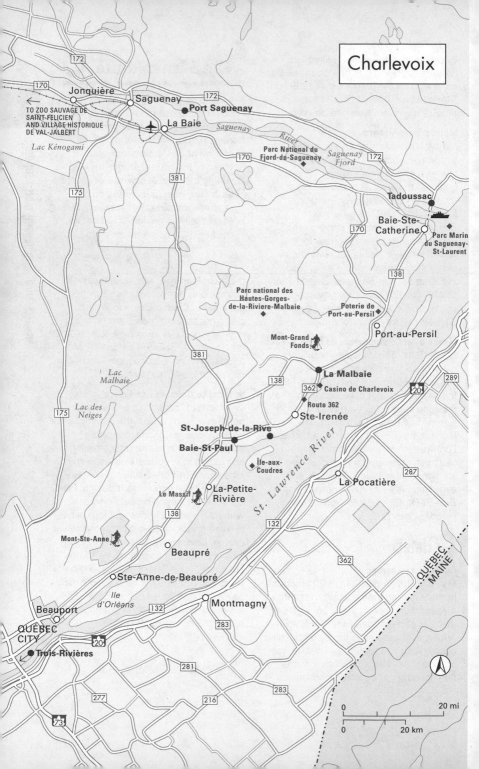

St-Joseph-de-la-Rive

20 km (12½ miles) northeast of Baie-St-Paul.

A secondary road descends sharply into St-Joseph-de-la-Rive, with its line of old houses hugging the mountain base on a narrow shore route. Enjoyed for its warm microclimate, the town features peaceful inns and inviting restaurants. Drive through and see the traces of early town life and the beginning of local industry: an old firehouse and a hydroelectric building that houses a generator dating back to 1928.

GETTING HERE AND AROUND

From Baie-St-Paul, drive northeast on rue Leclerc (Route 362).

Sights

Île-aux-Coudres

ISLAND | A free, government-run ferry from the wharf in St-Joseph-de-la-Rive takes you on the 15-minute trip to the island where Jacques Cartier's men gathered *coudres* (hazelnuts) in 1535. Since then, the island has produced many a *goélette* (a type of sailing ship), and the families of former captains now run several small inns. You can bike around the island and see windmills and water mills, or stop at the stores selling paintings and crafts, such as traditional handwoven household linens. ✉ *St-Joseph-de-la-Rive* ☎ *877/787–7483 ferry schedules* 🌐 *www.traversiers.com/en/our-ferries/lisle-aux-coudres-saint-joseph-de-la-rive-ferry/contact-information.*

Musée Maritime de Charlevoix
(*Maritime Museum*)

OTHER MUSEUM | This museum, housed in an old shipyard, commemorates the days of the St. Lawrence *goélettes*, the feisty little wooden freighters that were the chief means of transporting goods along the north shore of the St. Lawrence River well into the 1960s. Very large families lived in cramped conditions aboard the boats, some of which are part of the exhibits. To modern eyes, it doesn't look like a comfortable existence, but the folklore of the goélettes, celebrated in poetry, paintings, and song, is part of the region's strong cultural identity. ✉ *305 rue de l'Église, St-Joseph-de-la-Rive* ☎ *418/635–1131* 🌐 *www.museemaritime.com* 🎟 *C$11.*

Hotels

Hôtel Cap-aux-Pierres

$ | **HOTEL** | New ownership invested in a substantial renovation of the Cap-aux-Pierres, and the rooms now have a modern and stylish décor and many have river views. **Pros:** good food; indoor and outdoor pools; beautiful environment. **Cons:** restaurant is a little pricey; rooms are somewhat outdated; no air-conditioning. [$] *Rooms from: C$159* ✉ *444 chemin la Baleine, Île-aux-Coudres, St-Joseph-de-la-Rive* ☎ *888/554–6003, 418/438–2711* 🌐 *www.hotelcapauxpierres.com* 🕒 *Closed mid-Oct.–Apr.* 🛏 *98 rooms* 🍴 *Free Breakfast.*

Shopping

BOOKS

Papeterie Saint-Gilles

STATIONERY | This paper factory produces handcrafted stationery using a 17th-century process. There's also a small museum, which explains through photographs and demonstrations how paper is manufactured the old-fashioned way. Slivers of wood and flower petals are pressed into the paper sheets, which are as thick as the covers of a paperback book. The finished products—made into writing paper, greeting cards, and one-page poems or quotations—make beautiful, if pricey, gifts. Visitors can wander through the museum for free, and guided tours can be arranged for groups. ✉ *354 rue F.A. Savard, St-Joseph-de-la-Rive* ☎ *418/635–2430, 866/635–2430* 🌐 *www.papeteriesaintgilles.com.*

La Malbaie

35 km (22 miles) northeast of St-Joseph-de-la-Rive.

La Malbaie, one of the province's most elegant and historically interesting resort towns, was known as Murray Bay when wealthy Anglophones summered here. The area became popular with American and Canadian politicians in the late 1800s, when Ottawa Liberals and Washington Republicans partied decorously all summer with members of the Québec bourgeoisie. William Howard Taft built the "summer White House," the first of three summer residences, in 1894, when he was the American civil governor of the Philippines. He became the 27th president of the United States in 1908.

Many Taft-era homes now serve as handsome inns, offering old-fashioned coddling with such extras as breakfast in bed, whirlpool baths, and free shuttles to the ski areas in winter. Many serve lunch and dinner to nonresidents, so you can tour the area going from one great French or Québécois meal to the next.

GETTING HERE AND AROUND

Even if you don't want to visit St-Joseph-de-la-Rive, Route 362 between Baie-St-Paul and La Malbaie is much more scenic and well worth the extra half hour it adds to the trip from Québec City. Le Train de Charlevoix offers a day trip to La Malbaie Thursday through Sunday from mid-June to early July and Wednesday through Sunday until mid-October. It departs Chute Montmorency station at 9:10 am, with a stop en route at Baie-St-Paul; the round-trip takes 11 hours including time to get off and explore, and the fare, including breakfast and a four-course dinner, is C$369 (plus C$60 for a guaranteed riverside seat).

◉ Sights

Casino de Charlevoix

CASINO | The casino is one of four gaming halls in Québec (the others are in Montréal, Gatineau, and Mont-Tremblant) owned and operated by Loto-Québec. Charlevoix's, the smallest of the lot, still draws around 800,000 visitors a year—some of whom stay at the Fairmont Le Manoir Richelieu, which is connected to the casino by a tunnel. Largely renovated in 2016, it offers 21 gaming tables and more than 800 slot machines. The minimum gambling age is 18, and a photo ID is required to enter the casino. ⊠ *183 rue Richelieu, Pointe-au-Pic* 📞 *418/665–5300, 800/665–2274* ⊕ *casinos.lotoquebec. com/fr/charlevoix/accueil.*

Musée de Charlevoix

HISTORY MUSEUM | The museum traces the region's history through a major permanent exhibit. Folk art, paintings, and artifacts help reveal the past, starting with the French, then the Scottish settlers, and the area's evolution into a vacation spot and artists' haven. Temporary exhibits change every season. ⊠ *10 chemin du Havre, La Malbaie* 📞 *418/665–4411* ⊕ *www.museedecharlevoix.qc.ca* ⊠ *C$8.*

Parc national des Hautes-Gorges-de-la-Rivière-Malbaie

NATIONAL PARK | **FAMILY** | A 40-minute drive from La Malbaie will bring you to a stunning stretch of the Malbaie River, surrounded by impressive steep slopes and rocky peaks. There are plenty of beautiful views to take in—whether it's from a kayak on the river or while hiking a network of trails—and lots of fresh air, in this central part of the Charlevoix Biosphere Preserve. ⊠ *25 boul. Notre-Dame, Clermont, La Malbaie* 📞 *418/439–1227* ⊕ *www.sepaq.com/pq/hgo* ⊠ *Park access, daily: C$9. Camping from C$24 per night.*

A hiker takes in the view of an ancient glacial valley in Parc national des Hautes-Gorges-de-la-Rivière-Malbaie.

☕ Coffee and Quick Bites

Pains d'exclamation

$ | **BAKERY** | **FAMILY** | This lively café-and-bakery offers a wide variety of classic and unique pastries and breads (hello, preserved-lemon bread!), sandwiches and quick breakfast and lunch options. It's a favorite with locals, who either eat in or take out after a quick chat with the friendly staff. **Known for:** quick, delicious lunches; great pastries; patio dining. $ *Average main: C$10* ⊠ *398 rue Saint-Étienne, Pointe-au-Pic* ☎ *418/665–4000* ⊕ *www.painsdexclamation.com* ⊘ *Closed Sun. and Mon.*

🛏 Hotels

Auberge des Peupliers

$ | **B&B/INN** | About half the guest rooms at this hilltop inn overlook the St. Lawrence River, and the country-style accommodations are spread among three buildings, including a farmhouse more than two centuries old. **Pros:** scenic location; lounge with fireplace and bar perfect for relaxing; excellent service. **Cons:** complaints of average food at a high price in the restaurant; some rooms may not have air conditioning; need to drive to downtown La Malbaie. $ *Rooms from: C$156* ⊠ *381 rue St-Raphaël, La Malbaie* ☎ *418/665–4423, 888/282–3743* ⊕ *www.aubergedespeupliers.com/en/charlevoix-hotel/home* ⊅ *22 rooms* ⧒ *Free Breakfast.*

Chez Truchon Bistro Auberge

$$ | **B&B/INN** | Located in a quiet neighborhood within easy walking distance to the heart of La Malbaie, the Auberge Chez Truchon is a distinctively elegant inn that was originally constructed in 1902. **Pros:** friendly, professional service; beautiful historic building; above an excellent bistro. **Cons:** the rooms along the second floor veranda are less private; some rooms don't have river views; some guests on the lower floors have complained about noise from the restaurant below. $ *Rooms from: C$135* ⊠ *1065 rue Richelieu, La Malbaie*

☎ *888/662–4622, 418/665–4622 bistro* 🌐 *www.aubergecheztruchon.com* 🛏 *9 rooms* 🍴 *No Meals.*

Fairmont Le Manoir Richelieu
$$$$ | **RESORT** | **FAMILY** | Linked to the Casino de Charlevoix by tunnel, this castle-like building and its sweeping grounds come with stunning views and some great sports and leisure facilities. **Pros:** variety of dining options on-site; good for families, with kids' club, kids' menu, and babysitting; scenic location. **Cons:** complaints of inadequate amount of and attitude of staff; not the best room service; some rooms could use updating. [$] *Rooms from: C$310* ✉ *181 rue Richelieu, Pointe-au-Pic* ☎ *418/665–3703, 800/463–2613* 🌐 *www.fairmont.com/richelieu-charlevoix* 🛏 *422 rooms* 🍴 *Free Breakfast.*

Performing Arts

Domaine Forget
MUSIC | This music and dance academy has a 604-seat hall in Ste-Irenée, 15 km (9 miles) south of La Malbaie. Musicians from around the world, many of whom teach or study at the school, perform during its International Festival. The festival, which runs from mid-June to late August, includes Sunday brunches with music, a buffet, and a view of the St. Lawrence. Some weekend concerts are also held in the fall and spring. ✉ *5 rang St-Antoine, St-Irénée* ☎ *418/452–3535, 888/336–7438* 🌐 *www.domaineforget.com.*

Activities

GOLF

★ Club de Golf Fairmont Le Manoir Richelieu
GOLF | Be warned: if you play this course, you'll have to work hard to focus on the game and not the gorgeous scenery overlooking the St. Lawrence River. Originally established in 1925 and recently restored and expanded, this is a links-style course with three 9-hole courses that offers quite a bit of challenge, thanks to the design (the fairways are relatively wide but feature a number of strategically placed bunkers, trees, and mounds) and to the course's hilltop undulations. ✉ *181 rue Richelieu, Pointe-au-Pic* ☎ *418/665–2526, 800/665–8082* 🌐 *www.fairmont.com/richelieu-charlevoix/golf/club-de-golf-fairmont-le-manoir-richelieu/* 🎫 *From C$65* 🏌 *St-Laurent Course: 9 holes, 3178 yards, par 36; Richelieu Course: 9 holes, 3148 yards, par 36; Tadoussac Course: 9 holes, 2918 yards, par 35* ☞ *Facilities: driving range, putting green, golf carts, rental clubs, restaurant, bar.*

SKIING

Mont-Grand Fonds
SKIING & SNOWBOARDING | This winter-sports center 12 km (7 miles) north of La Malbaie has 20 downhill slopes (including four recently opened glades in an area called The Lynx), an 1,105-foot vertical drop, and three lifts. It also has 184 km (113 miles) of cross-country trails. Two trails meet International Ski Federation standards, and the ski center occasionally hosts major competitions. You can also go dog sledding, sleigh riding, ice-skating, and tobogganing here. ✉ *1000 chemin des Loisirs, La Malbaie* ☎ *418/665–0095, 877/665–0095* 🌐 *www.montgrandfonds.com* 🎫 *Full day tickets: C$58.*

Tadoussac

71 km (44 miles) north of La Malbaie.

Most people come to Tadoussac for the whale-watching excursions and cruises along the magnificent Saguenay Fjord. Beluga whales, highly recognizable because of their all-white color, small size, and high-pitch call, live here year-round and breed in the lower portion of the Saguenay in summer. The many marine species that live at the confluence of the fjord and the seaway

In Tadoussac from May to October, you can see whales living in the Saguenay River.

attract other whales, too, such as pilots, finbacks, and humpbacks.

Sadly, the beluga is endangered; the whales, together with 35 other species of mammals and birds and 21 species of fish, are threatened by pollution in the St. Lawrence River. This has spurred a C\$100 million project (funded by the federal and provincial governments) aimed at removing or capping sediment in the most polluted areas, stopping industrial and residential emissions into the river, and restoring natural habitat. There's still much work to be done, but greater attention is being given to this unique ecosystem, now a National Marine Conservation Area.

The short drive here from La Malbaie leads past lovely villages and views along the St. Lawrence. Jacques Cartier made a stop at this point in 1535, and from 1600 to the mid-19th century it was an important meeting site for fur traders. As the Saguenay River flows south from Lac St-Jean, it has a dual character: between Alma and Chicoutimi, the once rapidly flowing river has been harnessed for hydroelectric power; in its lower section, it becomes wider and deeper and flows by steep mountains and cliffs en route to the St. Lawrence.

GETTING HERE AND AROUND
From La Malbaie, drive northeast on Route 138. You must take a free 10-minute ferry ride from Baie-Ste-Catherine to get to Tadoussac. The ferries leave every 20 minutes, from 4 am to midnight, then every half hour until 4 am. For more information on ferry schedules, call *418/643–2019.*

VISITOR INFORMATION
CONTACT Tourist Information Center Tadoussac. ⊠ *197 rue des Pionniers, Tadoussac* ☎ *418/235–4744, 866/235–4744.*

Sights

Centre d'Interprétation des Mammifères Marins

VISITOR CENTER | You can learn more about the whales and their habitat at this interpretation center run by a locally based research team. They're only too glad to answer questions. In addition, explanatory videos and exhibits (including a collection of whale skeletons) serve as a good introduction to the mighty, but endangered cetaceans. ✉ *108 rue de la Cale-Sèche, Tadoussac* ☎ *418/235–4701* 🌐 *www.baleinesendirect.org/en* 🎟 *C$15.*

Parc Marin du Saguenay–St-Laurent

NATURE PRESERVE | The 800-square-km (309-square-mile) marine park, at the confluence of the Saguenay and St. Lawrence rivers, has been created to protect this marine area's three fragile ecosystems. ✉ *Park office, 182 rue de l'Église, Tadoussac* ☎ *418/235–4703, 888/773–8888* 🌐 *parcmarin.qc.ca/home.*

Hotels

Hôtel Tadoussac

$$$ | **HOTEL** | **FAMILY** | A stunning natural environment and the 1942 Victorian-style building make this an equally great choice for an active or romantic stay. **Pros:** good spa; views over the bay; summer kids' club with day care. **Cons:** walls very thin; a little pricey for largely unrenovated rooms; no air-conditioning in rooms. [$] *Rooms from: C$240* ✉ *165 rue du Bord de l'Eau, Tadoussac* ☎ *418/235–4421, 800/561–0718* 🌐 *www.hoteltadoussac.com* 🕒 *Closed Nov.–mid-May* 🛏 *149 rooms* 🍴 *Free Breakfast.*

Activities

WHALE-WATCHING

The best months for seeing whales are August and September, although some operators extend the season at either end if whales are around. Fjord tours are also available.

Croisières AML

WILDLIFE-WATCHING | This outfitter offers two- and three-hour whale-watching cruises starting at C$84.99. The tours, in Zodiacs or larger boats, depart from Tadoussac pier. Tours of the Saguenay Fjord are available, and you can also take a daylong excursion on a chartered bus from Québec City, including a three-hour whale-watching cruise. ✉ *Tadoussac* ☎ *418/692–1159, 800/463–1292* 🌐 *www.croisieresaml.com.*

Port Saguenay

This seaport is appreciated more for its natural beauty than for its shipping industry. Although it's interesting to see the big vessels and the huge equipment used to load and unload them, the scenes simply can't compete with the surrounding wilderness of cliffs, fjords, and the bare rock faces of the Canadian shield, not to mention the whales that inhabit the waters seasonally.

Sights

★ **Parc National du Fjord-du-Saguenay**

NATURE SIGHT | Colossal rock cliffs and forest-covered mountains meet the still waters of the Saguenay Fjord, one of the longest in the world, and the namesake national park runs its entire 105-km (65-mile) length. Of the park's three regions, the Baie-Éternité, which hosts the visitor center, is about 60 km (37 miles) south of the city of Saguenay, where you can visit the Fjord Museum (Musée du Fjord). Outdoor enthusiasts have much to do here, including kayaking, fishing, hiking, camping, bird-watching, whale-watching, and mountain biking, and the park can supply equipment and guides. The spectacular Baie-Éternité escarpments provide thrilling climbs and a via ferrata. Or you can take it easy on sailboat and sightseeing boat cruises, or enjoy a thrilling whale-watching experience.

☎ 418/272–1556 🌐 *www.sepaq.com/pq/sag/index.dot?language_id=1* 🎫 *C$9.*

★ Village historique de Val-Jalbert
MUSEUM VILLAGE | FAMILY | Powerful Ouiatchouan Falls, higher than Niagara Falls, overlook and long ago powered this once thriving mill town. Ultramodern in its day, the village had electricity and running water 25 years before the rest of Québec, but administrative and production pitfalls closed the mill and by 1927 all the residents had departed. Today, you can see the beautifully restored mill, post office, general store, and butcher shop, then hike to the top of the falls, where a glass platform puts you directly over the center of the cascade. Modern accommodations are available within the general store and some restored period houses, and campgrounds and rustic cottages to rent are other options. ✉ *95 rue St.-Georges, Chambord* ☎ *418/275–3132* 🌐 *valjalbert.com/en* 🎫 *C$31.*

★ Zoo Sauvage de Saint-Felicien
ZOO | FAMILY | Cougars, polar bears, grizzly bears, Canadian lynx, American bison, and Japanese macaques are among the 75 species that roam open environments here. Between June and October, guides lead overnight tours in The Land of the Caribou, including hiking, a campfire meal, and canoeing on Lac Montagnais, where caribou may swim right by your boat. ✉ *2230 boul. du Jardin, St-Félicien* ☎ *418/679–0543* 🌐 *zoosauvage.org/en* 🎫 *C$20; Land of the Caribou tour C$382.*

🍴 Restaurants

Le Restaurant La Cuisine
$$$ | ECLECTIC | World cuisines influence chefs who are well-versed in French techniques and fond of using local ingredients. Thai cuisine inspires five-spice chicken with cashew nuts, rice noodles, vegetables, and sweet chili sauce; a taste of Italy is clearly evident in the veal flank with mushrooms, truffle oil, and Parmesan risotto. **Known for:** good selection of beer and wine; local produce; chic décor. [$] *Average main: C$30* ✉ *387 rue Racine E, Chicoutimi* ☎ *418/698–2822* 🌐 *www.restaurantlacuisine.ca* 🕘 *No lunch weekends.*

Rouge Burger Bar
$$ | BURGER | Towering gourmet burgers are made exactly to order with a choice of lamb, chicken, salmon, local beef, or a vegetarian patty. Dress it up with one of several cheeses (maybe fresh chevre), various garnishes (how about caramelized onions and smoked bacon?), and a range of sauces (a dab of citrus tarragon mayonnaise?). **Known for:** several TVs make it perfect for sports fans; their own line of barbecue and other sauces; popular so reservations necessary. [$] *Average main: C$12* ✉ *460 rue Racine E, Chicoutimi* ☎ *418/690–5029* 🌐 *www.rougeburgerbar.ca* 🕘 *Closed Mon. and Tues.*

☕ Coffee and Quick Bites

Boucherie Davis Ltee
$ | CANADIAN | Come hungry—really hungry—to this foodie destination, where the full-service, family butcher shop dating back to 1943 also hosts a café and gourmet food market featuring locally made artisanal products. Tuck into a thick rib steak with a local *saison* beer, select from the hot and cold buffets, or go for the "menu of the day" and watch butchers in action as you dine. **Known for:** wide variety of products available for purchase on-site; high-quality produce and products; warm welcoming environment. [$] *Average main: C$20* ✉ *1959 rue Davis, Jonquière* ☎ *418/548–5243* 🌐 *www.boucheriedavis.com* 💳 *No credit cards.*

🛏 Hotels

Auberge de la Riviere Saguenay
$ | B&B/INN | Set on a slope overlooking the Saguenay Fjord, this lovely inn is a fine launching place for waterway or mountain adventures. **Pros:** beach

access; most rooms have stunning fjord views; convenient base for exploring. **Cons:** breakfast is not included; décor is a little dated; no air-conditioning. [$] *Rooms from: C$129* ✉ *9122 chemin de la Batture, La Baie* ☎ *418/697–0222, 866/697–0222 toll-free number* 🌐 *www.aubergesaguenay.com* 💳 *No credit cards* 🛏 *15 rooms* 🍴 *No Meals.*

★ Gite Du Haut des Arbres

$ | **B&B/INN** | With nine tastefully decorated modern rooms in a spectacular setting overlooking the fjord, this family-owned and operated "gite" is a nature lover's paradise located less than 10 minutes from the center of Chicoutimi. **Pros:** modern rooms; beautiful grounds; swimming pool. **Cons:** small parking spaces; can be noisy; no commercial establishments within walking distance. [$] *Rooms from: C$119* ✉ *Gite Du Haut des Arbres, 744 Rue Du Ruisseau-Lachance, Chicoutimi* ☎ *418/306–1963* 🌐 *www.giteduhautdesarbres.com* 🛏 *9 rooms* 🍴 *No Meals.*

Motel Panoramique

$ | **MOTEL** | Set back from the road and nestled along the banks of the Saguenay river just 4 kilometers from downtown Chicoutimi, Motel Panoramique is a pleasant, unassuming motel that feels a world away from the hustle and bustle of the nearby city. **Pros:** great value; friendly service; excellent location. **Cons:** the rooms in the front of the establishment are off of a busy road; rooms on ground floor may lack privacy; some rooms may feel outdated. [$] *Rooms from: C$109* ✉ *Boulevard du Saguenay Ouest, 1303, Chicoutimi* ☎ *418/549–7102, 418/590–7455* 🌐 *www.motelpanoramique.ca* 🛏 *54 rooms* 🍴 *No Meals.*

Shopping

Bons Délices et Péchés

CHOCOLATE | Chocolatiers here make truffles, cream-filled chocolates, spirits-spiked bonbons, chocolate-dipped ice cream in chocolate-dipped cones and dark, white, and milk chocolate. Fancy cookies and custom cakes are sold, too. ✉ *244 rue La Fontaine, Chicoutimi* ☎ *418/545–1660.*

Domaine de la Savonnière

OTHER SPECIALTY STORE | **FAMILY** | Herbs, flowers, fruit, spices, and essential oils are used to make soaps prepared on the premises. The soap maker is usually in and happy to explain the process and answer questions about the soaps' healthful properties. Soap-making workshops are available for adults and kids. ✉ *3289 boul. de la Grande-Baie Sud, La Baie* ☎ *418/544–8484.*

Trois-Rivières

Where the Rivière St. Maurice divides into three channels, the town that grew up around it came to be known as Trois-Rivières (Three Rivers). Today it's a busy industrial hub but still retains pleasant shady streets and historical sites; a bygone iron and steel mill are worth a look. The town is also a good base for exploring the waterfalls and rock faces of the Parc National de la Mauricie, just 64 km (40 miles) away.

Sights

Boréalis

FACTORY | **FAMILY** | Back when Trois-Rivieres was a lumber, paper, and pulp industry leader, this plant's machinery whizzed and whirled. Built in the early 1920s, it pumped, filtered, and stored water for the paper mill. By the mid-1950s, the plant filtered more than 20 million gallons of water a day that was used to produce 1,000 tons of newsprint. Today, it is eerily quiet, especially the long-abandoned underground vaults, which are part of the original architecture and machinery that's on display. ✉ *200 av. des Draveur, Trois-Rivieres* ☎ *819/372–4633* 🌐 *www.borealis3r.ca* 🎫 *C$15.*

Sanctuaire Notre-Dame-du-Cap

RELIGIOUS BUILDING | Built in 1955, on the site of earlier churches dating back to 1659, this is Canada's national shrine to Notre Dame (Our Blessed Mother) and an important pilgrimage site. As impressive as the great European cathedrals, this white granite, octagonal building hosts up to 1,660 people, and its lofty dome is topped by a pyramid and cross 258 feet above the ground. Reinforced concrete arches outline the building. Five bells ring A, Bb, D, F, and G notes, and the sanctuary's organ has 5,425 pipes. Inside, the altar is a single block of marble, and nary a pillar blocks views of magnificent architecture and stained glass masterpieces. ✉ *626 rue Notre-Dame E, Trois-Rivieres* ☎ *819/374–2441* 🌐 *www.sanctuaire-ndc.ca* 🎫 *Free.*

Vieille Prison de Trois-Rivières

JAIL/PRISON | Dating to the early 1800s, this was the oldest continuously operating prison in Canada prior to its closure in 1986. The stark, stone structure with thick bars on the windows makes it clear that nobody is getting out. Originally built to house 40 inmates, the facility at times hosted up to 100 convicted criminals. If only the old doors and cedar basement joists could talk, what tales of mayhem might they tell? Tour guides share a few. The prison is attached to the Musée Québécois de Culture Populaire. The museum's collection of more than 70,000 objects, plus traveling and changing exhibitions, showcase Québec's history and culture, including crime and prison life. ✉ *200 rue Laviolette, Trois-Rivieres* ☎ *819/372–0406* 🌐 *www.culturepop.qc.ca* 🎫 *C$17 for jail; C$15 for museum; C$24 combined ticket.*

🍴 Restaurants

Le Sacristain

$$ | ECLECTIC | What was once a Wesleyan church has become a sanctuary for salads and grilled sandwiches. Ingredients stretch beyond ham and cheese; choose capers, smoked salmon, grilled mango, and hearts of palm. **Known for:** unique location in a converted church; great stop between Montréal and Québec City; English-speaking staff. [$] *Average main: C$15* ✉ *300 rue Bonaventure, Trois-Rivieres* ☎ *819/694–1344* 🌐 *www.lesacristain.ca* 🕒 *No dinner.*

Poivre Noir

$$$$ | FRENCH | Sleek and modern, this friendly restaurant hits all the right spots—it's devoted to local ingredients and its dining room and deck overlook the St. Lawrence River. While the menu items is constantly evolving, expect creative plates: bison tartar, pickled mushrooms and salt foie gras; sablefish, lime mousseline, and clementine white butter; and savarin, elderberry, and white chocolate Chantilly as dessert. **Known for:** accommodating to food allergies; creative cocktails; outside bar and terrasse overlooking the St-Lawrence. [$] *Average main: C$35* ✉ *1300 rue du Fleuve, Trois-Rivieres* ☎ *819/378–5772* 🌐 *www.poivrenoir.com* 🕒 *Closed Sun.–Tues. No lunch.*

Restaurant le St-Antoine

$$$ | BISTRO | This family-owned restaurant is rooted in French classics but has a taste for pizza and pasta, too. Escargots, steak tartare, veal scallops with mushroom cream sauce, grilled steaks, and various steamed mussel presentations join numerous Italian-style linguini dishes including alfredo, Bolognese, and carbonara. **Known for:** pleasant terrasse; bring-your-own alcoholic beverage; seafood and pasta dishes. [$] *Average main: C$22* ✉ *151 rue St.-Antoine, Trois-Rivieres* ☎ *819/378–6420* 🌐 *www.lestantoine.ca* 💳 *No credit cards* 🕒 *Closed Mon. and Tues. No lunch.*

Hotels

Motel Canadien
$ | **HOTEL** | A nice cross between a hotel and an inn, the rooms are not fancy but well-appointed and clean, and the innkeepers are friendly and helpful. **Pros:** electric fireplaces in rooms; free Wi-Fi; air-conditioning. **Cons:** interior design feels dated; small rooms; 50% deposit required when booking. [$] *Rooms from: C$105* ✉ *1821 rue Notre-Dame E, Trois-Rivieres* ☎ *819/375–5542* 🌐 *www.motelcanadien.ca* 💳 *No credit cards* 🛏 *10 rooms* 🍴 *Free Breakfast.*

Motel le Marquis
$ | **HOTEL** | **FAMILY** | On the historic Chemin de Roy linking Québec to Montréal, this motel offers comfortable, good value close to attractions like the charming sanctuary and lovely gardens of Ste-Marthe-du-Cap church. **Pros:** free Wi-Fi; family-friendly; hearty breakfast. **Cons:** few decorative touches; small rooms; innkeepers don't speak much English. [$] *Rooms from: C$85* ✉ *989 rue Notre-Dame E, Trois-Rivieres* ☎ *819/378–7130* 💳 *No credit cards* 🛏 *12 rooms* 🍴 *Free Breakfast.*

Shopping

Cabane à Sucre Chez Dany
OTHER SPECIALTY STORE | **FAMILY** | Maple syrup, maple taffy, maple candy, maple everything—when it's "sugaring time" in Québec, this shack is busy. Visitors get to not only purchase the fruits of this labor, they may also see how maple sap becomes syrup and how to make taffy in the snow. There's an all-you-can-eat restaurant with a maple-centric menu, and live music of the region. ✉ *195 rue de la Sablière, Trois-Rivieres* ☎ *819/370–4769* 🌐 *www.cabanechezdany.com.*

Les Jardins Dugré
FOOD | Just a few minutes from downtown, the Dugré family tends a large vegetable farm. Besides selling their own berries, asparagus, and sweet corn, among other produce, the farm market offers various other local choices, including baked goods, cheeses, jams, pickles, honey, vinaigrettes, fresh pasta, maple products, and more. Arrive in the right season and you may pick your own strawberries. ✉ *3861 rang St-Charles, Trois-Rivieres* ☎ *819/377–3108* 🌐 *www.fermegagnon.com/lesjardinsdugre.*

Photo Credits

Front Cover: Walter Bibikow/ Getty Images [Description: Canada, Quebec, Mont Tremblant Ski Village, dusk -Located in the Laurentians] **Back cover, from left to right:** Simon Eizner/ Shutterstock, Songquan Deng/ Shutterstock, Marc Bruxelle/ Shutterstock. **Spine:** Pierre Lecrerc/Shutterstock. **Interior, from left to right:** Pinkcandy/Shutterstock (1). iPIX Stock/Shutterstock (2-3). **Chapter 1: Experience Montréal and Québec City:** Pierre Leclerc/ Shutterstock (6-7). Susanne Pommer/Shutterstock (8). Kristi Blokhin/Shutterstock (9). Carnaval de Québec (9). J.schultes/Dreamstime (10). Rabbit75/Dreamstime (10). Kristi Blokhin/ Shutterstock (10). Wickedgood/Dreamstime (10). Jiawangkun/Dreamstime (11). Rob Crandall/ Shutterstock (11). Kristi Blokhin/Shutterstock (12) Rabbit75/Dreamstime (12). Dennizn/ Dreamstime (12). Bill_comstock/Flickr, [CCC BY 2.0] (12). Benoit Daoust / Shutterstock (13). William Manning / Alamy Stock Photo (13). Stephane Audet (13). Rabbit75/Dreamstime (13). Mbruxelle/Dreamstime (14). Cybernesco/Dreamstime (14). Beaustock/Dreamstime (14). Bigjohn3650/ Dreamstime (14). Jiawangkun/Dreamstime (15). Michael L Brown/Shutterstock (18). Georges Alexandar Hashtag Media/ Juliette & Chocolat (Plateau) (18). Vsl/Shutterstock (18). Caroline Perron (19). Jen Lobo/iStockphoto (19). Eva Blue / Montréal Tourism (20). Charles Prot (21). Alexi Hobbs (22). Marie / Reine Mattera (22). Dylan Stewart Page/Sibéria Spa (22). Spa Bolton (22). Balnea Spa and Réserve Thermale (23). Grogl/ Shutterstock (23). Bianca Des Jardins/Strøm Nordic Spa (23). Bianca Des Jardins/ Strøm spa nordique (23). Andriy Blokhin/Shutterstock (24). iPIX Stock/Shutterstock (24). Kristi Blokhin/Shutterstock (24). Maridav/Shutterstock (24). Mathieu Dupuis (25). **Chapter 3: Montréal:** Griffinyx/Dreamstime (61). Felix Lipov/Shutterstock (73). Studio du Ruisseau (75). Vlad2003/ Dreamstime (91). Louriv/Dreamstime (93). Le Mount Stephen (104). Canadian Tourism Commission (112). Benoit Aquin (125). Quartier des spectacles, Martine Doyon (129). Tourisme Montréal, Stéphan Poulin (148). C.I.I.O/iStockphoto (151). Bakerjarvis/Dreamstime (155). Sandyprints/ Dreamstime (161). Meunierd/Shutterstock (165). Ververidis Vasilis/Shutterstock (171). **Chapter 4: Side Trips from Montréal:** Vlad G/Shutterstock (173). Design Pics Inc/ Alamy Stock Photo (181). Hadimor/iStockphoto (188-189). Benoit Aquin (194). Mustafa Quraish/Shutterstock (205). **Chapter 5: Québec City:** Edwin Tseng/Shutterstock (207). Mervas/Shutterstock (217). Meunierd/Shutterstock (221). Rusty426/Dreamstime (231). Emperorcosar/ Shutterstock (237). Andriy Blokhin/Shutterstock (238). Chris Cheadle / Alamy Stock Photo (240). Photorebelle/ Dreamstime (254). **Chapter 6: Side Trips from Quebec City:** Magnus L/Shutterstock (263). Brizardh/Dreamstime (271). Melanie Marln (275). Kavram/Shutterstock (278). Sebastienlemyre/ Shutterstock (280). Julien Robitaille / Alamy (285). Sylvie Bouchard/Shutterstock (287). **About Our Writers:** All photos are courtesy of the writers except for the following: Chris Barry/ credit: Mark Bouchett.

*Every effort has been made to trace the copyright holders, and we apologize in advance for any accidental errors. We would be happy to apply the corrections in the following edition of this publication.

Notes

Notes

Notes

Fodor's MONTRÉAL & QUÉBEC CITY

Publisher: Stephen Horowitz, *General Manager*

Editorial: Douglas Stallings, *Editorial Director;* Jill Fergus, Amanda Sadlowski, Caroline Trefler, *Senior Editors*; Kayla Becker, Alexis Kelly, *Editors;* Angelique Kennedy-Chavannes, *Assistant Editor*

Design: Tina Malaney, *Director of Design and Production*; Jessica Gonzalez, *Graphic Designer*

Production: Jennifer DePrima, *Editorial Production Manager;* Elyse Rozelle, *Senior Production Editor;* Monica White, *Production Editor*

Maps: Rebecca Baer, *Senior Map Editor;* Mark Stroud (Moon Street Cartography), *Cartographer*

Photography: Viviane Teles, *Senior Photo Editor;* Namrata Aggarwal, Payal Gupta, Ashok Kumar, *Photo Editors;* Eddie Aldrete, *Photo Production Intern*

Business and Operations: Chuck Hoover, *Chief Marketing Officer;* Robert Ames, *Group General Manager;* Devin Duckworth, *Director of Print Publishing*

Public Relations and Marketing: Joe Ewaskiw, *Senior Director of Communications and Public Relations*

Fodors.com: Jeremy Tarr, *Editorial Director;* Rachael Levitt, *Managing Editor*

Technology: Jon Atkinson, *Director of Technology;* Rudresh Teotia, *Lead Developer;* Jacob Ashpis, *Content Operations Manager*

Writers: Chris Barry, Marie-Eve Vallieres, Elizabeth Warkentin, Barbara Woolsey

Editor: Angelique Kennedy-Chavannes

Production Editor: Monica White

Production Design: Jessica Gonzalez

31st edition

ISBN 978-1-64097-502-6

ISSN 1525-5867

SPECIAL SALES
This book is available at special discounts for bulk purchases for sales promotions or premiums. For more information, e-mail SpecialMarkets@fodors.com.

PRINTED IN CANADA

10 9 8 7 6 5 4

MIX
Paper from
responsible sources
FSC® C016245

About Our Writers

 Chris Barry is a native Montrealer and freelance journalist who has contributed to scores of publications over the years and has been writing for the *Fodor's Montréal and Québec City* guide since 2002. He's currently finishing a book documenting his years as a professional rock-and-roll musician in the 1970s, '80s, and '90s.

 Marie-Eve Vallieres Born and raised in Montréal, Marie-Eve Vallieres knows the city like the back of her hand, despite that it is constantly evolving. Marie-Eve has written for *AFAR Magazine,* Expedia Canada, and Viator, and she has been interviewed regularly on CBC Radio One. Check out her blog, To Europe And Beyond, at www.toeuropeandbeyond.com.

 Elizabeth Warkentin is a freelance writer who was born and raised in Montréal and is enjoying getting reacquainted with her native city after a 20-year absence. She is an avid photographer and freelance journalist and has contributed to a variety of publications including BBC Travel, the *Boston Globe,* the *Toronto Star,* and the *Vancouver Sun.*

 Barbara Woolsey is a Canadian journalist who's trekked across the world by plane, train, and motorbike. She currently spends most of her time in Berlin, producing for Reuters TV and contributing to publications such as *The Guardian, The Telegraph,* and *Thrillist.* Barbara studied French at the Université de Montréal and has returned regularly to cover the city for different outlets. Barbara updated the Travel Smart chapter this edition.